Legacies of Race

Legacies of Race

Identities, Attitudes, and Politics in Brazil

Stanley R. Bailey

Stanford University Press
Stanford, California

Stanford University Press
Stanford, California

Printed in the United States of America on acid-free, archival-quality paper

Library of Congress Cataloging-in-Publication Data
Bailey, Stanley R.
  Legacies of race : identities, attitudes, and politics in Brazil / Stanley R. Bailey.
    p. cm.
  Includes bibliographical references and index.
  ISBN 978-0-8047-6277-9 (cloth : alk. paper) — ISBN 978-0-8047-6278-6 (pbk : alk. paper)
  1. Ethnic attitudes—Brazil.   2. Blacks—Race identity—Brazil.   3. Racially mixed
people—Race identity—Brazil.   4. Race awareness—Brazil.   5. Race—Government
policy—Brazil.   6. Brazil—Race relations—Political aspects. I. Title.
  F2659.A1B34 2009
  305.800981—dc22

                            2008042351

Typeset by Thompson Type in 10/14 Minion

*In honor of my mother, Bernice Prosen Bailey,
and my father, James Palmer Bailey (1919–2003)*

Contents

1   Introduction   1

2   Understanding Racial Attitudes   13

3   Racial Boundaries   39

4   Race and Culture   66

5   Stratification Beliefs   88

6   The Black Movement   117

7   Affirmative Action   145

8   Racial Sorting   169

9   Race Making in Black and White   190

10 Conclusion   214

    Notes   227

    References   265

    Index   287

Legacies of Race

1 Introduction

SOCIAL SCIENCE RESEARCH on racial dynamics in Brazil identifies the myth of racial democracy as comprising in large part the national common sense on "race."[1] This myth provides the cognitive framework for understanding a great deal about attitudes toward racial issues in present-day Brazil and perhaps for most of the twentieth century. Gilberto Freyre, a Brazilian social scientist, is credited with popularizing the ideas behind Brazil as a racial democracy among elites beginning in the 1930s.[2] Confronted with the period's scientific racism, which posited the existence and unbridgeable nature of distinct human races, the superiority of a white race, and that mixed blood created degeneracy, Freyre proposed something quite different. He believed instead that "cross-breeding" produced hybrid vigor in humans and thereby heralded a bright future for the otherwise condemned dark Brazilian nation.[3] His statements were bold when read against the backdrop of Jim Crow U.S. and even Nazi German emphases on white racial purity. Through emphasizing a special character and an uncommon flexibility of Portuguese colonizers that made possible extensive miscegenation, Freyre claimed that Brazilians of three races—Africans, Europeans, and indigenous—had mixed and were giving birth to a new race constituting a new world in the tropics, a Brazilian "meta-race," a *moreno* (an ambiguous brownish color) people.

This new race would flourish as an ethnic or racial democracy, where "Men [sic] regard each other as fellow citizens and fellow Christians without regard to color or ethnic differences."[4] Freyre championed "the broad, though not perfect opportunity given in Brazil all men [sic], despite race or colour, to assert themselves as full Brazilians."[5] This view on "equal opportunity" coexisted, however, in a society that was decidedly hierarchical in nature, where dramatic social inequalities were rarely questioned; rather, they seemed almost naturally preordained.[6] Nonetheless, through this Freyrean ideological framing, miscegenation became the motor behind Brazilian racial dynamics and the foundation on which the *idea* of racial democracy was constructed.[7]

According to this perspective, the type of violent and virulent racism and separatism common in the Jim Crow United States was impossible in Brazil. The potential boundaries of racial groups were said to have blurred, and particularistic ethnic and racial classifications yielded to a more universal national identification. Unlike the United States, where stubbornly ascribed and/or asserted ethnic and racial group identities determined national organizing principles, Brazil supposedly transcended these rigid racial categories and many of their attendant consequences. What in other societies were incompatible social segments were united in Brazil to form the basis of national belonging.

In sum, Freyre suggested that *mestiçagem,* or racial mixture/miscegenation, was the essence of Brazilianness and was strengthening the national community into a meta-race.[8] He predicted that there would be "a growing lack of difference on the part of a great number of Brazilians—a tendency to consider themselves *moreno* not only a white *moreno,* as before, but the *pardo*[9] in various degrees of brownness, from light to darkest, through the effects of racial mixing, and even the *preto*—a *amorenamento* [browning]."[10] This vision of racial mixing creates the foundation for Brazil as a racial democracy, especially primed for the dominance of a racially ambiguous or mixed type. Munanga explicates this connection: "From the ideal of a mixed people . . . the myth of racial democracy was gradually elaborated . . . We have a mixed origin and, today, we are neither *pretos* nor *brancos* but, yes, a miscegenated people, a *mestiço* [mestizo] people."[11] Hence, it would appear that, according to Freyre, Brazil's racial democracy has two central ingredients: (1) the construction of a metaracial Brazilian type resulting from the blurring of racial boundaries through miscegenation and (2) the broad "though not perfect" acceptance of persons of all skin color types as full and equal participants in the benefits of citizenship in the Brazilian nation.

This seemingly innocuous understanding of racial dynamics in Brazil would appear to suggest that skin color is relatively unimportant in the lives of Brazilians, that they may have moved beyond the problem presented by prejudice and discrimination based on racial characteristics. It may even suggest a type of color-blind society. Some have gone as far as to claim that it implies a racial paradise scenario in Brazil.[12] Indeed, this mid-twentieth-century positive view of Brazilian racial dynamics led the United Nations to look to Brazil in the aftermath of Nazi racism and during the reign of Jim Crow in the United States for an alternative model of how race could be lived. To that aim, in 1950 the United Nations Educational, Scientific and Cultural Organization (UNESCO) funded an extensive exploration of the "enchanted" nature of race relations in Brazil in order to share it with the world.[13]

Needless to say, the prestigious social scientists of the UNESCO group did not find a racial paradise in mid-twentieth-century Brazil. Although they did find that the three "racial stocks" had "mingled and mixed to form a society in which racial tensions and conflicts are especially mild," these researchers also documented racial prejudice and the disadvantaged position of individuals of varying degrees of African ancestry.[14] They described, for example, starkly negative attitudes toward *negros*,[15] whose physical features were "universally considered ugly,"[16] and reported that much of the studied region of northern Brazil was characterized by remnants of a *branca* aristocratic class. Membership in this class was closed to "the Negro, the dark *mestiço*, and even those who have Negro ancestry or marked Negroid features."[17] In another studied area, Minas Velhas, the research documented that "residential segregation actually occurs . . . [along with] overt exclusion of Negroes from the Social Club."[18]

Notwithstanding these findings, one of UNESCO researchers' central theses continued to suggest that prejudice and discrimination based on race were subdued in Brazil. However, this thesis must be understood relative to the United States, which was their yardstick case characterized by legalized segregation, discrimination, and overt racial violence. They posited that in Brazil class was the most important stratifying factor and that physical features associated with race or ethnicity combined with other factors, such as education level, occupation, economic situation, and family connections, to give people their social position in Brazilian society.[19]

Regardless, these UNESCO findings of racial prejudice and discrimination were not given much attention at the time in Brazil. A military dictatorship had risen to power in the 1960s soon after the reports were published, and the new regime was unreceptive to criticism of the Brazilian nation. Although not as brutal as some of its South American counterparts during approximately the same years (e.g., Argentina and Chile), this authoritarianism would last into the early 1980s. During its waning years, the dictatorship loosened its hold just enough to allow civil society to think more freely and organize. In this climate, social movement actors rose from many corners of that society and demanded a voice in the nation's affairs. Among them were *negro* movement participants who strongly rejected the view of Brazil as a nation where skin color was unimportant. In stark contrast to the sunny belief that Brazil was a racial democracy often propagated by the Brazilian state,[20] these activists knew that racial discrimination and prejudice were a part of their daily lives and that the picture many elite and state actors painted of Brazil was a deleterious myth.

According to a growing critical vision, this elite framing of the myth of a racial democracy constituted a denial of the daily experiences of discrimination and prejudice suffered by persons of varying degrees of African ancestry. As such, the myth itself became a target, and *negro* movements began to organize against it.[21] Their struggle was not merely to correct a distorted understanding of racial dynamics among the elite and by the Brazilian state that had long constituted the official race story but also to address the common understanding of race among everyday Brazilians. The romanticized myth of racial democracy was believed to have thoroughly colored the societal fabric of Brazil, penetrating deep into the psyche of the general common sense.

According to *negro* movement actors, the perceived embrace of this myth by the general population plagued progress toward racial equality in three important ways. Primarily, they held that a majority of Brazilians, including nonwhites, denied the existence of racial discrimination. Social movement actors secondly believed that the myth therefore hampered antidiscrimination mobilization: If people did not believe in the existence of racial discrimination, surely they would not mobilize for its eradication. Lastly, the myth was said to restrict the formation of positive racial identification among Brazilians of varying degrees of African ancestry.[22] In essence, the myth of racial democracy was believed to severely limit the possibilities of the advancement of nonwhite Brazilians.

At the same time that *negro* movements began to organize more openly in the late 1970s and early 1980s, social scientists also began to directly challenge the myth of a Brazilian racial democracy. Similarly suggesting that the Brazilian mind-set was characterized by a fundamental denial of the existence of racial discrimination, social demographers Carlos Hasenbalg and Nelson do Valle Silva published quantitative analyses demonstrating the correlation between nonwhiteness and disadvantage.[23] Other social scientists followed suit, and the published work on racial inequality in Brazil grew. This literature documents disadvantage in diverse areas—income, education, labor market, and marriage market, and so on.[24] Standing on this platform of evidence, some researchers and many *negro* movement actors heralded the death of the racial democracy myth.[25] They had conclusively proven that skin color constituted an independent factor creating disadvantages for Brazilians of varying degrees of African ancestry and statistically refuted the fiction that Brazil's history of miscegenation resulted in equality.

The importance of this proof cannot be overestimated: It continues today to provide crucial impetus and backing for race scholars and social movement actors.[26] Brazil is no longer considered a paradisiacal counterexample to the United States in terms of race, and it is no longer believed to have found the key to moving beyond race through miscegenation. Once considered a hopeful alternative, merely blurring the boundaries of blackness and whiteness is no longer seen as a viable strategy in and of itself to fight racial discrimination. In fact, as I will discuss later, the opposite soon became the guiding belief: Only through clarifying and strengthening a dichotomously structured classification scheme in *negro* and white through fomenting race consciousness and robust racial identification could progress be made.[27]

Given the research of the last decades regarding the lack of racial democracy in Brazil, one might assume that the Freyrean myth has been necessarily expurgated. However, some question whether the newer characterization of myth was even correct. Was the myth of racial democracy about denying the existence of racial discrimination, and did it in turn foster that denial among the majority of Brazilians? There is no doubt that Brazilian political elites boasted of existent racial democracy, at times heralding a level of congeniality, equality, and oneness between individuals of varying skin color unmatched anywhere in the world.[28] But can the *sensus populi* regarding the significance of skin color variation be reduced to a strategic lie or ignorance-laden empirical description? Do elite interpretations and discourses, such as Freyre's or even those of contemporary social scientists, correspond to popular majority belief systems and the understandings of everyday Brazilians?[29] An assumed correlation between elite and nonelite interpretations has been commonplace, resulting in a thesis of Brazilian ignorance, i.e., that Brazilians are blind to racial discrimination.[30] However, it is possible that there is in fact a significant disconnect between the elite perspective and that of the nonelite.

What is the essence of this myth as understood by *everyday* Brazilians? Moreover, what types of attitudinal stances are born of such a myth? Herein lays the crux of contemporary debate among social scientists to which this book hopes to contribute.

In addition to the above alluded movement actors and social scientists whose ideas constitute the dominant stance in the literature and discourse concerning Brazilian race politics, there is another group of social scientists who resist reducing the set of ideas known as the myth of racial democracy to a pernicious deception.[31] These scholars, perhaps in large part more anthropological in orientation, also recognize and document discrimination and prejudice in Brazil. However, rather than blame the myth of racial democracy for fostering a denial of widespread inequality, they suggest that the myth acts as a utopian ideal for which Brazilians yearn and against which they measure reality. As stated exemplarily by Sheriff, "[Racial democracy] summons the collectively-held notion of the moral force of a shared heritage, a common family, a unified nation. Racism is repugnant. It is immoral. It is, above all, un-Brazilian."[32] Some scholars posit, then, that this utopian ideal may act as an incentive to construct a more equal Brazil.[33]

This alternative view of the myth of racial democracy might be compared, albeit imperfectly, to the "American's Creed" or "American Creed" in the United States.[34] This creed amounted to an early statement of values and principles, like democracy, freedom, equality, and justice, that Americans espouse and hold dear. However, the everyday reality of millions of Americans throughout the history of that nation has fallen decidedly short of these ideals. The creed, nonetheless, is neither blamed nor discarded. Similarly, Americans have been socialized into believing the Horatio Alger myth that suggests that with hard work anyone can "make it." This is certainly not true; structural impediments have confounded even the hardest of workers throughout American history. However, instead of framing the American Creed or the Horatio Alger myth as pernicious lies, insistence on the values espoused in them can and have formed the basis of dialogue and struggles for inclusion.[35] Might the same be true of the racial democracy myth in Brazil? Does the myth buttress racial inequality, or could it actually help in the struggle to challenge that inequality?

To more thoroughly investigate the question of the essence and effects of the myth of racial democracy in Brazil, researchers need to hear from all strata of Brazilian society. Unfortunately, however, the beliefs and attitudes of a great number of people to whom this conversation pertains have largely

been left out of the debate. There has been an absolute lacuna of public opinion research on racial attitudes in Brazil.[36] The assumed common sense of
racial democracy has thus been studied mostly through localized ethnogra-
phies like those of the UNESCO project and more recently by important field
research, including Twine's popular in-depth portrait of racial attitudes in a
rural Brazilian community in the 1990s and Sheriff's ethnography of an urban
favela, or shantytown.[37] While these have contributed significantly to the social science literature on racial dynamics in Brazil, they are limited methodologically in their ability to speak directly to the attitudes of the general public. Addressing this limitation, this book explores contemporary large-sample
attitudinal surveys that may uniquely capture the racial common sense of
everyday Brazilians.

Will a focus on public opinion research, as opposed to elite discourse or
ethnography, settle debates on the nature of this myth? It will not. However,
missing this large piece of the puzzle certainly hampers our understanding of
racial issues in Brazil. The importance of using survey methods to study Brazilian racial attitudes is made apparent by the aforementioned prominent Brazilianist social scientists Carlos Hasenbalg and Nelson Silva. They claim:

> With the exception of elections research, the academic literature on race and
> politics in Brazil has been developed without the benefit of knowledge of the
> general public's attitudes on matters of race relations. We know much more
> about what the elite think about these matters, whether they be black or white,
> than we know about the general public. The best example of this is the overused
> ideology of racial democracy, an idea invented by intellectuals and appropri-
> ated by the government—which made it the official story of race relations in the
> nation. It has been presumed to constitute the common sense about race in the
> population. Yet the ways in which this ideology is translated into concepts and
> attitudes among white and black Brazilians continue to be largely unknown.[38]

Addressing that research gap, this book captures the racial common sense in
Brazil through three major surveys of racial attitudes conducted from 1995
through 2002: the 1995 DataFolha national sample survey of racial attitudes,
the 2000 CEAP/DataUff survey of racial attitudes in the state of Rio de Janiero, and the 2002 PESB national social survey.[39]

In addition to helping understand more fully racial attitudes in contemporary Brazil, it is also my hope that this book illuminates through comparison the changing nature of racial attitudes in the United States. The United

States is actually in the midst of important changes in racial understandings, as evidenced by the institutionalization of multiracialism in the 2000 census through adopting the "mark one or more" races format. Prior to that, for most of the twentieth century, individuals of European and African ancestries in the United States were officially identified as either of a white or a black race, but never both. The census change, along with the growing size of the U.S. Latino population (now second only to whites), has led some to claim that the United States is becoming more like Latin America in terms of racial dynamics.[40] That Latin Americanization includes such phenomena as increased focus on racial ambiguity and mixed racial parentage influenced by greater rates of racial and ethnic intermarriage and Latin American immigration to the United States. Hence, a more thorough understanding of Brazil could aid in anticipating attitudes and dynamics that may develop in the United States.

Furthering this counterpoint, it is worth noticing that just as the United States seems to be moving in the direction of Latin American racial dynamics, Brazil seems to be heading in the opposite direction. Seemingly tracing a path back through U.S. history, Brazil is experimenting with single-race understandings of racial group membership, or monoracialism, as opposed to multiracialism. For example, many institutions of higher learning in Brazil are instituting affirmative action legislation; and, rather than using the mixed-race category of the Brazilian Census, they are opting for a single-race *negro* versus white classification scheme to identify recipients. If the idea of racial democracy in Brazil exalts racial mixing, it is understandable that this attempt to "unmix" the population for race-targeted intervention has already created much debate, an issue I delve into later. Regardless, it appears to be the case that racial dynamics in the United States and in Brazil are like two ships passing in the night, one showing signs of movement toward mixed-race framings and the other toward single-race identification. Sociologist G. Reginald Daniel uses the metaphor of "converging paths" to describe these dynamics.[41] If this is the case, a contemporary comparison is crucial.

In addition, this book seeks to clarify issues that will help us better understand not only the United States, but many Latin American countries as well. Colombia, Cuba, Venezuela, and Ecuador are just a few of the countries in that region with populations of varying degrees of African origin, whose citizens therefore contend with similar issues. As in Brazil, there has been a lack of data that capture racial attitudes of the general public in these countries. Hence, the importance of the large data sets that are becoming available in

Brazil cannot be overestimated as a means of shedding light on other similar Latin American contexts.

To these ends, the Brazilian racial common sense as framed by the myth of racial democracy is in need of further study to gain a deeper and, most importantly, representative picture. I begin this exploration in Chapter 2 by commenting on the attitudinal complex itself as regards its value as an object of study. I lay out three basic perspectives that dominate the general literature on the study of racial attitudes: group conflict theories, sociocultural theories, and social identity theory. Although differing in important ways, all three perspectives appear especially apt, I argue, for studying dynamics in societies robustly divided along racial lines and characterized by strong subjective racial identification that I label "racialist" contexts.[42] In contrast I call forth an alternative conceptualization of racial commonsense understandings called "antiracialism" that may better frame a context of weak racial subjectivity and in which the population embraces racial ambiguity.[43] Debate continues regarding the more adequate framing in Brazil, and I lay out how the antiracialist and racialist perspectives have alternatively held sway in twentieth-century Brazilianist race scholarship. I then briefly propose a way to reconcile and conceptualize the differences between these two competing framings through taking into account variation in levels of racial "groupness."[44] I hold that the general literature has not adequately considered the variable salience of racial group boundaries in part due to its reliance on the U.S. case, where black and white racial group boundaries tend to be uniformly robust and historically have appeared "natural and immutable."[45] Lastly, I introduce at the end of this second chapter the data I employ in my analyses.

In Chapter 3 I address more directly the central analytical concept used in the analysis of public opinion on racial issues—the racial group. Racial attitudes are most generally and simply understood as the opinions and perspectives of racialized individuals, members of differing racial groups, on racialized issues. Hence, to study racial attitudes in Brazil, I first need to explore the nature of racial boundaries in that context and delineate its boundaried collectivities. This first empirical chapter draws on extensive data on racial identification, both self- and other-classification, as well as classification of self and others in comparison to photographs, a very unique methodology, to say the least. Seeking to understand racial boundary dynamics, I examine issues of the degree of consistency of interviewer- versus self-identification, the degree of loyalty individuals show toward the category in which they self-classify, and the preferences individuals reveal for alternative category schemas. Through this examination I show that the boundaries of racial formations in Brazil continue to be quite tenuous, multiple, and overlapping and may be resistant to the concept "racial group." I conceptualize this dynamic as variation in the levels of "groupness." This understanding of racial identification in Brazil as exhibiting lower levels of groupness will form the basis of much of my argumentation in subsequent chapters.

After exploring and mapping racial boundaries in Brazil, Chapter 4 is an empirical look at the assumed content of those boundaries: culture. Researchers note that racial group subjectivity in Brazil has historically not been considered very robust at the same time that newer classification trends suggest the increasing salience of the racially affirmative term *negro*. Importantly, some even propose the census adoption of that category to unify nonwhites. I argue that to understand the effects of a possible change in census labeling, it is necessary to take into account a central element the label is believed to enclose—*negro* cultural specificity. I explore four areas that speak to the state of "*negro* culture": ethnic self-classification, *negro* cultural repertoires, perceptions of ethnic distinctiveness, and perceptions of common ancestry. My findings suggest that, partly through a process of nationalization, many African-derived cultural elements were transformed into symbols of national identity. Hence, identification with these symbols is not clearly delineated along racial lines. I conclude that the absence (or weak state) of an exclusive set of *negro* cultural symbols may condition the *negro* label's ability to unify nonwhite Brazilians.

Chapter 5 is truly a core chapter in this book. In it I address a specific result that the literature claims flows from the Brazilian racial common sense: a denial of racial discrimination in Brazil. The myth of racial democracy and a denial of racial discrimination have been intimately linked most forcefully and repetitively during the last two decades of the twentieth century. In this chapter I ask, Do Brazilians actually deny racial discrimination? It is a straightforward empirical question that many survey items address. I look, for example, at Brazilian explanations of racial stratification, and I also examine differences between white and nonwhite explanations of that stratification. My findings strongly contradict the literature at every turn. A majority of both white and nonwhite Brazilians identify the important role of discrimination in that society, and I offer data that suggest they may have done so consistently since at least 1986.[46] Hence, I argue against a facile conceptualization of the myth of racial democracy as constituting a denial of racial discrimination.

Chapter 6 is the first of two chapters that explore the posited consequences of the myth of racial democracy on antiracism strategies. Scholars of Brazilian racial dynamics have long asked why, in a country so clearly stratified along color lines, the Brazilian *negro* movement has struggled at mobilizing a constituency.[47] Frequently offered explanations include the aforementioned denial of racial discrimination and/or a resistance to unified *negro* identification. I explore this question and report surprising results. First, Brazilians do recognize a clear basis for *negro* mobilization (*negros'* rights are not equally respected in Brazil), and they overwhelmingly express support for that mobilization. Furthermore, a majority of Brazilians express willingness to participate in antiracism activities and many even to become members of antiracist organizations. Color is not generally a significant determinant of these attitudes. Instead, age most decisively predicts attitudinal stances (a negative relationship to support for antiracism). With these unexpected findings, I attempt an alternative framing addressing the *negro* movement's issues with mobilizing a constituency.

Chapter 7 explores consequences of the Brazilian racial common sense for the question of race-targeted policy initiatives. In a context that has been characterized as gripped by a denial of racial discrimination, one would think that race-targeted policy would have little chance of enactment. However, Brazil is in the midst of an affirmative action boom. Dozens of Brazilian universities now employ a racial quota system to redress the historical exclusion of nonwhites from the realm of higher education. How did this dramatic shift occur? What do ordinary Brazilians think about these policies? What factors are associated with the varying opinions that Brazilians hold? I find, contrary to predictions drawn from general framings, that there is significant support for race-targeted intervention in Brazil, including by white Brazilians. In addition, I find that social class appears most strongly associated with that support. Hence, I offer a revised understanding of the effects of the myth of racial democracy on antiracism.

Chapter 8 examines how state actors in charge of administering affirmative action in Brazil are opting for a dichotomous *negro* versus white scheme for sorting beneficiaries, even though that society has historically embraced racial ambiguity. What are the consequences of adopting a dichotomous classification in a thoroughly multiracial society? Will this strategy prove efficient for sorting beneficiaries from nonbeneficiaries? I find, for example, that there is significant disagreement as to who qualifies as nonwhite and who as white in terms of both self- and other-classification. In addition, almost half of the mixed-race sample opts for whiteness when constrained to black and white terms. Finally, a strong majority of a national sample of Brazilians rejects multiracials as candidates for *negro* racial quotas. Results point to the possible unintended exclusion of many multiracial individuals from beneficiary status whether through self- or other-elimination.

In Chapter 9 I continue to explore the adoption of racial dualism for affirmative action policies but this time in terms of its symbolic consequences on shifting identification trajectories. In contrast to the United States, where fewer than 3 percent of the population self-classified as mixed race in the 2000 census, almost 40 percent of Brazilians did so in its 2000 census. Will Brazil's adoption of de jure dichotomous classification in *negro* and white for the distribution of scarce resources affect how individuals choose to self-classify? Chapter 9 addresses that question and documents, for example, through a split ballot survey that the mere mention of quotas for *negros* nearly doubles the percentage of a national sample choosing that term. I argue, then, that the adoption of inclusionary race-targeted public policy will have a race-making effect in the direction of traditional white versus black dynamics in the United States.

Finally, in my conclusion in Chapter 10, I briefly summarize my analyses and argument and lay out their importance for both racial theorizing and public policy debates in Brazil. My findings tend to contradict dominant perspectives on race in Brazil, and I attempt to explain these counterintuitive results. A good portion of the explanation may be methodological in nature. As noted, the Brazilian context has suffered from a lack of public opinion research on racial attitudes. The result has been a disconnect between elite interpretations of the Brazilian racial understandings and the actual common sense as lived by the masses of poor Brazilians, *negro,* white, and in between. My hope is to help bridge that gap and present a more bottom-up, representative picture. In addition, the reliance on general theories of race that have been unduly influenced by one central case, that of the United States, has also hampered comparative social research. Those theories carry embedded within assumptions about the nature of racial dynamics, especially regarding the robust nature of boundaries in black and white, that compromise their application in racially ambiguous contexts like Brazil. I argue for taking seriously the challenges that the Brazilian case presents for the comparative study of race. Rather than trying to force round pegs into square holes, a comparative, two-way conversation will most benefit the social scientific study of the legacies of race.

Understanding Racial Attitudes

The Attitudinal Complex

Before delving into the data, we should pose the question of the value of the study of attitudes as social scientific endeavor that can shed light on complex racial dynamics. That is, what is the worth of the attitude as an object of study? I begin this exploration of racial attitudes in Brazil, then, with a clarification of the conceptualization of the attitudinal object. Schuman and his colleagues offer this straightforward interpretation: "In most social science writing, the term 'attitude' refers to a favorable or unfavorable evaluation of an object. The object may be a person, a group, a policy, an idea, or indeed anything at all that can be evaluated."[1]

Although this definition covers a wide range of question types, it does not necessarily encompass some of the survey items that I will be presenting. Those hard-to-categorize items deal not with evaluative objects per se but address beliefs such as those that Brazilians have regarding racial inequality. Schuman and his coauthors, however, find it easy to incorporate beliefs into the general definition. They write: " . . . some [questions] do depart from [the evaluative form] more noticeably and seem to inquire about beliefs rather than about attitudes in a purely evaluative sense . . . Yet in common parlance such inquiries are usually referred to as attitude questions also. Moreover, this and other belief questions that we analyze all have obvious evaluative implications."[2]

Surveys of public opinion also may inquire directly about behavior patterns. For instance, in Schuman and his colleagues' study, they report on surveys where respondents were asked about their voting practices. In addition, throughout this exploration of public opinion on race, I hold that racialized populations are not things in the world but visions of how the world is or should be organized in terms of human population diversity. Hence, I conceptualize racial classification dynamics, both self- and other-assigned, as racial attitudes that are subjective, contextual, and changing over time. (I discuss this perspective in greater detail in Chapter 3.) In sum, what I call the attitudinal complex in this book is all of those subjective opinions and beliefs about racial issues, including one's own and others' racial identity, expressed in large-sample public opinion surveys.

Public opinion surveys, however, have not always been afforded high credibility in the social sciences. Perhaps the most frequent criticism of public opinion data is that attitudes may not correspond with behavior.[3] Krysan attempts to confront this criticism by claiming that there is no reason to expect a one-to-one correspondence between an attitude and a behavior. What should be expected is "correlational consistency rather than literal consistency."[4] As she points out, longitudinal data do reveal patterns of general correspondence, for example, in the case of trend data on intermarriage: As attitudes captured in public opinion surveys toward racial intermarriage have grown more accepting of this practice, rates of racial intermarriage have also increased. While actual intermarriage lags behind its corresponding attitudinal trend, there is nevertheless change in the same direction.

Offering two further examples of correlational consistency, Krysan makes reference to the passage of civil rights legislation and that of anti–affirmative action policies in the United States. She points out that Burstein showed that supportive public opinion was key to the passage of the 1964 Civil Rights Act.[5] Likewise, negative public opinion toward affirmative action led both the states of California and Washington to approve ballot measures aimed at eliminating those policies. Hence, it is this correlational dynamic that speaks most directly to the relationship between attitudes and behavior in the study of public opinion.

Bobo discusses another criticism leveled at public opinion surveys: "It is argued that studies of racial attitudes and beliefs, as the subjective properties of individuals, tell us little about the broader historical, political, and socio-economic—in a word, structural—dynamics said to truly drive race and ethnic relations."[6] There is no doubt some truth to this criticism. Public opinion data are not a tell-all but rather a complement to those studies on broader structural processes affecting social life. In fact, I believe structural factors are central but subjective interpretations of how those structural elements affect the lives of individuals, and collectivities in a society, for example, are also crucial to study.

One more caveat is in order. There is no doubt that the survey context is artificial. Due to situational variability, moving from survey context to real life can easily complicate beliefs and attitudes. Krysan considers this multifaceted dynamic, stating:

> Another way of looking at it is the clash of abstract values in concrete form. Abstract values run into competition in the real world due to the competing values that are present (in contrast to the survey context which is in isolation). No one would expect a abstract principle in survey context to win out in all situations regardless of the other values with which it competes—commonsense tell us that most people work out compromises depending upon the exact balance of positions.[7]

In sum, although an attitude is a complicated expression that does not automatically mirror behavior, there is significant evidence of directional correlation between the two. My goal, then, is to detect, explore, and attempt to explain attitudinal patterns that may suggest real-world behavior and consequences in Brazil.

Racial Attitudes Research

Notwithstanding the limitations, there is an extensive and growing body of social scientific research in contexts other than Brazil that uses survey methods to examine public opinion on racial issues. This research largely concerns the United States and fits into the larger body of literature on intergroup relations and theories of group-based oppression in general. The specific focus on capturing racial attitudes in large-sample public opinion surveys, as well as an extensive use of survey methods for hypothesis testing, is characteristic of this kind of research. It is decidedly interdisciplinary and has been extensively published in top journals and academic presses. Premier practitioners include sociologist Lawrence Bobo, political scientist David Sears, and social psychologist Jim Sidanius, whose 2000 edited volume, *Racialized Politics: The Debate about Racism in America,* I call on frequently in the following pages.[8] The lion's share of this research is based on the United States (although, as I discuss, Sidanius and his colleagues do propose a more general framing). In addition, this literature's U.S. focus is mainly on white versus black racial group

dynamics, and its hypothesis testing centrally addresses only white racial attitudes. Krysan explains that this focus flows from two factors, one theoretical
and the other methodological.[9] Theoretically, it was generally assumed that
only white racial attitudes were in need of explanation. Methodologically, the
necessary data on nonwhite racial attitudes were not available because they
had not been collected. Nonwhite voices in this matter, ironically, were under-
valued. It should be mentioned, however, that the attitudinal literature is currently expanding in the United States to include studies of other populations,
such as Latinos and Asian Americans, a trend that should certainly result in
the continual reformulation of dominant framings.[10]

Does this body of research offer promise for understanding racial attitudes
in Brazil? In order to evaluate its utility and to find an adequate way of approaching the Brazilian case, I briefly review the two dominant competing
theory clusters addressing racial attitudes, sociocultural approaches[11] and
group conflict framings.[12] In addition, I add a third perspective, social identity
theory, due to its influence on several framings in the area of intergroup relations[13] and its potential worth in confronting dynamics specific to the Brazilian case. Each perspective offers a different model of how the idea of race
functions and what factors shape racial attitudes; nonetheless, I will show that
all three also share several core assumptions in their attempts to explain the
attitudinal dynamics surrounding race.[14]

Sociocultural Approaches

Sociocultural approaches explain racial attitudes as configured through a
gradual socialization process that results in negative affect toward racialized
out-groups.[15] One prominent example of this approach is a perspective labeled
symbolic racism.[16] Symbolic racism in the United States, the central context it
addresses, attributes negative affect to sociocultural learning, thus fitting into
traditional views of racial prejudice.[17] Children and adolescents acquire prejudice along with other values and attitudes that are normative in their social
environment. Conformity pressures, as well as the intrinsic strength of early-
learned attitudes, ensure that prejudice persists through later life.

Almost all whites, then, are said to have a "solid core of prejudice" that forms
the basis of antiblack affect, no matter how anachronistic it may be.[18] Symbolic
racism is viewed as a blend of this affect with the traditional American moral
values embodied in the Protestant ethic of individualism and self-reliance, the
work ethic, obedience, and discipline. Those afflicted with the type of prejudice

that symbolic racism addresses resist change in the racial status quo "based on moral feelings that blacks violate such traditional American values."[19]

Four main attitudinal stances of whites toward blacks stem from symbolic racism: (1) Blacks are no longer especially handicapped by racial discrimination; and (2) they still do not conform to traditional American values; however, (3) they continue to make illegitimate demands for special treatment; and (4) they continue to receive undeserved special treatment from government and other elites.[20] Rather than bigoted beliefs expressed openly as in the Jim Crow era, the current manifestation of racism is opposition to implementing equality.[21] This is justified through the view that blacks now want *special* treatment rather than *equal* treatment.

It is key to mention that the antiblack affect addressed by symbolic racism is not a defense against the personal material impact possibly suffered by whites because of a changing racial status quo. On the contrary, in symbolic racism, whites do not centrally fear losing privilege or power but just resent blacks as challenging other moral and symbolic goods.

In sum, symbolic racism, like sociocultural framings in general, finds that antiblack affect is the basis of white racial attitudes. This framing does not generally deal directly with black racial attitudes. However, it follows that their attitudinal stances on racial issues should be substantially different than those of whites due to alternative socialization processes. These theories, then, generally posit a racial divide in public opinion between whites and blacks.[22] Subjective racial identities and clear group membership lines are taken for granted in sociocultural approaches.

Group Conflict Theories

A second approach to the study of racial attitudes includes the variants on group conflict theory.[23] These theories also perceive and emphasize a divide in public opinion concerning racial issues and seek to explain it as the result of the divergent racial interests of whites and blacks.

Bobo bases his theorizing regarding this racial divide on Blumer's group position model.[24] Blumer focused on group-based dynamics as influenced by feelings of entitlement to social resources, status, and privileges, and perceived threats to those entitlements.[25] Following that lead, Bobo agrees that the core factor influencing attitudes is the subjective image of where the in-group *ought* to stand vis-à-vis the out-group.[26] He claims, then, that any social system with long-standing inequalities defined along racial lines sets the stage for "realistic" or meaningful struggle over group-based interests.[27]

Quite contrary to symbolic racism, Bobo finds little room for antiblack affect as an explanation for the divide between black and white racial attitudes. Although negative affect toward blacks exists, the level on which it operates is within the individual rather than the more dominant forum of the group. Along with See and Wilson, Bobo agrees that racism is best conceptualized as a property of social systems; antiblack prejudice, on the other hand, is the property of individuals, and as such is not as powerful an actor on group dynamics.[28] In sum, according to Bobo, "Why 'race matters' would appear to reflect group-based interests. This, [I] submit, is the only reasonable interpretation of the powerfully robust racial difference in opinion that separates the views of blacks . . . from those of whites."[29]

Sidanius and his colleagues (social dominance theory) also find that antiblack affect has little to do with white racial attitudes on decisive issues (e.g., implementation of equality).[30] They claim that in fact there is no real evidence that the American racial hierarchy has ever been centrally characterized by this kind of prejudice.[31] According to this theory, racism is defined by ideologies of superiority—a belief in the moral, intellectual, or cultural supremacy of one group over another—but does not necessarily associate negative affect with the under-group. Sidanius claims that in the pre–Civil War era in the United States, an absolute certainty of black inferiority was quite often accompanied by positive affect toward blacks. Also discussed as "paternalistic racism," this disposition continued in some areas up to the civil rights era.[32]

Social dominance theory has three elements at its core: (1) Societies are typically organized around group-based hierarchies; (2) politics can be thought of as an exercise in intergroup competition over scarce material and symbolic resources; and (3) one of the primary functions of values and ideologies is to legitimize the disproportionate allocation of desired social outcomes to the dominant group and to maintain the structural integrity of the system of group-based social hierarchy.[33] Central to this perspective is a "social dominance orientation" (SDO), which reflects the degree to which people desire unequal, dominance-oriented relationships among groups within the social system.[34] According to Sidanius and his colleagues, the social dominance orientation is the central driving factor behind the racial attitudes of whites in the United States and in other contexts where racial hierarchies exist.[35]

In sum, both Bobo and Sidanius view the racial divide in public opinion as reflecting competition over group-based interests. They claim that what their group conflict framings hold in common are (1) that individuals identify with their own racial group, (2) that racial groups have competing racial interests that generate conflict, and (3) that dominant groups develop ideologies to justify and legitimize their hegemony.[36]

Social Identity Theory

Social identity theory is also a group-oriented framing of social interaction. That is, similar to both the previous theories I laid out, it focuses principally on in-group and out-group dynamics.[37] However, different from the sociocultural theories and group conflict perspectives, the social identity perspective does not find that group-centered dynamics need involve differing group interests or even primarily out-group prejudice. Rather, its focus is on in-group favoritism. At the same time, however, according to this perspective, out-group hostility can arise from the mere perception of belonging to differing social categories. Tajfel and Turner refer to an experiment where individuals were placed in differing categories but where differences that might motivate in-group/out-group dynamics were absent. They found that "intergroup discrimination existed in conditions of minimal in-group affiliation, anonymity of group membership, absence of conflicts of interest, and absence of previous hostility between the groups."[38]

Social identity theory possibly provides, then, an alternative way of framing intergroup conflict, showing that conflicts of interests and histories of hostility may not be the absolute determinants of intergroup attitudes and behavior. It claims that, besides striving always for enhanced self-esteem through a positive self-concept, individuals also strive to achieve or maintain positive social identification. Therefore, the mere perception that there are categorical differences between groupings of individuals leads to intergroup differentiation and conflict in attitudes and behavior. According to Tajfel and Turner, "the basic hypothesis, then, is that pressures to evaluate one's own group positively through in-group/out-group comparisons lead social groups to attempt to differentiate themselves from each other."[39]

The Racial Groupness Continuum

In subsequent chapters, I discuss the empirical and theoretical fit of the above-mentioned perspectives in the multiracial Brazilian context. What is important to note now, however, is that all three theories, whether focusing on out-group prejudice, group-based interests and ideologies, or in-group favoritism, are predicated on salient group identification by "members of discrete and discontinuous categories," as described by Tajfel and Turner.[40] Not only do Sears and his coauthors begin their volume with the assumption that individuals "identify with their own racial group,"[41] but Dawson writes in his overview chapter of that volume that all the chapters contained therein, including a wide range of pieces from top researchers using sociocultural and group conflict approaches, presuppose that "racial attitudes are structured across racial groups."[42]

This presupposition of strong group divisions and identification that characterizes these theories can be viewed as one assuming high levels of "groupness."[43] "Groupness" is a concept I draw centrally from Loveman and Brubaker, and their colleagues, that suggests a scale of racialized population cohesion and subjectivity, high to low.[44] To be clear, although contexts characterized by high levels of groupness do exist, the level characterizing any society or referring to any social boundary in any context is an empirical question to be explored. In contrast, the facile assumption of high levels of groupness embedded within many social theories becomes a research perspective and methodology, a point to which I return.

In terms of the empirical question of the variable nature of social boundaries on a groupness continuum, what would the racial common sense look like at different points along that continuum? I can address that question by offering examples of what researchers frame as racialist and nonracialist common senses. According to Appiah, "racialism" describes that context, typified in the research of the three major perspectives reviewed above, characterized by a belief "that there are heritable characteristics, possessed by members of our species, that allow us to divide them into a small set of races, in such a way that all the members of these races share certain traits and tendencies with each other that they do not share with members of any other race. These traits and tendencies characteristic of a race constitute, in the racialist view, a sort of racial *essence*."[45]

For example, Zack characterizes the U.S. racialist context as follows: "Almost everyone in American society assumes that people are derived into natural groups with common physical traits that can be studied in the biological sciences, and that the groups are the referents of racial terms."[46]

I believe that the racialist worldview involves the establishment of the following three core assumptions about human population diversity. These assumptions may be formulated somewhat differently across contexts due to particular historic configurations of population mixing and exploitation. However, in general, in the racialist context, a population:

1. Conceives of distant, diffuse, and multiple ancestral geographic-origin categories as singular, important, and enduring (as African or European in the United States).
2. Equates those ancestries with inheritable biological differences called races (as the European race or the African race in the United States).
3. Establishes discrete sets of physical criteria associated with each race (centrally a white/less-than-white skin-color palette in the United States, delimiting white and black races).[47]

Appiah goes on to remark, importantly, that as a racial common sense, racialism does not have to assume racial hierarchies: "Racialism is not, in itself, a doctrine that must be dangerous, even if the racial essence is thought to entail moral and intellectual dispositions. Provided positive moral qualities are distributed across the races, each can be respected, and have its 'separate but equal' place."[48]

Unambiguous racial boundaries, robust racial identification, and social interaction framed as "race relations" all characterize the racialist context. Interestingly, although Appiah claims that "in theory" high levels of racial groupness may be "benign," the dominant theories on attitudinal stances do not generally address benevolent situations. Rather, they generally appear to frame racialism as an inherently destructive belief set that causes out-group prejudice, group-based competition over scarce resources, and in-group favoritism. In fact, Sears, Bobo, and Sidanius contrastingly define "racialism" as "the belief that blacks were inherently inferior to whites because of their race."[49] I, instead, adopt Appiah's definition.

If a multiracial society marked by a high level of groupness can be characterized as racialist, then how do we conceptualize multiracial societies toward the other end of the groupness continuum? Mary Waters offers a framing that attempts this task in her study of West Indian immigrants in the United States. In that study, she contrasts what she denotes as a "lack of racialism" characteristic of the cultural mentality of some first-generation immigrants to the United States with the racialist worldview they find themselves confronted with in the United States.[50] According to Waters, "'Racialism' . . . refer[s] to a heightened sensitivity to race, a tendency to racialize situations and relations between people."[51] A "lack of racialism," which she views as representing the native cultural mind-set of West Indian immigrants, describes a context where race is not of primary importance for defining subjective identities, where individuals generally interact "not as representatives of their race."[52]

In the following statements, Waters lays out key elements that characterize a "lack of racialism" as opposed to "racialism," comparing racial imagery in the United States and the Caribbean:

> The social construction of race in the Caribbean has historically been different than in the United States. Nowhere in the Caribbean is race a simple bipolar distinction between white and black. Race is more of a continuum in which shade and other physical characteristics, as well as social characteristics such as class position, are taken into account in the social process of categorization. The determination of race is quite variable . . .

and

> In the United States the "one-drop rule" has defined anyone with any black ancestors as black. An intermediate category for mixed-race people or colored people is socially recognized in the West Indies but not in the United States. Finally, conflict in the Caribbean that is seemingly about race is often one where race is better understood as a marker of socioeconomic inequality; fights about race are more about the gulf between rich and poor.[53]

This "lack of racialism," then, may be characterized as the counterposition of racialism, that is, referring to dynamics in a multiracial context where racial group affiliation and identification are not primary or ideologically legitimate sources of social organization. Variable or ambiguous racial identification, a focus on color as opposed to race, and an emphasis on social class all are assumed characteristics of the nonracialist context.

Racialism and Antiracialism in Brazil

Might Waters's juxtaposition of racialism and nonracialism advance the understanding of attitudinal stances in Brazil? It is a promising place to start. Waters's characterization of the West Indies certainly appears to resonate with Brazil: ambiguous racial calculus, including the embrace of mixed-race identification, a focus on a color continuum, and the central importance of class. However, I follow Guimarães for the case of Brazil and instead use the concept "antiracialism" as a counterposition to racialism.[54] The major difference between antiracialism and Waters's "nonracialism" or "lack of racialism" is that an antiracialist orientation, such as that in Brazil, is formulated in direct opposition to and as a rejection of racial dynamics in the U.S. context.[55] As this may not necessarily be the case in the West Indies, the distinction is important. In addition, "nonracialism" may intimate that racial dynamics are completely lacking, whereas antiracialism does not.

Following Guimarães, if racialism characterizes a context where the popular belief holds that everyone belongs to discrete racial groups that determine social interaction, antiracialism characterizes a rejection of that assertion and vision. In the place of a racial group focus, the antiracialist context recognizes color differences but not as the basis of social group formation. Instead, class- and nation-based identifications are primary.

According to Guimarães, the origin of antiracialist thinking in the Brazilian social sciences was forged in early twentieth-century Brazil in large part through the writings of Gilberto Freyre, Sérgio Buarque de Holanda, and Caio Prado Jr., much of whose elite discourse on Brazilian modernity was aimed at forging a common national destiny in "overcoming racialism."[56] They sought to marginalize the discourses of scientific racism, eugenics, and other quasi-scientific theories on race as subdivisions of the human population prevalent at the time in elite circles. In antiracialist thought,

> the concept of race, in addition to expressing the ignorance of those who used it, came also to denote racism. "Race" [in Portuguese] came to mean only "determination," "will power," or "character" but almost never "subdivisions of the human species"; these came to be designated only by a person's color: *branca* ("white"), *parda* (roughly, "mulatto"), *preta* (roughly "dark black"), and so on. The colors came to be considered objective, concrete, unquestionable realities without moral or intellectual connotations. Such connotations were rejected as "prejudice."[57]

To clarify the definition of antiracialism, I further cite Guimarães:

> It is very interesting to observe how this anti-racialist ideal was absorbed into the Brazilian way of being. Indeed, the perception became a cliché that for Brazilians races do not exist and that what is important in terms of life opportunities is a person's social class (which more than economic position means a certain lifestyle guaranteed through education and cultural habits).[58]

Antiracialism, then, entails most clearly a rejection of viewing race as dividing the Brazilian population into discrete subgroups of the national population, at the same time that it recognizes color variation. Antiracialism is also a perspective that may privilege class, although not exclusively, in explaining social stratification.

It is important to understand that the antiracialist perspective in Brazil was not formulated in a vacuum. Rather, Brazilian writers and to some extent the populus measured and understood Brazilian racial dynamics as counter to those in the United States, a perspective that researchers have subsequently echoed. Silva writes that "the racially segregated US was the privileged contrast for distinguishing Brazilian culture."[59] Explaining the effects of this, she claims, "The prevailing racial discourse in Brazil celebrates the fact that, unlike the US, our society lacks clear-cut criteria for racial classification, and cele-brates the absence of racial separation and conflict."[60] Peter Wade similarly writes, "In Brazil, Freyre also gave credibility to the notion of 'mixture' as one element in a 'tropical' society, and his characterization of paternalistic race relations as a corollary of mixture was implicitly opposed to the USA's vigorous discrimination against blacks and the strict maintenance of social boundaries."[61] U.S. racialism, then, becomes the oppositional backboard for understanding Brazilian antiracialist ideas and dynamics.

Perhaps the distinguishing mark of antiracialism in general is an emphasized belief in a "miscegenated people," to use Munanga's phrase.[62] In this aspect, Brazil has much in common with the other Latin American countries with populations displaying varying degrees of African ancestry. These countries—Venezuela, Colombia, Ecuador, Nicaragua, the Dominican Republic, Cuba, Costa Rica, and so on—generally uphold national ideologies of *mestizaje* or mestizization.[63] Researchers have used a variety of images and concepts to describe this ideology: "*café con leche*,"[64] "racial mixture" or "ethnic homogenization,"[65] "racial homogeneity" and "Hispanic,"[66] "deracialized consciousness,"[67] the "*moreno*"[68] or "*morenidade*,"[69] and, finally, Freyre's "meta-race."[70] As Wade posits, the "particularity of Latin American identity" resides in the phrase "*somos todos mestizos*" (we are all mestizos).[71] Altered slightly to "*somos todos morenos*," this phrase exemplifies the antiracialism perspective in Brazil.

Stages of Brazilian Racialism and Antiracialism

Racialism and antiracialism can be viewed, then, as framing common-sense racial understandings located along a continuum of racial groupness, high and low, respectively. These contrasting orientations, however, are not only empirically relevant in terms, for example, of describing racial identification tendencies but are also general ideological stances. That is, these perspectives describe, explain, and/or justify relevant social patterns on the part of everyday people living in multiracial contexts. They can also be viewed as embedded in social science theories and hence constituting competing research perspectives. That is, social scientists throughout the twentieth century employed racialism and antiracialism to explain racial dynamics within Brazil, and these competing framings continue to organize debate in the twenty-first century.[72]

To understand how both perspectives have been alternately used in framing Brazilian racial dynamics, I lay out four key stages in the development of Brazilianist social scientific thought regarding race in twentieth-century Brazil and into the twenty-first. Each stage in the following typology reveals a pendulous dynamic of competing notions. For example, at one point social scientists find the racialist "race relations" approach inefficient for the Brazilian context, while at another the pendulum swings toward racialist interpretation. I offer this succinct overview of the stages:

1. The first post-Freyrean period of racial theorizing in Brazil is that of *antiracialism.* It privileges the contrast between racial dynamics in Brazil and the United States. A celebration of miscegenation characterizes this period.

2. The second stage, *challenging antiracialism,* is marked by a swing toward quantitative analyses that dispute the myth of a Brazilian racial democracy and point to an underlying racial division in Brazil.

3. With the "debunking" of the myth of racial democracy, a third stage, *racialism,* privileges the similarities between the United States and Brazil. The dominant "race relations" paradigm is embraced to frame the Brazilian context.

4. Finally, there is a nascent reaction to a racialist interpretation in Brazil, and the stage of *challenging racialism* begins to form. There is a return to privileging the U.S./Brazil contrasts and marked criticism of the "race relations" framing for Brazil.

The following four sections review, then, some of the central academic thinkers from each stage of Brazilianist literature on race. In devising neat typologies, some complexity is sacrificed. For example, the subtlety of chronological and theoretical overlaps may be lost. Likewise, some theorists may be placed in more than one stage as their perspective changes over time and from issue to issue. However, in spite of these limitations, the general time-order relationship can be clearly seen, and the stages are unmistakably distinct. The contemporary stages three and four are treated more briefly because they are addressed extensively in subsequent chapters.

Stage One—Antiracialism

The first body of literature on skin-color dynamics in Brazil that I address here emerged in the "post-Freyre period" after the publication of *Casa Grande* in 1933.[73] Writers of that time emphasized three dynamics as characteristic of this context: robust class identification, the color continuum, and racial group ambiguity. Primary exponents of this early antiracialist perspective are Pierson, Harris, Wagley, Willems, Hutchinson, and Degler.[74]

Regarding class, Wagley, for example, concludes in an introduction to an edited volume on his study of racial dynamics in rural Brazil that "it was found that the most important and most crucial alignment in rural Brazilian society was that of social classes, and that racial type was generally but one criterion by which individuals were assigned to a social class."[75] According to Harris, evidence of the subordination of racial to class identity is the fact that individuals of approximately equal socioeconomic rank are categorized with similar "racial" terms regardless of their location on the color continuum.[76] Furthermore, the adage in Brazil that "money whitens" is also presented as support for the primary importance of class over race. Exemplarily, Harris concludes, "It's one's class and not one's race which determines the adoption of subordinate and superordinate attitudes between specific individuals in face-to-face relations."[77] This theme of the primacy of class is also found in Pierson and Hutchinson.[78]

These early studies also emphasize a color continuum in Brazil. Harris (1964) claims,

> Racial identity in Brazil is not governed by the rigid descent rule. A Brazilian child is never automatically identified with the racial type of one or both of his parents, nor must his racial type be selected from one of only two possibilities. Over a dozen racial categories may be recognized in conformity with the combination of hair color, hair texture, eye color and skin color which actually occur. These types grade into each other like the colors of the spectrum and no one category stands significantly isolated from all the rest.[79]

This is not to say, however, that various racial categories are equal. Rather, the color continuum is tilted to favor its lighter end. As Harris explains, "all racial segments see race as one of the diagnostics by which an individual's value is measured . . . [and] everybody believes it is better to be white."[80] He goes on to explain,

. . . no amount of wishful thinking about the lack of "race prejudice" in Brazil can alter these facts . . . (1) Racial stereotypes are well-developed, (2) The stereotypes are graded and arranged in ascending-descending order, (3) The *negro* occupies the lowest level, and (4) The white occupies the highest level.[81]

Similar to Harris, Nogueira also classified Brazil's patterns of prejudice as corresponding to appearance.[82] While these researchers highlight racial prejudice, however, they shy away from linking this prejudice with the kind of discrimination that determines socioeconomic status: Again class is the privileged operator. As Wagley claimed, "The expression of prejudice against Negroes, the *mestiços* and people of Indian physical type is mainly manifested verbally and not in behaviour. Other factors (wealth, occupation, education, etc.) are of greater importance in determining the actual patterns of interpersonal relations than race."[83] Hence, class is of greater importance than race in terms of discrimination.

In a very early study on Brazilian racial attitudes published in the *American Journal of Sociology*, Willems reaches two conclusions regarding the nature of prejudice and discrimination in Brazil: (1) "Color prejudice and discrimination exist to some extent, at least in São Paulo; yet sometimes it seems difficult to draw a sharp line between class and race prejudice," and (2) "Contrary to what happens in the United States, public opinion is strongly opposed to any kind of racial discrimination. Any deviation from what is considered to be the general pattern of race behavior [i.e., cordiality] is severely condemned and often violently reproved."[84]

Perhaps understandably, given the noted prominence of classism over racism, as well as the emphasis on miscegenation in some of the founding literature of Brazilian racial discourse, these researchers emphatically dismiss racial group formation. Harris claims, "Despite the 'ideal' stereotypes, there is no 'actual' status-role for the Negro as a Negro, for the white as a white, or for the mulatto as a mulatto. There are no racial groups."[85] Instead, the emphasis is on racial ambiguity and intermediate categories.[86] According to Harris, the "subordination of race to class, absence of descent rule, and terminological efflorescence" all contribute to "ambiguous racial calculus" in Brazil.[87]

This view of the ambiguity resulting from miscegenation leads several other prominent researchers (in addition to Harris) to specifically deny the existence of racial groups in Brazil. For example, Hutchinson concludes, "Thus race is but one of a number of elements ranking people in a social scale, rather than a separating factor which divides them into distinct groups."[88] Wagley introduces the concept of "social race," as opposed to race, a conceptualization where social interaction is not predicated on caste distinctions but on color, class, and the like: "Social races do not form self-conscious groups and 'race relations' do not take the form of interaction between 'racial' groups."[89] Significantly, Wagley concludes, "It almost might be said that 'race relations' do not exist in Brazilian society."[90] Moreover, according to Harris, "The failure to state this fundamental principle [that self-conscious racial groups do not exist] . . . easily leads to a distorted picture of the race situation in Brazil."[91]

The view of race as a subordinate factor in the politics of discrimination—as well as an emphasis on miscegenation, class, and the color continuum—frames the post-Freyre literature on Brazilian racial dynamics. Because of this, many researchers subsequently viewed this work as supporting a particular version of racial democracy ideology, which later began to be associated with the complete negation of racism.[92] Skidmore, for example, characterizes this period as supportive of an "establishment mentality," and governed by elitist, assimilationist discourse and an "indifference to race."[93] The next stage challenged this supposed mentality.

Stage Two—Challenging Antiracialism

Challenges to the antiracialism literature appeared on three fronts: (1) from the so-called São Paulo school, led by Florestan Fernandes;[94] (2) from social activists of the emerging *negro* social movements;[95] and (3) from a new generation of demographers with access to "hard" data on racial structuring.[96] The activities and writings of the São Paulo school primarily came after the initial writings of the antiracialism stage (thereby viewed as a reaction to them), but there is some significant overlap. The *negro* movement and the new generation of demographers developed later out of the social environment surrounding the gradual easing and eventual demise of the military dictatorship in power from 1964 to 1985.

The central concerns in the writing of the São Paulo school that distinguished them as a reaction to the antiracialism stage were (1) a beginning assumption that racial prejudice and discrimination did exist in Brazil and were a serious problem, (2) a negative view of miscegenation, and (3) a view of racial democracy as inducing a denial of that discrimination.[97]

The literature mentions at least three factors that influenced this alternative reading of the Brazilian context. First, contrary to the social scientists of the antiracialism stage, whose most prominent members were U.S.–educated researchers schooled in the "race relations" theories of the Chicago school, Fernandes and his students had favored a Marxist theoretical paradigm.[98] Roger Bastide also figured prominently in this school.[99] Although they privileged class relations as the determinant factor of social structuring in this industrializing capitalist nation, they sought to establish a view of "racism" as an independent variable for explaining social inequality in Brazil. To this end, the Marxist formulation of "class consciousness" appears to have influenced their conception of race relations, especially as regards the mystifying effects of racial democracy on race consciousness. According to Fernandes, the most crucial ideological effect of this myth was the responsibility placed on nonwhites for racial inequalities.[100] As Fernandes is best known for writing, this ideological effect was manifested in "the prejudice of having no prejudice."[101]

Another important difference between the São Paulo school and the antiracialism orientation was the former's negative view of miscegenation. Guimarães views this counterpoint as differentiating social scientists and elites living in São Paulo and those living and working in the more traditional Northeast: "For the intellectual elites of São Paulo . . . miscegenation was never viewed in a positive light."[102] São Paulo had experienced a large influx of European and Asian immigrants that established a diversity of ethnoracial formations that were unknown in other cities of Brazil, especially the traditional Northeast. In this Southeast context, nonwhite Brazilians were the clear minority. Furthermore, the ideology of "whitening" appeared the strongest in São Paulo. According to Guimarães, this more oppressive climate led to a devaluing of miscegenation and an emphasis on ethnoracial identification.[103]

In addition, Fernandes's close relationship and ideological affinity with the *negro* movement, which sought out a specific cultural domain for *negro* identity, may also have influenced his negative evaluation of miscegenation.[104]

An even clearer criticism of traditional racial understanding in Brazil began during the waning years of the military dictatorship, a special period labeled the *abertura democrática* (circa 1974 through 1985). Like other Latin American dictatorships, this totalitarian period was marked by repression of all opposition perceived by the military as a threat to the stability of the national community. Guimarães claims that during those years the military adopted a racial democracy orientation that became a type of "dogma" or official "ideology of the Brazilian state."[105] The essence of the military's take on racial democracy was the negation of racism in Brazil. Guimarães holds that the myth of racial democracy "eventually becomes a racist ideology, that is, a justification of the discriminatory order and of the racial inequalities that really exist."[106] It was in this context that the myth of racial democracy came to be viewed most strongly by researchers as a type of *legitimizing ideology* of the powerful in Brazil and a *mystifying ideology* for the *povo*, or nonelite classes.

During the *abertura democática*, Brazilian *negro* movements reentered the scene.[107] Some participants in these groups likewise at times equated the racial democracy myth with a "mystifying function" and even with racial genocide.[108] Furthermore, they viewed racial ambiguity as an obstacle to creating solidarity among nonwhites; instead, they favored the building of positive racial identification or *negro* racial subjectivity,[109] an endeavor that the myth of racial democracy supposedly neutralized. Therefore, it became the task of the reemergent *negro* movements to challenge what was now viewed as the essence of antiracialism—the denial of racism.

Perhaps the most important influences in this battle are Carlos Hasenbalg and Nelson do Valle Silva.[110] These authors changed the focus of Brazilian "race relations" research by demonstrating that the social inequalities in Brazil could not be reduced to class dynamics. Using quantitative methods on census and survey data, they "established an unequivocal racial component [to socioeconomic inequality] that could not be reduced to differences in education, income, class, and, what is decisive, could not be diluted in the color continuum."[111]

Most importantly, Hasenbalg and Silva propose that "it is possible and correct to aggregate data on color into two groups (whites and non-whites), as there are no substantive differences between the non-white groups (*pardos* and *pretos*)."[112] These quantitative researchers, then, reveal an underlying bipolarization of social relations in Brazil as concerns socioeconomic inequality. They also crystallize the designation of racial democracy as a legitimizing and mystifying ideology.[113] According to Guimarães, the process initiated by Hasenbalg and Silva make the concept of race inevitable for theorizing skin-color dynamics in Brazil, which leads the way to the third phase in the Brazilianist literature on race.

Stage Three—Racialism

I refer to racialism as constituting a perspective similar to the one described by political scientist Michael Hanchard as "a race-centered focus" in the analysis of Brazilian skin-color dynamics.[114] According to Segato, this stage is marked by a new generation of researchers, whom she calls "North American students," who increasingly focus on a comparison of Brazil with the United States, or more precisely, who read the Brazilian scene from the North American perspective and use the latter as a model or yardstick of racial progress.[115] With the quantitative evidence to show the underlying nonwhite and white divide, the stage was set for an explicit introduction of racialism. Segato mentions Gilliam, Winant, and Hanchard as exemplifying this point of view.[116] These researchers appear to be especially motivated by the emerging possibility of a race-centered emancipatory project in Brazil. Toward this struggle for racial equality, they prioritize race in the analysis of social structuring and interaction and are encouraged by the fact that antiracialism has been undermined through the research of Hasenbalg and Silva.

Guimarães, educated at the University of Wisconsin, Madison, and a primary architect of the racialist orientation, explicitly rejects antiracialism: "That model . . . acted to hide, rather than reveal, to deny, more than to affirm, the existence of 'races' in Brazil."[117] In strong contrast, he argues for the introduction of explicit racialism:

> My opinion, moreover, is that it is very difficult to imagine a way to fight against an imputation or discrimination [based on race] without granting [that concept] a social existence. If it were not "race," to what should we attribute the discriminations that only become intelligible through the idea of "race"?[118]

For the emancipatory project to be successful, therefore, it is necessary to bring to life, in Guimarães' phrasing, "the race concept just as it is used in common sense understandings."[119] This requires "the recognition of racism, the admission of cultural and racial differences in Brazil, the defense of strategies that are *prima facie* not universalist in nature," all tasks to be aided through social scientific research.[120]

Another key task of racialist social science was to reevaluate the color continuum and racial ambiguity concepts that appeared to devalue racial subjectivity. For example, Hanchard claims,

> Contrary to many popular as well as academic claims, phenotypic self-identification does not operate as a free-floating signifier for Brazilians, but within long-standing parameters of white and *negro,* with qualified but nonetheless oppositional meanings attached to both phenotypic categorizations.[121]

Winant is similarly suspicious of antiracialism, claiming that in Brazil, as in the United States, "racial difference, racialized subjectivity, is a permanent feature."[122] He further theorizes the emancipation project, writing that the "liberation of racial identity is as much a part of the struggle against racism as the elimination of racial discrimination and inequality."[123]

Integral to this stage was a continuation of the framing of the myth of racial democracy as a racist ideology with an obscurant function and "devastating effects."[124] Among the effects receiving the analytical attention of scholars during this stage are (1) inducing a denial of racial discrimination, (2) discouraging nonwhite identity formation, and (3) derailing the possibility of antiracism strategies.[125] Importantly, the ideology was believed to be embraced equally by white and nonwhite Brazilians.[126]

Lastly, even though this perspective views racial democracy as an obstacle to effective antiracism, Brazil is in the midst of adopting race-targeted approaches to historic racial inequality, as I discuss extensively in this book. One last characteristic of this racialism stage is a strong support of those approaches. One illustration of that support was the presentation of a document to the national congress arguing a vision of Brazil in *negro* and white and urging nationally legislated *negro* racial quotas in various spheres of public life, including in all federal universities.[127] It was signed by many scholars supporting the racialist interpretation of Brazilian population diversity.

In sum, five elements appear to characterize this racialism stage: (1) the centrality of race for sociological analysis; (2) recuperation of *negro*/white racial subjectivity; (3) the view of racial democracy or antiracialism as a legitimizing and mystifying ideology leading to a denial of racial discrimination; (4) a focus on the devastating social effects of antiracialism, e.g., neutralizing racial identity mobilization and antiracist organization; and (5) strong support for race-targeted public policy to combat racialized inequality. This phase, having its roots in the 1990s, remains dominant. However, it is not unchallenged.

Stage Four—Challenging Racialism

The "challenging racialism" stage contests racialism as a model of analysis on the grounds that it is heavily predicated on the exceptional U.S. case. Viewing this model as lifted from its roots and applied elsewhere, Silva dubs it "ethnocentric universalism." Similarly, Bourdieu and Wacquant controversially deem it "cultural imperialism."[128] Fry, Sansone, Segato, Barrios, Harris and his colleagues, Camara, Reis, and others perceive this approach as an incorrect universalization of the terms, concepts, experiences, and politics of race from the United States.[129] All of these researchers appear to challenge the idea that the United States represents the mature embodiment of a universal model of modern "race relations" while Brazil is a less-advanced variation.

In many ways, this stage's discourse on race is an updated version of many of the antiracialism ideas laid out by Pierson and Harris: An emphasis on multipolar schemas of classification, the view that color categories do not represent racial groups, the importance of social class, and the emphasis on miscegenation as the interpretative key to the Brazilian context are all re-examined. However, new to the literature is a suspicion of using race-targeted public policy to confront racial inequality.[130]

The challenges of many of the researchers of this stage to racialism focus primarily on the works of Hanchard and Winant.[131] Antiracialist scholars reject, for example, the conceptualization of race as understood in contemporary "race relations" analyses that presuppose racial divisions as concomitant with cultural group formations.[132] According to these researchers, the construction of racial (group) identities or racial subjectivity in the United States is particular to the U.S. history of legalized discrimination and segregation. Through the perversity of separation and segregation, and through the politics of contestation,[133] a very strong and particular concept of "black subjectivity"[134] or "racial consciousness"[135] or an "African niche"[136] was constructed in the United States. Silva claims, "this particular construction of black subjectivity surreptitiously colonizes [Hanchard's] analysis" in Brazil, writing that Winant, too, "remains prisoner to [that] particular construction of race."[137]

Further confronting Winant's writings, Silva claims that his "view [of racial formation] is premised upon the acceptance of racial difference as a substratum of social relations," or "organized around the idea that races are indeed god-given pre-social groups."[138] The essence of racialism, then, "envisions a society organized as a collection of 'races.'"[139] The problem arises "when this perspective provides the basis for analyzing racial politics in multiracial spaces where 'racial difference' does not correspond to a view of society as composed of distinct racial groups," as is the case in Brazil.[140]

While the racialism perspective emphasizes a bipolar underpinning to Brazilian racial dynamics, antiracialist theorists, for example, place importance on the situational nature of multiple color classifications in Brazil.[141] Fry, for example, posits that these multiple classifications, rather than branching off an underlying biracialization, may "permit the deracialization of the individual identity," making it "radically different" from the bipolar model.[142] The Brazilian system views racial differentiation "in terms of phenotype rather than origin in accordance with the view that Brazilians of any colour share a common (mixed) racial origin."[143] This both reflects and allows the view of the nation as of one race, again Freyre's "meta-race," through the process of miscegenation.

The "challenge to racialism" stage most differs from the "racialism" stage in its view of the set of ideas referred to as the myth of racial democracy. Rather than viewing it as the basis for and perpetuator of racial subordination, racial democracy in this stage is more a "myth of an interrelating people";[144] it suggests "a conjunction of powerful ideas and values that makes Brazil be Brazil."[145] Instead of an elitist message that legitimizes white supremacy while confounding Brazilians of varying degrees of African ancestry into believing they live in a racial paradise, the racial democracy orientation is viewed as a deep-seated belief in the desirability of a society truly not segmented along racial lines and in the essential equality of all peoples. This belief is so strong that even positive racial identification is viewed with "ambivalence, confusion [and] antipathy."[146] Nobles explains that "the discursive construction of racial identity in Brazil is one of an all encompassing national identity which not only questions the propriety of racial identities other than 'Brazilian' but which supersedes their existence."[147]

Lastly, many of the leading theorists of this challenging racialism stage also express opposition or concern regarding race-targeted approaches for confronting social disadvantage in Brazil.[148] Much of the basis of this opposition concerns a possible racializing effect of the state's adoption of official race categories and the racial divisions and antagonisms that may ensue.[149] Many scholars holding this antiracialist perspective also signed a document or manifesto that, like the theorists of the racialism stage, was sent to the national congress, but this one to express opposition to the federal government's adoption of racial quotas.[150] These scholars recognize the dramatic social inequalities in Brazil, but they argue that the best way to combat social exclusion in Brazil is through the construction of universally available, high-quality public services in the areas, for example, of basic education and health services. The establishment of racial quotas in higher education, according to many of the antiracialist perspective, will do little to challenge the dramatic inequalities that exist among the masses of disadvantaged Brazilians of all colors; rather, those policies might only mask the most significant causes of that inequality and thereby hamper the society's ability to actually reduce widespread disadvantage.[151]

General Guiding Hypotheses

In sum, the "racialism" and "challenging racialism" stages form the basis of what I see as two competing paradigms for the contemporary interpretation of Brazilian racial dynamics and hence of racial attitudes. The configuration of racial attitudes under each should be quite different, as should be the determinants of those configurations. The racialist perspective holds that the racial group concept is primary: Identities are racial, interests are organized racially, and ideologies are racial-group specific. Thus, attitudes should reveal the prominence of that concept through attitudinal divides along racial lines. The antiracialist approach, on the other hand, would decenter the racial group as the primary analytic concept. Thus, racial or color groupings from an antiracialist analytical lens would not robustly organize attitudinal stances in Brazil, whether according to identities, interests, or ideologies. These two guiding hypotheses organize much of the empirical analyses I present in the chapters that follow.

Presentation of Attitudinal Data Sets

To evaluate the adequacy of racialist versus antiracialist approaches, I employ data from three probability surveys to describe, explore, and explain patterns of racial attitudes in Brazil. They were created in 1995, 2000, and 2002, two from national samples (1995 and 2002) and one from the state of Rio de Janiero. Although generalizability occasionally becomes an issue that I note when appropriate, the three together provide a rich and novel picture of racial attitudes in contemporary Brazil. I do not pretend, however, that the attitudes captured in the span of years covered by these surveys directly speak to previous configurations of attitudes in Brazil; nor do I pretend that the attitudes on which I report have continued unchanged in the time since the surveys were conducted. Regarding the latter, to the contrary, as I will reiterate later, attitudinal stances in Brazil are in flux.

The 2000 Racial Attitudes Survey

The 2000 Rio de Janeiro survey is an original data source in whose elaboration I participated; it is the central data set for this study. The Ford Foundation in Brazil funded the *Centro de Articulação de Populações Marginalizadas* (CEAP) (in English, Center for the Study of Marginalized Populations), a *negro* movement/nongovernmental organization in Brazil, to head this survey project.[152] For the elaboration of the survey instrument, I spent one year (August 1998 through August 1999) in the city of Rio de Janeiro. Tasks consisted of the following: (a) weekly work sessions with the research staff of CEAP, (b) directing focus groups, and (c) conducting informal field interviews with key informants.

Through this extensive process the research team came to understand what and how to ask about race in Brazil. As in all contexts, careful question construction is essential, and an understanding of context-sensitive vocabulary and racial perspectives is required. To this end, a group of three to six CEAP members and I participated in the weekly working sessions, lasting anywhere from one to four hours during the yearlong period. The focus group research varied in setting (rural versus urban), age, skin color, and socioeconomic levels of the participants. I conducted six groups of approximately ten persons each. Focus group sessions lasted approximately one hour, and insights gained there were used for questionnaire construction. I also conducted key informant interviews with several local community leaders, two parish priests, and four schoolteachers. The end result of this process was a questionnaire comprised of eighty items. Topics include nonwhite disadvantage, Afro-Brazilian religions, perceptions of group conflict, police brutality and racial profiling, African-derived culture, interracial marriage, discrimination, prejudice, and the like.

The application of the instrument was entrusted to a professional, university-based survey research center, DataUff—*Núcleo de Pesquisas, Informações e Políticas Públicas da Universidade Federal Fluminense*. Affiliated with the Federal Fluminense University in Rio de Janeiro, this center specializes in instrument elaboration and application. I participated in various meetings with the research group to evaluate the validity of our instrument.[153] DataUFF conducted pretests of the survey. The sampling frame consisted of Brazilian adults, aged eighteen and older, residing in the state of Rio de Janeiro and was defined through official census tract data gathered in 1996 by the *Instituto Brasileiro de Geografia e Estadísticas* (IBGE). The sampling method was a stratified, multistage technique to draw a random sample of 1,200 elements. The state of Rio de Janeiro was initially divided into three regions. After selecting municipalities at random from within the region strata, successive random samples were taken of neighborhoods, then streets, then households, then individuals. Three weights were included to correct for the oversampling of the interior of the state, for the within-household probabilities of selection, and for the sampling variance on age and gender. Special care was taken regarding the training of the interviewers for the discussion of racially sensitive topics. Also, an effort was made to employ interviewers of diverse skin colors, and "race of interviewer" effects were taken into account and can be tested.

The 1995 Racial Attitudes Survey

In addition to the CEAP/DataUff data set, I also employ data from a 1995 face-to-face survey on racial attitudes conducted by the *DataFolha Instituto de Pesquisas*. The *DataFolha* Research Institute is the survey unit of the *Folha de São Paulo*, one of Brazil's major daily newspapers. Data are based on a multistage national probability sample. The sampling frame is the entire urban population sixteen and older. Approximately 76 percent of the population was considered urban at the time of the survey.[154] Municipalities were selected at random from within representative socioeconomic level, region, and size strata. Successive random samples were then taken of neighborhoods, then streets, and then individuals. The full sample consists of 5,014 persons sampled across 121 municipalities.[155] The data set roughly matches data from the 1991 census on several important variables, including race, age, and sex.[156]

The 2002 Brazilian Social Survey

The final data set I use in this book is from a national probabilistic attitudinal survey (the *Pesquisa Nacional Brasiliera*, or PESB) conducted in 2002 and funded by the Ford Foundation.[157] The PESB model follows that of the U.S. *General Social Survey* (GSS) and the *British Social Attitudes* (BSA) survey and benefited from collaboration with their research scientists. The 2002 PESB included a module on racial attitudes, with one of its stated goals being to speak to the topic of race-targeted policy. The frame was defined using census tract data gathered in 1996.

The sampling method was a stratified, multistage technique to draw a sample of 2,362 adults (eighteen and older). The nation was first divided into two strata, region and municipality. The region stratum sorted twenty-seven states and the Federal District into five regions (Midwest, North, Northeast, South, and Southeast). The municipality stratum was based on 5,507 municipalities. Of these, 102 were chosen for the sample. Capital municipalities were automatically selected. To reduce costs, municipalities with fewer than 20,000 inhabitants in the vast North and Midwest regions were excluded (approximately 3.1 percent of the total population). The other seventy-five municipalities were chosen through a stratified method according to number of domiciles as well as urbanization and literacy indexes. After municipalities had been selected, successive random samples were taken of neighborhoods, households, and individuals. The survey utilized a split-ballot method. Weights were included to correct for oversampling by region and by the questionnaire version, as well as by sex, age, education, and working and nonworking populations and were used for all the analyses included in this paper. The response rate was 77 percent.

3 Racial Boundaries

THE EXPLORATION OF RACIAL ATTITUDES in the U.S. context assumes the existence of racial groups. Researchers in that context study white racial attitudes and black racial attitudes, both of which generally reflect opinions and ideas expressed by members of one racial group concerning their relationship to the other racial group. While this is overly simplistic, the basic assumption that "racial attitudes are structured across racial groups," and that these groups undoubtedly differ from one another, underlies various dominant research perspectives.[1] Tapping this belief, Kinder and Sanders write, "Blacks and whites [in the United States] look upon the social and political world in fundamentally different and unintelligible ways."[2]

In fact, I would argue that the racial group is the central concept of dominant framings in the social science literature on racial attitudes, and it is also a central unit of analysis.[3] Thus, if we are going to use this literature to explore patterns of racial attitudes in a given context, we need to locate the putative racial groups and explore the nature of that unit of analysis.[4]

On a basic level, parsing groups means searching for boundaries and divisions. Thus, mapping out a context's racial dynamics inevitably brings into question the salience and strength of those boundaries. Although not always recognized in the literature, this is an important empirical question given that racial boundaries can be actually quite unstable and context dependent. As various scholars note, social boundaries can be "bright" or "blurred,"[5] "hard" or "soft,"[6] "thick" or "thin."[7] However, dominant perspectives on racial attitudes, like group conflict theories, tend to ignore this variability. Instead they address racialized populations as social groups in the sociological sense, as a collection of individuals who share a common identity, interact with one another, and accept membership obligations and expectations. For this to be unambiguously true, the boundaries around these groups should be hard, bright, and strong. Although this is sometimes the case, the possibility for variation over multiple contexts is enormous. Given that the actual strength of any boundary determines so much about the nature of the population it defines, an investigation into boundary salience is critical in attitudinal research.

Before I begin this empirical exploration of racial boundaries in Brazil, it is important to address the question of how racial group membership is determined. Although some students of racial dynamics may view racial group membership as a static demographic datum attached to individuals, such as sex or age, it is in fact much more subjective. In their study of census racial classification in the United States, Hirschman, Alba, and Farley comment, "For most census questions, the demographic and social characteristics are regarded as objective phenomena that are knowable if appropriate tools of measurement are designed. The question of race is different, however, because it includes an inherently subjective component."[8]

There are no objective racial group boundary markers: An individual's racial identity today clearly is what he or she says it is, especially in the survey context. Racial groups, then, should be viewed not as things in the world but as ideas couched in ideologies about how the world is organized, on the nature of human diversity, and concerning one's own identity and place in the world.[9] Therefore, to ask about someone's racial identification is an attitudinal question whether it is via self- or other-classification. The hard biology of race has been relegated by most scientists to the realm of outdated, quasi-scientific musings.

In this chapter, I examine questions requiring respondents and interviewers to self- and/or other-classify according to various formats, including in comparison to photographs. Through their answers I explore what the central racial boundaries are in Brazil and suggest whether any of these appears strong enough to define a "self-conscious social group."[10] If so, dominant perspectives from the general literature, such as group conflict theory and sociocultural perspectives, may prove helpful for framing the Brazilian context. If my results point away from the existence of robust racial subjectivity, then our theoretical lens may need adjusting.

Brazil's Racial Composition

Fernando Henrique Cardoso, ex-president and eminent sociologist, stated in a speech at a conference in 1996: "We wish to affirm . . . the existence of distinct races in Brazil."[11] Cardoso did not name those "races," perhaps considering them so obvious that specification was unnecessary. However, to map racial attitudes effectively, I need to define my unit of analysis. A logical place to begin is to find an official accounting of racial groups, which in Brazil and other multiracial contexts generally leads to the racial and ethnic categories of a nation's census.[12] As researchers have done in the United States, one can document the changing racial and ethnic composition of that nation by tracking census records.[13] Of course, to do so is to find a myriad of changing taxonomies through the years. Even through official bureau statistics, the question about existing boundaries and their salience remains contingent and in debate. In Brazil, the national censuses have been administered since 1870 and most contained a "color/racial composition" question.[14] Hence, looking to the categories of the national census is a promising place to begin the task of mapping racial boundaries.

The Brazilian Institute of Geography and Statistics (IBGE) is responsible for Brazil's decennial census. Since 1940, excepting the 1970 census in which a color-race question was not included, the IBGE has employed the categories *branco* (white), *pardo* (brown), *preto* (black), and *amarelo* (yellow or of Asian ancestry), adding *Indígena* (Indigenous) in 1991.[15] According to its 2000 census, Brazil's racial or color composition is approximately 54 percent *branco,* 39 percent *pardo,* 6 percent *preto,* 0.5 percent *amarelo,* and 0.4 percent Indigenous. This accounting is derived from a self-identification question using the above listed categories in a closed format: "Considering the following categories, what is your color or race?" The term *race* was added in 1991 after over 100 years of asking only about color. Nobles claims that the addition of the term *race* was designed to reflect the new inclusion of the indigenous category in the national census in 1991 at the bequest of the International Monetary Fund.[16] Formerly, persons of indigenous descent were generally labeled *pardos.*

As an important side note, I will be focusing on the categories *branco* (white), *pardo* (brown), and *preto* (black) and excluding individuals who consider themselves primarily of Indigenous or of Asian ancestries. Because these two populations together make up less than one percent of the national population as measured through the 2000 census, their numbers are too small in existing attitudinal surveys to provide much confidence in most statistical operations regarding those populations. Regarding the decision on whether or not to translate the census terms into English in subsequent discussions, this is a delicate question, for their translations can lead to some confusion and misleading oversimplification. For instance, the category *branco* is often translated into English as "white." However, the idea of a "white" population embedded in the social science literature on race is many times predicated on notion of white racial purity developed in the United States through its historic *de jure* adoption of the rule of hypodescent.[17] The facile transference of that notion of whiteness into Brazil is wrongheaded. A Brazilian *branco,* for example, may be considered non-*branco* by a third party using the U.S. notion of whiteness as a universal yardstick for measuring racial classification. Moreover, the term *pardo,* if simply translated as "brown," may wrongly conjure up the idea of Hispanic for many non-Brazilianists. Some translate it into English as "mulatto." Finally, substituting black for *preto* may erroneously equate that category with black racial group membership as also understood in the United States. Guimarães, for example, translates *preto* as "dark black" in English.[18] In a spirit of compromise and to lessen the burden for non–Portuguese-speaking readers, I will use the English translations of *branco* (white) and *pardo* (brown), relying on the reader to recall the above-mentioned caveats, but I will continue using the *preto* (black) census term without translation. Maintaining *preto* in Portuguese enables its important sociological distinction from another "black" category not used in the census, *negro,* that I introduce below, and from the category "nonwhite," which is a statistical summation category of *pardos* and *pretos.*[19]

The first question to be addressed here is: Do the census white, brown, and *preto* terms identify racial groups? In other words, do they constitute social groups possessing distinct racial subjectivity and cohesion? If so, we will be studying white racial attitudes, brown racial attitudes, and *preto* racial attitudes, following the assumed correlation between group boundaries and attitudinal stances. White, brown, and *preto* would become the values of our racial group unit of analysis, and these values could be simply referred to as "races" from that perspective. Secondly, we need to ask if there are other salient racial group boundaries in Brazil not represented or captured incorrectly in the census. For example, the labels *moreno* and *negro,* whose meanings I discuss below, are used frequently in Brazil but are not census terms. If these represent salient racial boundaries and exhibit high levels of cohesion and subjectivity, then the list of racial groups may need to be modified or expanded. Finally, a third question differs from both of its predecessors: Might the terms of the national census refer to color categories rather than racialized social groups?

All of these are very contentious questions in contemporary Brazil and in the literature. Scholars, government bureaucrats, politicians, and social movement actors disagree on which terms should be used by the census and what they represent.[20] Before delving empirically into the Brazilian census terms, I briefly lay out these competing scholarly positions as to the nature and/or correctness of the census categories in Brazil.

Triadic Racial Group Framing

In a study on the effect of commercial television in Brazil on racial attitudes, labeled a "cultivation effect," Leslie states one of his central research questions as follows: "How does the cultivation effect differ for each of the four major ethnic groups in Brazil?"[21] He then divides Brazil's "ethnic groups" into the following: white, brown, *preto,* and *amarelo.* Leslie continues this usage throughout his study, at times substituting *race* for *ethnic group.* Similarly, Brazilianist historian George Reid Andrews mentions at one point in his expansive and sophisticated work a view of the Brazilian census categories as representing distinct racial groups. Although this perspective is not dominant in his research, he writes:

> Ever since the colonial period Brazilians have drawn a distinction between *pardos* and *pretos,* who they see as two related but different *groups.* Hallowed by centuries of usage, and now deeply engrained in Brazilian culture and attitudes, the distinction is a real one. . . . I acknowledge the existence of . . . the *pardo* and *preto racial groups.*[22]

In the majority of his book, Andrews alternatively collapses brown and *preto* categories into a collective black or *negro* classification to emphasize a white versus nonwhite racial dichotomy in Brazil (a practice I explore later). However, this is notwithstanding his comments on the existence of culturally and attitudinally distinct brown and *preto* racial groups. Adding to the discussion of racial categories, Roberto Da Matta also hints at the distinctive nature of browns as opposed to *pretos* and whites, saying that although *mulatos* and *mestiços* (mixed-race individuals who are captured under the *brown* term on the census) also exist in the United States, they "are explicitly recognized culturally and ideologically" in Brazil rather than being "submerged as whites or as *negros*."[23]

Other researchers adopt the same treatment of the census categories as racialized social groups. Although in some cases the use of the concept "group" may only be what Brubaker calls "an intellectual bad habit" rather than a statement of position regarding the racial groupness of these categories,[24] employing race-centered language and methodologies to analyze the Brazilian context supports, explicitly or not, the census racial group view. Consequently, this triadic framing suggests the interpretation of contemporary racial dynamics in Brazil as "race relations" between the white, brown, and *preto* racial groups.

Other Racial Groups

Some scholars, sectors of government, and *negro* movement actors disagree with the view that the white, brown, and *preto* categories are the best way to capture racial or ethnic group salience in Brazil and suggest various modifications to the official categories. Harris and his colleagues, for example, argue explicitly for the inclusion of *moreno* as an official census category.[25] These authors base this proposal on two principal factors: their support for a strictly emic system of classification[26] and the high level of saliency of the *moreno* category as a preferred descriptor of "color-race." Although they confirm *moreno* as highly ambiguous due to its popular use "across a wider spectrum of etic phenotypes than any other color-race term," they claim that "this ambiguity cannot be eliminated from the Brazilian system of color-race identity without compromising its emic integrity."[27] Thus, color-race ambiguity and ambivalence *about* color-race identification are not synonymous for these researchers: *Moreno* corresponds to a social identity that the census must capture. They further suggest that it is an important civil right to be able to self-identify in the national census with this term of choice.[28] Other researchers also at times treat the *moreno* grouping directly as a racial group.[29]

In contrast to the proposal to widen the choices (and increasing the potential ambiguity) of the census categories, a second proposal collapses the brown and *preto* terms into a unified "Afro-Brazilian" racial category called *negro*.[30] Sansone's extensive ethnographic studies address the popular understanding of *negro* in Brazil.[31] He offers the following approximate definitions: *Preto* is "a traditional term that refers primarily to color" whereas *negro* is "originally a very offensive term that in the last decades became a term for ethnic affirmation."[32] Implicit in these two definitions is that *preto* refers to the darker end of the traditional Brazilian dark-to-light color continuum and that ethnic affirmation refers to persons emphasizing an identity rooted in African ancestry. This division between *preto* as color and *negro* as ethnicity or race may oversimplify complex dynamics, but it is represented in that fashion by *negro* movement actors and race scholars.[33] Some *negro* movement actors also refer to the difference as between the "common black" (*preto*) and the "Africanized black" (*negro*).[34]

This "collective black"[35] category represents a politicized strategy[36] to correct what the *negro* movements view as the detrimental masking of binary "race relations" between *negro* and white racial groups.[37] Within this discourse, *negros* are a majority racial group that includes all nonwhites of varying degrees of African ancestry and that extends to its members a collective *negro* classification. Although this idea may have been initiated by social movement discourse, its logic is echoed in academic circles where researchers write of Brazil as having the largest national "black" or *negro* population outside of Nigeria,[38] and discuss a reduction of the census categories to *negro* and white.[39] Prominent *negro* politician, academic, and activist Nascimento clarifies the meaning of the *negro* term:

> Official Brazilian census data use two color categories for African descendants: *preto* (literally, "black") for the dark-skinned and *pardo* (roughly, mulatto and mestizo) for others. It is now accepted convention to identify the black population as the sum of the *preto* and *pardo* categories, referred to as *negro, afro-brasileiro,* or *afro-descendente*. In English, "black," "African Brazilian," and "people of African descent" refer to this same sum of the two groups [*preto* and *pardo*].[40]

In this practice, *negro* becomes the Brazilian equivalent to the U.S. category African American, which may be translated as Afro-Brazilian by researchers using (bi)racial terminology.[41]

Hence, both the terms *moreno* and *negro* have been evaluated at different times as identifying social groups in Brazil by divergent academic and social movement actors who propose their adoption into the national census. If true, my unit of analysis in the study of racial attitudes would then necessarily include *moreno* and/or *negro* racial groups.

Census Terms as Color Categories

A third position holds that the official census categories do not represent racial groups at all; rather, they capture important color dynamics. Silva writes:

> The collection of data concerning color in the official census form is based on the supposition that, whatever a respondent's racial identity or verbal preference might be to indicate his or her color, the question in the closed form in predetermined categories is understood as a reference to the demographic characteristic of skin color. And, as such, is answered in the approximated correct way by the respondent.[42]

The assumptions behind viewing the census categories as color descriptions instead of racial group designations may originate with IBGE officials. This institution has historically interpreted the population as being so mixed in terms of "racial" origins that it would be impossible to ask respondents to define themselves in discrete racial classifications.[43] According to this stance, extensive miscegenation has led to a point where the question of color or race may be generally understood as it was by Noguiera: Brazil's color awareness responds to *marca* or appearance, in opposition to the explicitly racial U.S. model based on *origem* or ancestry.[44] IBGE officials, then, originally chose color instead of race, focusing on phenotype and excluding cultural and historic or ancestral criteria.[45]

In this view, the white category is commonly understood as comprised of lighter skin-toned individuals, and category membership may be relatively straightforward within that context. It is less clear what skin color corresponds to the brown category. The literal meaning of *brown* in Portuguese refers to an unflattering, arid color, perhaps grayish brown, that in popular parlance would rarely be used for self-identification. Butler suggests that its contemporary usage encompasses "brownness" and includes the various intermediate shades, each with its own name.[46] *Preto* refers strictly to the darker end of a color continuum.[47]

In sum, this perspective embraces the notion that the census categories, as put by Piza and Rosemberg, capture "physical characteristics that have nothing to do with racial or ethnic membership."[48] Hence, these categories may not robustly structure racial attitudes.

Social Boundaries: Internal and External Processes

To explore these various perspectives, which I do in an extensive empirical analysis that follows, it makes sense to discuss the nature of racial and ethnic boundaries and how these are constructed in the first place. It is widely accepted that social identities in general may be viewed as practical accomplishments, rather than static forms, resulting from the interplay of external and internal (or other- and self-) definition.[49] External definition refers to the way one person or group of persons defines another and takes place through several different strategies. Exclusionary tactics, such as discrimination, and official labeling through the national census or identity documents are two examples of external definition processes.[50] Internal definition, conversely, refers to dynamics in which "actors signal to in- or out-group members a self-definition of their nature or identity,"[51] using language, religion, or culture to create a sense of group belonging.[52]

The interplay between internal and external definition processes often creates we/they boundary formation: Ethnic and racial identities are examples of this general process. Supporting this idea, Barth writes that ethnic groups "are categories of ascription and identification by actors themselves."[53] Thus, as Barth posits, an ethnic group "has a membership which identifies itself, and is identified by others, as constituting a category distinguishable from other categories of the same order."[54]

In terms of racial group formation, external dynamics are generally considered more influential.[55] Jenkins' extensive work, for example, focuses specifically on the power of external definition in the formation of racial group boundaries.[56] Central to that framing is the sociological distinction between a category and a group.[57] A category is a collection of individuals whose nature and composition are defined by the categorizer, usually a higher-status or more powerful "other." In that case, the categorized might not necessarily view themselves as belonging together. A group, however, involves an experience of membership or belonging; it is more generally internally defined. Hence, in theory, we can distinguish, for example, a racial category and a racial group, thereby noting the variability in boundary salience that can exist among differing racialized populations.

Along with the recognition that the boundaries of racialized collectives may differ in terms of their comparative solidity, it also follows that they might change over time. Jenkins explores, for example, external factors that produce racialized social groups *out of* racial categories of individuals.[58] In this way, racial groups might form out of a sense of cohesion, solidarity, and subjectivity among a population characterized as racially distinct by a more powerful other. In the United States, for example, the formation of contemporary black racial group subjectivity may be viewed as resulting from legalized discrimination and segregation, official naming by state censuses, and later by the politics of recognition.[59]

Of course, the internalization of categorization is always contingent; one cannot clearly predict when a category of individuals may assimilate, in whole or part, the terms by which it is defined by an "other."[60] Brubaker and Cooper, for example, conclude, "Identification—of oneself and of others—is intrinsic to social life; 'identity' in the strong sense is not."[61]

To help further understand the variable nature of the boundaries of racial populations, we can locate both groups and categories on the "groupness" continuum. Groupness measures "the sense of belonging to a distinctive, bounded, solidary group."[62] On the high end of this continuum we find the social group, in which there is a feeling of commonality, connectedness, and shared identity. The social group, therefore, has a clear and definite boundary. Brubaker and Cooper describe this type of collective phenomenon as follows: "This is the emotionally laden sense of belonging to a distinctive, bounded group, involving both a felt solidarity or oneness with fellow group members and a felt difference from or even antipathy to specified outsiders."[63] That is, "Strong notions of collective identity imply strong notions of group boundedness and homogeneity. They imply high degrees of groupness, an 'identity' or sameness among group members, a sharp distinctiveness from nonmembers, a clear boundary between inside and outside."[64]

On the other hand, categories have much more porous boundaries and thus exhibit relatively lower levels of groupness.[65] There may be shared characteristics that promote a sense of sameness, but the relationship between category members does not carry the emotional weight, for example, of belonging to a social group.

Thus, as Yancey and his colleagues state, "ethnicity [and race] should not be regarded as an ascribed attribute with only two discrete categories, but as a continuous variable."[66] They further comment, "We echo Cohen's recent statement that: 'unless we recognize differences in degree of manifestation we shall fail to make much progress in the analysis of ethnicity. To put it in the idiom of research, ethnicity is a variable.'"[67] In sum, because internal and external definition processes vary across contexts and over time, and because they are not always consistent with one another, different kinds of boundaries emerge that create looser or tighter divisions. The nature of these divisions then determines the nature of attitudes involved. This basic premise will guide my analysis of racial boundaries in Brazil.

Empirical Exploration of Boundaries

To assess Brazilian racial boundaries, I begin by looking at the internal- and external-definition processes surrounding the census terms. I do this first by testing the consistency of self- versus other-classification, and second by assessing whether a person shows in-group category loyalty by self-classifying similarly in a variety of circumstances. Next, I look at the robustness of alternate color-race classifications by exploring one factor frequently associated with the "hardness" of racial boundaries: whether or not they enclose phenotypically distinguishable individuals. Finally, I ask whether or not the census categories represent color classifications rather than racialized social groups by using photographs to test the consistency of phenotypic classification. None of these empirical operationalizations alone speaks unambiguously to the issue of groupness. As a whole, however, these empirical inquiries address levels of groupness, thus suggesting whether or not a racialized social group perspective is an adequate framing in Brazil and, if so, which are the salient racial groups.

Consistency of Self- versus Other-Categorization

Integral to the premise that social identity is the result of both internal and external processes, Jenkins stresses that group identity formation is never unilateral. On the one hand, "it is not enough to assert an identity. That identity must also be validated (or not) by those with whom we have dealings."[68] On the other hand, nor is it enough to be ascribed an identity. As Brubaker and Cooper remark, "[We should not] presuppose that such identifying (even by powerful agents, such as the state) will necessarily result in . . . internal sameness . . . distinctiveness . . . [and] bounded groupness."[69] Clearly there is ample room for disjunction between external and internal dynamics that may affect levels of groupness.

To test the coming together of asserted and ascribed boundaries, we can compare a person's own perception of his or her racial classification to a third party's perception of the same (self- versus other- or interviewer-classification). Following theory, it would seem a straightforward assumption that the greater the similarity between these two, the more robust the boundary. Conversely, a lack of mutual agreement may suggest more porous or blurred social boundaries.[70]

Buttressing this assumption is the example of the United States, where white and black racial identification is very strong. Thus, in that context we should expect a high level of consistency between interviewer- and self-classification. Although data that measure interviewer- versus self-classification in the United States are difficult to find, due in part to the fact that possible disagreement between the two has rarely been considered an issue, at least one study by Harris and Sims looked at racial identification consistency making use of data from the National Longitudinal Study of Adolescent Health.[71] In that survey of adolescents in the United States (n = 5,000), they found an almost perfect correspondence between the way an interviewer classified adolescents and the way those same adolescents self-classified. Of adolescents that self-identified as white, 99.9 percent were labeled the same by interviewers, as were the 99.8 percent that self-identified as black.[72] Because we know the United States to be characterized by strong racial group boundaries, these findings support the positive association between classification consistency and robust racial group identification.

Several researchers have performed similar measurements of interview- versus self-classification consistency in Brazil.[73] Telles and Lim, for example, show how divergence between these two classification schemes in Brazil leads to different estimates of racial inequality, and they conclude that interviewer- versus self-classification inconsistency is characteristic of ambiguous racial boundary formation in Brazil and in Latin America in general.[74] They contrast this ambiguity with the U.S. and South African contexts.

Following the lead of those previous studies, I cross-tabulate survey data that capture both interviewer- and self-classification of color from the 2000 CEAP/DataUff, the 1995 DataFolha, and the 2002 PESB datasets. The theoretical assumption, again, is: The greater the level of consistency between self- versus interviewer-classification, the higher the level of groupness, thereby suggesting the existence of racialized social groups.

Table 3.1 provides a summary glance of all three surveys on this issue of consistency. Beginning with the CEAP/DataUff data, column 1 shows that when cross tabulating self- versus interviewer-classification, only 77 percent of persons who self-classified as whites were classified the same by interviewers. Although relatively high compared to the other two classifications, this number is very low compared to the results from the United States. Only 60 percent of self-classified browns and 56 percent of self-classified *pretos* were placed in the same categories by interviewers. This means that interviewers evaluated 23 percent of self-classified whites, 40 percent of self-classified browns, and fully 44 percent of self-classified *pretos* as belonging to different categories.

Table 3.1 Percent distribution of consistency between interviewer-classification and self-classification of color in census format, 2000, 1995, 2002

Census category	CEAP/DataUff	DataFolha	PESB
White/White	77%	88%	78%
Brown/Brown	60	71	74
Preto/Preto	56	69	51
TOTAL	100	100	100
N	1,034	4,516	2,281

SOURCES: CEAP/DataUff 2000, DataFolha 1995, PESB 2002.

Also reported in Table 3.1, both the national DataFolha and PESB surveys produced similar results. In the former, 88 percent of whites, 71 percent of browns, and 69 percent of *pretos* were consistently classified. The 2002 PESB results show consistent classification for 78, 74, and 51 percent of whites, browns, and *pretos,* respectively.

The external and internal definitions are divergent enough, therefore, to suggest significant relative ambiguity between color categories in Brazil, in turn suggesting lower levels of groupness in populations named by the census. This is especially true of *pretos,* whose likelihood of being identified the way they identify themselves approaches 50:50 in the national PESB sample. In comparison to the U.S. context where, according to the Harris and Sim study, consistency is close to 100 percent, these data suggest that significantly lower levels of groupness characterize all three categories of the Brazilian census.

Category Loyalty

If the official census categories represent robust racial groups, we might also expect respondents to self-identify similarly whether or not the options are expanded or an open format is used. In other words, a high level of groupness is positively associated with category loyalty.[75] A feeling of belonging and allegiance to a label would flow from the sense of group solidarity and boundary recognition that mark internalized identities.[76] This is further supported by social identity theory, which holds that mere sorting of individuals into categories creates strong in-group favoritism, which in turn should theoretically promote category loyalty.[77]

The U.S. case is again instructive. In 1996, the Census Bureau carried out a survey (Race and Ethnic Targeted Test) that, according to Hirschman, Alba, and Farley, was designed "to determine how the American population would respond to alternative questions on the measurement of racial and ethnic origin."[78] The research experiment included "variations in the order of the questions, in question wording, in the inclusion of a multiracial/biracial category, in directions that allowed for multiple responses to the race question, and in a combined race and Spanish-origin question."[79] They report that: "unmistakably consistent conclusions emerge from the results produced by the different experiments. The reporting of race by non-Hispanics appears to be affected only slightly by changes in format. The smallest changes are registered in the white and black sample."[80] Hirschman concludes, regarding this dynamic, "The overwhelming majority of African Americans, Asian Americans, and whites will classify themselves in the same categories regardless of what classifications are used."[81] This degree of category loyalty suggests high levels of groupness within black and white communities in the United States, the points of comparison in Brazil.

How do the three official census categories hold up when surveys change formats in Brazil? Do respondents remain loyal to their "groups"? In all three data sets at which we are looking, respondents were asked expanded-option (CEAP/DataUff) and open-ended (DataFolha and PESB) questions before self-classifying in the official census format. For the expanded-option question in the CEAP/DataUff survey, we employed focus groups to develop a list of the most prevalent categories in Brazil. Table 3.2 contains the results from open-ended and expanded-option self-classification formats from all three surveys.

Beginning with the 2000 CEAP/DataUff data from the state of Rio de Janeiro, we see a pattern emerge. The proportion of the population self-classifying as white is 48 percent in the closed census format, compared to 33 percent in the expanded format. In other words, 31 percent of census-classified whites opted for another category in the open format: This suggests that "whiteness" may be significantly less coveted than might be assumed.[82] The brown category suffers an even greater loss, moving from 35 percent in the closed format to 15 percent in the expanded format. That is a loss of 57 percent of browns from the census format. The greatest movement came from the *preto* classification, falling from 17 percent to 4 percent in the expanded format, meaning that over three-fourths of census-classified *pretos* choose other labels when given the option. Clearly, category loyalty is not robust in Brazil.

Results from the PESB and DataFolha national survey data, also in Table 3.2, reveal the same dynamic. For example, in the PESB sample, those self-

Table 3.2 Percent distributions of self-classification in census and expanded/open formats, 2000, 1995, 2002

Color/Race	CEAP/DataUff		DataFolha		PESB	
	Census	Expand	Census	Open	Census	Open
White	48%	33%	47%	42%	49%	43%
Moreno	—	29	—	31	—	24
Brown	35	15	33	6	39	15
Negro	—	9	—	3	—	7
Preto	17	4	21	5	12	3
Moreno claro	—	—	—	7	—	3
Mulato	—	5	—	1	—	1
Mestiço	—	5	—	0	—	0
Others	—	—	—	5	—	4
TOTAL	100	100	101	100	100	100
N	1,034	1,035	4,516	4,447	2,225	2,306

SOURCES: CEAP/DataUff 2000, DataFolha 1995, PESB 2002.

classifying as white fell by six percentage points. Even more dramatically, the brown category was reduced by twenty-three percentage points, or by about 60 percent, and the *preto* category lost over 75 percent of its members: Only three percent of respondents claimed the *preto* label when given a completely open choice.

One might see this as a question of semantics and suggest that although individuals of the three racial "groups" sometimes prefer different terms, these terms all refer to the same population. In the United States, for example, one might prefer to be called "black" instead of "African American," or "European American" instead of "white," but in both cases the two terms would generally be judged as descriptors of the same social group. In Brazil, many people do prefer a different set of terms in general than those in the census, as I will address in the next section. However, if the original three terms are truly capturing social groups that self-classify using interchangeable terms, then category membership in the expanded- and open-format categories would correspond to (or collapse into) those of the closed format categories. This is far from true. Table 3.3 is a cross-tabulation of the census format with the expanded format of the 2000 CEAP/Datauff sample. It reveals in its column-percentaged format that, when given the chance, 38 percent of census browns (see column 2) move to the *moreno* term. However, they are also joined by

Table 3.3 Percent self-classification of color-race in the expanded format by the census format: Adult population in the state of Rio de Janeiro, 2000

	Self-classification		
Self-classification	White	Brown	Preto
White	68%	0%	0%
Brown	0	43	1
Preto	0	1	22
Mulatto	1	8	10
Mestiço	4	7	3
Negro	1	3	42
Moreno	26	38	21
TOTAL	100	100	100
Percent distr.	48	35	17

SOURCE: CEAP/DataUff.

$N = 1035$

26 percent of census whites (column 1) and 21 percent of census *pretos* (column 3). That is, the *moreno* label is not simply a substitute label for brown; those preferring to self-classify as *moreno* are a cross-selection of all the groupings. Thus, entirely new groupings are formed, which challenges the triadic racial group view of the census terms. Very similar dynamics are repeated in the 1995 DataFolha and the 2002 PESB samples. (Cross-tabulations not shown.)

In sum, regarding the triadic racial groups view, the lack of category loyalty and the inconsistency between interviewer- and self-classification suggest that the current census categories' levels of racial groupness are not robust; hence, these findings lend some support to the view that these census categories do not represent three distinct racialized social groups.

Alternate Category Preferences as Social Groups

Returning to the question of category choice, research reveals that many Brazilians express significant preference for categories outside the census list to describe their color or race.[83] Table 3.2 revealed that in the CEAP/DataUff survey, a full 29 percent of respondents self-identified as *moreno,* making that the largest color/race segment after white. In addition, about 7 percent of respondents chose the *negro* term. The remaining 8 percent were split among various extra-official terms popular in everyday talk. This trend is continued in the other datasets. *Moreno* remains the second most popular term after white (31 percent in 1995 and 24 percent in 2002, as reported in Table 3.2), and the *negro* term more than doubled in popularity from 3 percent in 1995 to 7 percent in 2002. Is it possible, then, that the *moreno* and *negro* populations exhibit high levels of groupness, hence representing racialized social groups?

Because of questionnaire construction, I was not able to test self- versus other-classification or category loyalty to answer this question in the case of noncensus terms. However, there is another way to gauge groupness in terms of the *negro* and *moreno* populations. Most scholars would agree that, in contemporary contexts, racial constructions largely stem from a perceived biological difference manifested in phenotype distinctions.[84] That is, phenotype becomes the central marker through which members assert their in-group similarity and are ascribed out-group membership by nonmembers. Conversely, if third parties are unable to ascribe someone to a racial category, and membership is known only to insiders, the robustness of the category is questionable.[85] Alba calls this a case of "blurred boundaries" and states: "Boundary blurring implies that the social profile of a boundary has become less distinct: the clarity of the social distinction involved has become clouded, and individuals' location with respect to the boundary may appear indeterminate."[86] Because status clarity is disrupted, boundaries may become porous and less effective organizers of social dynamics, meaning that ambiguity about who belongs and who does not may be negatively associated with levels of groupness.

Membership ambiguity in some cases, then, may be approximated by exploring perceived skin-color distinctiveness: If members of a collective appear to exhibit a distinguishable range of phenotypic characteristics, then there may be more of a chance of racial group formation. One way to explore this is to look at how individuals self-classifying themselves as *morenos* or *negros* responded in the alternative closed-format census questions. Are these categories pulling together similar skin-tones as delineated by the white, brown, and *preto* categories? I conceptualize this operationalization as measuring the census color content of alternative category preferences.[87]

Morenos. Regarding *morenos,* Table 3.4 presents a row-percentaged cross tabulation of self-classification in the census format versus self-classification in the expanded format from the 2000 CEAP/DataUff survey. It shows which categories these respondents chose in the census format, and thus these results may approximate one view of the color content of the *moreno* category. The table reveals that fully 43 percent of those choosing to self-classify as *moreno* in the expanded format self-classified as white in the closed format. Another

Table 3.4 Percent self-classification of color-race in the census format by expanded format: Adult population in the state of Rio de Janeiro, 2000

	Census format				Percent distr.
Expanded format	White	Brown	Preto	Total	
White	95%	5%	0%	100%	33%
Brown	1	98	1	100	15
Preto	0	5	95	100	4
Mulato	6	59	35	100	5
Mestiço	37	50	13	100	5
Negro	7	13	80	100	9
Moreno	43	45	12	100	29

SOURCE: CEAP/DataUff.

$N = 1035$

12 percent self-classified as *preto* in the closed census format, and the remaining 45 percent self-classified as brown. The DataFolha and PESB national data sets follow the same pattern. In 1995, the *moreno* category was comprised of 24 percent census whites, 60 percent census browns, and 16 percent census *pretos;* in 2002 it was made up of 19 percent census whites, 64 percent census browns, and 17 percent census *pretos* (cross-tabulations not shown). Hence, those who choose the term *moreno* come from all over the color spectrum. It is a broad category without clear color distinction, which suggests lower levels of groupness.

Based on that analysis, the *moreno* term may not represent a robust social group at all. It is true that many people call themselves *moreno,* as Harris and his colleagues document.[88] However, evidence suggests that the *moreno* category lacks significant we/they boundary clarity and may instead be an umbrella term not tightly attached to a specific phenotype. Indeed, if, as some suggest, *moreno* represents "Brazilianness,"[89] then almost any Brazilian can potentially be considered *moreno.* In fact, people may be choosing this category precisely because it is not a segmented group identity, but a collective whole, thus nullifying the we/they divisions that may be crucial to group formation.

Negros. Does the *negro* label represent a racialized social group that is defined by collective identity and cohesion? Returning to Table 3.2 we see that the *negro* category is far less popular than the *moreno* label. For example, the results show that only 9 percent of respondents chose to self-identify in this manner when given the choice in the 2000 CEAP/DataUff survey of the state of Rio de Janeiro. Only 3 percent did so in the 1995 national survey. Who are those who feel that the *negro* category best describes their color-race? Table 3.4 shows that 80 percent of those who chose to self-classify as *negro* in the open format in the CEAP/DataUff survey called themselves *preto* in the census format. Additionally, 13 percent self-classified as brown in the census format, and another 7 percent self-classified as white. Clearly, if the *preto* category, which makes up 80 percent of the *negro* population, is comprised of respondents from the darker end of the color spectrum (as researchers hold[90]), then the *negro* category can be similarly characterized in that survey context. Hence, this suggests significant census color homogeneity among those of the *negro* category, which also suggests the possibility of higher levels of groupness.

However, putting these data into a larger perspective, we see from Table 3.3 regarding the CEAP/DataUff data set that of those who identified as *preto* in the closed format, only 42 percent actually chose the *negro* category in the expanded format. Twenty-one percent chose *moreno*, and 22 percent chose to remain with the *preto* classification. Hence, the *negro* category may represent a subgrouping of the *preto* population, meaning, again, that external validation of a *negro* identity may be problematic. Because a majority of the census *pretos*, who may share the same phenotypic characteristics as *negros*, do not choose to self-identify as such, the *negro* term may not represent a unique, bounded racial group. Alternately, if the two are interchangeable terms, then the low levels of groupness that characterize the *preto* term established in our earlier measurement of the inconsistency between self- versus other-classification might also apply to *negro* as well. Either way suggests low levels of groupness for the self-identified *negro* population as captured in these survey contexts.

Moreover, according to *negro* movement actors and race scholars, *negros* are defined as all browns and *pretos*.[91] Using that definition, there is no doubt about the low level of groupness of the *negro* population. Table 3.3 shows that only 3 percent of the brown population in the CEAP/DataUff survey chose to self-classify as *negro* in the expanded format question. In the 1995 and 2002 national datasets, 2 and 5 percent of browns chose *negro*, respectively. Hence, *negro* clearly does not substitute for brown or *preto*, nor does it appear to be an umbrella nonwhite term that represents a racialized social group. Nobles states that even the *negro* movement "recognizes that the vast majority of those who self-identify as *moreno* (and *pardo*, for that matter) most likely do not see themselves as part of a collective black racial group or even as partners in a common cause."[92] In fact, she writes that "Brazil's black majority [that is, the *negro* population] is a paper creation."[93] Telles similarly claims: "*Negro* in the popular system, like *preto,* refers only to those at the darkest end of the color continuum. Thus, while the *negro* movement has succeeded in giving *negro* wide currency in the government and the media, the popular use of the term continues to be limited."[94] In fact, Burdick's ethnographic work documents a dynamic of nonwhite Brazilians rejecting the *negro* label. Referring to a process he calls "color-identity alienation," he shows how *negro* movement organizations have distanced many nonwhite Brazilians by insisting that they self-label as *negros.*[95] Not only does this clearly violate the principles of self-classification,[96] but it also suggests that there is no internally defined racialized group that includes all nonwhites in Brazil.

The Census and the Color Continuum

If the national census categories do not clearly reference robustly defined racial groups, do they generally refer to color? I can explore this possibility in a similar manner to the ways in which I approached the existence of racial groups based on the consistency of external versus internal category definitions but employing a different rationale. That is, if phenotype color is an "understood" criterion, then there should be significant correspondence between interviewer and self-classification. However, as Table 3.1 showed, this is not the case at all. Interviewers evaluated 23 percent of self-classified whites, 40 percent of self-classified browns, and fully 44 percent of self-classified *pretos* as belonging to different categories. In other words, these categories may not be effective organizers of phenotypic information, or phenotype may not be as "understood" as the research assumes.

Could it be in those cases, however, that the perceived external objectivity of the physical characteristic color is lost due to such variables as race-of-interviewer bias[97] or the effect of the social class of the respondent on the interviewer's judgment (a "class-of-respondent" bias)? To carry color to a more objective level and format, it makes sense to control the dynamic set of information that is present in the survey context. Generally, the interviewer and respondent both could allow the context (the house of the respondent in household interviews) and other social class clues such as body language, mannerisms, speech, and dress to influence how they self- or other-identify. However, the 2002 PESB used a method that allows us to evaluate the respondents' levels of agreement on who belongs in which categories controlling for most of the social class proxies and for race-of-interviewer effects. Respon-

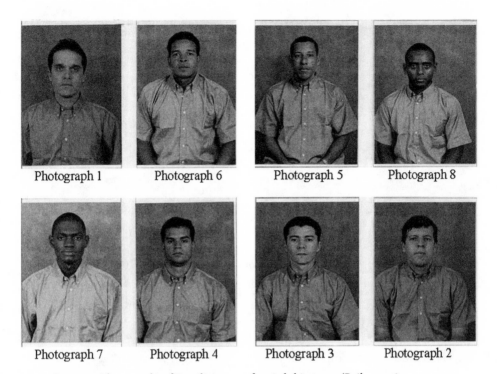

| Photograph 1 | Photograph 6 | Photograph 5 | Photograph 8 |

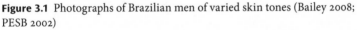

| Photograph 7 | Photograph 4 | Photograph 3 | Photograph 2 |

Figure 3.1 Photographs of Brazilian men of varied skin tones (Bailey 2008; PESB 2002)

dents were shown eight photographs of young Brazilian men whose colors span the color continuum all in the same context wearing identical clothing. (See Figure 3.1.)[98] They were then asked to classify the eight photographs according to the census format.

The results are presented in Table 3.5. They reveal that there was a great deal of consensus on who was white, brown, or *preto:* Close to 90 percent or more of the respondents classified seven of the eight photographs similarly into these categories. For example, 96, 88, and 86 percent of all respondents placed photographs 1, 2, and 3 into the white category (column 1). Likewise, 87 and 89 percent (column 2) placed photographs 5 and 6 in the brown category, and 96 percent of all the respondents (column 3) placed photographs 7 and 8 in the *preto* category. The only photograph that caused a lower level of agreement was photograph 4. Twenty-five percent judged him as white and 73 percent as brown. These generally very high levels of agreement on the placement of individuals in the white, brown, and *preto* categories suggest some

Table 3.5 Percent distribution of other-classification of photographs in census format: Adult population in Brazil, 2002 (row-percentaged)

Photograph	White	Brown	Preto
1	95.6%	3.9%	0.2%
2	87.8	11.5	0.8
3	85.9	13.1	1.0
4	25.2	73.0	1.8
5	4.7	86.8	8.5
6	3.8	88.7	7.5
7	0.9	3.1	96.1
8	1.0	2.6	96.4

SOURCE: PESB 2002, data adapted from Bailey 2008.

consensus on an external evaluation of these individuals, and it may be reasonably assumed that the central factor used to sort them was phenotype.

In addition, in contrast to racial group subjectivity, if the official terms were merely color descriptions, there would be no reason to presume category loyalty. In other words, when given a choice, respondents may choose a variety of other terms to capture their unique color. As indicated in Table 3.2, we already know Brazilians will choose from at least a handful of other descriptors when give the option. In fact, Brazilians literally use dozens of terms to describe color or race. Table 3.6 lists a random selection of 45 of the 134 of these unique, largely color-oriented terms that an open format question produced from a 1976 national survey. The variability of the unique color labels is fanciful, to say the least. These results support the belief that Brazilians understand categorization of this type to be more about color description than racialized social group membership.

Taking into account all of these factors, my analysis suggests, then, that the census terms may in fact represent primarily color categories rather than robust racial groups. It is, of course, a question of degree and not of one or the other; however, attributing social group status to groupings that may tend more toward category status appears to produce unsavory results, as I discuss below. Moreover, an interpretation of the categorical nature of these terms has been well represented in the literature: Nogueira, for example, noted:

> The expressions "*preto* or *negro* group," "white group" or "brown group" when used in relation to Brazil, connote primarily a sense of a grouping of individuals with this or that physical appearance rather than a sense of "social groups," since the latter implies a specific organization, not a mere statistical summation.[99]

Table 3.6 Selected self-classification responses in the open format:
Adult population in Brazil, 1976

1. *Acastanhada* (cashewlike tint; carmel colored)
2. *Alva-escura* (dark or off-white)
3. *Alva-rosada* (or *jambote,* roseate, white with pink highlights)
4. *Amarelada* (yellowish)
5. *Amorenada* (tannish)
6. *Azul-marinho* (deep bluish)
7. *Bem-clara* (parchmentlike; translucent)
8. *Branca-avermelhada* (peach white)
9. *Branca-plida* (pallid)
10. *Branca-suja* (dirty white)
11. *Bronze* (bronze)
12. *Burro-quando-foge* (burro running away implying racial mixture of unknown origin;
    the opposite of *cor-firma*)
13. *Caf* (coffee)
14. *Canelada* (tawny)
15. *Castanha-clara* (clear, cashewlike)
16. *Clara* (light)
17. *Corada* (ruddy)
18. *Cor-de-cuia* (tea-colored; prostitute)
19. *Cor-de-rosa* (pink)
20. *Encerada* (waxy)
21. *Escura* (dark)
22. *Galega* (an often derogatory term for a Galician; features considered gross and misshapen)
23. *Laranja* (orange)
24. *Loira-clara* (pale blond)
25. *Malaia* (from Malabar)
26. *Meio-amerela* (mid-yellow)
27. *Meio-preta* (mid-*preta*)
28. *Miscigenao* (mixed—literally miscegenated)
29. *Morena-bem-chegada* (very tan)
30. *Morena-castanha* (cashewlike tan)
31. *Morena-jambo* (dark red)
32. *Morena-fechada* (very dark, almost mulatta)
33. *Morena-roxa* (purplish tan)
34. *Moreninha* (toffeelike)
35. *Negra* (negro)
36. *Paraba* (like the color of marupa wood)
37. *Polaca* (Polish features; prostitute)
38. *Preta* (black)
39. *Quase-negra* (almost *negro*)
40. *Queimada-de-sol* (sunburned)
41. *Rosa* (roseate)
42. *Roxa* (purplish)
43. *Sapecada* (burnished red)
44. *Tostada* (toasted)
45. *Verde* (greenish)

SOURCE: 1976 Brazilian Household Survey (PNAD). Selection of the original 134 terms (1st, 4th, 7th)
presented in IBGE 1999.

Discussion and Conclusion

I began this first empirical chapter as an exploration of racial boundaries due to the centrality of the racial group concept to studies of racial attitudes. If indeed racial attitudes are in large part structured across racial groups, we must begin by naming those populations. In addition, recognizing that racial boundaries are actually variable in nature on a continuum of category to group, I sought to understand the degrees of groupness exhibited by Brazil's racialized populations. The Brazilian national census seemed the logical place to begin an accounting of racial boundaries in that context, and I briefly summarize the results.

I first posed the question of whether the official census terms white, brown, and *preto* exhibit high degrees of groupness and thus represent social groups. This triadic racial group approach is frequent in the literature.[100] To address that question I devised two empirical approximations of "groupness." First, I posited that the coming together of internal versus external definition is associated with social group formation, which I looked at by cross tabulating interviewer- versus self-identification. I contended that the greater the consistency of interviewer versus self-identification, the higher the level of groupness. Supporting this premise, data from the United States suggest a near-perfect correspondence between interviewer- and self-identification regarding whites and African Americans.[101] My data, however, revealed relatively high levels of inconsistency between interviewer- and self-classification in the census categories in all three studies. Thus, in comparison to the United States, the Brazilian census terms appear to be characterized by lower degrees of groupness.

Second, I proposed that category loyalty was characteristic of social group formation, and I operationalized this concept through accessing category switching from closed to open or expanded formats of racial classification. I contended that the lesser the degree of category switching, the higher the level of groupness. This approach was supported through using the example of the U.S. case, where category loyalty was found to be generally maintained even in alternative expanded question formats.[102] All three data sets revealed high levels of category switching.[103] This lack of category loyalty also suggests the lower degree of groupness that characterizes the census terms.

I then inquired as to whether or not racialized social groups could be located under alternative names. Examining open and expanded formats, I found that significant segments of the samples preferred the *moreno* and *negro* terms. To approximate the degree of groupness characterizing these populations I examined membership distinguishability, which I operationalized via perceived skin-color distinctiveness. The greater the perceived skin-color distinctiveness, the greater the degree of groupness. Regarding the *moreno* term, I found very high levels of skin-color variation. This heterogeneity of skin-color types would seem to hamper out-group/in-group membership recognition (an essential dynamic for racial groups). Therefore, although popular, my data suggest that a low degree of groupness characterizes the *moreno* population.

As to the other proposed racial group in Brazil, *negro*, I did find a more homogeneous in-group makeup in terms of perceived skin color: Eighty percent of individuals who self-classified as *negros* were self-classified *pretos* from the census format according to results from the 2000 sample. However, when given a choice, a majority of *pretos* preferred non-*negro* terms, meaning that the in-group homogeneity was not accompanied by out-group heterogeneity, thereby again hampering population distinguishability of those stating a preference for the *negro* label. Thus, the data suggest the label's lower degree of groupness.

Finally, I looked at the view of the census terms as color categories, that is, as concerning a "physical characteristic" skin color having little or nothing to do with social groups. To confront this position, I measured a sample population's ability to agree on the placement of eight photographs of individuals of varying skin color into the census categories. Overall, the ability of the respondents to agree at very high levels in seven out of eight cases appears to lend some support to the "physical characteristic" view of the census categories.

In this chapter, then, I have questioned whether or not the white, brown, *preto, moreno,* and *negro* labels represent self-conscious racial groups. The complexity of the phenomenon of social group formation and the tentative nature of my empirical approximations do not provide, of course, a definitive answer. I will continue to explore Brazil's potential racialized boundaries in subsequent chapters. However, through this empirical analysis, it is clear that some leading perceptions about racial dynamics in Brazil are misguided and that the underlying assumptions of those perceptions should be questioned.

As I previously discussed, the general theories on racial attitudes carry embedded in them the assumption of robust racial groupness. They intimate racial group formations that are cohesive, solidary, bounded, and that create strong collective identities. This is true of the bulk of "race relations" literature, which in large part focuses on white versus black race relations in the United States.[104] These assumptions are not surprising given the U.S. history of racialism, which remains intact to a large degree today. Therefore, that Sears, Bobo, and Sidanius, for example, state squarely the premise that individuals "identify with their own racial and ethnic groups" is not generally problematic in the United States.[105] However, incorporating that premise into general theory leads to unwarranted assumptions about racial identification and other racial attitudes in contexts outside of the United States.

A recent piece by sociologist Richard Alba that compares second-generation immigrant assimilation and exclusion in France, Germany, and the United States points out this problem.[106] Alba claims that to truly understand how processes of assimilation and exclusion will play out regarding immigrant populations, we must pay attention to the boundary processes in which immigrants are involved. Making a conceptual distinction between "bright boundaries," which create certainty about membership, and "blurred boundaries," where in-group/out-group distinctions are not easily made, Alba finds that the nature of the boundary greatly affects the assimilation processes under study. Hence, to assume bright boundaries is problematic. He claims, "theorizing in the US (where most theorizing occurs, in fact) has largely taken for granted the structural features of American society, such as the salience of race."[107] This, of course, weakens comparative social science. Alba continues,

> The argument here is that boundary concepts, such as bright vs. blurred boundaries, provide a productive basis for comparison. These concepts subsume features like race that have proved their explanatory power in the U.S. and enable them to be matched with their equivalents (or near equivalents) elsewhere.[108]

I propose a similar argument using the idea of groupness to enable comparative social science in the case of racial attitudes. The groupness concept makes room for the empirical case of race in the United States, where degree of groupness is high, while also allowing for multiracial contexts whose groupness quotient may differ significantly.

Racial dynamics do characterize the Brazilian context: individuals do express racial attitudes and varying degrees of racial or color identification. However, to frame the discussion as one of "race relations" is to assume that the strongest organizing structures of the context are racialized social groups and thus to possibly overlook other processes at work. This problem was clearly pointed out decades ago by the seminal work of Fredrik Barth. He wrote: "The analysis of interactional and organizational features of inter-ethnic relations has suffered from a lack of attention to problems of boundary maintenance. This is perhaps because anthropologists have reasoned from a misleading idea of the prototype inter-ethnic situation."[109] I believe the same may be happening in the study of racial attitudes. General theory has incorporated a conceptualization of racial boundary salience from a prototype "race relations" situation of the United States, thereby compromising its ability to apply in other contexts.

Why does it matter whether or not we determine how strong racial boundaries and racial group formation are? High degrees of racial groupness are associated with a clear organization of attitudes along racial lines. In such a context, everyone identifies with his or her own racial group, and in-group/out-group boundaries are generally unambiguous. It follows, then, that contexts marked by lower degrees of racial groupness would be less likely to organize cognitive processes along racial lines. Based on her ethnographic work in Brazil, Segato, for example, conceptualizes the difference I am suggesting in the following way: "My contention is that the cognitive, psychological operations at work in Brazil are of a different kind and embedded in a different structure of relationships than those in the US."[110] Following this, I agree with Brubaker and his colleagues that "we [too often] make cognitive assumptions about the way in which people parse, frame, and interpret their experience" based on group-based visions of the social world.[111] To remedy this approach, we must, then, make the nature of racial boundaries an empirical question. Only then can we understand their association with attitudinal stances.

What do racial attitudes look like in a context where group-based assumptions do not necessarily hold? In other words, using Guimarães's conceptualization, how are racial attitudes different in antiracialist versus racialist contexts?[112] In Chapter 4, after having looked at the nature of the boundaries in Brazil in this chapter, I turn to the "content" of those boundaries, which, following Barth's conceptual language, can be called "culture." I center that discussion in the ongoing debate about whether or not to incorporate the *negro* category into the national census.

4　Race and Culture

ONGOING DEBATES IN BRAZIL and in the United States concerning census race categories pit "monoracial" classification schemes, that is, those recognizing single-race heritages, against multiracial classification.[1] Throughout most of the twentieth century, the United States used a white/black binary system for European Americans and African Americans. That dichotomous system helped contribute to strong group-based subjectivity where ambiguity was seldom tolerated legally or socially: A person was either white or black and nowhere in between. However, the 2000 U.S. Census institutionalized a type of multiracialism that allows respondents to mark more than one race and thus assert a more ambiguous identification.[2] Some scholars in the United States have called this shift in census format a racial revolution.[3]

Interestingly, Brazil appears to be shifting in the opposite direction. At present, the country continues to use the ternary system that includes white, *preto,* and the third intermediate category *brown.* However, as mentioned in the previous chapter, some government officials, academics, and activists seek to eliminate category intermediacy in favor of a binary *negro*/white distinction.[4] Recall that *negro* is a label used as a collective black term unifying *pretos* and browns in a single racial group similar to African Americans or blacks in the United States. There is irony in this trend. As Lovell states, "It may be the case that racial identity in the United States is becoming more Brazilian [i.e., multiracial] in character while Brazil appears to be more like North America [i.e., dualistic]."[5]

Although growing in opposite directions, does the change in both countries stem from a similar root? In the United States, increasing rates of racial and

ethnic intermarriage may be largely responsible for its move toward multiracialism.[6] Brazil, on the other hand, has historically experienced higher rates
of racial intermarriage than the United States, and this trend continues unchanged.[7] Thus, if not decreasing rates of intermarriage, what has prompted the
Brazilian move toward monoracialism?[8] The principal stimulus appears to be
the necessity to redress historic and contemporary racial discrimination.[9] Robust collective identities have proven strategic in other contexts, like the United
States, for mobilizing against racial disadvantage.[10] With that goal in mind,
monoracial advocates argue that the intermediate term in the Brazilian census
creates division within the nonwhite population that undermines the racial solidarity believed necessary for antiracist mobilization.[11] Many *negro* movement
actors, then, perceive the need to strengthen *negro* racial "grouphood," or to
increase the level of *negro* racial "groupness," producing "a strong attachment
to black identity."[12] That identity would become a vantage point from which to
interpret nonwhite discrimination as well as to mobilize against it.

In the promonoracial argument, external labeling is considered a major
influence in racial or ethnic group identification. In the historic absence of
strong racial subjectivity defined along dichotomous lines, the census in Brazil may therefore be eyed as a group-building stimulus.[13] Census categorization in general is an example of what Cornell and Hartmann call a "contextual
construction site of ethnic group formation."[14] However, as we have discussed
earlier, the process of racial and ethnic boundary construction is a multifaceted product of both external contextual conditioners, such as the census, and
internal group dynamics.[15] The latter comprises "existing intragroup attachments and the assertion of an ethnic identity by group members employing
the raw materials of history, culture, and pre-existing ethnic constructions."[16]
Cornell argues that variation in *intragroup dynamics* has important consequences via *interaction effects* with *external conditions* for patterns of ethnic
identity formation. Importantly, the nature of the intragroup dynamics often
determines how external labels are accepted, applied, and processed.

What is the state of the intragroup ties among *negros* in Brazil? Are *negros*
joined by a strong ethnic culture? To explore the state of intragroup cohesion or ethnic definition in Brazil, and thus to understand how the proposed
change in external census labeling might affect group-based identification, I
address attitudes toward the following four elements of internal *negro* ethnic
definition: ethnic self-classification, cultural repertoires, perception of ethnic distinctiveness, and perceptions of common ancestries. The interaction

of these elements with external labeling, what Cornell calls "the mediating effects of [ethnic] content," is important to take into account: It may significantly condition the goal of racial identity construction at the heart of current antiracism strategies.[17] Given that many mobilization efforts rely on substantial cohesion of the group in question, different strategies might be sought when internal group definition is less robust. To analyze this internal ethnic definition, I draw on data from the 2000 sample of racial attitudes in the state of Rio de Janeiro and on the 2002 PESB national survey.

Background

As noted in the previous chapter, color or race classification is complex and unstable in Brazil. For example, an individual may self-classify in one category at one point in time or in one context and choose a different category in another instance or place.[18] In the context of the national census, the most prevalent switch is from *preto* to brown.[19] Whether due to the influence of a "whitening ideology" or to a perceived "mulatto escape hatch," one cannot assume category stability in Brazil.[20]

In contrast to the U.S. Census, which uses racial ancestry as its yardstick to capture diversity, Brazilian census categories are often said to correspond with positions along a color continuum.[21] To claim, however, that the United States measures ancestral descent and that Brazil measures color is simplistic and somewhat deceptive. Ancestry matters in the United States but is narrowly limited by the "rule of hypodescent."[22] According to that rule, for any person whose lineage includes a person of African descent, all other ancestries are nullified. In terms of ancestry in Brazil, due to its history of European conquest and immigration, extensive involvement in the African slave trade, as well as to separate categories for indigenous and Asian descent populations, the brown and *preto* categories are most generally considered to be composed of persons of some "discernible" African ancestry. Some researchers even translate the term *pardo* into English as "mulatto," thereby clearly assuming this lineage.[23]

Some research suggests that although persons of varying degrees of African descent many times occupy different color categories along the continuum, these individuals may be treated similarly by Brazil's systems of social stratification.[24] To be nonwhite in Brazil means to expect lower wages and disadvantaged life chances in general.[25] However, in spite of their shared disadvantage, persons of varying degrees of African descent in Brazil, that is, browns and *pretos,* may not generally view themselves as belonging to a single *negro* racial group.[26] For example, Winant writes of nonwhites' ability in Brazil "not only to deny, but to *avoid* their own [black] racial identity."[27] Hanchard, too, calls attention in his work to Brazilian nonwhites' "negation of their identity."[28]

Along with this lack of robust *negro* subjectivity, there have historically been few mass mobilizations against racial stratification in Brazil.[29] *Negro* movement actors and academics have long connected these two phenomena, claiming that the former causes the latter.[30] Burdick writes, "The refusal of the majority of Afro-Brazilians to acknowledge their blackness . . . obviously erodes the movement's efforts to build a unified ethnic identity, regarded as a precondition for the building of an effective antiracist struggle."[31] What has arrested the development of racial subjectivity among nonwhite Brazilians? As discussed earlier, some blame the census categories brown and *preto* for purposefully dividing a collective population what would otherwise have cumulative power.[32] Santos writes, for example, "Built into the official census is what we call deformation—the prevalence of arbitrary designations in relation to the item 'color' that seek, fundamentally, to establish fissures in the identity of blacks."[33] Working from this belief, researchers and activists propose instituting the monoracial category *negro* for all persons of some "discernible" African ancestry,[34] thereby making it the rough equivalent to the U.S. "black" category.[35]

The term *negro* has a long history of usage by *negro* organizations in Brazil, such as the *Frente Negra Brasileira,* or Brazilian *Negra* Front, in the 1930s; the *Teatro Experimental do Negro,* or *Negro* Experimental Theater, in the 1940s and 1950s; and the *Movimento Negro Unificado,* or Unified *Negro* Movement, in the 1970s and 80s. However, none of these organizations was successful in building a unified *negro* identity in Brazil; neither did they always show interest in promoting *negro* cultural specificity. In fact, according to Lélia Gonzalez, the orientation of the earlier two of those three movements was assimilationist.[36]

How can contemporary movement actors act to strengthen racial subjectivity of nonwhites in Brazil to effectively challenge racial inequalities? One strategy focuses on building African-related subjectivity by reclaiming *negro* as a term of ethnic affirmation, using it to "reethnicize" blackness.[37] Those who pursue this strategy view *negros* as the sum of the brown and *preto* categories of the census even though the individuals in these two categories appear resistant to that classification.[38] Nonetheless, movement actors see browns and *pretos* as their putative constituency joined, if not presently by a strong common culture, at least historically by common disadvantage. Hence, to fill in the boundary marked by disadvantage in order to unify nonwhites, that is, *negros,* for antiracism, *negro* movement actors seek to strengthen the diluted ethnic content of blackness in Brazil. As opposed to inventing something new, many view the strategy of the *negro* movement to reethnicize blackness as "nothing more than a re-working of the substance of a group whose boundaries and identity have already been delimitated by the system of racial domination."[39] In a sense, then, movement leaders want to shift *negros* from being a group "in itself" to a group "for itself" through a process of ethnicization at the service of antiracism.[40] They look to increase the "degree of groupness" through building a group-specific culture, in the idiom of Brubaker and Cooper.[41]

African-Derived Culture in Brazil

Because building *negro* racial subjectivity in Brazil has been difficult, one might think that African-derived culture, that is, cultural elements whose origins are traceable to African slaves and their descendents in the colonial era, is not prevalent in Brazil.[42] Such a conclusion would be difficult to sustain, however, for African-derived cultural elements are quite widespread.[43] Perhaps most important among these elements is Afro-Brazilian religious expression,[44] as it may be that which is most widely practiced and most directly identified as African in origin. Unlike in the United States, where African-origin religious expressions were systematically diluted and even lost, African slaves in Brazil were able to maintain significant fragments of their ancestral religions, and these continue to be practiced today.[45] However, because African-descent populations quickly learned that to be Brazilian meant to be Catholic, they adapted and disguised the roots of these fragments to keep them alive. African-origin expressions were strategically mixed with and even masked by Catholic rituals to become Brazilian cults.[46] African deities were given the names of Catholic saints, for example, and rituals became more hybridized. Although the end of slavery in the late nineteenth century allowed for these adapted religious fragments to reemerge from the shadows and organize centrally into the Afro-Brazilian religion *Candomblé,* they have since been outlawed in the past and repressed many times.

The twentieth century saw two important developments that further affected the evolution of Afro-Brazilian religious expressions, as well as that of many other African-derived cultural elements. These were the "nationalization" of African-origin cultural symbols by the state and elites from the 1920s through the 1970s,[47] and a subsequent reappropriation or "re-Africanization" of these symbols by *negro* organizations from the 1970s to the present day.[48] Brown refers to this dual process as the "whitening" and then "blackening" of "black culture."[49]

Nationalizing African-Derived Culture

The nationalizing project began most earnestly at the state level during the first regime of Gertulio Vargas (1930–1945).[50] Andrews documents how the official discourse of that era in Brazil, as well as in several other countries of Latin America (for example, in Cuba, Venezuela, and Mexico), began "sharply shifting course."[51] The oligarchic regime focus on the importance of all things European gave way to a populist value of racial mixing in the strategic interest of unifying populations for nation building.[52] This new populist turn toward the integration of America's three "races," Europeans, Indians, and Africans, became the foundation of the myth of racial democracy that emphasized a fusion of racial boundaries. Andrews writes, "Instead of ignoring and rejecting the region's African and Indian heritages and its history of race mixture, Latin Americans acknowledged both and even went so far as to propose them as the foundation on which to construct new national identities."[53] To do so, African-derived cultural elements particular to African slaves and their descendents were celebrated as a common national heritage "much in the same way that oil wells, tin and copper mines, and other strategic political and economic resources were [nationalized] at the same time."[54]

Elements that were appropriated to symbolize Brazilian national identity include samba music and dance, Afro-Brazilian religious expressions, and the slave-origin sport of *capoeira*.[55] Samba music and dance, for example, although formerly repressed by white elites as barbaric, gained legitimacy in the early twentieth century, especially in European-origin *carnaval* parades.[56] During the years of Vargas, "who did much to promote certain forms of popular culture as both national and nationalist culture," the combination of samba and *carnaval* celebrations was formally legalized and even subsidized by government agencies.[57] Sheriff writes that "samba and . . . *carnaval* became simultaneously identified both with images of an authenticating 'blackness' . . . and with those of the uniquely hybrid, 'mixed' national culture of Brazil."[58] Both samba and *carnaval* soon were seen in the eyes of Brazilians (and in those of the world) as symbols par excellence of Brazilianness. They also became fodder for the tourist industry and the "cultural industry" that tapped into powerful commercial interests in music sales.[59]

In the religious sphere, Umbanda appeared in the first part of the twentieth century as a Brazilianized or nationalized form of the African-derived religion Candomblé.[60] Brown refers to Umbanda as a deraciated form of African Brazilian religion.[61] According to her research, it was invented by a group of middle-class whites who attempted to "whiten" Candomblé by eliminating what were considered to be uncivilized aspects, such as animal sacrifice and the ritual use of blood, and adding traditions drawn from European culture. These included a reorientation toward spiritist philosophy and Catholic moralism.[62] For example, much of the power of the ancient African *orixás,* or deities, was reduced in the pantheon of Umbanda rituals to the figure of the *preto velho,* or "old slave."[63] Like many of the Catholic saints, the *preto velho* was "poor, humble, accepting of his fate, submissive, docile, helpful, curing the ills of Brazil."[64] Umbanda soon became more popular than Candomblé and by the 1980s had an estimated 20 million followers.[65]

Although the adoption of many African-based cultural elements as national symbols may be viewed as a positive change from their previous repression and marginalization during slavery, researchers and activists also view this process as strategic cooption on the part of the state and elites and as a form of cultural violence or "cultural colonization."[66] Nationalization meant "the progressive loss of African cultural forms and the 'whitening' of Afro-Brazilian culture through progressive admixture, or 'syncretism,' with other traditions."[67] Through nationalization, Afro-Brazilian markers were made generic and less powerful: as Andrews explains, "when a valuable resource is nationalized for the public good, its previous owners no longer control it."[68] Furthering this logic, many researchers and activists posit that the nationalization of African-based cultural symbols helped to inhibit contrastive identity formation and thus subverted antiracist mobilization.[69]

Re-Africanization of African-Derived Culture

Countering this homogenizing force, a process of re-Africanization further marked the contemporary evolution of African-derived symbols. In the 1970s, the waning power of Brazil's military dictatorship, strong since 1964 and ending in 1985, corresponded with a nascent democratizing process. This transition period witnessed a boom of social movements for those demanding full citizenship. The "Black cultural movements"[70] that were a part of this boom converged "to establish a difference: that of 'being black.'"[71]

According to Cunha, these movements "advocated the advancement of 'black culture' as a strategy for the mobilization, politicization, and consciousness raising of the black population."[72] As Agier writes, their central effort was "a search for a cultural specificity capable of providing its holders a place within the new realignment of social and political forces."[73] One clear starting point for establishing that *negro* "difference" or creating *negro* "cultural specificity" was to reclaim nationalized African-derived symbols and purify them by weeding out admixture and syncretism.[74] As Agier explains, it was a "racial reappropriation . . . of a vast cultural repertoire already distributed (by means particular to racial domination) throughout a population much larger than just *negros* and *mulatos*."[75]

Examples of re-Africanization can be found within the celebration of *carnaval*. *Blocos,* or local groupings that marched, danced, and sang together in *carnaval* parades, had expressed African themes for many years. However, they did so in ways that favored traditional and nonthreatening portraits of African elements. In the 1970s and 1980s many of these groups changed their orientation in the direction of "black pride" and explicitly racial interests.[76] They contested the domination of *carnaval* by white elites, and some *blocos* allowed only nonwhite participation.[77] They were what Hanchard calls "race-first" entities,[78] a rarity in Brazilian society. Although many of their themes were born of syncretism, incorporating, for example, elements from Afro-Caribbean reggae and following models provided by the aesthetic-political movements of African Americans,[79] the struggle was to "blacken their 'very real cultural specificity.'"[80]

In addition to the revisions to *carnaval,* Riserio reports that "the vanguard of Candomblé became involved in a campaign for breaking with the complex phenomenon of religious syncretism."[81] During the 1970s and 1980s, the practitioners of this Afro-Brazilian religion began to examine issues of authenticity. This pursuit took some as far as Nigeria "in search of ritual knowledge and authentic ritual materials."[82] Leaders of African-derived religions from South America, the Caribbean, Nigeria, and the United States held international conferences in which the central theme was African orthodoxy. At the 1983 Second Conference of the Tradition of the Orixás, held in Brazil, the "leaders of the most prestigious [Brazilian] Candomblé houses" supported a proposal "to banish the Catholic saints and other aspects of Catholic practice and worship from Candomblé."[83] The influence of reinvigorated Africanism in Candomblé even touched Umbanda, where Brown reports that leaders began to add formerly extricated African rites to their ceremonies.[84]

In sum, as is evident through this discussion, the status of African-derived cultural elements in Brazil has been in flux. Cultural expressions that once

belonged to African slaves and their descendents were hidden and transformed to survive the brutality of slavery and were later heralded by the government and elites as national symbols of a generic Brazilian identity. Still
later they became the object of reappropriation as markers of difference with
which to build a *negro* ethnic community.

These historical negotiations around who owns African-derived culture
speak strongly to social boundary formation. Do attitudes toward African-
derived culture reflect a distinctly bounded *negro* culture? As Nobles so aptly
states, "[*negro*] movement leaders [in Brazil] use the census to create identities as much as to energize preexisting identities, yet securing a new census
category and galvanizing a self-conscious group of people with new political
and social allegiances are two different tasks. The second does not necessarily
follow the first."[85] Before pursuing this question in the data, I briefly situate
the role of culture in racial and ethnic group formation according to general
theoretical perspectives on ethnic identity construction.

Theoretical Perspectives

As noted in the previous chapter, "boundary construction is the drawing of
contrasts."[86] The expansive literature on ethnic and racial group formation
speaks to the multiple ways that distinctions become salient. A well-accepted
perspective emphasizes a circumstantialist position whereby "social and historical forces organize persons into differently-situated groups, providing the
raw material for contrastive identity-formation."[87] This can be thought of as
a focus on contextual determinants of group formation. Many of these determinants are "defined by economic relationships and opportunities, patterns
of discriminatory behavior and formal entitlements, and the classificatory
schemes of other, often dominant, populations."[88] Yancey, Ericksen, and Juliani mention, for example, the "ecological structure of cities" that condition
common occupational positions and residential concentration that lead to social group formations.[89]

From a circumstantialist perspective, the structural disadvantage of nonwhite Brazilians should result in strong contrastive identity formation. However, researchers generally recognize that this has not happened to the degree
expected,[90] and that circumstance may not be always enough to result in group
subjectivity.[91] According to Cornell, "while circumstances constrain and shape
ethnic identities, the content of those identities mediates the effect of circumstance": It is this interaction "that drives the trajectory of group life."[92] A social

constructivist approach, then, views it as essential to take into account both the content and the circumstances that shape ethnic group formation.[93]

The content of ethnic identity refers to, in Barth's words, "the cultural stuff that [an ethnic boundary] encloses."[94] Nagel describes the components of ethnic content or culture as including: "art, music, dress, religion, norms, beliefs, symbols, myths, and customs."[95] These elements are what people within the ethnic boundary share, the ties that bind them together or, most simply, intragroup attachments.[96] Although these attachments can be very broad,[97] Cornell proposes a typology of the central dimensions of ethnic group content that includes institutions, interests, and culture.

An ethnic group whose shared ties are forged through ethnic-specific institutions may be labeled an "institutional community." Members are most closely linked by "their common participation in a set of more or less exclusive institutions designed to solve particular life problems," including spiritual, health, and education-related needs.[98]

An ethnic group in which its members are united on the basis of a shared set of perceived interests is called a "community of interests." This type of community is generally "the consequence of a set of economic and political circumstances that place persons in common positions in the social order."[99] They may develop a sense of their group's disadvantaged position vis-à-vis other groups that unites them in pursuit of particular interests.

The third dimension of Cornell's typology of ethnic group content is culture. When group members share a distinct culture, one that is exclusively identified with and shared by group members and that sets them apart from nongroup members, this group may be considered a "community of culture."[100] Members share a sense of group-based identity rooted in the perception that they think and act alike. They develop worldviews and behaviors that capture the essence of the group's peoplehood and reinforce a sense of solidarity among group members. Cornell and Hartmann mention elements such as stories, ritual events and celebrations that act as symbolic resources in ethnic "communities of culture."[101]

Cornell's argument works, then, from three basic assumptions: (1) internal definition varies; (2) it varies according to three dimensions of institutions, interests, and culture; and (3) this variable internal definition has important consequences for boundary formation.[102] For instance, racial groups with robust boundaries, such as African Americans in the United States, may embody all three dimensions at high levels. Alternately, groups with weak internal definition, which Cornell refers to as "symbolic communities," contain individuals who are "unattached to any set of substantial and distinctive interests, exclusive institutions, or more elaborate cultural constructions."[103]

The ethnic dimension of institutions, interests, and culture "animates and authenticates ethnic boundaries by providing a history, ideology, symbolic universe, and system of meaning."[104] Looking, then, specifically at the ethnic content conceptualized as culture, my analysis in this chapter attempts to understand the potential impact of a change in census labeling in Brazil, or the formalization of a monoracial boundary, through an examination of the cultural elements that the proposed *negro* label might enclose. Does a *negro* "community of culture" exist in Brazil? Are there intragroup attachments comprised of cultural symbols and ethnic understandings particular to Brazilians of varying degrees of African descent? To suggest an answer, I turn to the 2000 CEAP/DataUff survey from the state of Rio de Janeiro and to the national PESB survey from 2002 to explore attitudes toward ethnic self-identification, African-derived cultural repertoires, ethnic distinctiveness, and ethnic ancestries.

Findings

As discussed, *negro* movement actors and some academics have proposed that the national census adopt the term *negro;* they believe this term could act as a label of ethnic affirmation unifying all persons of some "discernible" African ancestry. Data presented in Chapter 3, however, revealed that only a limited number of nonwhite Brazilians prefer to self-classify using this term. In the expanded format question in the CEAP/DataUff survey from the state of Rio de Janeiro, while 67 percent of the sample self-identified using nonwhite terms, only 9 percent of those nonwhites self-identified as *negro.* The national PESB data set showed similar results: Fifty-seven percent opted for nonwhite terms in an open format question, but only 7 percent of those nonwhites chose the *negro* term. Finally, in 1995, analysis of the DataFolha national survey reveals that 58 percent chose to self-classify using nonwhite terms in the open format, while only 3 percent opted for *negro.* Hence, although *negro* movement actors and most researchers use *negro* as a monoracial category that mirrors the term "black" in the United States (that is, a label for all persons of some "discernible" African ancestry), a large majority of nonwhite Brazilians do not.

Group-Specific Cultural Repertoires

To explore the question of a group-specific *negro* culture in Brazil, the CEAP/ DataUff survey included several questions regarding elements that are connected to *negro* culture in the literature and that arose in focus groups. Respondents were asked about the personal level of importance they attributed to each of these items on a four level scale: "very important," "important," "a little important," "not important." A first group of questions addressed music genres: samba, *pagode* (considered a derivative of samba most popular among lower-class Brazilians; it also indicates the informal gathering of small groups of musicians and singers playing this genre),[105] *axé* music (a music style associated with the state of Bahia, which is approximately 80 percent nonwhite),[106] and *funk* (a new style of urban youth music with roots in U.S. rap and Jamaican reggae). Bossa nova was also included as a contrast: Due to its association with middle and upper classes, it may be less popular among nonwhite Brazilians.

Table 4.1 presents percentage distributions of those who claimed that the item in question was either "important" or "very important" in their lives (a combined category) by several color or race terms. The results reveal that all color categories attribute similar levels of importance to the music genres, resisting the gaps that would indicate *negro* cultural specificity. For example, 53 percent of whites and 58 percent of nonwhites (browns and *pretos* combined) viewed samba as "important" or "very important." Forty-three percent of whites and 41 percent of nonwhites embraced the bossa nova genre. Perhaps one exception, revealing instead category-specific differences, was *funk* music. Sansone describes it as "a highly popular genre among lower-class black youth in Rio de Janeiro and Salvador."[107] It is the least popular of all the music genres presented here. Nevertheless, twice as many *negros* (isolated via the expanded format question) as whites and browns viewed it as "important" or "very important," 16 percent and 8 percent respectively. The fact that, similar to whites, only about half as many browns viewed *funk* as important when compared to *negros* (and *pretos*), suggests that *funk*'s attraction is greatest among the darkest segment of the nonwhite population.

Respondents were also asked to rate the importance in their lives of various elements associated with African-derived religious beliefs. Results presented in Table 4.1 indicate a very similar pattern to the one laid out regarding music genres. Although there are some differences in a few percentage points between color categories, no difference is so great as to indicate *negro* cultural niches.

Table 4.1 Percent distributions of combined "important" and "very important" response categories for culture items and of beliefs about cultural differences by selected color/race classifications, Brazilian adult population in the state of Rio de Janeiro, 2000

Culture elements	Various self-classification schemes				
	White[a]	Brown[a]	Preto[a]	Nonwhite[a]	Negro[b]
Music					
Axé	38%	45%	43%	44%	47%
Pagode	47	55	57	56	58
Samba	53	56	62	58	68
Bossa nova	43	41	40	41	47
Funk	8	8	15	11	16
Religion					
Orixá	15	17	23	19	21
Jogo de búzios[c]	8	12	14	13	12
Iemanjá[d]	15	17	23	19	23
São Jorge[e]	31	29	34	31	31
Ervas[f]	25	27	33	29	27
Roupa branca[g]	8	11	13	12	11
Sports					
Capoeira	31	34	43	37	51
Volleyball	63	65	65	65	69
Soccer	69	74	77	75	78
Tennis	42	43	42	43	42
Auto racing	47	44	47	45	49
Other					
Carnaval	41	40	38	40	47
Negro versus white culture					
No differences	68	65	62	64	62

SOURCE: CEAP/DataUff 2000.

[a]Categories from the census format question. "Nonwhite" is brown and *preto* combined.

[b]Category isolated via the expanded format question.

[c]A rite of divination.

[d]Ritual offerings in the sea in honor of *Iemanjá*.

[e]Commemorating the day of São Jorge, who also represents a particular *orixá*.

[f]Ritual bathing in prepared herbs.

[g]Wearing white clothing on Saturdays in honor of Oxalá, god of creation.

For example, 15 percent of whites and 19 percent of nonwhites said that *orixás,* the "spiritual beings who rule and represent the natural forces of the universe and human life" in the Candomblé religion, were "important" or "very important" to them.[108] Likewise, 15 percent of whites and 19 percent of nonwhites embraced Iemanjá, "the Orixá of the oceans and mother of the waters."[109]

Next, the survey addressed the realm of sports. Capoeira, a type of martial arts with roots in slave communities, was the only sport that was clearly associated with African-derived culture in the literature.[110] However, the survey included a variety of other sports in an attempt to capture some color-based differences. Of all of these, capoeira was the only one that revealed difference. Thirty-one percent of whites compared to 37 percent of nonwhites embraced the form, yet when those who self-classified as *negro* in the expanded format were isolated, that percentage rose to 51. However, the fact that such a large percentage of whites viewed it in the same light as nonwhites challenges the idea that capoeira is a group-specific element of *negro* culture. The other sports were all fairly close. Nonwhites and whites even equally embraced tennis and auto racing, which might be viewed as "whiter" sports due to their association with higher levels of income.[111]

Finally, the survey addressed *carnaval*, which is perhaps the most recognized cultural symbol of Brazil and is viewed as saturated with African symbolism. In spite of this, however, Table 4.1 reveals no appreciable differences in its value to whites and nonwhites. Forty-one percent of whites compared to 40 percent of nonwhites in Rio de Janeiro said it was "important" or "very important" in their lives.

Perceptions of Ethnic Distinctiveness

Furthering the investigation into culturally-specific communities, CEAP/ DataUff interviewers asked respondents the following question: "Do you believe that (1) *negros* in Brazil have different customs and traditions than the rest of the population or that (2) there are no differences between the customs and traditions of *negros* and the rest of the population?" Table 4.1 presents those results: Approximately two-thirds of the population said that they believe there are no differences in the customs and traditions of *negros* compared to everyone else (68 percent of whites and 64 percent of nonwhites). Very suprisingly, this includes 62 percent of those self-identifying as *negro*, a term that is believed to represent Africa-derived ethnic affirmation.

In all, the results presented in Table 4.1 speak to a milieu in which cultural specificities are not easily delineated by race or ethnicity. Additionally, Table 4.2 presents a distribution of selected cultural items by educational level, sex, age, and region. Some differences arise. For example, *carnaval* is least popular among the poorest segment of the sample population from the state of Rio de Janeiro (at 27 percent) and most popular in the municipality of Rio (at 49 percent) in contrast to the interior or metropolitan areas (36 and 37 percent, respectively). *Capoeira* is most strongly embraced by the youngest

Table 4.2 Percent distribution of combined "very important" and "important" response categories for selected African-derived cultural items by educational level, sex, and age, Adult population in the state of Rio de Janeiro, 2000

	Carnaval	Capoeira	Samba	Orixás
Educational level[a]				
Low	27%	36%	45%	17%
Medium low	41	36	67	15
Medium	45	38	54	19
High	47	31	60	17
Sex				
Female	38	33	54	16
Male	46	39	60	19
Age				
18-25	51	47	54	16
26-40	35	38	55	15
41-60	45	32	61	21
61-93	37	25	54	14
Region				
Interior	36	37	50	14
Municipality	49	35	65	21
Metropolitan	37	34	55	15

SOURCE: CEAP/DataUff 2000.

[a]Low (illiterate/primary incomplete); Medium low (primary complete/junior incomplete); Medium (junior complete/secondary incomplete); High (secondary complete/superior incomplete and superior complete) (combined due to small number of "superior complete").

grouping of the sample population (eighteen- to twenty-five-year-olds). Taken as a whole, however, the similarities across the board stand out. We see, then, that these other sociodemographic variables fare similarly to racial category in terms of their structuring effect, further contributing to the idea of the widely distributed nature of African-derived culture across social spheres in Brazil.

In sum, in terms of the relationship between color categories and cultural repertoires, Sansone writes, "White people of all classes . . . participate in *Candomblé, capoeira,* samba, and *carnaval* associations."[112] Similarly, Walker remarks, "In fact, some Euro-Brazilians are more culturally Afro-Brazilian than some Afro-Brazilians."[113]

Perceptions of Ethnic Ancestries

Next the CEAP/DataUff survey asked about perceptions of ethnic or racial ancestries. Rhetoric of common descent or ancestry is the defining mark of ethnic subjectivity.[114] White and brown respondents were asked if they had any *negro* ancestors.[115] Then brown and *preto* respondents were asked if they had any white ancestors. Finally, all three categories of individuals were asked

Table 4.3 Percent distributions of perceived ancestry by self-classification in census format, 2000 and 2002

	White	Brown	Preto
	PANEL 1		
Have white ancestors	—	80%	59%
Have *negro* ancestors	37%	80	—
Have Indian ancestors	28	48	44
	PANEL 2		
Africa	5%	16%	37%
Portugal	25	17	14
Brazilian Indian	10	20	20
Europe	13	5	3
Brazil	45	62	60

SOURCE: CEAP/DataUff 2000, PESB 2002.

if they had indigenous ancestors. The results are presented in Table 4.3, Panel 1. In terms of nonwhites, 80 percent of browns and almost 60 percent of *pretos* claimed to have white ancestors. In addition, 80 percent of browns and 37 percent of whites claimed to have *negro* ancestors. Finally, as to indigenous ancestry, 48 percent of browns, 44 percent of *pretos,* and 28 percent of whites claim to have indigenous ancestors. These results suggest a worldview and presentation of self as of mixed ancestry for a majority of the population. Specifically, the results may reflect the myth of national origin that proclaims that Brazilians are a unique mixture of three "races": European, African, and indigenous.

Notwithstanding, does this mindset allow a separation into the types of ethnic group ancestries with which academics generally categorize populations? The 2002 PESB national survey included a question about ancestry. Respondents were asked, "From which country or continent do you believe your ancestors came?" Survey participants were then presented with a list of fifteen "countries or continents" to which they responded "yes" or "no." Table 4.3, Panel 2, shows the top five ancestry responses in a cross-tabulation with self-classification in the census format. It reveals that about 5 percent of *brancos*, 16 percent of browns, and 37 percent of *pretos* claim African ancestors. Hence, the great majority of browns and *pretos,* defined as *negros* in the monoracial idiom, do not recognize the African ancestry of their forbearers in this survey context. The question from the CEAP/DataUff survey discussed above found a greater recognition of the *negro* ancestry in the state of Rio de Janiero. However, in that case, interviewers asked respondents specifically about *negro* ancestors, not about Africa. Hence, the results suggest that the two items are not entirely comparable, as the term *negro* may not be so straightforwardly identified with Africa in the Brazilian mindset.

Furthering this suggestion of divergent meanings of the terms *negro* and African ancestry, in a cross-tabulation (not shown) of those who self-classify as *negro* in the open format (7 percent of the PESB sample) with the question about African ancestry, only 49 percent claim African ancestry. Thus, even for those who seem to squarely recognize an African-based ethnicity by self-identifying as *negro,* a slight majority respond that their ancestors did not come from Africa in that survey context. As this finding indicates, ethnic boundary formation is a complicated process that is many times about perceived commonalities among a long list of possible ones.

Examining further the Brazilian mindset regarding ancestry, Table 4.3, Panel 2, also shows the cross-tabulation of self-classification in the census format with several of the other ancestral "countries or continents." In terms of the myth of national origin, of special interest in addition to the Africa response is the recognition of Portuguese and Indian heritage. *Branco*s are more likely to recognize Portuguese heritage than browns and *pretos,* but the great majority of all three groups do not. Browns and *pretos* are equal in their recognition of Indian ancestry. More browns say that their ancestors are of indigenous than of African origin. Lastly, nearly two-thirds of browns and *pretos* claim Brazilian ancestry compared to 45 percent of *branco*s. The high level of responses recognizing Brazilian ancestry combined with the low level of recognition of particularist ancestries seem to speak to the idea of the formation of a Freyrean-type metarace or racial fusion. Ethnic and racial boundaries appear blurred in the popular mindset in favor of a more inclusive nationalist category of Brazilianness.

In sum, the results from both data sets suggest a disconnection between color and ancestry in the Brazilian imagination. While in the CEAP/DataUff data set 80 percent of browns and 30 percent of *branco*s claimed to have *negro* ancestors (and conceivably 100 percent of individuals identifying as *pretos*), only 13 percent of the national population claimed to be of African ancestry, according to the PESB survey. As discussed in the previous chapter, then, in the popular imagination color rather than ancestry appears to be the defining mark of category membership in Brazil. If asked about origin or ancestry, the majority of Brazilians simply reply "Brazilian," which suggests a very murky situation for the categorization of Brazilians by ancestries or into ethnic groups.

Discussion

The survey results presented in this chapter suggest that it may be difficult to characterize the collective *negro* population (browns and *pretos*) in Brazil as a "community of culture," employing the conceptual language of Cornell's typology.[116] In Segato's words, there appears to be no "discrete African niche" in Brazil.[117] This is certainly due not to the absence of African-derived cultural elements, but to their apparent dispersion throughout the general population, as the survey suggests. The differing color categories are generally quite similar in the levels of importance that they attribute to African-origin cultural expressions of the most varied types. Moreover, two-thirds of Brazilians in Rio de Janeiro, non-*branco*s included, state there are no traditions or customs that actually distinguish *negro*s from the rest of the population. Finally, there is little preference for recognizing African origins when asked in a survey; and, as reported from the previous chapter, the term that many researchers and activists equate with African-derived ethnic affirmation, *negro*, appears decidedly nonsalient among non-*branco*s.

Was the dispersion of African-derived culture throughout the Brazilian nation the product of state cooption?[118] There is no doubt that nationalist projects did support that dispersion. However, Segato proposes an alternative explanation, claiming that state elites were forced to expand their ideas about national culture from the bottom up. She writes regarding the lack of discrete culture niches, "this is not the outcome of a process of expropriation and cannibalization of black symbols by Brazilian society at large but is, much to the contrary, the result of a strong African presence that has invaded and conquered the white cultural space in an irreversible process."[119] Other possible contributing explanations include that the lack of de jure segregation in postabolition years resulting in relatively high rates of racial intermarriage and that relatively low rates of residential segregation did not support the development of distinct cultural niches nor robust ethnic sentiments. Regardless of the explanation, however, the results are invariant: Brazil is best characterized by a "pervading African presence in culture and society instead of a discrete African niche."[120]

Hence, my results employing a quantitative methodology support a central finding of Sansone's extensive ethnographic research in Brazil: "there can be blackness [i.e., peoples of varying degrees of African descent] without (black) community or black culture of the traditional sort."[121] The findings also lend some credence to what anthropologists Peter Fry and Yvonne Maggie recently wrote about exclusive cultural realms in Brazil:

> Many intellectuals . . . share a belief that our country is divided into distinct "races" and "ethnicities," each one with its own "culture." *Negra* culture, for example, is spoken of as if it were something practiced only by *negros* in *negro* spaces. However, others, probably including the majority of Brazilians, follow a more modernist tradition, believing that we are all mixed . . . For these people "cultural diversity" is in each Brazilian. They affirm that many whites know how to samba and that not all *negros* can do it very well, that all Brazilians eat *feijoada*,[122] speak the same language and can at some point worship African-religion deities. For them, the notion of ethnicity, race, and separate cultures in Brazil is an out-of-place idea.[123]

Finally, and along that same line of reasoning, Reis, Segato, Silva, and Costa also argue against the view that color clearly correlates with culturally distinct populations in Brazil.[124]

Mediating Effects of Content

According to Cornell, ethnic group responsiveness to changing external conditions, such as official classification through national censuses, varies with the nature of group attachments.[125] What, then, do these results reveal in terms of the mediating effect of content on monoracial identity construction in Brazil through the possible census adoption of the *negro* label? I believe they suggest that the effect may not be wholly positive in the view of those who wish to construct a contrastive *negro* identification for all non-*brancos*. Rather, the absence or weakness of a particularist cultural niche could result in an ambivalence toward, or rejection of, the label *negro* as a solo racial group. In effect, a forced choice between white and *negro* could result in many browns opting for the former.[126] I further elaborate on this resulting ambivalence and possible whitening of the population in Chapters 8 and 9, which look at the institutionalization of dichotomous racial classification in affirmative action legislation.

In essence, the proposed change from ternary to binary in census naming may not reverberate clearly in the experiences of most Brazilians. As Sansone writes, "in Latin America most definitions of blackness employed by academics as well as by government agencies and political groups correspond very little if at all with definitions used in daily life by ordinary people, both black and non-black."[127] Whether viewed as positive or negative, it appears that the nationalizing process with its cultural syncretism has resulted in the pervasiveness of African-derived elements within Brazilian national culture rather than a robustly distinct *negro* "community of culture."

This is not to say, however, that building a unified *negro* identity is impossible in Brazil or even that cultural elements are not available for this project. I have only investigated the widely recognized elements attributed to *negro* culture in the literature, in the focus groups, and by *negro* movement actors, and although they may resist easy operationalization, there are surely many others that might magnetize a *negro* community of culture. Also, the relative absence of a "community of culture" at one point in time does not proscribe its eventual formation. Moreover, although cultural distinctiveness is a process, usually unconscious, that takes place over great periods of time, ethnic entrepreneurs or "political innovators," in Barth's words, can also stimulate the growth of contrastive culture.[128] This is obvious in the process of the re-Africanization of African Brazilian culture mentioned above. Barth described this dynamic as follows:

> . . . much of the activity of political innovators is concerned with the codification of idioms; the selection of signals for identity and the assertion of value for the cultural diacritica, and the suppression or denial of relevance for other differentiae . . . but a great amount of attention may be paid to the revival of select traditional culture traits, and to the establishment of historical traditions to justify and glorify the idioms and the identity.[129]

In addition, I have not systematically explored Cornell's other internal elements of contrastive identity construction: ethnic-specific institutions and interests. Regarding the first, according to Hanchard, race-specific, self-sufficient institutions such as black churches in the United States are "the perverse silver-lining of racial segregation," supporting contrastive identity construction and mobilization.[130] However, because there is little history of such *negro*-only institutions in Brazil,[131] it does not appear that a *negro* "institutional community" is at present a reality that can be counted on to affirm the *negro* label.

It is Cornell's "community of interests," where "members of the group consciously share a distinctive set of positional interests,"[132] that may provide the strongest leverage for advocates of building a unified *negro* identity using the

national census. The theory long supported by many researchers and activists
that a widespread denial of racial discrimination exists in Brazil is being challenged.[133] Survey-based research instead suggests that Brazilians in fact have
a keen awareness of the inequity that nonwhites face.[134] I will return to this
issue in the next chapter and present findings supporting that conclusion. It
suffices to say at this point that the disadvantaged structural position of nonwhites in Brazilian society may be an *unexpected* construction site for building contrastive identity, and an emphasis on shared interests stemming from
common structural disadvantage could be pivotal for building intragroup attachments in support of the *negro* label.

A focus on strengthening racial subjectivity through fortifying a "community of interests" as opposed to a "community of culture" speaks to an important ongoing debate raised most forcefully by Michael Hanchard in terms of
antiracism mobilization in Brazil.[135] Hanchard claims that one of the down-
falls of Brazilian *negro* movements and organizations has been their tendency
toward "culturalism." That is, many *negro* organizations have focused much
of their energy on recuperating remnants of African bits of history and rites
as unifying symbols of blackness and for building *negro* racial subjectivity
(part of the process of re-Africanization).[136] In doing so, these groups, according to Hanchard, have not moved toward strategies to counter racism;
furthermore, he believes that relying on this "excavation" merely leaves *negro*
cultural elements further open to strategic appropriation. Hanchard proposes
instead that the foundation of *negro* movement strategy and energy be based
on a more issue-oriented mission—the explicit politicization of race, that is,
defining more clearly *negros'* positional interests vis-à-vis whites in Brazil. He
forcefully states, "explicitly racial politics without issue orientation in a country where race identity is up for grabs has been, and will be, a dead end."[137]

My analysis also suggests the limits of using "cultural strategies" in the
service of ethnic mobilization and antiracism in Brazil.[138] However, it does
so *not* due to a fear of further strategic cooption, as Hanchard cautions. In
contrast, I believe that because people of all colors in Brazil now embrace
African-derived cultural symbols as part of a Brazilian national identity, a
reversal of this fusion would be a monumental task that might even hamper
antiracism efforts.

One last issue merits note in terms of external definition and the possibility of creating a "community of interests" via the use of the term *negro*. As I
will further explore in Chapters 7, 8, and 9 Brazil has recently developed race-

based public policies. Most notably, several state and federal universities are adopting a racial quota system (employing the term *negro*) to counteract the drastic underrepresentation of nonwhites in higher education. These strategies are controversial but mark a growing trend.[139] This novel development in Brazilian politics would certainly have to be considered one form of external definition that could help delimit a "community of interests" and provide backing for a possible change in census categorization.

Conclusion

At least in terms of governmental, social movement, and academic discourse, there certainly is an appearance that Brazil is developing more dualistic racial dynamics, some of these similar to those in the United States, as also argued by Daniel in his recent book *Race and Multiraciality in Brazil and the United States: Converging Paths.*[140] This trend is toward building racial groupness in terms of *negro* racial identification, as I will argue in Chapter 9. It seems clear that for *negro* movement actors, U.S. dualism or monoracialism is viewed as a privileged path toward greater effectiveness in the struggle against historic and contemporary nonwhite disadvantage in Brazil[141] and that perspective appears to be supported by many social scientists.[142] Others appear less enthusiastic about the trend toward *negro* versus white identification in Brazil.[143] Only time will tell if monoracialism via the *negro* term will indeed take hold among the masses of poor and working-class Brazilians who comprise the majority of the population: The absence of a *negro* "community of culture" surely adds to this uncertainty. In sum, Munanga reminds researchers that, "We should not forget that at present white and black Brazilians share, more than they realize, common models of behavior and ideas. The former are more Africanized, and the latter more Westernized, than they believe."[144]

How does the less-than-robust state of group-based culture in Brazil, as laid out in this chapter, and the ambiguity of the boundaries defining racialized populations, as explored in Chapter 3, affect the study of attitudes on other racial issues? In the following chapter, I explore whether the myth of racial democracy, which forms the core of the Brazilian racial common sense, constitutes a denial of racial discrimination. The low levels of groupness created by ambiguous boundaries and cultural diffusion become very important for understanding how Brazilians interpret this myth.

5　Stratification Beliefs

EVEN THOUGH THE LITERATURE identifies the myth of racial democracy as the "national common sense" on race,[1] and although it has been at the center of academic and social movement discourse since at least the second half of the twentieth century and now into the twenty-first, it was and is not always clearly defined. One of the reasons, of course, is that it is an attitudinal complex, a set of informal beliefs, and not a formal doctrinal proclamation or political constitution. This myth has been incorporated into the worldviews and mind-sets of millions of individual Brazilians in so many distinct ways and forms, consciously or subconsciously. However, as Hasenbalg and Silva claim, we really seem to have little idea what everyday Brazilians think about it.[2]

Nonetheless, the myth has several components that can be pieced together from the literature and discourses on race in Brazil, some of which I mentioned in previous chapters and others of which I address here and in subsequent chapters. Briefly, it foremost refers to interracial mixing and/or miscegenation.[3] The modern Brazilian nation was envisioned by many of its prominent thinkers as a comparative melting pot that was to become something "neither black nor white"—populated by a Brazilian metarace.[4] As a consequence, racial or color ambiguity and racial democracy are closely associated. In addition, racial democracy speaks to interracial intimacy and presumed cordiality among individuals of differing skin colors.[5] The type of racial conflict and segregation witnessed in other nations such as the United States and South Africa are generally not a part of postabolition Brazilian history. Importantly, racial democracy is also about equality before the law regardless of skin color or race.[6] Finally, it is a discourse about national belonging cemented in the "fable of the three races," which points to the birth of the Brazilian nation as equally springing from three racial stocks: African, European, and Indian.[7]

Notwithstanding its arguably progressive foundations, the influence of the myth of racial democracy on social dynamics in Brazil is generally viewed as negative by a dominant perspective in the social sciences and by many *negro* movement actors. It is said to mask the realities of racism,[8] discourage positive *negro* identification,[9] and create ambivalence toward antiracism strategies.[10] In this light, the myth is generally viewed as a social stratification belief, that is, a popular explanation for a society's hierarchical structure in terms of socioeconomic outcomes.[11] Although the myth may be more than just a stratification belief, the dominant research perspective has all but reduced it to those narrow terms. For example, Bairros, one of the few to attempt to lay out clearly the differing elements of the myth, writes:

> This belief [the myth of racial democracy] is widely circulated in greater or lesser degree to this very day, and can be seen in such convictions as:
>
> - Afro-Brazilians encounter no racial discrimination in Brazil;
> - The "natural temperament of the Brazilian people prevents racial distinctions";
> - Afro-Brazilians are satisfied with their social condition;
> - There does not exist, there has never existed, and there will never exist any problem of social justice for Afro-Brazilians.[12]

This identification of the myth almost completely with a denial of racial discrimination is so prevalent that when studies began to appear documenting discrimination in Brazil, some academics and social movement actors proclaimed the "death" of the myth of racial democracy,[13] proposing that the supposed popular belief that there is no racism in Brazil was no longer defensible.

As is perhaps obvious, I believe that there is room for legitimate debate as to whether or not the myth of racial democracy can be reduced to an erroneous stratification belief. There is no doubt, however, that Brazilian beliefs about social stratification are important and that this part of the Brazilian racial common sense is in need of analysis. In fact, outside of Brazil, there is a growing body of research addressing the importance of beliefs about racial stratification,[14] and this focus is primarily due to the view that explanations for racial stratification condition the attitudes of individuals and groups toward strategies for confronting racial disadvantage.[15] This literature generally divides stratification beliefs into individualist and structuralist accounts.[16] The former posits that racial inequality is due to nonwhites themselves (a type of victim-blaming) and is associated with inaction regarding that inequality. The structuralist type holds that there are external factors systematically disfavoring the disadvantaged individual or group such as racial discrimination. Structuralists, therefore, tend to support transformative actions such as antidiscrimination policy in the form of affirmative actions.[17]

Differing racial ideologies influence the distinct stratification beliefs that individuals adopt. These ideologies include racial prejudice as theorized through sociocultural theories of intergroup relations[18] and assertions of group-based racial interests as framed by conflict theory.[19] All of these generally find that race is the most robust predictor of an individual's explanation for racial inequality. That is, they conceive of the social world as divided in discrete races whose interpretations of societal dynamics diverge or are at times mutually unintelligible.[20] Hence, as one group of researchers remarks, blacks and whites are "naturally expected" to differ in their explanations for black disadvantage.[21] This position, however, may discount the effects of other variables, such as educational level, on stratification beliefs, as it may at the same time overestimate the strength of subjectively defined racial group identification, as I discuss below.

In this chapter I examine the ways Brazilians understand the disadvantaged position of nonwhites using data from the 2000 CEAP/DataUff and the 1995 DataFolha surveys. I take special note of the association between stratification beliefs and race that is central to the general literature, and I explore whether that association holds in Brazil. That is, do Brazilians recognize racial discrimination as causing nonwhite disadvantage or do they blame some other factor? In addition, do the opinions of whites and nonwhites differ? In examining these issues, I hope to bring into the debate on the nature of the myth of racial democracy a missing piece of the puzzle—how everyday Brazilians explain racial inequality as expressed in public opinion surveys.

Racial Attitudes and the Myth of Racial Democracy

Historical Background

For Freyre, miscegenation became the motor behind Brazilian racial dynamics and racial democracy. According to this historic view, potential racial boundaries blurred due to extensive "mixing," rendering racism in the manner of U.S. segregation and polarization impossible in Brazil. Racism in the United States was considered a by-product of a racialist context that bred separatism, contempt, and violence. However, even within the antiracialist discourse of the Brazilian context, few disputed that darker-skinned individuals faced socioeconomic disadvantage. The racial democracy ideology was thought to help explain away the origin of that disadvantage as unconnected to racial discrimination. As Hasenbalg and Huntington write, "The popular Brazilian ideology of racial democracy holds that there is no prejudice or discrimination against non-whites in Brazil, certainly not when compared to the United States."[22] Therefore, the white versus nonwhite gap must be primarily due to other factors, such as an epiphenomenon of class.[23] Degler summarizes this traditional view: "After all, so the argument went, racial prejudice was virtually unknown in Brazil, so how could the low social and economic position of blacks be ascribed to racial discrimination? This view has come to be called the Brazilian 'myth of racial democracy.'"[24] Therefore, it was concluded that if a nonwhite individual was differentially unsuccessful in improving his or her social position compared to poor whites, that individual was primarily at fault.[25] Hasenbalg and Huntington claim that this individualist interpretation of racial inequality was held "by whites and non-whites alike."[26]

Researchers historically endorsed, then, a perspective on nonwhite disadvantage as "fostering a false concept of the reality of Brazilian race relations,"[27] leading to the denial of racial prejudice and discrimination. The myth of racial democracy was described, for example, as the prejudice of not having prejudice[28] and as an ideology of nondiscrimination.[29] As such, it appeared to provoke two specific assumptions that permeated Brazilian society: (1) The problems of nonwhites must be due to their own incapacity and irresponsibility, and (2) whites are exempt from moral obligation or responsibility regarding racial inequality.[30]

Contemporary Brazilian Attitudes

Since those earlier writings on the myth of racial democracy, many studies have been published challenging reductionist class-based interpretations of inequality in Brazil and documenting links between color and socioeconomic status unexplained by human capital models that control for educational level, for example.[31] However, considering that ideologies can exist above and beyond scientifically endorsed interpretations of social phenomena,[32] the question remains whether the racial democracy ideology continues to exercise its confounding influence on public opinion. That is, does it lead to a denial that discrimination is the basis of racial inequality and thereby legitimize the racial status quo?

Legitimizing Myth.   Contemporary research heavily endorses the view of racial democracy as an "antiracialism imagery"[33] that fosters a denial of racial
discrimination.[34] Hanchard, for example, claims, "What remains from the
previous belief system of racial democracy . . . is the denial of the existence of
the ongoing racial oppression of Afro-Brazilians."[35]

This newer body of literature of the "racialism" stage detailed in Chapter 2
also clearly repeats at least two specific effects of this ideology on beliefs about
racial inequality. Firstly, it holds that white Brazilians deny racial discrimination. Winant writes that "there is little evidence that white racial attitudes are
changing significantly in Brazil. . . . Whites continue to uphold the familiar
position: 'Racism does not exist in Brazil.'"[36] Secondly, the newer research
repeats the claim that nonwhite Brazilians also continue to deny discrimination. Twine writes, "Despite a body of social science literature documenting
racism, this mythology of the Brazilian racial democracy is still embraced
and defended by non-elite Brazilians."[37] Twine's category "nonelite" refers
"particularly to Afro-Brazilians."[38]

Guimarães sums up this contemporary view as follows:

> Understood as an ideology of domination by Fernandes (1965), the myth of
> racial democracy in Brazil would be just a cynical and cruel way of main-
> taining the socio-economic inequality between whites and blacks, covering
> and silencing the reality of color prejudice and racial discrimination. It is in
> that way that the majority of *negro* Brazilian intellectuals understand "racial
> democracy" and make the denouncing of its cruelty (as an ideology that anes-
> thetizes and alienates its victims) the principal instrument for political mobi-
> lization and the formation of a combative racial identity.[39]

Hasenbalg clarifies further: "The notion of myth to qualify 'racial democracy'
is used here in the sense of illusion or deception and signifies the distance between representation and reality, the existence of racial prejudice, discrimination and inequalities and their negation in the discursive realm."[40]

Therefore, in this perspective, which remains largely dominant in *negro*
movement and academic realms in the twenty-first century, racial democracy
is a "legitimizing ideology" of racial oppression.[41] It protects white privilege
by confounding perceptions of racial inequality and through blaming the individual for a lack of social mobility.[42] This vision of the effect of the myth of
anesthetizing and deceiving the victims of racial oppression I call the "Brazilian ignorance" stance.

Legitimate Utopia. There is an alternative view of the racial democracy orientation and its contemporary effects. Some scholars mentioned in the "challenging racialism" stage from Chapter 2 believe that the myth of racial democracy may have a positive side, acting as a utopian dream that envisions Brazilian society as one based on a "myth of an interrelating people."[43] Guimarães also summarizes this view, although generally does not endorse it:

> A few anthropologists (Fry 1995) have come out against [the above-mentioned] interpretation holding instead that racial democracy is the founding myth of the Brazilian nation, a fundamental element of its civilizing matrix. Even though it does not completely exclude prejudices and discrimination, it allows for greater intimacy and interpenetration between blacks and whites, thereby providing a more solid basis for overcoming racism.[44]

According to this perspective, a majority of Brazilians view the U.S. history of interracial conflict and separation as absurd and posit that there are no essential differences between individuals of the white, brown, or *preto* categories.[45] Racial rifts should have no place in Brazil. In this view, even positive racial identification is met with "ambivalence, confusion [and] antipathy,"[46] and, hence, an antiracialism stance prevails.[47] Although skin-color inequality exists, the racial democracy orientation may constitute a moral high ground common to all Brazilians that both recognizes and repudiates discrimination. According to Sheriff, "[Racial democracy] summons the collectively-held notion of the moral force of a shared heritage, a common family, a unified nation. Racism is repugnant. It is immoral. It is, above all, un-Brazilian."[48] Similarly, but earlier, Oracy Nogueira wrote: "[Racial democracy] has a positive side, when taken as a proclamation of an ideal or a contrasting value with which or inspired in which it is possible to criticize the existing conditions."[49]

Therefore, beyond an ideology leading Brazilians of varying degrees of African ancestry to believe that they live in a "racial paradise"[50] or legitimizing white privilege, racial democracy may reflect a deep-seated desire for a society that is not segmented along racial lines and that is essentially equal for all peoples. As such, this antiracialism imagery may provide Brazilians a yardstick with which to measure their unequal status, thereby enabling a structuralist account or recognition of racism. Hence, far from precluding antiracism, in supporting a discrimination-based interpretation of racial inequality, the myth may act as a valued and accepted principle, a legitimate utopian ideal, that can be invoked to confront nonwhite disadvantage.

Prevailing Framings of Stratification Beliefs

As discussed in Chapter 2, the competing frameworks of sociocultural theories and variants on realistic group conflict theory dominate the literature
on racial attitudes. Although the reach of these theories may extend beyond
the U.S. context, examining their application in the United States regarding
stratification beliefs provides a useful point of comparison for Brazil. Among
the ample U.S. public opinion data on racial issues, there appears a striking
division between blacks and whites regarding explanations for racial inequality. The 1994 General Social Survey posed the following question: "On the average, blacks have worse jobs, income, and housing than white people. Do you
think these differences are mainly due to discrimination?" In response, 67
percent of black Americans said "yes," while 68 percent of white Americans
said "no." However, although both sociocultural and group conflict theories
posit that blacks overwhelmingly point to discrimination while whites overwhelmingly point away from it, they disagree as to what motivates this divide,
as I presented in Chapter 2 and briefly summarize here.

Sociocultural Approaches

Sociocultural approaches explain racial attitude development as a gradual socialization process that results in negative affect toward outgroups.[51] In terms
of white racial attitudes toward blacks, this negativity comes in large part
from believing that blacks violate basic traditional American values such as
individualism, self-reliance, obedience, and discipline. This post–civil rights
perspective says that even though blacks are no longer especially handicapped
by racial discrimination (because it was outlawed) they still do not conform to
American values.[52] In other words, if formal discriminatory measures are no
longer responsible for black disadvantage, it must now be blacks themselves.
This type of racial ideology, then, influences an individualist explanation for
black disadvantage based in antiblack animus.

Group Conflict Theories

A second approach comprises the variants on group conflict theory.[53] These
framings generally posit that prejudice, for example antiblack animus, has
little to do with explanations for black disadvantage. Rather, whites blame
blacks for causing racial inequality as a way to justify white privilege. Hence,
the "lack of motivation" explanation serves as a legitimizing ideology of white
social dominance.[54] Sidanius and Pratto claim that in situations of group-

based dominance, the superordinate group holds this kind of hierarchy-enhancing ideology to legitimize its dominance. These authors state, "socially constructed groups . . . at different points along the social power continuum are naturally expected to differentially endorse legitimizing ideologies in relatively predictable ways."[55] That is, blacks would not support ideologies that enhance racial hierarchy or the status quo (for example, individualist explanation of racial stratification), while whites would do so.

Hypotheses

To set up a set of hypotheses, I first turn to Brazilianist framings that cast the myth of racial democracy as the "prejudice of not having prejudice"[56] or "the mythic construction of a society without racial prejudices or discrimination."[57] *Racial prejudice* is generally distinguished by social scientists as referring to an attitudinal stance, while *discrimination* refers to maltreatment or actions. Prejudice, therefore, can theoretically be a private stance that does not necessarily manifest itself in overt acts. Discrimination, on the other hand, is never a private issue and necessarily creates victims. The general populace most likely does not make that distinction, so prejudice and discrimination may be closely associated in Brazilian minds. Several of the survey items that I employ in this analysis, however, distinguished between them, and a first hypothesis drawn from the Brazilianist literature addresses prejudice alone:

H1: Brazilians deny the existence of racial prejudice in their society.

In terms of racial discrimination, the dominant Brazilian literature posits that Brazilians do not recognize that phenomenon as the root of Brazilian social inequality.[58] Hence, my second hypothesis:

H2: Brazilians deny the existence of racial discrimination.

In addition, the Brazilianist literature is very explicit about this denial being consensual, that nonwhites are similar to whites in this respect.[59] Thus, the third hypothesis:

H3: White and nonwhite Brazilians agree in their denial of racial discrimination.

On the other hand, the general literature on the same subject would generally posit stark racial divides in Brazilian public opinion regarding discrimination. According to the sociocultural approach, whites are induced by prejudice into blaming blacks for their own disadvantaged position.[60] Although not directly addressed, it would appear that because blacks are not equally socialized in antiblack affect, they would view themselves as structurally disadvantaged. Group conflict theories see whites blaming blacks for racial inequality based on strategic efforts to maintain and justify white privilege or white racial interests. Blacks would most commonly hold an opposite position, attempting to delegitimize white privilege.[61] Hence, based on general theory, my fourth hypothesis:

> H4: White Brazilians deny the existence of racial discrimination, while nonwhite Brazilians affirm it.

Finally, the Brazilianist literature frequently claims that everyday Brazilians may recognize the existence of a socioeconomic gap between whites and nonwhites in their country, but they offer a class-based explanation for it.[62] Hence, my fifth and final hypothesis:

> H5: Brazilians blame class not race for apparent racial inequalities.

Findings

Racial Prejudice

I explore my first hypothesis using several questions on the CEAP/DataUff survey from the state of Rio de Janeiro regarding the existence of racial prejudice in Brazil. Those items are listed in Table 5.1. The first question, wider in breadth than the second, asked whether the respondent believes there is a lot, a little, or no racial prejudice in Brazil. The first column of Table 5.1 reveals that fully 64 percent of the population recognizes a lot of prejudice, 31 percent say there is a little, and only 5 percent say that there is no prejudice in Brazil.

Two more survey items delve even deeper into the issue of prejudice. The first of these asked specifically if "whites" are prejudiced against *negros,* as opposed to a generic "in Brazil" of the earlier question, thereby specifying who the prejudiced ones are. Exactly half of the population felt that whites have a lot of prejudice against *negros,* whereas only 7 percent said there was none (question 2, Table 5.1, column 1). The last question of this set (question 3, Table 5.1) introduced a twist, asking if *negros* are prejudiced against whites. In response, 20 percent of Brazilians in Rio claimed that *negros* are very prejudiced against whites, and 32 percent claimed that *negros* were not at all prejudiced against whites (column 1).[63]

The responses do show some racial category differences on perceptions of prejudice. Whites are slightly less willing to recognize prejudice in general

Table 5.1 Percent distributions of items on the existence of racial prejudice in Brazil
by select color classifications: Adult population in the state of Rio de Janeiro, 2000

	All	Nonwhite	White	Preto	Brown
1. In Brazil there is . . .					
. . . a lot of racial prejudice?	64%	69%	58%	68%	70%
. . . a little racial prejudice?	31	28	35	29	28
. . . no racial prejudice?	5	3	7	3	2
2. Whites in relation to *negros* have . . .					
. . . a lot of prejudice?	50	55	45	55	54
. . . a little prejudice?	43	41	46	39	41
. . . no prejudice?	7	5	10	6	5
3. *Negros* in relation to whites?					
They are not at all prejudiced.	32	37	27	37	37
They have some prejudice.	48	45	51	44	46
They are very prejudiced.	20	18	23	19	17

SOURCE: CEAP/DataUff 2000.

1 Do you believe that in Brazil there is...

2 Do you believe that in Brazil, in general whites in relation to negros have . . .

3 Do you believe that in Brazil negros are color prejudiced in relation to whites?

than are *negros* and a little more willing to recognize *negro* prejudice against whites. On question 1, whereas 58 percent of whites claim that there is a lot of racial prejudice in Brazil (column 3), 69 percent of nonwhites agree (column 2). In addition, whereas 37 percent of nonwhites claim that *negros* are not prejudiced against whites (question 4, column 2), 27 percent of whites claim the same (column 3). However, in general, the differences between white and nonwhite responses are not dramatic, and overwhelming majorities of both groups clearly resist "the prejudice of not having prejudice," thereby contradicting my first hypothesis (H1). In sum, Brazilians, both white and nonwhite, in the state of Rio de Janeiro are quick to recognize that Brazil is fraught with prejudice.

Racial Discrimination

Moving now to explanations for racial inequality, recall that the Brazilianist literature posits that all Brazilians deny that racial discrimination is involved. To tap this dynamic, the respondents in the CEAP/DataUff survey were reminded that some studies show that in general *negros* have worse jobs, salaries, and education levels than whites, and then they were asked to explain why (see Table 5.2, question 1, for question wording and format). This

Table 5.2 Percent distributions on explanations for racial inequality by select color classifications, 2000 and 1995

	All	Nonwhite	White	Preto	Brown
1. Some studies show that in general negro persons have worse jobs, salaries, and education than white persons. I am going to mention some reasons that people say explain that situation. What do you think of each explanation? (agreement responses)					
Racial discrimination impedes *negros* from getting good jobs and bettering their lives.	82%	86%	77%	91%	84%
Negros are less motivated than whites.	14	13	16	13	12
Negros are still suffering from the effects of slavery.	70	73	67	76	72
2. *Negros* were freed from slavery about 100 years ago. In your opinion, who is the most responsible for the fact that the *negro* population still lives in worse living conditions than the white population?					
The prejudice and the discrimination that exists among whites against *negros*?	72	72	72	67	74
Negros who don't take advantage of the existing opportunities?	28	28	28	33	26

SOURCE: CEAP/DataUff 2000, DataFolha 1995.

construction could potentially reveal a structuralist stance, if discrimination is blamed, or an individualist stance, if *negros* were blamed due to a lack of motivation. Results in Table 5.2 (column 1, question 1) show that an overwhelming majority of Brazilians in the state of Rio de Janiero (82 percent) point squarely at white discrimination as the explanatory factor.

We can compare these results to a national sample as the 1995 DataFolha survey asked a very similar question. Following a statement that *negros* had been freed from slavery for over 100 years but still live in worse conditions than whites, respondents were then asked who was responsible for this (see Table 5.2, question 2, for wording and format): Seventy-two percent pointed to the prejudice and discrimination that exists among whites against *negros* (question 2, column 1). Only 28 percent claimed that *negros* themselves were at fault for not taking advantage of existing opportunities.[64] Clearly, then, my second hypothesis (H2) regarding a Brazilian denial of racial discrimination receives no support.

Are there racial divisions in these responses? The dominant Brazilianist stance holds that there should be none,[65] and the general literature clearly posits that whites and blacks disagree because of race-specific interests and/ or prejudice. However, according to the 1995 DataFolha survey, there are no racial divisions between whites and nonwhites: Seventy-two percent of both categories affirm the existence of racial discrimination (Table 5.2, question 2, columns 2 and 3). The 2000 CEAP/DataUff survey (Table 5.2, question 1) does reveal a small difference between whites and nonwhites on this question. The 83 percent majority of the sample that affirmed discrimination included 77 percent of whites (column 3) and 86 percent of nonwhites (column 2). In addition, when asked directly if *negros* are less motivated in the 2000 survey, an individualist explanation, 16 percent of whites and 13 percent of nonwhites said they were (columns 3 and 2, respectively). These differences are relatively minimal when one considers that overwhelming majorities of whites and nonwhites agree in their evaluation of discrimination. Moreover, in the 1995 DataFolha survey, which asked about *negros* not taking "advantage of existing opportunities" (question 2, Table 5.2), whites and nonwhites opined exactly the same—only 28 percent agreeing with the individualist interpretation.

Hence, regarding my third hypothesis (H3) that both whites and nonwhites agree as to that denial of discrimination, this perspective is not supported by the data. While it is true that color is generally not associated with the Brazilian view of the causes of racial inequality, the direction of the belief is not what is hypothesized by the dominant Brazilianist stance. Rather, both white and nonwhite Brazilians overwhelmingly point to discrimination, not away from it.

Regarding the fourth hypothesis (H4) from the general literature on a possible racial divide, whites do not disagree with nonwhites in offering a structuralist explanation for racial inequality, and thus neither whites nor nonwhites blame the victims for their own disadvantage. Hence, there is no support for that hypothesis.

In addition and as an important side note, Andrews comments, "Afro-Brazilians are more likely to see racial inequality as caused by present-day discrimination. Euro-Brazilians, by contrast, are more likely to explain such inequalities in terms of the heritage of slavery."[66] However, contradicting that assertion, results from question 1 in Table 5.2 show that a majority of both categories do view the effects of slavery as a factor and that nonwhites are even more likely to do so than whites (73 and 67 percent, respectively, in columns 2 and 3).

Delving deeper into perceptions of discrimination in Brazilian society, the CEAP/DataUff survey questioned respondents about the possible discrimination suffered by *negros* at the hands of the police. This discrimination is, in fact, documented and is quite common.[67] Nonwhites are more likely to suffer violence at the hands of police and even be killed by them without any apparent justifying motive. Does Brazilian public opinion recognize that differential, unjust treatment? Respondents were first asked about the frequency with which *negros* are questioned (*abordados*) by police during police operations such as raids or police checkpoints (*blitz* or *revista*) (Table 5.3, question 1). Results in column 1 reveal an amazing 95 percent of the population (including 94 percent of whites) saying that *negros* are targets in these situations "always" or "almost always." When asked the same about whites in similar situations (question 2), only 41 percent of the sample (including 38 percent of nonwhites) claimed whites were "always" or "almost always" targeted. Clearly whites and nonwhites agree strongly that *negros* receive a differential, discriminatory treatment from Brazilian law enforcement.

Next, respondents were asked if during the last year they had ever witnessed an act of discrimination against a *negro*. Results presented in Table 5.3 (question 3, column 1) reveal that 26 percent of the sample said "yes." Nonwhites, at 30 percent, were more likely to witness instances of ongoing discrimination than whites, at 22 percent (columns 2 and 3). In the self-classification format, *pretos* were most likely at 32 percent to witness discrimination (column 4), while browns, 24 percent, were less likely (column 5).

Respondents were then asked if they themselves had experienced discrimination based on their color or race. Results in Table 5.3, question 4, show that about 15 percent of Brazilians in Rio say "yes" (column 1). Color differences occur on this item, as might be expected: Twenty-four percent of nonwhites (column 2) compared to only 6 percent of whites (column 3) responded that they had personally been victims of discrimination. Importantly, when broken down further by color, it is the population self-classifying as *preto* that

Table 5.3 Percent distributions of items on discrimination by select color classifications: Adult population in the state of Rio de Janeiro, 2000

	All	Nonwhite	White	Preto	Brown
1. Frequency you believe *negros* are questioned during police operations.					
Always	64%	66%	61%	68%	66%
Almost always	31	29	33	28	29
Sometimes	3	3	4	2	3
Almost never	2	2	2	2	1
Never	1	1	0	1	1
2. Frequency you believe whites are questioned during police operations.					
Always	13	10	17	13	9
Almost always	28	28	28	27	28
Sometimes	18	17	18	14	18
Almost never	33	35	33	35	35
Never	7	10	4	11	10
3. In the last year, have you ever witnessed an act of discrimination against a *negro*?					
Yes	26	30	22	32	24
4. Could you tell me if at some point you have felt discriminated against because of your color or race?					
Yes	15	24	6	36	18
5. In the last 20 years the social and economic situation of *negros* in Brazil has . . .					
. . . gotten much better	29	24	34	23	24
. . . gotten a little better	43	46	40	47	46
. . . gotten much worse	14	14	14	14	14
. . . gotten a little worse	5	5	4	6	4
. . . stayed the same	10	11	8	10	12

SOURCE: CEAP/DataUff 2000.

claims to have felt the brunt of the discrimination. Fully 36 percent of *pretos* (column 4) compared to 18 percent of browns (column 5) claimed to have personally suffered discrimination because of their color or race.

Lastly, one survey item attempted to gauge how Brazilians in the state of Rio de Janeiro see the overall situation of *negros* over time by asking, "Do you believe that in the last twenty years the social and economic situation of *negros* in Brazil improved or worsened, a little or a lot?" Results are listed in Table 5.3, question 5. Collapsing the first two responses "much better" and "a little better," column 1 shows that a strong majority, a full 72 percent, does believe that progress has been made in the last twenty years. Only about one-fifth believes the situation has worsened. There is some color difference in these results: Thirty-four percent of whites compared to 24 percent of nonwhites (columns 3 and 2) claim things have gotten much better. However, overall judgments are very similar, 70 percent of whites and 73 percent of nonwhites seeing a decline in racial discrimination over the prior two decades.

Race versus Class

As regards the relative weight of class versus race explanations for the disadvantaged situation of nonwhites in Brazil, the literature posits that part of the mystification that racial democracy produces comes from blaming class for racial inequalities.[68] Two survey items suggest some insights into this posited effect. First, recall the question about the actions of police toward different populations at checkpoints. The survey also asked about how the police treat individuals that appear to be poor (see Table 5.4, question 1). According to the responses presented in column 1, poor people fare much worse than whites, as judged in comparison to responses to question 2 presented in Table 5.3. (Of course, these are overlapping categories—tens of millions of Brazilian poor are white.) Ninety-one percent of the sample claim that the poor are always or almost always targets of the police, which is a similar number to the 95 percent of the sample that said the same of *negros* (Table 5.3, question 1, column 1). This survey item reveals that both class and race discrimination are obvious realities for almost all Brazilians in the state of Rio de Janeiro.

A final question was much more direct regarding how class factors into explanations for racial inequality. Respondents were asked whether or not they agreed with the following statement: "In Brazil, *negros* are discriminated against not because of their color but because they are poor." Results in Table 5.4, question 2, reveal that 57 percent of the sample expressed some level of agreement with that statement (column 1). Nonwhites were actually more likely to agree with that statement than whites, 62 and 52 percent, respectively (columns 2 and 3). Hence, on this issue, the dominant Brazilianist position receives some qualified support. When forced to choose between race or class discrimination, class appears the more important explanation for everyday Brazilians in Rio de Janiero. As I will discuss below, however, in measuring the relative

Table 5.4 Percent distributions of items on class discrimination by select color classifications: Adult population in the state of Rio de Janeiro, 2000

	All	Nonwhite	White	Preto	Brown
1. With what frequency do you believe the poor are questioned by police during police operations?					
Always	50%	52%	46%	55%	51%
Almost always	41	38	43	36	40
Sometimes	5	4	5	2	6
Almost never	3	2	4	3	2
Never	2	2	2	4	1
2. In Brazil *negros* are not discriminated against because of their color, but because they are poor.					
Agreement	57	62	52	64	60

SOURCE: CEAP/DataUff 2000.

weight of race and class variables for determining socioeconomic outcomes, much of the scientific literature also points to class variables as the core, but not exclusive, determinant socioeconomic disadvantage.[69]

Discussion

Results presented in this chapter point to a very different character of the myth of racial democracy than the dominant literature on Brazil purports in terms of everyday Brazilian attitudes. Contradicting my first hypothesis, there is overwhelming recognition of racial *prejudice* in Brazil. Second, that both white and nonwhite Brazilians deny the existence of *discrimination* addresses the cornerstone of the racial democracy edifice, according to both the earlier literature and contemporary research.[70] However, contradicting my second and third hypotheses, overwhelming majorities of whites and nonwhites in the samples from Rio de Janeiro and the 1995 national survey point to discrimination as behind *negro* disadvantage. Contradicting my fourth hypothesis, that whites but not nonwhites will deny discrimination, an overwhelming majority of whites agree with nonwhites that discrimination explains *negro* disadvantage. In sum, not only do my results suggest that the view of the myth of racial democracy as a "prejudice of not having prejudice" is at the very least outdated, but they also suggest that this "myth" does not blind people to discrimination.[71] The "Brazilian ignorance" stance does not fit the data.

Because this issue has always lived in relation to the United States, it is important to return to that comparison. Degler believed that "Americans more than Brazilians recognize discrimination,"[72] yet my results do not back up that historic contention for the time period covered by my data. The support I find that all shades of Brazilians show for a structuralist explanation is strikingly high relative to the United States, where public opinion is rigidly divided along racial lines and where there is strong white support for an individualist interpretation. Recall that 68 percent of white Americans rejected discrimination as the cause of black disadvantage in the United States, according to the 1994 General Social Survey, compared to the 28 percent of Brazilians classified as white regarding racial inequality in Brazil in 1995. Likewise, 68 percent of black Americans affirm that discrimination is the cause of black disadvantage in the United States in comparison to the 72 percent of Brazilians categorized as nonwhite regarding their own unequal status. The opinion of blacks/nonwhites in both contexts appears similar, but whites differ greatly in the United States and Brazil.

My fifth hypothesis revealed that a majority (57 percent) of Brazilians chose class over skin color to explain discrimination in a forced choice, either/or survey scenario. Is this proof that Brazilians do actually deny racial discrimination? I believe such an interpretation would be misleading. Scholars continue to debate this very complicated issue of the determinants of racialized inequality in Brazil. Current studies attempt to measure what percentage of socioeconomic inequality—for example, differences in income—is due to human capital differences and other factors or to skin color. Although estimates vary, educational differences controlling for race are decisive, while race controlling for human capital differences still exerts an independent influence.[73] Thus, racial inequalities cannot be explained away by class proxies such as education; likewise, racial inequality cannot be understood without taking into account the core class effects. Telles (2004) ends his discussion of structural racial discrimination in Brazil as follows, revealing a glimpse of the complexity surrounding the issue of forcing a choice between class and race to explain inequality:

> Racism has been more hidden and indirect in Brazil [compared to the United States] for many reasons, including the greater importance of class-based mechanism for reproducing racial inequality, the apparent absence of either formal or de facto extreme segregation in schools, and the greater role of so-

cial networks rather than direct exclusion in employment. However, Brazil's class discrimination and high levels of inequality have racial components, including race as a criteria for mobility into the upper reaches of that system and greater inequalities where the nonwhite population is larger.[74]

Other researchers point squarely to education, a social class proxy, as the most significant factor accounting for difference in socioeconomic outcomes between color groupings in Brazil. Hasenbalg explains, for example, "it seems clear that in contemporary Brazil the nucleus of disadvantage that *pretos* and browns appear to suffer can be located in the process of educational achievement. . . . In terms of the differences between groups of color, educational inequality is the principal factor explaining disparities in income."[75]

It is not surprising, then, that a majority of Brazilians weigh class more heavily than race in a closed-ended, either/or question. They may, in fact, be right on many accounts, as the literature posits. This does not mean, however, that they would reject the notion of an independent effect of skin color controlling for "class, family, neighborhood, and a host of other social- and cultural-capital factors."[76] In other words, as my survey results on prejudice and discrimination suggest, Brazilians recognize the complexity of historic and contemporary racial inequality in their country, and they may not be as reductionist as scholars and activists have stipulated.

Explaining Brazilian Stratification Beliefs

Can the consensus structuralist view on racial inequality that my results suggest be squared with the general and Brazilianist literature on racial attitudes, or does that consensus represent a counterintuitive contradiction? Beginning with general theory, are sociocultural and conflict framings useful in this analysis?

According to sociocultural framings employed in the United States, whites hold an individualist interpretation for racial inequality. They deeply resent blacks for not living up to American values and possess an antiblack affect created through white socialization processes and a view of blacks as having the same opportunities as whites. Transported to the Brazilian context, because racial discrimination was outlawed with abolition in 1888 and did not manifest itself in later de jure discrimination, such as Jim Crow in the United States, it seems plausible that Brazilian whites would blame nonwhites for their own disadvantage. This framing is at a loss, then, to explain why whites would recognize discrimination and prejudice in Brazil even in the presence of formal equality before the law.

The variations of group conflict theory are also inconsistent with the re-sults presented here. They hold that white racial interests lie in a continuation of the racial status quo and therefore that whites will deny the existence of structural disadvantage or discrimination to maintain the current structural arrangement. Doing otherwise, it is theorized, would jeopardize white privilege. However, cognizant of racial inequality, Brazilians of the white category do not offer a justifying explanation for their privileged position. Rather, they appear to delegitimize white privilege by endorsing a structuralist account.

Sidanius and Pratto do raise the possibility that ideologies appearing to delegitimize racial inequality may, in reality, prove to be what they label "hierarchy-enhancing" stances that actually buttress the status quo.[77] It is difficult, though, to imagine how the type of racial common sense revealed through my data that specifically conditions a strong awareness of white discrimination could be hierarchy enhancing. This is especially true in the Brazilian context that is, according to the dominant stance I challenge, characterized by a historic racial common sense that denies racial discrimination. In such a context, to admit racism would appear to be decidedly out-of-place, seemingly "unBrazilian." Nonetheless, the empirical test of such a hypothesis would be that the white recognition of racial discrimination be accompanied by white opposition for policies and strategies that might challenge that discrimination. I test that hypothesis in subsequent chapters where it becomes clear that the perspective on the hierarchy-enhancing quality of a white structuralist stance in Brazil needs revision.

For the most part, the general theories do correctly predict that nonwhite Brazilians will consistently recognize prejudice and structural discrimination as the force behind their disadvantaged position. However, Sidanius and Pratto's version of the group conflict perspective, social dominance theory, errs significantly. According to that framing, nonwhite Brazilians are induced by a "false consciousness" into sharing a white denial of racial discrimination.[78] Again, to the contrary, my results show that: (a) Whites in Brazil do not legitimize inequality through denying racial discrimination; and (b) both whites and nonwhites point to white discrimination as the cause of racial inequality.

Why do these theories generally do so little to explain stratification beliefs in Brazil? A central emphasis of sociocultural approaches and group conflict theories is that group orientations mold racial attitudes, as is found to be the case in the United States.[79] These theories conjure up very strong divisional boundaries between and around racialized social groups. In his formulation of differing types of racial boundaries, Banton, for example, describes the United States as characterized by "hard" boundaries.[80] Alba writes of "bright" boundaries in the United States as compared to "blurred" ones in other contexts.[81] Hence, as discussed in Chapter 3, racialized social boundaries are clearly variable in terms of their robustness, and I hold that the existence of blurred or ambiguous boundaries, as opposed to bright ones, has consequences for the cognitive organization of attitudes.

To explicate how differential boundary salience may affect explanations for social group inequality, Kluegel and Smith provide an example of stratification beliefs concerning sex-based inequality.[82] They find that although blacks and women in the United States held similar subordinate positions in the hierarchy of inequality, both men and women tended to offer a structuralist account of gender inequality. This is radically different from the racial division of individualist versus structuralist that whites and black hold, respectively, regarding racial inequality. In other words, gender was not a determinant of beliefs about gender discrimination, while "race" was a decisive determinant of beliefs about racial discrimination in the United States. In discussing this comparison, the authors conclude that the lack of a gender effect was due to a "lesser degree of salience of the group membership," along with a general lack of segregation and a lack of negative affect between women and men.[83]

These same conditions—a general lack of segregation, lower negative affect toward the disadvantaged population, and weaker divisional boundaries—are apparent in the Brazilian racial context, especially as concerns boundary salience and group membership.[84] As I addressed in Chapter 3, Brazil is known for ambiguous racial or color boundaries.[85] Racial ambiguity may be defined as "the failure effectively (and successfully) to maintain the line separating blackness and whiteness."[86] Alternatively, Harris describes "ambiguous racial calculus" in Brazil as a situation where the "ego lacks a single socio-centric racial identity."[87] Both definitions of boundary ambiguity are complementary and point to a context where skin-color dynamics may be characterized by "a lesser degree of group membership salience" or by a lesser degree of "racial subjectivity."[88] When socially constructed boundaries are porous or ambiguous, their significance as markers of distinct, self-identifying social segments with diverging worldviews is reduced,[89] and convergence of opinions becomes a real possibility.

In sum, contrasting race-centered notions, I suggest that when boundaries are ambiguous, as in Brazil, their divisional power in the cognitive domain may be compromised. Weak boundary salience may create a situation that results in the inability of the color or race construct to predict attitudinal stances. In other words, racial or color boundaries in Brazil may not mold cognitive processes along group membership lines, at least not in ways predicted by the dominant theories.[90] Hence, the inefficiency of those theories in the Brazilian context becomes obvious.

Racial Democracy as Antiracialism's Centerpiece

If robust group-based racial subjectivities rife with disaffect for the out-group (a sociocultural perspective) or galvanized behind protecting group-specific privilege (a conflict perspective) do not resonate in Brazil, what does drive Brazilian stratification beliefs? I believe that the answer brings us full circle back to the myth of racial democracy, but not in the way envisioned by the dominant stance. My results support the conclusions of Fry, Reis, Segato, and de la Fuente, for example, who hypothesize the character of the myth as "a proclamation of an ideal or a contrasting value with which or inspired in which it is possible to criticize the existing conditions."[91] It is even, as Guimarães calls it in a more encompassing conceptualization, an "antiracialism imagery."[92] However, it may almost be the opposite of what Guimarães had in mind and posited when he wrote: "The antiracialist imagery of the negation of the existence of 'races' later prompted the negation of racism as a social phenomenon."[93] To the contrary, the myth of racial democracy is associated with a structuralist, discrimination-based explanation for racial inequality during the period under study (1995–2002). Hence, the interpretation of the myth of racial democracy as a possible legitimate utopian ideal during that period better fits the data.

Why do so many social scientists apparently misinterpret the myth as an individualist stratification belief? Critics of my research might claim that the previous stance offered by Fernandes and Degler, for example, was an accurate interpretation for the time, and that my findings reflect a significant shift in public opinion that occurred by the year of my earliest data set. However, while it is certainly true that my data from 1995 and 2000 cannot straightforwardly speak to much earlier attitudes in Brazil, there was one previous large-sample survey of political public opinion that asked respondents about their stratification beliefs and hence can give us a possible glimpse of attitudes a decade earlier. This 1986 electoral survey in São Paulo, reported by Hasenbalg and Silva, posed the following question:

Some people say there is discrimination against blacks and mulattos in employment—that it is much more difficult for them to get a good job than for whites. Others feel that to progress in life, everything depends on the person and has nothing to do with the color of one's skin. In your opinion, is there discrimination against people of color, or is the opportunity to advance in life equal for whites and blacks?[94]

In response, 67 percent of whites and 67 percent of "blacks" said that there was discrimination against people of color. These results are very significant and match almost exactly the results I obtained from 1995 and 2000 surveys. Hence, although it might be conceivable that racial attitudes prior to 1995 may have been significantly different than those reflected in my data sets, these results from 1986 *suggest* otherwise as concerns ten years earlier.

Taking this argument a very cautious step further, however, was public opinion in the 1970s characterized by a denial of racial discrimination or prejudice? There were no large-sample surveys that I know of that can address this issue. However, Michael Mitchell's doctoral dissertation contains results from a survey using a nonrandom sample of nonwhite Brazilians that he conducted in 1972.[95] The sample size was just under 400; and although the survey is not generalizable to the entire nonwhite population, Mitchell claims its systematization (which he details) provides some confidence that it can speak to a large segment of the "black" population in the city of São Paulo at that time. The questionnaire contained the following item: "Do you believe that prejudice exists in Brazil?" Fully 74 percent responded affirmatively, that prejudice is manifested either openly or in hidden form; 18 percent agreed that prejudice exists, but very little; and only 8 percent said there is no prejudice in Brazil. Many caveats must accompany such a sample; however, the results again appear to contradict the common assertion in the dominant literature that nonwhites deny racial prejudice and/or discrimination in Brazil. Sticking with large-sample survey results, however, and thus pushing Mitchell's results aside, as far as I know, no scholar has posited such an early shift from a general denial of racism to a general recognition of racism in Brazil that would have been reflected in that 1986 survey in São Paulo. Telles notes a much later shift, suggesting that "popular and elite support for the idea of racial democracy ended in the 1990s."[96] However, not only does this leave the 1986 results unexplained, but most scholars, in contrast to Telles, have continued to describe an ongoing denial of racism.[97] For example, in 1996 Andrews wrote, "Thus racial democracy, and its dark underside of frank, unreflective racism, remain much in evidence in Brazilian society at both the elite and popular levels, and will continue to exercise influence over that society for some time to come."[98] In 1999, Winant also claims that "there is little evidence that white racial attitudes are changing . . . "[99] Hence, I want to suggest here that the apparently counterintuitive results I present are not because attitudes had changed drastically by time of the 1995 DataFolha or the 2000 CEAP/DataUff surveys, much less by 1986 election survey in São Paulo. Instead, I am of the opinion that Brazilianist scholars, in large part, have wrongheadedly generalized from the top down regarding the formation of racial attitudes in Brazil through making claims about the opinion of the masses based on those of dominant elite.

Moreover, if, in fact, mass opinion did shift by the 1986 survey, or excluding those results, by the 1995 DataFolha survey, how could we explain that change? Major shifts in public opinion do not happen quickly or easily. Entrenched belief systems are not changed by decree, especially in a country the size of Brazil. In fact, theorists of shifts in public opinion place a high premium on documenting the exact mechanisms that, when present, are capable of producing them. Two prominent perspectives on this issue are those of John Zaller's in *The Nature and Origins of Mass Opinion* and Taeku Lee's in *Mobilizing Public Opinion.*[100] Lee agrees with Zaller's seminal piece on how mass opinions are generally formed and shift, although, as I mention below, Lee then adds a new angle.

Zaller's theory represents a top-down approach. He posits that the masses form political preferences of all types based on the information diffused centrally in the mass media. Those opinion preferences specifically include racial attitudes. Importantly, the individuals responsible for the content of that information are political elites: "politicians, higher-level government officials, journalists, some activists, and many kinds of experts and policy specialists."[101] Therefore, when, for example, elites uphold a clear picture of some political reality made proximate through coverage in varied mass media outlets, Zaller posited that "the public tends to see events from that point of view."[102]

Research in Brazil does document that some dominant members of the economic, political, military, and intellectual elite had tended to deny the existence of discrimination and prejudice for decades. Perhaps most influential in terms of propagandizing the idea of a Brazil without racism was the military dictatorship of 1964 through 1985, or at least it is the most cited example by contemporary scholars.[103] What elite shifts, then, stimulated the dramatic about-face captured in the 1986 and 1995 surveys? Moreover, which were the mass media mechanisms that transformationally transmitted those elite shifts to the general masses of Brazil? These questions must be answered if a shift in public opinion is argued.

Elements of the "challenging antiracialism" stage laid out in Chapter 2 can provide some clues to suggest answers to the first question regarding elite events. That stage, marked by the waning of the dictatorship's authoritarian zeal, witnessed the birth of new quantitative studies that painted the picture of a very unequal Brazil along the lines of color or race. These studies certainly became fodder in later years for social science and social movement debates about the nature of racial stratification in Brazil. In addition, *negro* movements were constituted during those same years, arguing as many other associations at the same time for some voice after years of the marginalization of civil society under military rule. Although significant, were those few academic studies and/or the ideas of movement elites even mirrored in the ideas that characterized the elite in general, and especially the elite whose opinions mattered in terms of influencing the opinions of the masses? I suspect that they were not in the years prior to the 1986 and 1995 surveys.

Then there is the second question that would have to be addressed in terms of those that posit a shift in mass opinion before the 1986 or 1995 surveys: What mass media mechanisms might that very small number of academic and movement elites have used to transform mass opinion in the years preceding these surveys and thus captured in them? It would indeed be an incredible feat to lay out a convincing scenario of how that could have occurred. As I posit in subsequent chapters, movement and academic elites are in fact now in the twenty-first century possibly influencing a shift in mass opinion; however, their power to do so, as I argue, is constituted only through the collaboration of a third very powerful actor whose actions do affect the masses and mass media, the Brazilian state. However, the Brazilian state, with the return of democracy in 1985, was silent on racial issues until the assumption of the presidency of Fernando Henrique Cardoso in 1995 and then only slowly began to move in the direction of recognizing racism. As I argue in Chapter 7, not until at least 2001 did the mass media begin to transmit in a concerted fashion a new discourse on Brazil, characterizing it as a country struggling with racism.

Hence, absent the evidence of radically changed ruling elite ideas and of the presence of specific mass media mechanisms influencing an earlier shift in the mass opinions in Brazil, I cannot claim that the 1986, 1995, or 2000 surveys, which all registered a keen recognition of discrimination on the part of the masses, represent something new. All the evidence I can muster, then, points to an overgeneralization on the part of social scientists regarding the nature of public opinion in Brazil whereby they equated the opinion of elite actors with those of the masses. In some ways they employed a type of top-down approach similar in some respect to Zaller's, but these social scientists did so by making facile assumptions without apparent supporting evidence.

As mentioned above, although Lee agrees with Zaller on the general origin and nature of mass opinion, he does add a new twist. Lee argues that in some special circumstances, a bottom-up dynamic creates the mechanisms for shifts in public opinion. Lee examined the civil rights era in the United States, and he argues that it was black insurgency that caused a shift in that country's general patterns of racial attitudes during that time. Lee writes, "When black insurgency successfully mobilizes a groundswell of protest, a sequence and process are set in motion that move racial attitudes out of relative quiescence into activated mass opinion."[104] That is, he writes that insurgencies capable of mobilizing disruptive, visible, and mass participation can bypass the normal channels through which elites transmit political ideas to the masses; in contrast, the masses become active participants and influence a wider shift.

Could Lee's bottom-up approach explain a shift in public opinion in Brazil that would have been captured in the 1986 and 1995 surveys? That, indeed, would be another argument very difficult to conceive. In the next chapter, I show, for example, that in the 2000 survey respondents in Rio de Janeiro were asked if they had ever heard of the *negro* movement; only 14 percent of the sample responded "yes," in equal percentages for all color groupings. Furthermore, I will report in that chapter on the general absence of racial protests in Brazil, and much less those involving the masses, during the 1980s and 1990s, with very few exceptions. Lee concludes that his framing explains attitudinal shifts in moments of social chaos or widespread protest movements mobilizing the masses. That description does not appear to coincide with societal dynamics in Brazil during those decades, nor even into the third millennium. I am left with the question, then, of how to explain a possible shift in mass opinions in Brazil if one were to argue that a shift is represented in the data I present from 1986, 1995, and 2000 on the recognition of racial discrimination.

Turning the entire question on the origin of public opinion around, however, if it appears that some elite in those earlier decades tended to deny racial discrimination in Brazil, how can I suggest that nonelites were different? I think I can do so turning to a key variable affecting the formation of public opinion in both Zaller's and Lee's framings. According to these theorists, an intervening variable needs to be added to understand a possible disconnect between elites and nonelites. That is, Zaller holds that variation in mass public opinion is only partly explained by elite influence or "information." Rather, he claims that every opinion is a marriage of that information with another element: deep-seated predispositions. He states: "citizens are more than passive receivers of whatever media communications they encounter. They possess a variety of interests, values, and experiences that may greatly affect their willingness to accept—or alternatively, their resolve to resist—persuasive influences."[105] I believe that dominant scholars have oversimplified the influence of elites on Brazilian racial attitudes in part because they have not adequately theorized this predispositions element (combined with the aggravating fact of a lack of survey data on the opinions of the masses in Brazil). This element may act as a type of filter of elite influence, leading everyday Brazilians to parse elite opinions in a more nuanced way and to maintain a more critical perspective based in their own experiences.

This view receives some support from Hasenbalg and Silva. Hasenbalg writes, for example, "the notions about racial democracy were formulated by intellectuals using preexisting ideas,"[106] and with Silva, he adds, "Yet the ways in which this ideology is translated into concepts and attitudes among white and black Brazilians continue to be largely unknown."[107] Now, however, with several large-sample surveys to draw on, we are beginning to learn more about how Brazilians in general think about racial inequality. In finding that they contrast elite interpretations, I believe it is key to turn to that intervening variable—predispositions in the form of values, interests, and experiences—to understand racial democracy's influence on racial attitudes. Such a framing allows an exploration of the myth of racial democracy not as an elite-driven lie, but as a deep-seated belief based in the experiences, many of them involving discrimination, and in the dreams of ordinary Brazilians.

A Return to Racial Democracy as Legitimate Utopian Creed

In terms of more deeply understanding the ways in which the majority of Brazilians may understand this myth and why it is best framed as a legitimate utopian ideal rather than a legitimizing hoax, it may help to begin by exploring Guimarães' description and interpretation of historic views of the myth in *negro* movement circles. He reports that the expression "racial democracy" became popular and politically accepted because it "was used frequently by the *negro* movement in the 1950s."[108] For example, Guimarães claims that it was employed to extol certain characteristics of Brazil by Abdias do Nascimento and by the *negro* movement *Teatro Experimental do Negro* (TEN). During the inaugural First Congress of the Brazilian *Negro* in 1950, Nascimento gave a speech in which he stated: "We can observe that the long-practiced *mestizaje* as an imperative of our national formation from the beginning of colonization of Brazil is being transformed in inspiration . . . in a well founded doctrine of racial democracy that serves as a lesson and model for other peoples of complex ethnic formation, such as our own."[109] Later, in 1955, in the closing of a conference on race relations, the *negro* movement TEN proclaimed, "Brazil is a national community where the most advanced customs of racial democracy are alive and well, even with the survival among us of some vestiges of discrimination."[110]

These statements both reference a situation in Brazil where *negro* movement actors recognized and praised the rare context of interracial mixing, while also recognizing the very real burden of discrimination. These praises, of course, must be understood in relation to the United States at the time, where racial violence, forced segregation, and prohibitions against interracial marriage and intimacy were the norm, and in fact the law. This contrast is so salient that Guimarães recounts that racial democracy as an idea "was rapidly transformed into a racial democracy *tout court,* in direct relation to the racial conflicts that became the beginning of the end of legal racism in the US."[111] He writes:

> To the contrary of what happened in that country [the United States], scholars and militants [in Brazil] thought that they already counted with the legacy of racial democracy coming from Abolition. For *negro* movements, however, abolition was not a complete movement because it did not represent the economic and social integration of the *negro* to the new capitalist order: for both the generation of the 1930s (*Frente Negra Brasileira,* or FNB), and the generation of the 1950s (TEN), a second Abolition was necessary.[112]

According to Guimarães, racial democracy, then, signified the recognized possession of full rights to something not yet materialized. He even claims that as late as 1982 the *Movimento Negro Unificado* (MNU) campaigned for "an authentic racial democracy,"[113] clarifying: "On one hand, the stated principle [racial democracy] signified a right that could be called upon at any moment, and therein resides the progressive side; on the other hand, its lack of realization and it being a promised ideal always indicated its conservative aspect."[114]

The historic ideas behind Brazil as a racial democracy, then, may have first included the recognition of a Brazilian character born of considerable racial mixing, which was long viewed as creating degenerate mulatto types by modern science and outlawed in the United States. At its heart, this Brazilian character may have consisted in a widespread belief in true equality, and racial intimacy, ambiguity, and cordiality were its expected corollaries. Thus, to point out that there was still much to be done in an unequal Brazil to combat the socioeconomic disadvantage of nonwhite Brazilians, movement actors could invoke this national character as a goal. Guimarães writes: "It has to be recognized that in ideological terms, the belief in a racial democracy and a mixed origin of the Brazilian people served to solidify the formal position of equality of *negros* and mulattos in Brazilian society."[115] Hence, Guimarães concludes: "The ideas and the name racial democracy, far from constituting an achievement created by the white dominant classes, as some activists and sociologists want to make it today, was for many years a way of integration forged by *negro* militancy."[116]

The ideal behind the myth of racial democracy that Guimarães documents is squarely that of an antiracialism imagery, a stance born of a history of the relative blurring of racial boundaries through miscegenation and forged against the backdrop of racist racialism of the U.S. Jim Crow period and of the era's scientific racism. Far from being a legitimizing myth, racial democracy might best be understood, then, as a collective predisposition; as a set of values, interests, and experiences embraced by the masses; as a principled idea of a society in opposition to the United States and its formalized racial divides. As Silva writes, "The prevailing racial discourse in Brazil celebrates the fact that, unlike the US, [Brazil] lacks a clear-cut criteria for racial classification."[117] This collective predisposition has likely filtered some of the effect of elite influences, thereby helping to produce the disconnect between elite opinions and those of the masses.

So, is the myth of racial democracy an ideology that legitimizes the unequal racial status quo, or is it a utopian dream or ideal that may be called on to challenge nonwhite disadvantage? The majority interpretation, clearly stated by Bacelar, is that "The myth of racial democracy is reinforced in an articulated and legitimizing, rather than contradictory, manner."[118] Guimarães, whose very sophisticated historical analysis reveals a more nuanced and heretofore generally unanalyzed history of the myth, nonetheless echoes the view that the myth became a "racist ideology" with an "obscurantist function."[119] However, the results presented here extrapolated from public opinion surveys suggest that it is not that at all, at least for the period under study and perhaps even as far back as 1986.

Conclusion

How might an understanding Brazilian public opinion on racial issues contribute to the struggle against racial equality? A deeper knowledge of attitudes and beliefs can help determine whether or not antidiscrimination actions and perhaps which kinds of actions will gain the crucial support that they need to be successful. For example, in the United States, the attitude of white Americans that black Americans are responsible for their own disadvantaged position has kept whites from supporting strategies that confront inequality.[120] Schuman and his colleagues conclude in their exhaustive study of racial attitudes in the United States:

> We have seen . . . that the majority of whites deny the importance of discrimination and place most of the burden for black disadvantage on blacks themselves. . . . Given these findings, we have little reason to expect that . . . [policies] characterized as giving any hint of preference to blacks . . . will have much support in the white population.[121]

There was a time when white Americans appeared cognizant of their responsibility for black disadvantage. Schuman and Krysan claim that a 1963 Gallup poll reveals that 70 percent of whites felt that whites were more to blame for the situation of blacks than blacks themselves.[122] Just five years later, however, this figure dropped dramatically: Only 28 percent of whites blamed whites, and 72 percent of this group now blamed blacks themselves. Although the authors suggest possible reasons for this devolution in white attitudes,[123] most important for the purpose of comparison with Brazil is that the attitudes in Brazil expressed in the three surveys on which I report appear very similar in at least one respect to those of the civil rights era in the United States: There is a societal consensus that much of the nation's inequality is to be blamed on racial discrimination. Brazilians, then, may be in a unique position that could motivate public debate on the issue of racialized inequality and lead to challenges to the racial status quo.

It is clear now, at least to this social scientist, that Brazilians are aware that discrimination plays a key role in reproducing inequality and that the dominant "Brazilian ignorance" stance is not supported by evidence from large-sample surveys.[124] This leads to the next question: How might an antiracialist common sense affect the fight against racial inequality? I turn to this question in the next two chapters.

6 The Black Movement

A CENTRAL QUESTION CHALLENGES SCHOLARS of antiracism and social movements in Brazil: Why, in a country so clearly stratified along color lines, has the Brazilian *negro* movement been historically unsuccessful in mobilizing a constituency?[1] Frequently, those offering explanations find fault with the "*negro* constituency" itself, [2] centrally holding that the denial of racial discrimination on behalf of nonwhites, as described in the previous chapter, is the root of the problem.[3] Twine, for example, argues, "continued faith . . . in racial democracy is a primary obstacle to the development of a sustained and vital antiracist movement in Brazil."[4] Others mention one or more of the following obstacles: a resistance to *negro* racial identification;[5] the class differences between movement leaders and the proposed *negro* constituency;[6] the multiple color categories that discourage the *negro* identification necessary for mobilization;[7] and/or, the imposition of decontextualized models for racial mobilization that do not resonate with most Brazilians.[8]

The ability to isolate the contextual determinants of attitudes toward racial mobilization and antiracism has suffered from the aforementioned lack of probability-sample survey data that benefit scholars in other contexts.[9] As Hanchard pointedly remarks, "one of the difficulties in assessing levels of apathy, indecision, or resistance among black Brazilians is the paucity of survey data."[10] Again, we have relied heavily on localized ethnography,[11] in-depth interviewing of *negro* activists,[12] and writings from *negro* movement actors themselves to explain nonwhite "apathy."[13] Until very recently, then, generalizable survey data constituted a major missing piece of the "Brazilian puzzle."[14]

Turning to the 2000 racial attitudes survey from the state of Rio de Janeiro, I focus this chapter on those items addressing the Brazilian *negro* movement and antiracism. These questions measure perceptions of the need for *negros* to organize, willingness to participate in antiracism activities, and, finally, willingness to join antiracist organizations. Hence, they tap ongoing questions on apathy toward *negro* movement activity in Brazil. To elaborate the questions posed to respondents regarding these issues, I collaborated with members of the CEAP/DataUff *negro* movement/NGO in Rio de Janeiro (Center for the Study of Marginalized Populations), as detailed in Chapter 2. Hence, these questions directly reflect the concerns of at least that sector of *negro* movement actors.

As we have already seen in previous chapters, some of the attitudinal dynamics posited in the literature on Brazilian racial dynamics, as well as in the general literature, have been off base. I believe this is due to what Jeffrey Alexander phrases as "theoretical overdetermination and empirical underdetermination."[15] To help correct that approach, in this Chapter, I examine public opinion data regarding the assumed apathy concerning antiracism and the *negro* movement in Brazil. I explore a possible polarization among whites and nonwhites and seek to isolate other sociodemographic determinants of these opinions, such as education and age. This information should advance our knowledge of public opinion on racial issues in Brazil for theory building and perhaps aid in the practical task of strategizing antiracism in that context.

The Brazilian *Negro* Movement

Background

In many societies where there is a history of population-specific discriminatory dynamics group-specific mobilization has been key for social change. This may be especially true regarding issues of racial and ethnic exclusion. There is no doubt, for example and as Bobo remarks, that "the political activism and the demands of black Americans are a major force in changing black–white relations in the United States."[16] While perhaps less clearly articulated, there is also a significant history of *negro* activism in Brazil. Various attempts at *negro* mobilization in modern Brazil date back at least to the founding of the Brazilian *Negro* Front (*Frente Negra Brasileira*) in 1930, a fledgling *negro* movement and political party that was later declared illegal by Vargas and disbanded.[17] The Front's central concern was to solidify the image of the *negro* population as fully Brazilian. Rather than using a particularist discourse during that time period, the Front sought fervently to distance the *negro* population from "Afro-Brazilian cultural traditions felt to be behind the stereotypes that stigmatized blacks" and to denounce "the color prejudice that distanced Brazilian blacks from the job market in favor of foreigners."[18]

Subsequent *negro* organizations, though, were not as explicitly "political" as the Brazilian *Negro* Front in the sense of claiming a party identity and instead focused on promoting African-rooted culture.[19] The clearest example of this is the *Negro* Experimental Theater (*Teatro Experimental do Negro*) in Rio de Janeiro in the 1950s, the founding project of which was to make room for *negro* actors in the arts. However, it soon widened its mission to include recuperating the image and self-esteem of the *negro* Brazilian. In the discourse of this movement, *negro* was rhetorically equal to *povo* (or "the people"), which fit well within the nationalist and populist rhetoric of its time.[20]

Later, the military coup of 1964 clearly marginalized civil society, usurping the direction of these political and cultural ideas and participation through repression and authoritarianism. However, with the so-called *abertura democrática*, or waning of military authoritarianism in Brazil (late 1970s and early 1980s), many diverse sectors of formally marginalized identifications began to struggle for political space, including the *negro* movements. Hence, the growth of the contemporary scene began with the Unified *Negro* Movement to Combat Racial Discrimination (MNU) in 1978. The MNU was organized with what Andrews calls an "explicitly political orientation."[21] According to Guimarães, "politically, it aligned itself with the revolutionary left; ideologically, it assumed, for the first time in the country, a radical racialism."[22] Its three biggest influences, among others, were the criticism of Florestan Fernandes on the state of race relations in Brazil, the American black movement, and the struggles for independence in Africa.[23]

Regarding its political agenda, the immediate goal of the organization was to raise consciousness about racial discrimination at the same time that it fought for the larger mission of "the eradication of capitalism from Brazil."[24] According to Andrews, "Its platform analyzed racism as an inevitable consequence of capitalist development, and argued that the only way to create genuine racial democracy in Brazil was to replace capitalism with socialism."[25] With the waning of revolutionary socialism in Brazil in the 1980s, the MNU put aside its strategy of fighting for a noncapitalist context in which to forge a racial democracy.

It was, however, successful in forging greater acknowledgment of racial discrimination in some spheres of elite discourse. For example, the MNU convinced most of the major political parties that the problem of racial discrimination deserved the national spotlight.[26] As a testament to the influence of the MNU, all but the governmental party (Democratic Social Party) included anti-racism in their platforms during the general elections of 1982 and 1986.[27] Most impressively on the political front, however, has been the movement's recent successful promotion of affirmative action strategies in Brazil. Racial quotas have been put in place in several public universities at the state (for example, State University of Rio de Janeiro) and federal (for example, University of Brasília) levels and in some federal government ministries and state level public agencies, as I will address in Chapter 7. Perhaps the event that has most greatly spurred the growing strength of the *negro* movement in twenty-first-century Brazil was its participation in the United Nation's 2001 International Conference on Racism in Durban, South Africa, where it had the second-largest delegation.[28] The conference received extensive coverage from major Brazilian news organizations, further shedding light on the problem of discrimination in Brazil.[29]

The *negro* movement in Brazil continues its struggle to construct a race-centered interpretation of social dynamics in *negro* and white, as I address in subsequent chapters. According to Guimarães, the *negro* movement's racialism resides in "evoking the charisma of the black race and making one of its goals the formation of a [unified] black racial identity."[30] To this end, the Brazilian *negro* movement seeks an identity for its constituents built on racial descent. Whereas the Brazilian census continues to use the five categories to classify the population (white, brown, *preto, indígena,* and *amarelo*), the *negro* movement promotes the unification of all nonwhite Brazilians considered by the movement to be of some African descent (browns and *pretos*), under the label *negro*.[31] This label is preferred because it is believed to connote race consciousness, in contrast to the *preto* term that refers more centrally to the chromatic color "black."[32] As a measure of its success, much of the media, the executive branch of the federal government, and many academics have cleanly dispensed with color gradations in their work and discourse and have adopted a *negro* versus white lens on Brazil.[33]

A Lack of Constituency

Although the movement has been effective in recent times in bringing the interests of its organization to the stage of public debate and policy, it has been generally ineffective in mobilizing popular support among its "constituency"—nonwhite Brazilians.[34] According to Hanchard, absent in the *negro* movements of the 1970s and 1980s were the practical dimensions of constituency organization: community outreach and grassroots politics. In addition to these organizational deficiencies, there was also an absence of significant antiracist mobilization: "There were no Afro-Brazilian versions of boycotting, sit-ins, civil disobedience."[35] To a large extent, these absences carried over into the 1990s.[36] Andrews more recently reports on the movement's "failure to attract popular support beyond a very small constituency based mainly in Afro-Brazilian middle class."[37]

Moreover, if the *negro* label itself is indicative of racial consciousness and African-based identification, then its very popularity could be a gauge of the *negro* movement's influence on a wider constituency. In this line of reasoning, as has already been discussed, the great majority of nonwhite Brazilians do not prefer this label when given the chance to self-classify in an open format: Again, only 7 percent chose to self-classify as *negro* in the national 2002 PESP survey in a country that is approximately 50 percent nonwhite. Although its history of racial exclusion is frequently compared to the United States,[38] Brazil clearly lacks the sense of black racial group membership and many of the types of participation in antiracism found in the U.S. context. The *negro* movement is, however, growing in terms of its weight within the Brazilian political arena, a fact that will certainly influence attitudes toward it in the future. Nonetheless, below I review three core explanations that are frequently offered to account for the apparent historic apathy or negativity toward the mobilization of *negro* antiracism in Brazil.

Lacking a Target Due to a Denial of Discrimination. The most prominent and widely accepted reason given in the literature for an absence of significant *negro* mobilization concerns the posited denial of racial discrimination on the part of all Brazilians, including nonwhites and, hence, the lack of a target around which to mobilize.[39] As I discussed in the previous chapter, many researchers point to this denial as a key component of the myth of racial democracy interpreted as a naïve or even perverse belief in the deracializing effects of miscegenation in Brazilian history. Hence, Burdick writes that the *negro* movement's common argument is "that the lack of popular black participation in the black movement can basically be understood as due to vague, distant, or secondary awareness of color prejudice."[40]

This posited vague awareness may stem in part from the subtle nature of discrimination and prejudice in Brazil. Unlike in the United States, Brazil has never legally mandated discrimination or segregation. Winant writes:

The informality alone of the Brazilian system—in contrast with segregation in the US—went a long way to mask its character. Indeed, it was precisely the formality of the US racial order, its politicization and enforcement by the state, that provided the black movement with a suitable target for mobilization.[41]

This lack of target is also pointed out by Guirmarães: "In contrast to the US and South Africa, where explicit racial oppression gave legitimacy to black peoples' organized struggles, the racial democracy ideology deprives the dominated population its base for collective self-defense and self-uplifting."[42] Hence, due to either to ignorance about or the subtlety of racial discrimination in Brazil, some researchers and activists hold that Brazilians have believed they live in a "racial paradise,"[43] thereby neutralizing the possibility of significant antiracist mobilization.[44]

Class Differences.   A second explanation given for the lack of race-specific mobilization is that some consider the *negro* movement a middle-class social organization, not wholly representative of the interests of the masses of poor nonwhites.[45] Burdick remarks, "Black consciousness groups are composed primarily of professionals, intellectuals, and upwardly mobile students, a pattern that has characterized the movement from the start."[46] As a result, Bacelar remarks, "because [the *negro* movement] comprises a sector of the black community that ascended socially and has an intellectualized perspective, it does not attract the poor and largely illiterate black masses."[47]

Andrews makes it clear how these divergent class positions may affect the ability of the *negro* movement to attract nonelites in Brazil:

> Even when middle-class activists and poor blacks do make contact, they often end up talking past each other, and finding that they have little in common beyond the color of their skin. To unemployed blacks and those living on the fringes of the urban economy, racial discrimination seems the least of their worries. The differences between these people and the poverty-stricken whites and near-whites who live among them are negligible in comparison to those which divide middle-class blacks from their white counterpart.[48]

This major disjuncture between the vital interests of middle-class *negro* movement activists and those of the poor nonwhites named as their constituency could prevent participation in that movement. In addition, as Andrews comments, "the middle class constitutes only about 10 percent of the total Black population; and even among the middle-class Afro-Brazilians, attitudes toward the civil rights movement are very mixed."[49]

Resistance to Blackness.   A third explanation found in the literature for the absence of significant *negro* mobilization is the resistance of most nonwhites to self-classify as *negro*.[50] The Brazilian *negro* movement has targeted, then, the large array of color categories as an impediment to antiracism.[51] For some *negro* movement leaders and academics, these categories allow nonwhites to deny that they are actually *negros*, distancing them from *negro*-specific agendas and interests.

This stance is exemplified by Santos-Stubbe in her study of domestic workers in Rio de Janeiro.[52] For her study, she handpicked 130 *negra* domestics to interview based on what she considered clear *negra* phenotype. However, when they were asked to self-classify using the census terms, the color-race composition of the 130 "*negras*" was 61 percent *preta*, 35 percent white, and 4 percent *parda*. Santos-Stubbe offers an explanation for this dynamic: "They [*negras*] rebel against the fact of being *negras* and try to distance themselves from that group by denying their *negra* racial characteristics."[53] Fiola agrees, commenting, "Most blacks run away from . . . *negritude*."[54]

Along those lines, Nobles analyzed a campaign that took place in preparation for the 1991 census called, "*Não Deixe Sua Cor Passar em Branco: Responda com Bom C/Senso*" ("Don't Let Your Color Pass in White: Respond with Good Sense").[55] Its goal was to attempt to convince nonwhites to favor the darker end of the color spectrum when filling out the 1991 census (to resist "whitening"). Nobles called this campaign "a search for black bodies" or a *negro* constituency on the part of the *negro* movement. The characteristic *negro* movement stance toward nonwhite non-*negros* (that is, those preferring labels like *moreno, mestiço, mulato*, and the like) can be summed up by the statement of a prominent *negro* activist cited in Burdick: "We see that for every 100 *negros*, 70 reject their identity. So we must convince the *negro* to reject the ideology of 'whitening.' And the way to start is for him to call himself a *negro*."[56]

In sum, when nonwhite Brazilians do not show preference for the *negro* category and appear to prefer multiple color categories, this is evaluated an impediment for antiracism.[57] Such individuals are considered "avoiders" who need to adopt racial consciousnesses and *negro* racial identity,[58] a step that would lead them more readily to embrace antiracism and the *negro* movement.

Realistic Group Conflict Perspectives

Before turning to our data to sort out these context-specific explanations, I briefly touch on general framings for explaining attitudes toward black social movements. As discussed earlier, this literature comes most frequently from the U.S. context, where it has been generally concerned with attitudes toward the civil rights movement and toward black movement leaders.[59] Bobo's work stands out in this area and generally employs a realistic group conflict framing. Although it is possible to apply other perspectives "in abstract," I will mainly focus on Bobo's framing in this chapter as a theoretical backboard for the Brazilian case and for formulating hypotheses.

Bobo's central premise is that any social system with long-standing racial inequality sets the stage for "realistic" or meaningful struggle over group interests defined along racial lines. "Group conflict attitudes" are the result. These concern the distribution of values and limited resources between social groups, as well as attempts to affect the process and pattern of their distribution. Regarding the latter, Bobo focuses on "perceived threat" as that which drives opinions concerning the black political movement: "Perceived threat involves perceptions and evaluations of social groups or organized members of a group who are pressuring explicitly for change that might be beneficial to in-group members or harmful to out-group members. Attitudes toward the black political movement should tap these feelings of perceived threat."[60] Hence, he hypothesizes:

> From this viewpoint, groups occupying different positions in a system of racial stratification will differ sharply in their attitudes toward social movements that originate within the minority community. For the minority group, such a movement represents a voice for desired goals and should elicit positive evaluation. For the majority group, the movement represents an unwanted threat to an accepted social order and to a privileged group position and should elicit negative evaluation.[61]

Although Bobo's group conflict framing appears most robust for examining this question of attitudes toward the black political movement, he does explore other framings, most importantly, sociocultural theories of prejudice.[62] Although the nature of these two framings differs significantly, they both support an overall generalization that groups in different places along a racial hierarchy have very different attitudes toward social movements initiated within the minority community.[63] Hence, although I focus on the conflict framing, both sociocultural and conflict perspectives emphasize a racial divide in public opinion toward the political black movement. As detailed earlier, the difference between the perspectives is the cause each posits for this polarization. The former faults a negative affect toward the out-group and the latter a conflict over material interests.

Hypotheses

Borrowing from Bobo, I adopt the conceptual framing of "black political movement" for hypothesis construction.[64] I include under this label attitudes toward *negro* mobilization and its necessity in Brazil, willingness to participate in antiracism activities, and the desire for membership in an antiracist organization.

According to the group conflict perspective dominant in the literature on racial attitudes in the United States, there should be "substantial black–white differences in reactions to the black political movement."[65] That is, "each group should respond in a strategic, instrumental manner to shifts in the political context."[66] Hence, whites will oppose challenges to the status quo that antiracism might facilitate, and blacks will support it, each based on their own racial interests.

The Brazilianist literature, in general, points to a different set of interpretations concerning nonwhites. This literature predicts apathy or ambivalence from nonwhite Brazilians toward the *negro* political movement due to any or a combination of all the elements I discussed above: a denial of racial discrimination, class differences between activists and the masses of nonwhite Brazilians, and a resistance to self-identifying as *negro*. However, in agreement with the general literature, Brazilianists point to unfavorable opinions on the part of whites toward the *negro* political movement.

Based partly on the general literature and on the dominant Brazilianist stances, I test the following hypotheses:

H1: White and nonwhite Brazilians will deny a basis for a *negro* political movement, that is, racial discrimination (consistent with the Brazilianist literature).

H2: White Brazilians will generally express negative attitudes toward the *negro* political movement (consistent with the general and the Brazilianist literature).

H3: Nonwhite Brazilians will generally express negative attitudes toward the *negro* political movement (consistent with the Brazilianist literature).

H4: Nonwhite Brazilians will generally express positive attitudes toward the *negro* political movement (consistent with the general literature).

Findings

Recognizing the Need to Participate

As a corollary to the discussion in Chapter 5 of stratification beliefs, a first question from the 2000 CEAP/DataUff survey on racial attitudes in the state of Rio de Janiero asked respondents about the *negro* movement as follows: "Some groups that organize to protect the interest of *negros* are part of the so-called '*negro* movement.' Do you believe that the *negro* movement . . ."

1. . . . is right when it claims that there is a lot of racial prejudice in Brazil and that it should be fought against?
2. . . . is not right that there is racial prejudice in Brazil and is making a mountain out of a molehill?
3. . . . is right that there is prejudice, but that it is not necessary to fight against it?

Bivariate results are presented in Table 6.1. In the first column, question 1, it shows that fully 81 percent of the sample believed that the *negro* movement is right and that prejudice must be the object of a struggle to overcome it. There is very little difference between color categories: Eighty-three percent of nonwhites were joined by 77 percent of whites in recognizing the basis for the organization and the legitimacy of the struggle itself (columns 2 and 3, respectively).

Later in the survey, respondents were asked a very similar question: "In your opinion . . . (1) . . . do *negros* need to organize to fight to have their rights respected? (2) . . . is it unnecessary since their rights are already respected?" Results in Table 6.1, question 2, show that as regards this simplified question concerning the basis for *negro* movement mobilization, fully 94 percent (column 1) of the sample believed that *negros* need to organize to gain their due respect. Color differences here, too, were practically nonexistent.

Finally, respondents were asked whether they agreed with the following statement (Table 6.1, question 3): "The situation of *negros* in Brazil is going to change only if they organize to fight for their rights." Collapsing levels of agreement, again overwhelming majorities of both white and nonwhite categories expressed some level of agreement with this statement regardless of color category.

From these three survey items, it is clear that there is no support at all for my first hypothesis (H1) that white and nonwhite Brazilians deny a basis for

Table 6.1 Percent distributions of items on the *negro* movement and prejudice by select color classifications: Adult population in the state of Rio de Janeiro, 2000

	All	Nonwhite	White	Preto	Brown
1. Is the *negro* movement right about prejudice and that it should be fought against, or are they wrong and are making something out of nothing?					
Right	81%	83%	77%	81%	84%
Wrong	12	10	13	11	10
Right, but not necessary to fight	8	6	9	8	5
2. Do *negros* in Brazil need to organize and fight to have their rights respected, or is this not necessary because those rights already are respected?					
Need to organize	94	95	92	96	95
3. The situation of *negros* in Brazil is only going to get better if they organize to fight for their rights.					
Agreement	90	93	86	96	92

SOURCE: CEAP/DataUff 2000.

negro movement activity. This is consistent with results from Chapter 5 that show in general that Brazilians recognize the problem of racial discrimination in their midst.

Participating in Antiracism

How might these positive stances toward the need for *negro* mobilization translate into hypothetical willingness to participate in mobilizations against racial prejudice and discrimination? A first question asked: "If you were invited, would you participate in some activity to combat racism?" Bivariate results presented in Table 6.2, question 1, show that a majority of the population claim they would participate in an antiracism activity, including 52 percent of individuals of the white category. The highest positive response came from persons self-classifying as *preto*, at 65 percent. When collapsing "yes" and "perhaps" responses, about two-thirds of individuals in each color category express interest in participating in antiracism activities.

Table 6.2 Percent distributions of items on antiracism participation and organization by select color classifications: Adult population in the state of Rio de Janeiro, 2000

	All	Nonwhite	White	Preto	Brown
1. If you were invited, would you participate in some activity to combat racism?					
Yes	55%	58%	52%	65%	54%
No	32	30	35	27	31
Maybe	13	13	13	8	15
2. Would you like to become a member of an organization to fight against racism?					
Very much	24	28	19	33	25
A little	15	17	14	18	17
Perhaps	15	14	16	6	17
No	46	42	51	43	41

SOURCE: CEAP/DataUff 2000.

In addition, respondents were asked about openness toward actual membership in organizations dedicated to fighting racism: "Would you like to be a part of some organization for fighting against racism?" The possible answers were "very much," "a little," "perhaps," and "no." The bivariate results presented in Table 6.2, question 2, reveal less enthusiasm for the idea of being a part of some *negro* organization than for a willingness to simply participate in an antiracism activity. However, beyond that point of comparison, the interest appears very significant. Fully 48 percent of whites, 59 percent of browns, and 57 percent of *pretos* show some measure of interest in becoming a member of an organization dedicated to fighting racism. Hence, these results contradict the second and third hypotheses (H2 and H3) that predicted both white and nonwhite negativity toward antiracism. Only the fourth hypothesis (H4), based on the general literature, that nonwhites will generally express positive attitudes toward antiracism, receives support.

I now turn to regression techniques to isolate more efficiently those factors associated with interest in antiracist protest and organization. My first equation regresses willingness to participate in antiracism activities (Table 6.2, question 1) on several sociodemographic variables.[67] The dependent variable is comprised of three categories that are the response options to that item:

"yes," "no," and "maybe." I treat the "yes" response as the reference category. In the first model, the color variable is formed by collapsing the two nonwhite categories from the self-classification item in the official format (brown and *preto*) to form a unified nonwhite category. I juxtapose this category to the white category (omitted) as per *negro* movement discourse.

Results in Table 6.3 concerning Model 1 show that when comparing the omitted "yes" category of the dependent variable with the "no" response, there are no significant differences between the color groupings, controlling for age, sex, and education. Age, however, is the decisive variable. It is positively associated with the "no" response compared to the "yes" response. That is, as the respondents' ages increase, their openness to participate in antiracism activities decreases. Comparing the "maybe" response to the omitted "yes" category, age loses its significance.

Turning to Model 2 in Table 6.3, my color variable is formed according to self-classification in the official format: white, brown, and *preto*. White is the omitted category. Again there are no significant differences between the color groupings when comparing "no" and "yes" responses concerning willingness to participate in antiracism activities, controlling for age, sex, and education. Comparing the "maybe" response to the omitted "yes" category, one significant color difference does appear. *Pretos*, but not browns, are significantly more likely to choose "yes" over "maybe" in comparison to whites. That is, they appear to show less indecision about willingness to participation in antiracism. Age loses its significance in that category comparison.

A second similar analysis regresses willingness to become a member of an antiracist organization on the same sociodemographic variables, as opposed to just participating in antiracism protest. The dependent variable is comprised of the four response options: "no," "a lot," "a little," and "perhaps." Using multinomial logistic regression, I treat the "no" response as the reference category. Again, I present two models differing in the division of the color variable. In the first, color consists of white and nonwhite values.

Results in Table 6.4 show that when comparing the "a lot" response to "no," we see that education, color, and age are significant predictors. Education is negatively associated with the "a lot" response compared to "no," revealing that the less educated show more openness to being members than the more educated. This finding appears counterintuitive in the context of the argument that the *negro* movement is not very successful in mobilizing

Table 6.3 Multinomial logit regression predicting willingness to participate in antiracism activities: Adult population in the state of Rio de Janeiro, 2000

| Independent Variables | Comparison group "Yes" | | | |
| | Model 1 | | Model 2 | |
	No	Maybe	No	Maybe
Education	.045	−.019	.037	−.043
	(.071)	(.093)	(.071)	(.093)
Brown[a]			−.088	.078
			(.167)	(.215)
Preto			−.382	−.869*
			(.220)	(.339)
Nonwhite[b]	−.179	−.160		
	(.151)	(.202)		
Male	.037	.044	.035	.037
	(.156)	(.207)	(.156)	(.208)
Age	.403***	.080	.400***	.070
	(.049)	(.065)	(.050)	(.067)
Intercept	−1.976***	−1.610***	−1.941***	−1.509***
	(.333)	(.383)	(.333)	(.389)

SOURCE: CEAP/DataUff 2000.
[a] White is reference category.
[b] White is reference category.
*p < .05, **p<.01, ***p<.001

a constituency due to class differences between its members and the targeted constituency—the mass of nonelite nonwhites.[68]

As regards, color, importantly, the nonwhite category is positively associated with "a lot" as compared to "no." Therefore, for the question of membership, there is a statistically significant difference of opinion between the white/nonwhite categories, the latter showing greater interest in joining antiracist organizations. Nonetheless, recall from Table 6.2 that about half of all whites do express some interest in joining antiracist organizations. And finally, as age increases, the percentage choosing "a lot" as compared to "no" decreases. Older individuals of all colors are less likely to desire membership in a *negro* organization.

Still pertaining to the membership in antiracism organization question, Model 2 contains a color variable based on the expanded format question on color, and it parcels out the population into six color groupings all based on self-classification: *negro* (omitted), brown, *moreno*, white, *preto*, and "all others" (collapsing *mestiço* and *mulato*). This allows me to detect the effect on attitudinal stances toward possible membership in the *negro* movement of

Table 6.4 Multinomial logit regression predicting willingness to become a member of an antiracism organization: Adult population in the state of Rio de Janeiro, 2000

Independent Variables	Model 1			Model 2		
	A lot	A little	Perhaps	A lot	A little	Perhaps
Education	.236 (.078)	-.024 (.094)	-.024 (.087)	-.238** (.093)	-.025 (.091)	-.015 (.089)
Nonwhite[a]	.507** (.170)	.334 (.198)	-.031 (.196)			
Brown[b]				-.423 (.328)	.019 (.393)	.373 (.442)
Moreno				-.706* (.298)	-.140 (.356)	.334 (.405)
White				-.786** (.294)	-.393 (.357)	.299 (.405)
Preto				-.054 (.447)	-.390 (.644)	-.655 (.839)
Others				.007 (.342)	-.006 (.430)	-.932 (.643)
Male	-.005 (.174)	-.254 (.207)	-.002 (.202)	-.055 (.177)	-.201 (.205)	.039 (.202)
Age	-.320*** (.055)	-.480*** (.073)	-.279*** (.066)	-.333*** (.055)	-.479*** (.072)	-.273*** (.065)
Intercept	.752* (.343)	.411 (.430)	-.120 (.388)	-1.579*** (.395)	.738 (.487)	-.390 (.478)

Omitted category "No"

SOURCE: CEAP/DataUff.
[a] White is reference category.
[b] Negro is reference category.
*p < .05, **p<.01, ***p<.001

classifying in the various shades of nonwhite, especially as concerns *negros* and *pretos*. In this model, results show that the education effect and the age effect are similar to the other model. However, the color categories give us more information than does the simple bipolar white/nonwhite division. Results show that browns, *pretos*, and "all others" do not differ significantly from the *negro* category in the choice of "a lot" over "no," as it has been suggested.[69] This finding is important because it seems to go against the logic that it is key to antiracist mobilization for nonwhites to call themselves *negros*.

However, both *moreno* and white categories differ significantly from the *negro* category: Both are negatively associated with the choice of "a lot" over "no" when compared to *negros*, indicating that membership is a less attractive proposition for these two categories of respondents. The finding may reveal a difference between *morenos* and the rest of nonwhites as concerns attitudes toward the *negro* movement, lending some credence to the concerns of those who view splintered nonwhite identification as inhibiting the mobilization of a *negro* movement constituency. This difference between *morenos* and other nonwhites is important because the *moreno* category is indeed the most numerous nonwhite category by far in the open format, at 24 percent in the 2002 national attitudinal survey. However, even though the difference is statistically significant, a majority of *morenos* (54 percent) still express some interest in membership in antiracism organization.

Negro *Movement Visibility and Transparency*

Two final questions further help frame attitudes toward the *negro* movement as concerns the predicted apathy through exploring issues of movement visibility and perceived transparency. Regarding visibility, and as briefly mentioned in Chapter 5, respondents were asked: "Do you know of some group that has organized to protect the interests of *negros*?" As shown in Table 6.5, only 14 percent of the sample said "yes," regardless of their color category. Clearly, visibility is a serious problem for movement activists. While the current public debate over affirmative action, as well as Brazil's participation in the 2001 Durban conference on racism, has since increased general awareness, the *negro* movement's historic lack of relevance may be a real factor in low participation levels.

Finally, Brazilians often consider politics and politicians to be corrupt, and this attitude might foster skepticism toward the *negro* movement. Respondents were asked:

> In terms of the goals of those groups [i.e., *negro* movements], do you believe that these organizations that make up the *negro* movement defend the rights of all *negros*, or are they only concerned with defending the interests of their members?
>
> 1. They defend the legitimate rights of *negros*.
> 2. They are more concerned with defending the interests of their members.

Results in Table 6.5, question 2, show that a strong majority of the general public, as represented by the sample population, do not consider the *negro* movement corrupt. Interestingly, however, members of the *preto* category are the most suspicious: Forty-three percent affirm the view that the movement

Table 6.5 Percent distributions of items on the *negro* movement in Brazil by select color classifications: Adult population in the state of Rio de Janeiro, 2000

	All	Nonwhite	White	Preto	Brown
1. Have you ever heard of any group that is organized to protect the interests of *negros?*					
Yes	14%	14%	13%	14%	14%
2. In terms of the goals of the organizations that make up the *negro* movement . . .?					
. . . do they defend the legitimate rights of all negros?	63	64	61	57	67
. . . are they more concerned in defending only the interest of their members?	38	37	39	43	34

SOURCE: CEAP/DataUff 2000.

looks after only the interests of its members. Hence, better communication of goals and strategies might significantly ease suspicion among the *negro* movement's target constituency.

Discussion

I began this chapter with a key question for scholars and activists in Brazil: Why in a country so clearly stratified along color lines has the *negro* movement been unsuccessful in mobilizing a constituency?[70] The Brazilianist literature generally blames the nonwhite population itself. However, the results presented here clearly point away from such a conclusion in an entirely different direction.

First, contrary to the Brazilianist literature, my results show that an overwhelming percentage of Brazilians recognizes color-based discrimination (H1). Second, contrary to group conflict theory, which predicts racial polarization concerning attitudes toward the *negro* political movement, Brazilians of all colors strongly endorse the idea of *negro* mobilization. These results contradict the views that whites will express negative attitudes toward the *negro* movement (H2), while nonwhite Brazilians will be apathetic (H3). Only the view in the general literature that nonwhites will express positive attitudes toward the *negro* political movement receives support (H4). This broad-spectrum support for the *negro* political movement was also coupled with a general willingness to participate in antiracism activities. Finally, there was significant support, albeit somewhat contoured along color lines, for membership in antiracist organizations. Why do these outcomes so heartily contradict the well-trodden Brazilianist and general literature?

Group-Based Interests

Forming the core of group conflict theories are the following three premises: (1) Individuals identify with their own racial group; (2) the differing groups have divergent group-based interests; and (3) dominant groups develop ideologies to justify their privileged position.[71] These theories focus on racialized social groups that are pitted against each other in zero-sum struggles over scarce resources, each of whom develops racial ideologies to enhance or challenge their position.

How do these assumptions hold up when carried into the Brazilian context? In Chapter 3, I found that Brazilians actually do not automatically identify with "their own" racial group, as understood from a U.S. race relations perspective. Racial and color classification in Brazil is much more fluid, multiple, contextual, and not easily reducible, if at all, to racial group subjectivity in *negro* and white. Hence, bipolar dynamics predicated on *negro* versus white subjectivity are weakened. Subsequently, in Chapter 5, I examined the third assumption, asking whether Brazilians have created a legitimizing ideology of racial exclusion. Evidence presented in that chapter suggested that the Brazilian racial common sense is characterized by a structuralist or delegitimizing account of *negro* disadvantage consensually embraced by whites and nonwhites alike.

How does the evidence laid out in this chapter square with the second assumption of group conflict theory that the differing racial groups perceive divergent group-based interests? Bonilla-Silva writes, "All social divisions based on race are intrinsically about power and lead inevitably to divergent interests among the races."[72] Membership in what he labels the differing "races" automatically assigns collective racial interests and, importantly, the collective mind-set to protect them. Hence, regarding whites, he writes, "all members of the dominant race participate in defending and reproducing the racial structure."[73] Conversely, unless they are victims of hegemonic ideologies, all members of the subordinate "race" participate in challenging the racial structure.[74]

Thus, Bonilla-Silva highlights the inevitability of "conflict attitudes" among racialized individuals in societies where social inequality has a racial component.[75] In Sindanius and Pratto's formulation, whites are characterized by a "social dominance orientation,"[76] or a collective desire for white privilege through the perpetuation of the status quo, and hence oppose antiracism measures, including black movement mobilization.[77] Blacks, on the other hand, necessarily support antiracism. Similarly, regarding conflict attitudes, Bobo writes that, "for some [the black political movement] may represent a voice for desired ends, whereas for others, they constitute a threat to important values and interests."[78] The "others" here are whites, and the "important values and interests" constitute the perceived legitimacy of white privilege.

Generally, the data concerning nonwhite Brazilians are empirically consistent with this theory: A large percentage say they would participate in antiracism activities. However, the correlation ends regarding Brazilians of the white category. Instead of viewing the *negro* political movement as a threat to their racial interests, they overwhelmingly express support for *negro* mobilization and express willingness to participate in antiracism activities and organizations. Why do a large majority of Brazilians classifying in the white category appear to resist the pursuit of group-specific racial interests that Bonilla-Silva, Bobo, and Sidanius and Pratto stipulate?[79] In other words, why does the desire for and perceived legitimacy of white privilege not appear to dominate the attitudes of white individuals in the survey sample? I want to suggest here that those "white interests" are delegitimized by an egalitarian racial democracy creed couched in Brazilian antiracialism. That is, any "social dominance orientation" is overridden or partially neutralized by a creed that finds racial discrimination repugnant and un-Brazilian.

Supporting this view of an uneasy fit for the social dominance orientation in Brazil is the evident lack of white supremacy groups, the types of overt racial violence, and the racial segregation in Brazil's history that were so prevalent in the United States. Those phenomena are primary symptoms of group-based "conflict attitudes," and they clearly do not fit into the principled opinions of antiracialism. Brazilians of the white category, therefore, may consider the group bias that Bobo predicts to be incongruent with their ideology.

Some might point out, however, that perhaps the very recognition of the *negro* movement's struggle indicates the existence of racialized, group-specific interests. I believe, however, that an alternative interpretation is also plausible. Just as Brazilian antiracialism may keep whites from rallying around "white interests," that racial common sense may also view *negro* interests as common to all Brazilians, which explains the shared investment in antiracism regardless of color category. In other words, the racial democracy creed at the heart of Brazil's antiracialism may actually promote the idea of across-category national interests. Once again, the zero-sum game of opposing racial interests does not appear to dominate this context in terms of attitudinal stances.

Bobo does, however, make a distinction that also correlates with the data I have presented. He specifies "perceived threat," or the possibility of real conflict and redistribution of scarce resources, as a central determinant of attitudes toward the black movement. In light of this, perhaps Brazilians of the white category simply feel that their resources are safe, that the chances of real change and redistribution are quite low. Bobo writes,

> When black protest is high and is increasing, blacks should evaluate the black political movement positively. During such times whites should evaluate the movement negatively. When black protest is low and is decreasing, however, black evaluations should reflect a call for further action whereas white attitudes should become more moderate.[80]

Has the relative mildness or nonchallenging nature of the *negro* movement in Brazil's past permitted whites to embrace a principled support for antiracism, knowing that antiracism measures have little chance to effectuate change? This is indeed plausible. If so, the more that interests are framed in group conflict terms, according to zero-sum games that result in possible real loss for some, the more likely there will be negative reactions on the part of Brazilians of the white category, thereby possibly modifying the attitudinal map I have traced with my results.

Context-Specific Explanations

From exploring a group conflict framing of general literature, I turn now to the context-specific framings of Brazilianist literature. Similar to the general literature, context-specific arguments predict white negativity toward antiracism in support of white privilege. Unlike the general literature, however, Brazilianist literature assumes apathy on the part of nonwhites.[81] As I laid out in the beginning of this chapter, there are three common explanations for this: a comprehensive denial of discrimination, class differences between *negro* movement actors and their targeted constituency, and the nonwhite population's resistance to blackness.

Regarding the first explanation, if the myth of racial democracy successfully conditioned a denial of racial discrimination on the part of nonwhite Brazilians, they would find social movements formed to fight against it unnecessary.[82] On the contrary, however, nonwhite Brazilians do recognize racial inequality. This stance delegitimizes the status quo and is associated with hypothetical support for transformative antiracism action. Hence, these results appear more in line with a vision of the myth of racial democracy as a principled set of ideas that can stimulate debate and strategies concerning the inconsistencies between ideal and real conditions in Brazil than an obscurant, pernicious lie, as the dominant Brazilianist literature frames it.[83] It is my contention, then, that neither nonwhite Brazilians nor the reign of an ideology of nondiscrimination are to blame for the *negro* movement's historic lack of potency. The empirical evidence presented here suggests otherwise.

Assuming this is the case, a deeper dilemma appears. If nonwhite Brazilians recognize discrimination and support antiracism in the abstract, why have they not heeded the call of the *negro* movement to participate in antiracism activities? The literature mentions two central issues that are relevant to this question: resistance to blackness and class differences between activists and the masses.

Negro Movement Racialism.   Rather than supposing the targeted constituency to be "apathetic," perhaps a better explanation for the lack of *negro* movement success might be found in the social movement itself. That is, some scholars suggest that the Brazilian *negro* movement's discourse and strategies draw on models of social organization that do not fit easily in Brazilian mind-sets[84] and hence do not reverberate with a majority of Brazilians. For example, sociologist Denise Ferreira da Silva writes: "the problems faced by the black Brazilian movement derive less from the grip of an all-powerful racial ideology than from our effort to incorporate rhetorical strategies formulated elsewhere."[85]

That is, the movement embraces racialism in a society that has been long characterized as antiracialist. It views society as a collection of races and all individuals as members of either the *negro* or white race (if not "clearly" of Asian or Indigenous ancestries). Importantly, the Brazilian *negro* movement's discourse and strategies should be understood within the framework of strategic social movement essentialism and not necessarily scientific biologism, although that essentialism may hearken to perceived biological lineage or hereditary traits. That is, we are dealing with discourse designed to unite and mobilize a maximum number of the constituency to effectuate social change, not science. In doing so, social movements have often opted for strategic essentialism.

My working definition of racialism, following Appiah, is the popular belief "that there are heritable characteristics, possessed by members of our species that allow us to divide them into a small set of races."[86] In addition, according to Appiah, racialism does not necessarily denote racism because "provided positive moral qualities are distributed across the races, each can be respected."[87] Antiracialism, on the other hand, is a perspective that emphasizes mixture, evidenced, in part, through color ambiguity and the inability to divide a population into a small set of races. As such, it delegitimizes race as a rigid "principle of social vision and division."[88]

Is *negro* movement discourse in Brazil racialist? From both activist and academic literature, the strongest evidence suggesting so is the movement's insistence on using the term *negro* in place of brown and *preto* categories for persons of varying degrees of African origin. It is a term that belongs clearly to a bipolar racial scheme, juxtaposed to a white racial category. In protest of the ternary color scheme, for example, Nascimento and Nascimento write, "The 'white' and '*pardo*' categories are notoriously inflated, and the '*preto*' diminished, by the tendency of African-descent interviewees to classify themselves as white or mulatto."[89] Examining this argument that all persons of discernible degrees of African ancestry should belong to a single racial category, University of São Paulo sociologist Guimarães writes, "By defining *negros* as all African descendants and identifying these as the sum of the census categories *preto* and *pardo*, the movement . . . adopted as a criterion of identity not self-identification, as modern anthropology prefers, but biological lineage."[90] Later he makes more specific this connection in claiming the *negro* movement has opted for "the racialism of racial descent (made on the basis of physical traits or biological lineage)."[91]

To be clear, in my view, this racialist turn is effectuated through the following general steps that I laid out in Chapter 2 (at the same time applying them to the U.S. context): In the racialist context, a population

1. conceives of distant, diffuse, and multiple ancestral geographic-origin categories as singular, important, and enduring (as African or European in the United States).
2. equates those ancestries with inheritable biological differences called races (as the European race or the African race in the United States).
3. establishes discrete sets of physical criteria associated with each race (centrally a white/less-than-white skin-color palette in the United States, delimiting white and black races).[92]

Negro movement discourse in Brazil follows that racializing process through the following steps drawn from a recent article by Nascimento and Nascimento.[93] The authors:

1. conceive of African and European ancestral geographic-origin categories as singular, despite mixing, and enduring.
2. equate those ancestries with inheritable biological differences called races (as the European race or the African/*negro* race)
3. define "a range of color variations that most certainly indicate African race" (that is, the color of those that belong to the *negro* race is *pardo* and *preto*).[94]

Thus, *negro* movement racialism organizes ancestry to equate with discrete races delimited by a white/less-than-white (that is, white versus brown and *preto*) skin-color palette.[95]

This *negro* movement racialism, however, has not historically taken well in Brazil, and I believe that is precisely because Brazilian society has developed a racial common sense best framed as antiracialist. In fact, Guimarães claims that in Brazil antiracialism is associated with a denial of the existence of races.[96] While there may be some truth to that statement, it is important to note that a majority of Brazilians are probably not "nonracialist," but antiracialist. The former could not be the case in Brazil because of the existence of the myth of national origin. A majority of Brazilians apparently believe that the birth of their nation is the result of the mixing of populations of three distinct ancestries or "races."[97] However, the emphasis in Brazil is now on mixture, not the passage of those heritages untouched through time as present-day discrete races. Recall from Chapter 4 that two-thirds of Brazilians respond simply "Brazilian" when asked about their ancestry today, not African, Portuguese/European, or Indian.

Hence, the explanation that I outlined in the beginning of this chapter of a resistance to blackness, or to adopting *negro* versus white racial identification, may be partially helpful for explaining a lack of connection between the *negro* movement and its targeted constituency. However, I would frame the disconnect differently: The problem is not in the targeted constituency's resistance but in the movement's opting for a decontextualized framing as a *sine qua non* of antiracism in the first place. Gomes da Cunha explains:

> The strategy utilized by many segments of the black movement was to portray Brazilian society in black and white terms. Important themes and issues such

as color, phenotype, hair texture, and interracial relationships that shape race relations were ignored by accounts reducing the discussion of race in Brazil to black and white terms.[98]

Hence, the very framing of the *negro* movement's rhetorical strategies reflects explicit bipolar identity dynamics that are in many respects foreign to Brazilians.[99] As Fry points out, "giving credence to a discourse that speaks of *negros* and whites for a people that speaks a language of *morenos, pretos, mulatos, crioulos,* etc" can constitute an important hurdle for mobilizing a specifically *negro* constituency.[100]

Let me offer the following examples from Burdick on what can happen when couching antiracism in a racialist framing in an antiracialist context. Burdick reports that to be an active participant in the *negro* movement in Brazil "requires, de facto, that one call oneself *negro*."[101] However, my results from Chapter 3 suggested that this term does not resonate with all nonwhites and certainly even less with whites (48 percent of whom express some level of hypothetical interest in membership). Burdick's ethnographic research reveals two primary concerns on the part of his nonwhite research subjects that result in what he labels "color alienation" or a discomfort with "forced" *negro* classification. A first concern is Burdick's respondents' awareness that their social experiences may have been qualitatively different from those of people at the darkest end of the continuum whom they would label *negros*. One nonwhite respondent remarked, for example, "I have enjoyed privileges *negros* have not. I can say I am a *negro*, as an act of solidarity, but I don't feel it."[102]

The other concern is that by calling themselves *negros*, nonwhites are in effect denying the reality of their other ancestries and heritages. One informant was quite articulate about this point:

> Do I value my blackness? Of course! I take pride in it. But am I only black? No! I also am descended from Indians, and from Europeans. Should I disdain these heritages? Why shouldn't I value all my heritages? Why should I pretend I only have one heritage when this is just not true?[103]

Hence, the *negro* movement's insistence on unified *negro* classification may be an obstacle to wider mobilization, essentially derived from a model that may not resonate in Brazil.[104]

Moreover, my results suggest that an insistence on *negro* classification may be superfluous in that those who self-identify as *negros* in the survey sample were no more likely to support antiracism or express interest in antiracist organizations than those who self-classified as browns, *pretos, mestiços,* or *mulatos* (see Table 6.4). At the same time, the results did show that individuals self-classifying as *morenos,* the most popular nonwhite group in the open format, were significantly less willing than *negros* to express interest in becoming members of antiracist organizations. A plausible explanation for this attitudinal tendency of *morenos* could clearly be a rejection of *negro* identity in a racialist *negro* versus white framing.

In addition to framing identities in *negro* and white and the rejection that this may cause on the part of many Brazilians, there is a similar but conceptually distinct issue: the framing of interests in Brazil as *negro* versus white. Guimarães writes, "to recognize the idea of race and promote any antiracist action based on this idea, even if the author is black, is interpreted as racism."[105] I believe this statement has some truth to it. Brazilians may support antiracism, at least in principle, as my data reveal, but maybe not from a racialist perspective. That is, racial inequality is considered un-Brazilian by the racial democracy creed,[106] but so may be framing the issue as pitting supposed racial interests against one another. That is, my data suggest through across-category support for antiracism that the struggle is not considered as pertaining only to *negro* interests but to wider national interests concerning people of all colors.

In support of this idea of a popular rejection of the racialist framing of interests of the *negro* movement, I turn again to the 1986 survey in São Paulo reported on by Hasenbalg.[107] That survey included a question asking the sample, "In your opinion, what should *pretos* and mulattos do to defend their rights?" The possibilities were: (1) Each individual should demand alone that his or her rights be respected; (2) they should organize a movement in which only *pretos* and mulattos participate: and (3) they should organize a movement in which whites concerned with the problem also participate. Regarding this question, Hasenbalg concludes:

> The results indicate . . . that a solution to this problem should be found through collective mobilization. However, there is also a strong rejection of the idea that the collective movement be restricted to the discriminated group (only 5.2 percent of white and 7.2 percent of nonwhites approved that alternative). The solution endorsed by the great majority (83.1 percent of whites and 75.3 percent of nonwhites) is that of a movement of wider appeal, of an interethnic or inter-racial character, based then on the empathy on the part of whites in relation to the racial problem. The implication of this is that there is a rejection

of the possibility of a movement based on the confrontation between the two racial groups.[108]

These results led Hasenbalg to conclude:

> In the last 20 years the black social movement and race relations scholars have put emphasis both in particularism and in difference, in reference to the cultural plane, and in the universal in terms of citizenship. This tended to be done predominantly from an external reading of Brazil, inspired in the experiences of the United States and of the decolonization of African countries. Perhaps the new agenda should maintain the balance between the particularist and the universal, but do so from an interpretation of Brazil on its own terms, and not from an external reading.[109]

My results are consistent with the results from that 1986 survey and appear to also support Hasenbalg's conclusion.

In sum, I believe that the *negro* movement's insistence on a racialist framing of its strategies in which *negro* and white racial groups that have divergent identities and interests may have certainly been a reason for an apparent less-than-enthusiastic response to *negro* movement discourse in the last two decades of the twentieth century. It remains to be seen if that "apathy" will continue in a time when the racialist discourse is gaining strength.

Social Class Disconnect.   As to a final explanation for nonwhite apathy toward the *negro* movement, contrary to the expectations of the literature addressing class-based reasons for a lack of constituency,[110] individuals from lower classes in this analysis express more support for the *negro* political movement than those of the more privileged classes, using education as a class proxy. Hence, the differences between the social class position of the typical *negro* movement activist and the general nonwhite population does not appear problematic from the results of the 2000 survey in Rio. Two caveats are in order here, however.

First of all, studies reveal that racism increases with social class position.[111] In one such study, Telles looked at the effect of development on racial inequality in Brazil. He found that development "has clearly increased racial inequalities in professional and white-collar occupations while decreasing inequality in skilled blue-collar occupation."[112] He states that these findings support the claim "that racism in Brazil increases with income," and that "negative racial attitudes are clearly less intense among poor whites when compared to middle class whites throughout Brazil."[113] He concludes that for a lower stratum of Brazilian society, "race loses salience to class."[114] Hence, nonelite nonwhites may express support for antiracism in general, but when confronted with specific proposals of middle-class activists that pit whites against *negros*, these may not find echo due to the relative lack of conflict between poor whites and nonwhites who share much of the same social class position and space.

Secondly, Bailey and Telles report that preference for the use of the *negro* term is positively associated with educational level and that of the *moreno* term is negatively associated with the same.[115] That is, as one's social class position improves, there is more of an affinity for the term *negro*, whereas the *moreno* category is more readily embraced by the masses. Here, race and class appear to intersect in a way that disfavors the *negro* racialist movement discourse for nonelite nonwhites.

Practical Considerations for Mobilization Strategies

Some of my results presented here suggest some practical considerations for antiracism strategizing. First of all, although the data reveal very significant hypothetical support for participating in antiracism activities in general and even considerable interest in becoming members of the antiracism organizations, the same survey finds that only 14 percent of Brazilians in the state of Rio de Janeiro claimed actual knowledge of some type of *negro* organization. Of those, fully 26 percent responded that they could not even remember the name of the organization. Hence, there appears to be a visibility problem. More effective public campaigns could possibly convert willingness into actual participation or membership. As the *negro* movement gains prominence, especially through the affirmative action debate that I address in the following chapters, there is no doubt that the issue of invisibility is losing weight.

Secondly, age is the most decisive factor leading to positive attitudes toward the Brazilian *negro* political movement and especially for membership in antiracist organizations. Table 6.6 shows just how drastic that effect is. On the one hand, fully 75 percent of individuals of the youngest age group (eighteen to twenty-five years) express willingness to participate in antiracism activities, compared to 35 percent from the oldest category (sixty-one to ninety-three years). On the other hand, fully 62 percent of the oldest group responds "no" when asked about its openness to join antiracist organizations, whereas only 24 percent of the youngest responds the same. The origin of the age effect may be hard to establish; it may be influenced by the saliency of "black"

Table 6.6 Percent distributions of item on the willingness to participate in antiracism activities and join antiracist organizations by age groups: Adult population in the state of Rio de Janeiro, 2000

	18–25	26–40	41–60	61–93
1. Participate in antiracism activity				
Yes	75%	59%	51%	35%
No	12	27	36	54
Maybe	12	15	13	10
2. Join an antiracism organization				
A lot	34	24	23	18
A little	27	18	13	6
Perhaps	15	18	11	14
No	24	41	54	62

SOURCE: CEAP/DataUff 2000.

youth culture in urban Brazil that is actually shared across color categories[116] or by the general idealism of youth in contrast to older individuals who may be more skeptical about social change. Nonetheless, focused *negro* movement investment in younger individuals of the Brazilian population could be key to mobilization success.

Conclusion

In sum, in this empirical examination of attitudes toward the Brazilian *negro* political movement, I tested general premises from the literature that hypothesized either apathy or racial polarization. I reported surprising results—overwhelmingly positive attitudes toward the movement and the lack of robust significance of "race" or color for determining these stances.[117] My findings suggest the error in assuming that the lack of more active antiracist organization in Brazil stems from public apathy and therefore may shed new light on how to strengthen the antiracist struggle. In the following chapter, I examine attitudes toward another antiracism strategy—affirmative action.

7 Affirmative Action

JUST A FEW YEARS AGO THE POSSIBILITY of adopting race-targeted approaches to combat racialized inequalities in Brazil would have seemed impossible.[1] Andrews explains, "In a racial democracy, there doesn't exist any necessity for programs based on racial preference; to the contrary, these programs represent a negation of the most basic principles of this hegemonic ideology."[2] Hanchard, too, hypothesized, "the consequences of the ideology of racial democracy are quite real: no affirmative action programs for nonwhites."[3] In that public policy decisions are made at the elite level of state actors, and that the Brazilian state has traditionally denied the existence of widespread discrimination,[4] these researchers seemed to be proclaiming the obvious.

However, affirmative action strategies have burst onto the Brazilian scene,[5] beginning in earnest in late 2001 with the adoption of racial quotas at two state universities in Rio de Janeiro and subsequently legislated in many other universities and public spheres. How can we explain this unexpected development? Rather than resulting from a popular groundswell of public protest and demands, as I address below, the actual implementation of this strategy was prompted by struggles at elite levels between movement and state actors. Nonetheless, they are a surprising reality, considering Brazil's historic avoidance of both exclusionary and inclusionary race-targeted legislation.[6]

The attitudinal question addressed in this chapter, however, centrally focuses on popular support for those policies and the variables associated with that support. Do ordinary Brazilians, whose racial common sense is generally considered to be imbued with the myth of racial democracy, express support for or rejection of race-targeted strategies? What factors influence their opinions? The general reasoning behind the hypothesized rejection of affirmative action offered by dominant Brazilianist literature (represented by the Hanchard quote above) is that it is, again, the population's denial of discrimination acting as a type of legitimizing ideology of status quo, as discussed in Chapter 5, which leads to generalized opposition to antiracism strategies. Researchers in other contexts also hold that popular beliefs and ideologies, similar to the myth of racial democracy, can act to justify social arrangements and therefore negatively influence policy choices that may challenge the status quo.[7] Is the myth of racial democracy in fact a justifying ideology negating the possibility of popular support for affirmative action in Brazil?

All three surveys tapped opinions on race-targeted policies, and I draw on them centrally to attempt to answer that question. In confronting this debate, this chapter accomplishes the following: (1) It speaks to how the race-targeted approach came about in Brazil; (2) it sheds new light on how beliefs associated with the Brazilian racial democracy myth affect opinions regarding state intervention to ameliorate nonwhite disadvantage, namely affirmative action strategies; and (3) it explores the adequacy of perspectives from the general literature on the association between ideology and public policy for understanding the relationship between this myth and race-targeted policy in Brazil.

Race-Targeted Policy Debate in Brazil

Race-targeted strategies have a history of implementation in several national contexts, most notably in the United States, where they have aided the social mobility of many black Americans.[8] Nonetheless, these policies were one of the most controversial subjects in all of American society in the 1990s, leading Hochschild to write that the debate in the United States has constituted nothing less than a formidable "culture war" between white and black Americans.[9] In Brazil, where up until very recently these policies were relatively unknown and unused,[10] affirmative action already constitutes the most contested aspect of racial and gender politics.[11]

Brazil's first significant foray into the race-targeted policy debate has been in implementing racial quotas. The quota system is only one of at least five methods of race- and gender-conscious practices that have been historically covered under the umbrella of affirmative actions: (1) quotas, (2) preferences, (3) self-studies, (4) outreach and counseling, and (5) antidiscrimination.[12] Most commonly associated with discussion of affirmative action, however, are the first two methods. Under a quota system, increased representation of formerly excluded populations is accomplished by reserving a share of available positions for members of the targeted group, thus dividing the overall selection process into two separate, parallel competitions.[13] Under a preferences system, there is only one competition, but additional consideration is given to members of the targeted population in evaluating individual qualifications and thereby affecting applicant rankings.[14] Quotas are the subject of much of the rancor on the topic of affirmative action, and U.S. courts have consistently ruled race quotas as unconstitutional since the 1970s. Oppenheimer writes, "We may argue the merits of affirmative action quotas, but the Court [in the US] has foreclosed any further experiments with such plans. They are a dead letter."[15]

However, quotas are central to Brazil's new affirmative action programs in higher education, in part due to that country's traditional system of university entrance that differs significantly from the system employed in the United States. In Brazil, there are a very limited number of openings in the very limited number of public universities, which are sought after through a process called *vestibular*. According to Guimarães,

> Public universities, which offer the best quality higher education in Brazil, are accessible almost exclusively to upper-class students who have had access to private (paid) primary and secondary education. Ironically, these public universities are gratuitous, while middle- and lower-middle-class students at private universities pay very high tuition fees when measured against their income standards.[16]

Through the *vestibular* process, students take standardized tests, and their scores rank them for entry without generally taking into account other measurements of merit or alternative qualifications or considerations.[17] It is a highly competitive process, and only a fraction of applicants are accepted. Nonwhites are dramatically underrepresented among those accepted. According to Stubrin, whites make up about 52 percent of the Brazilian population, but account for about 72.9 percent of university students.[18]

With no extensive application files with which to consider various criteria as a part of the selection process, administrators in Brazil turn to racial criteria and reserve for the targeted population a percentage of openings for which only that population competes. In that parallel system for university entrance, there are variations in percentages, in labels for the disadvantaged populations, and in qualification criteria, and the like, due to the independence of local state actors who have taken the lead in implementing university quotas. In a general system of quotas, percentages are set equal to the proportion of the targeted population in the region.[19] Local state actors in Brazil are also attempting to follow that criterion to the extent possible.

The state of Rio de Janeiro is a case in point where race-targeted policies have passed into state law in the form of quotas for public university entrance. In October of 2001, the state legislature of Rio approved the following: "It is hereby established a minimum quota of up to 40% for brown and *negro* populations in the filling of openings at the university level at the State University of Rio de Janeiro (UERJ) and the State University of Norte Fluminense."[20] The results of this legislation will no doubt be studied closely. Since their implementation, some questions have arisen concerning identifying quota benefactors (due to the ambiguity of Brazil's traditional color continuum) and lawsuits by "white" students who feel their exclusion represented color discrimination.[21]

Since that initial legislation in Rio de Janeiro in 2001, racial quotas in higher education have become quite widespread in Brazil. As of July of 2007, some thirty Brazilian public universities have adopted race-targeted policies.[22] Moreover, legislation is now before the national congress mandating that all federal universities adopt racial quotas.[23] This turnabout in the Brazilian state's approach to racial disadvantage is nothing short of dramatic. Before turning to what Brazilians think about race-targeted policy, then, I briefly address the question of how this change came about. The state's official discourse has traditionally been one that denies the existence of racial discrimination in Brazil.[24] In addition, the *negro* movement has historically struggled to "matter" in Brazil.[25] How then did racial quotas come into being?

Cardoso and the Durban Conference

Against the backdrop of decades of generally failed attempts by a committed core of activists to influence state policy, the recent success of the *negro* movement in pressuring state actors to pass race-targeted legislation is remarkable. I believe that two events centrally facilitated the unexpected adoption of affirmative action in Brazil: the assumption of Cardoso to the presidency in 1995 and the participation of state and movement actors in the 2001 United Nations' World Conference against Racism, Racial Discrimination, Xenophobia, and Related Intolerance.[26]

Fernando Henrique Cardoso's assumption to the presidency in 1995 marked a turning point in the legitimization of antiracism politics in Brazil.[27] Since the founding of the Brazilian republic, political elites had generally ignored the racial component of social inequality.[28] In contrast, years before becoming president, Cardoso had been a prominent "race relations" sociologist,[29] and very early in his presidency he threw the weight of his office and intellect toward confronting racial inequality as part of a larger human rights agenda.[30] In 1996, his government endorsed the idea of affirmative action in its newly established National Human Rights Program.[31] Moreover, during Cardoso's tenure, which lasted until January 1, 2003, a few federal agencies adopted on a limited basis varying types of race-targeted initiatives.[32] Cardoso's personal influence as president on the state's openness toward antiracism strategies, according to some, would be hard to overstate. Among others acknowledging the centrality of Cardoso to the Brazilian turnaround regarding racial policy,[33] key *negro* movement actor Ivair dos Santos claimed in 2002, "If Fernando Henrique Cardoso had not been president, the debate would not have started."[34]

Yet Cardoso alone, however decisive, appeared unable or unwilling to adopt race-targeted policies on a large scale. Hence, the state's antiracism agenda had to be pushed forward through other means. The fortuitous participation of state actors in the United Nations' World Conference against Racism, Racial Discrimination, Xenophobia, and Related Intolerance in Durban, South Africa (August through September of 2001), and its numerous preparatory conferences, set the stage for more aggressive state-sponsored antiracism.[35] The state's renewed antiracism fervor, however, was sparked by the systematic and unrelenting pressure exerted by *negro* movement actors through the conference and the preparatory meetings. These encounters served as forums bringing state and *negro* movement actors together as never before, allowing the public airing of *negro* movement grievances and legitimizing the antiracism agenda.

In large part, then, as a result of both the agenda set forth by Cardoso and the decisive international antiracism conference, Brazil has witnessed a surprisingly rapid institutionalization of affirmative action on a larger scale in the early 2000s.[36] As mentioned, the first race-targeted legislation in higher education was adopted on October 10, 2001, at two state universities in Rio de Janeiro.[37] The following year, the State University of Bahia also adopted racial quotas.[38]

Thus, the historic disconnect between the state and the *negro* movement began to erode with the government of Cardoso and the Durban event. Lula's assumption of the presidency in 2003 has continued and deepened that partnership. Today the Brazilian state and the *negro* movement are clearly partners in developing race-targeted policy approaches to racial inequality, which are proliferating throughout the country. I now turn briefly to theoretical perspectives to frame my exploration of what everyday Brazilians opine as to the idea of affirmative action strategies.

Framing Opinions on Affirmative Action

What do Brazilians think about race-targeted public policy? The literature is mostly speculative at this point. There, again, is an almost total absence of data on public opinion regarding race-targeted policy from which to draw conclusions. This lacuna is due in large part to the novelty of the affirmative action approach in Brazil. Nonetheless, most of the difficulties that researchers and social movement actors have mentioned as possibly working against the adoption or continuance of these policies have one thing in common—they are linked to the myth of racial democracy.[39] The Brazilianist literature posits that a denial of the existence of racial discrimination, as discussed in Chapter 5 and inextricably bound to Brazilian antiracialism, generates opposition to antiracism initiatives in general, as addressed in Chapter 6, and specifically to race-targeted policy.[40] For example, Nobles reported in 2000 that "The racial democracy idea has disallowed positive policies by proclaiming them unnecessary."[41] This hypothesized relationship, then, is generally one that frames the myth of racial democracy as an ideology that justifies the status quo and thereby leads to opposition to strategies that could upset that status quo. Do theories from the general literature provide backing for such a framing? I briefly turn to that literature.

Theoretical Perspectives

Findings from general literature on racial attitudes bolster the validity of this perceived negative relationship between a denial of discrimination (believed to be embedded in the myth of racial democracy) and support for race-targeted policy. The consensus is that a lack of awareness of the structural determinants of inequality leads to opposition to policies that may challenge the status quo.[42] Hughes and Tuch summarize this consensus: "To the extent that acknowledgment of the existence of discrimination toward blacks . . . is a necessary prerequisite for support of policies aimed at dismantling discrimination's effects, those who deny that racism and discrimination are problems are likely to oppose race- or ethnic-targeted policies."[43]

Theories that study this relation generally emphasize the functional role of ideology in generating group-based oppression. These include realistic group conflict theory, group position theory, social dominance theory, and neoclassical hegemony models.[44] One way to label this similar approach is "group dominance perspective."[45] Although the models clustered under this label have much in common, I center the analysis on one variant of this perspective for hypothesis construction, social dominance theory (henceforward SDT).[46] I choose this framing over the other variants based on (1) the growing attention given to this perspective in the general literature;[47] (2) its vision of a general applicability beyond the United States (where the bulk of the literature on racial attitudes is centered) that specifically includes Latin America;[48] (3) its taking into account nonwhite racial attitudes as well as those of whites, a dimension few others actually do;[49] and (4) its provision of empirical standards for testing some of its derived hypotheses.[50] Although I focus on SDT, much of what I discuss as derivative of that model may also hold in important ways for the other group dominance framings.

Social Dominance Theory.   SDT endeavors to explain why and how group-based social hierarchies are produced and maintained. One of the central answers it provides is the naming of a persistent and universal tendency rooted in human psychology and biology that, according to its proponents, leads "individuals [to] desire and support group-based hierarchy and the domination of 'inferior' groups by 'superior' groups."[51] They label this tendency the "social dominance orientation." It is this orientation that significantly influences social ideologies and especially attitudes toward "the distribution of social value between social groups."[52] The level of the social dominance orientation displayed by an individual is centrally affected by that person's membership in and identification with salient and hierarchically organized social groups.[53] According to these theorists, it would usually be the case that dominants, and those that identify with them, would display higher levels of the social dominance orientation than subordinates.

However, unlike traditional group dominance perspectives that focus on the mind-sets and actions of oppressive dominants, SDT is more interested in "the manner in which subordinates actively participate in and contribute to their own subordination," remarking that "group oppression is very much a cooperative game" through both "active and passive cooperation."[54] Hence, they are interested in consensually held ideologies where subordinates and dominants share a same perspective. In this respect, SDT draws strongly from Marxist and neo-Marxist theorizing on "false consciousness" and "ideological hegemony."[55] Marx, for example, theorized that ideologies indeed function to justify and support hierarchical group relations, provoking on the part of subordinates what he labeled as "false consciousness": that dynamic wherein subordinates accept the hegemonic position of dominants as fair and legitimate. This allows dominant control over the social system without serious resistance from subordinates. SDT theorists specifically seek "the incorporation of this basic idea" into their framework, a notion to which "most social psychologists have not paid much attention."[56]

For this incorporation, SDT centers its argument on the manner in which ideological hegemony is established through "legitimizing myths." These myths "consist of attitudes, values, beliefs, stereotypes, and ideologies that provide moral and intellectual justification for the social practices that distribute social value within the social system."[57] For a construct to be considered a legitimizing myth, it should influence attitudes toward policy initiatives affecting social hierarchies (an SDT empirical standard). Ideologies generating support for policies that maintain and strengthen group-based domination are called hierarchy-enhancing legitimizing myths, and those that mediate support for policies that challenge hierarchies are called hierarchy-attenuating legitimizing myths (essentially a delegitimizing perspective). They further detail the nature of legitimizing myths as coming under two forms, as consensual (dominants and subordinates share a same perspective) or dissensual (where dominants and subordinates diverge in their perspectives on group-based hierarchy).

Social dominance theorists have begun testing their framework in Latin America. One recent study sought to understand the relationship between patriotism and race in the Dominican Republic, a context the researchers describe as molded similarly by a version of the myth of racial democracy.[58] SDT led them to predict that, as in the United States, dominant groups possess higher levels of attachment to the nation (expressed in more patriotic sentiments) than subordinate groups, a dynamic labeled "exclusionary patriotism." This dynamic would theoretically contribute to the maintenance of racial oppression in that context, thereby pointing to the hegemonic racial democracy myth as a hierarchy-enhancing ideology. I report some of their findings in the discussion section.

Hypotheses

The dominant perspective in the Brazilianist literature discussed above views the myth of racial democracy as what SDT labels a consensual hierarchy-enhancing legitimizing myth. Hanchard is clearly representative of this posi-tion.[59] He claims that the hegemonic ideology of racial democracy in Bra-zil sustains the dominant group's "passive revolution" in which that group's agenda is embraced by racial subordinates. He isolates the denial of racial discrimination provoked by the racial democracy myth as key to sustaining this revolution. Finally, he posits that the influence of this ideology precludes affirmative action programs for nonwhites in that context. Hanchard's rep-resentative view of the dominant Brazilianist position forms the basis of the following hypotheses, the first two of which I addressed in Chapter 5 and will only recall here:

H1: Brazilians deny that racial discrimination is behind *negro* disadvantage.

H2: This denial is consensual—embraced by both whites and nonwhites alike.

H3: The majority denial perspective acts as a legitimizing ideology leading to opposition to race-targeted policy.

These hypotheses fit comfortably within the SDT framework and its notion of a denial ideology (H1) that is consensually held (H2), leading to opposition to antiracism policies (H3), demonstrating the compatibility of this perspective with the dominant Brazilianist stance.

Findings

To address these hypotheses, I begin by recalling the nature of Brazilian be-liefs about racial stratification that I address in Chapter 5. In that chapter, I presented four items from the 2000 survey in Rio. One in particular accessed opinions on structural reasons for *negro* disadvantage flowing from racial discrimination. In addition, I presented an item from the 1995 DataFolha sur-vey that addressed that same structural explanation for racial disadvantage. To ascertain the consensuality of these racial stratification beliefs, I presented bivariate response distributions by color grouping on each item.

Table 5.2 revealed, first of all, that a majority of Brazilians in the 2000 Rio attitudinal survey recognized the role of discrimination in causing *negro* dis-advantage. Secondly, the same table revealed a near consensus as concerns that stratification belief on the part of individuals of both the white and non-white categories. Fully 77 percent of persons self-classifying in the white cate-gory pointed to discrimination, compared to 86 percent of those individuals in the unified nonwhite category. This consensus continued in the 1995 data set, also presented in Table 5.2. Following a statement that *negros* had been freed from slavery for over 100 years but still live in worse conditions than whites, when respondents were asked who was responsible, 72 percent of both categories pointed to white racial discrimination.

Therefore, regarding hypothesis #1 (H1—Brazilians deny that racial discrimination is behind *negro* disadvantage), the results reveal just the opposite. A vast majority of Brazilians point to discrimination. As to hypothesis #2 (H2—that the denial is consensually held between whites and nonwhites), there is support for this stance, but in the opposite direction predicted. Instead of a consensual majority denial of discrimination, there is a consensual majority recognition of it on the part of both white and nonwhite Brazilians. That is, if the racial common sense in Brazil, that is, the racial worldview of the vast majority of everyday Brazilians, is based in the myth of racial democracy, that myth is clearly not constituted by a denial of racial discrimination.

Turning now to race-targeted policies, in a series of items respondents were asked about levels of agreement with several types of quota legislation that had been employed or suggested in Rio de Janeiro: in higher education, in the job market, in state-sponsored television commercials, and in compiling candidate lists for election to public office (question wording listed in Table 7.1). In Table 7.2, I present univariate and bivariate statistics on each of these items. Those results reveal that, overall, a majority of Brazilians support the race-targeted approach. This is true for each of the distinct types that were presented to the respondents: quotas in university, in employment, for political candidates, and in commercials. For example, from the first row of the table, we see that 55 percent of Brazilians in the state of Rio de Janeiro express support for quota in universities. At the high end, 65 percent express support for the same in state-sponsored commercials. There is some variation in terms of the sociodemographic factors associated with that support, as I discuss below, but before examining those mediating factors in more detail, I first turn to advanced survey methods to look at the mediating role of Brazilian stratification beliefs.

Recall my third hypothesis: Do stratification beliefs affect opinions toward race-targeted policy in Brazil (H3)? The empirical standard offered by SDT scholars to capture a stratification belief's effect is whether that belief is positively or negatively associated with support for antiracism strategies.[60] To document that mediating role, I regress opinions on race-targeted policy initiatives from the 2000 CEAP/DataUff survey on racial stratification beliefs, along

Table 7.1 Survey items on race-targeted initiatives

In Brazil, there are very few negro students in universities. Some people believe that to change this situation the government should set aside openings for negros in public universities. Other people believe that setting aside openings for negros by the government would place other persons at a disadvantage. Do you believe . . .	1. . . . the government should set aside openings for *negro* in public universities? 2. . . . the government should not set aside openings?
Today, to increase the representation of women in politics, political parties are obligated by law to set aside 30% of candidate openings for women. Do you believe that to increase the representation of negros in politics . . .	1. . . . openings for negro candidates should also be set aside? 2. . . . it is not necessary to set aside openings.
Continuing with the question of setting aside openings, do you agree or disagree that openings should be set aside in good jobs for negro workers, since, in general, they have worse jobs than do whites?	1. Agree (strongly or in part) 2. Disagree (strongly or in part)
Presently the administration of the municipality of Rio de Janeiro mandates that 33%, or a third, of persons who participate in commercials paid for by the municipality have to be negro. Do you agree or disagree?	1. Agree (strongly or in part) 2. Disagree (strongly or in part)

SOURCE: CEAP/DataUff 2000.

with sociodemographic variables. The dependent policy variable is comprised of those four different items concerning race-targeted policy in the areas of education, of employment, for choosing political candidates, and for choosing actors in state-financed television commercials (listed in Table 7.1).[61]

The central independent variable is stratification belief. I construct this measure using the item from the 2000 CEAP/DataUff survey that asked respondents about whether they agreed that racial discrimination was responsible for *negro* disadvantage (Table 5.2) (1 = agreement, 0 = disagreement). Sociodemographic independent variables are educational level,[62] age, sex, color,[63] and income. I present two models of the regression results, the first using the three-color model (white, brown, *preto*) and the second the bipolar model (white versus nonwhite). The models include both metric and standardized coefficients.

In Table 7.3 we see, first, that the majority racial stratification belief variable recognizing the role of discrimination is positively associated with support for affirmative action policies, holding all other variables constant.

Table 7.2 Percent distribution of race-targeted initiatives by select color categories and education: Adult population in the state of Rio de Janeiro, 2000

| | Race-Targeted Initiatives | | | |
	Quotas in Universities, Yes	Quotas in Employment, Yes	Quotas for Candidates, Yes	Quotas in Commercials, Yes
All respondents	54.9%	57.4%	51.2%	64.8%
Two-color category				
White	46.3	48.0	43.4	64.3
Nonwhite	63.0	66.0	58.8	65.2
Three-color category				
White	46.3	48.0	43.4	64.3
Brown	59.7	63.5	55.9	66.1
Preto	69.8	71.2	64.7	63.5
Educational level				
Low	79.6	81.1	76.4	79.3
Medium low	68.0	68.5	59.1	67.6
Medium	46.2	49.0	44.6	59.0
High	30.0	35.6	30.6	56.9
Educational/Color				
White				
Low	74.8	74.5	67.3	80.7
Medium low	58.9	58.5	51.6	63.6
Medium	39.5	43.9	38.1	63.9
High	23.1	27.6	26.1	57.2
Brown				
Low	80.0	85.7	79.5	76.0
Medium low	70.7	71.7	60.0	70.4
Medium	52.6	54.7	52.6	62.7
High	38.8	44.9	36.5	57.1
Preto				
Low	90.5	88.1	92.9	82.5
Medium low	82.5	82.8	71.9	70.8
Medium	48.5	48.5	42.4	37.5
High	41.4	51.7	37.9	53.6

SOURCE: CEAP/DataUff 2000, adapted from Bailey 2004.

Note: $N = 990$

Table 7.3 Ordinal least squares regression predicting support for race-target policy: Adult population in the state of Rio de Janeiro, 2000

Variable	Model 1	Model 2
METRIC REGRESSION COEFFICIENTS		
Three-color (brown omitted)		
White	−.087***	
	(.024)	
Preto	.043	
	(.032)	
Two-color (nonwhite omitted)		
White		−.099***
		(.022)
Age	−.002*	−.002*
	(.001)	(.000)
Female	.047*	.048*
	(.022)	(.004)
Education	−.128***	−.130***
	(.010)	(.010)
Income	−.014***	−.015***
	(.004)	(.004)
Racial stratification belief (recognition of discrimination)	.066**	.069**
	(.028)	(.028)
Intercept	.989***	1.001***
	(.060)	(.058)
R^2	.21	.21
STANDARDIZED REGRESSION COEFFICIENTS		
Three-color (brown omitted)		
White	−.101	
Preto	.039	
Two-color (nonwhite omitted)		
White		−.132
Age	−.059	−.072
Female	.059	.061
Education	−.344	−.387
Income	−.150	−.096
Stratification belief	.070	.070

SOURCE: CEAP/DataUff 2000.

Note: $N = 990$

*p<.05, **p<.01, ***p<.001

Therefore, hypothesis #3 predicting that a majority denial perspective, reflective of the racial democracy myth, acts as a legitimizing myth (H3) leading to opposition to race-targeting policies does not receive support. Rather, as evidenced by that variable's positive sign, the majority belief in Brazil is shown to act as a hierarchy-attenuating or delegitimizing stance. That is, it is associated with support for affirmative action strategies. If the sign had been negative, we would have had to conclude that the recognition of racial discrimination in Brazil was actually a type of "neat trick" leading to opposition to challenges to the status quo—that is, hierarchy enhancing, as SDT predicts.[64]

Which others of the independent variables significantly affect policy choices? Beginning with the effect of color grouping, although there is a strong consensus between categories on the stratification belief item, this consensus loses some ground as regards policy preferences. That is, while the *preto* and the brown (omitted) categories do not differ significantly from each other in terms of support for race-targeted policies, the white category is less likely to favor those policies than is the brown grouping, holding constant the stratification belief and all other sociodemographic variables. Because the individuals of the white grouping would not be the benefactors of the policy preferences and possibly could be disadvantaged by them, an element of apparent group-based interest arises. This finding is consistent with the general group dominance perspective.

However, when compared to results on similar items in the U.S. context, the racial divide on race-targeted policy issues in Brazil appears less robust. In Brazil, the bivariate presentation in Table 7.4 reveals that 46 percent of whites compared to 63 percent of nonwhites favor quotas in higher education. In contrast, in the United States, in the 1986 National Election Study that included a very similar question on quotas, only 30 percent of whites compared to fully 80 percent of blacks favored the same.[65] Concerning quotas for good jobs, 48 percent of whites favor this policy in Brazil, compared to 66 percent of nonwhites. In the same 1986 study in the United States, only 15 percent of whites, compared to 68 percent of blacks, favored preferential hiring and promotion of blacks.[66] Therefore, although there is some evidence of possible group-based interests, these interests appear only moderately divided in comparison to the racially polarized U.S. context.

However, there may be alternative explanations for my regression results, that is, group-based interest may not be the driving force behind them. An alternative plausible explanation is that simple "self-interest" may be at play. White individuals, as nonbeneficiaries of race-targeted policies, may perceive

Table 7.4 Percent distributions of support for race-targeted intervention by racial categories in Brazil and the United States

	White	Black (U.S.)/ Nonwhite (Brazil)
Brazil		
University quotas	46.3%	63.0%
Job quotas	48.0	66.0
United States		
University quotas	29.7	79.7
Hiring preferences	15.4	67.7

SOURCE: Brazil—CEAP/DataUff 2000; United States—NES 1986 (adapted from Kinder and Sanders 1996).

these policies as possibly meaning tangible loss for themselves and their families, a stance that may have little or nothing to do with racial group subjectivity or solidarity.[67] Although it may be hard to distinguish between self- and group-based interests in predicting attitudinal stances, according to Kinder and Sanders, the possibility of the determinant effect of self-interest is increased when a question involves a policy where the benefits and harms are well publicized and when these are certain to take effect should a policy pass. They speculate that self-interest may be at play in the United States for "those whites who believed that affirmative action was likely to set back the education of their own children."[68] This same type of dynamic cannot be easily discounted in the case of quotas in Brazil.

The strongest determinant of opinion on race-targeted policy, however, is education. A cursory examination of bivariate distributions in Table 7.2 evidences this strong influence. It shows that about 80 percent of individuals with a low level of education support quotas in universities and jobs compared to 30 and 36 percent of those with higher education in the case of university and job quotas, respectively. This decisive relationship of education thoroughly holds controlling for color category. For example, Table 7.2 also shows that while fully 75 percent of whites with a low education support quotas in universities and jobs, only 23 percent of high-education whites do so in the case of university quotas (and 28 percent in the case of jobs). The regression results clearly further document the effect of education on policy opinions, revealing the strength of that relationship in comparison to the other determinants. For example, examining the standardized coefficients in Table 7.3 for Model 2, the coefficient for education is three times larger than that for color category

(–.387 versus –.132, respectively). Income is also highly significant, as may be expected due to the nature of both income and education as class proxies.

Younger adults are also significantly more likely to support intervention measures than older adults. This pattern contrasts, for example, findings by Bobo and Kluegel that in the United States, "there are no significant differences among the young and the old in support for race-targeted policies."[69] Regarding gender, according to the SDT researchers, males generally possess higher levels of the social dominance orientation than do females.[70] Hence, based on that premise, males will generally oppose policies that challenge the status quo, while women tend in the opposite direction, even when gender stratification is not at issue. The results reveal that Brazilian women are significantly more likely than Brazilian men to support race-targeted policies in that context, although I do not address the question of a causal connection to a social dominance orientation as in the SDT framing.

Discussion

These results speak directly to two issues located at the core of contemporary academic and public policy discussions regarding racism and antiracism in Brazil: (1) the determinant effect of the racial democracy myth on possible intervention strategies into nonwhite disadvantage; and (2) the adequacy of group dominance perspectives for analyzing Brazilian racial dynamics.

Affirmative Action and the Myth of Racial Democracy

Is the myth of racial democracy a consensual hierarchy-enhancing legitimizing myth, that is, a type of "false consciousness"? Warren, for example, claims that in Brazil "[racial] dominance is sustained less by force than consent."[71] Hanchard and others posit that the hegemonic racial democracy myth negates the possibility of race-targeted policies in Brazil.[72] My empirical analyses do not support these dominant Brazilianist perspectives. Rather, they show a near consensus between individuals of the white and nonwhite categories on the belief that racial discrimination *is* a causal factor of *negro* disadvantage. Moreover, this consensus is in the order of a delegitimizing belief, that is, it predicts support for race-targeted policies. In other words, this ideology appears not to be a "façade" or a "neat trick."[73] On the contrary, the results point to the racial democracy construct as a consensual hierarchy-attenuating (de)legitimizing myth or a "counterdominance" ideology, rather than one that enhances racial oppression.[74]

Hence, social dominance theory, which hypothesizes the functional role of the racial democracy myth as legitimizing racial hierarchy, does not capture the essence of this myth. The aforementioned study of the influence of racial democracy in the Dominican Republic also illustrates SDT's problematic nature in that Latin American context. Recall that the study sought to understand the relationship between patriotism and racial identification in the Dominican Republic, positing that, as in the United States, dominant whites would possess higher levels of attachment to the nation (expressed in more patriotic sentiments) than subordinate nonwhites. However, their results did not support this hypothesis. They write, "In stark contrast to our findings in the United States, . . . patriotic attachment to the nation did not differ by 'racial' category, nor was it positively associated with either Europhilic or Afrophobic tendencies within any 'racial' group."[75] In essence and in reference to these results, they did not demonstrate the myth of racial democracy to be a hierarchy-enhancing legitimizing ideology.

In explaining SDT's failure to predict how the ideology of racial democracy might affect levels of national attachment, they constructively remark, "there is reason to believe that the contextual differences between the US . . . on the one hand, and the Dominican Republic on the other hand, really do make a difference in the results of interest here [exclusionary patriotism]."[76] What, then, are the contextual differences that confound SDT in the Brazilian context (and perhaps also in the Dominican Republic)? I now turn the discussion to these contextual specificities.

Contextualizing Social Dominance Theory

Why does the ideological construct of racial democracy escape the prediction power of SDT? I posit an answer in what can be called the "groupist" assumptions on which SDT, in particular, and group dominance perspectives, in general, rest.[77] Specifically, "groupism" (as introduced earlier) involves the confusion and/or conflation of "the idea of 'group' with the ascription of social categories that are everpresent features of the process of interaction, and which are not necessarily associated with bounded groups."[78] That is, for SDT theorists, a "racial category" automatically connotes a "racial group."[79] In contrast, Jenkins argues for the retention of the necessary analytical distinction between a category and a group, claiming that group identities are rooted in processes of internal definition whereas categories are not.[80] Goldberg agrees that "the distinction between . . . 'group' and . . . 'category' [is] a *sine qua non* in the interpretation of ethnic and racial data."[81] SDT researchers do not necessarily retain this distinction moving from the racialist (where this conflation may, at first, seem less problematic) to the antiracialist context. In doing so, they fall into what Brubaker denotes as "groupism": "the tendency to take discrete, sharply differentiated, internally homogeneous and externally bounded groups as basic constituents of social life, chief protagonists of social conflicts, and fundamental units of social analysis."[82] Specifically as concerns dynamics of racial identification, Brubaker clarifies: "In the domain of . . . race, I mean by 'groupism' the tendency to treat . . . races as substantial entities to which interests and agency can be attributed . . . I mean the tendency to represent the social and cultural world as a multichrome mosaic of monochrome ethnic, racial or cultural blocs."[83]

In the following sections, then, I argue that SDT's automatic treatment of color differences as delimiting social groups leads to at least two assumptions that weaken that framework's efficiency in the Brazilian context. Specifically, they treat the differing racial or color categories as (1) homogeneous ideological agents and as (2) monochrome identities (to the neglect of intersecting and overlapping identifications, that is, class-based subjectivity).

Within-Category Ideological Homogeneity.   A first problem of SDT flowing from a groupist orientation is that it assumes within-category ideological homogeneity, that is, that "'whites'" and "'blacks'" ideological interpretations are unified and differ due to their contrasting and conflicting racial interests. Barbara Reskin labels this type of theoretical structure a "motive-based explanation for ascriptive inequality."[84] It is characterized by assigning causal status for ascriptive inequality to unobserved "allocator motives," or to that which prompts dominants to take actions resulting in or supporting ascriptive inequality. Figure 7.1 diagrams this causal model.

This model captures dynamics that most centrally focus on the *why* of ascription-based oppression, placing a "heavy load of inference" on ideology as the "engine of inequality." For example, "Sex inequality at work . . . has been attributed to men's hope to maintain their privileged status. . . . Inequality based on sexual orientation theoretically stems from a different motive— homophobia. . . . Among motive-based theories advanced to explain racial inequality are antipathy or fear by [white] employers."[85] For each group-based inequality, there is a group-based motive explaining the outcome.

SDT clearly exemplifies a motive-based approach. It singles out the "social dominance orientation" as the cause or engine of racial hierarchy. As

Figure 7.1 Causal model linking motives to inequality (adapted from Reskin 2003)

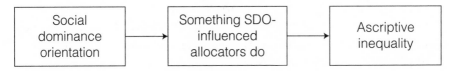

Figure 7.2 Causal model linking the social dominance orientation to inequality

discussed above, for SDT researchers the social dominance orientation is an apparent universal predisposition motivating "individuals [to] desire and support group-based hierarchy and the domination of 'inferior' groups by 'superior' groups."[86] The structure of the argument (see Figure 7.2) is much like that of conflict theories in general.

What is wrong with such an approach? Several criticisms regarding motive-based theories are possible. Among their weaknesses, Reskin mentions an inability to address inequality stemming from practices implemented in the past that persist in the present; the fact that inequality can result from "neutral" mechanisms that have disparate impacts on ascriptive groups; and the fact that motives are practically impossible to measure and differing motives can produce the same outcomes. Central to my concern, however, is their assumption of within-category ideological homogeneity. Reskin explains, "ascribing motives to individuals based on their group membership assumes within-group homogeneity on the causal variable."[87] As discussed above, theories that emphasize intergroup conflict all share the stipulation that "the differing groups have divergent group-based interests" and that dominant groups develop group-specific ideologies to ensure their dominance.[88]

This assumed homogeneity of inner-category perspectives on which motive-based explanations rest, however, may be untenable where subjective racial identification is not strong. Far from within-category homogeneity, the Brazilian context may be better described as marked by the lack of robust correlations between racial categories and attitudinal stances. Hasenbalg and Silva, for example, report that on the four questions involving racial issues included in a 1986 election survey in São Paulo, whites and nonwhites did not differ significantly.[89] As seen in previous chapters, category membership, as marked by the white and nonwhite classifications, are not robust predictors of perspectives on various racial issues, including cultural stances, stratification beliefs, and support for antiracist mobilization. In fact, it would appear that for many issues captured thus far in large sample surveys in Brazil, color category membership is not the decisive determinant. Rather than a negation of the significance of color as marking inequality in Brazil, these results speak to a context of decentered particularist racial identification,[90] and, along with it, an absence of unified group-based ideological perspectives.

Monochrome Identification.   A second issue regarding SDT that originates in its groupist assumptions is the overriding weight given to one group-based identity that leads to a neglect of the complexity of overlapping and nested identifications. As Brubaker remarks, the groupist vision has "a tendency to represent the social and cultural world as a multichrome mosaic of monochrome ethnic, racial or cultural blocs."[91] This emphasis on monochromatic identification, racial in this case, necessarily simplifies an individual's identity to one primary or overriding (racial) essence.

Reskin comments on this dynamic addressing what she calls the "balkanization of ascriptive identities" that is typical of motive-based theories.[92] When one finds inequality of outcomes according to sex, for example, motive-based theories focus on gender as the primary identity of participants explaining that dynamic. The same is true regarding inequality and sexual orientation (gays versus straights) and race (whites versus blacks). She explains, "Because we have constructed motive-based stories to account for these differently based expressions of ascribed inequality . . . the stories tend to be group-specific," which she claims leads to a type of "essentialism."[93] Hence, she discounts the fact that the dynamics surrounding ascriptive inequality can be productively understood in such group-specific ways.

The danger of focusing on monochrome racial identities may be especially hazardous in Brazil, where class-based identification may play a significant role in the cognitive organization of attitudinal stances. A possible race and class dynamic is not frequently focused on in the United States, where race is seen as the primary identity strongly determining attitudinal stances on racial issues. In a recent, unique study of class divisions on racial issues among black Americans, Hwang and colleagues summarize their findings as follows: "Our analysis suggests that blacks, regardless of class standing, join in a united front with their attitudes serving as grim reminders of the racial inequalities created and maintained by the current stratification system."[94] In this same vein, Kinder and Sanders regress race-targeted policy choice in the United States on class proxies and race. They conclude that in the United States it is "race, not class" that determines policy perspectives.[95]

However, in the regression analysis presented in this chapter, I find that class proxies are indeed quite significant in Brazil; and, judged by the size of the standardized coefficient in the case of education, that proxy's coefficient is three times as large as the race coefficient. These results reveal some support for an earlier view of race and class dynamics in Brazil reflected in Harris's classic study in which he reported, "It is one's class and not one's race which determines the adoption of subordinate and superordinate attitudes between specific individuals in face-to-face relations."[96]

Findings pointing to the importance of class-based identification are not surprising viewed in the context of extreme social class inequalities in Brazil. Shared histories of disadvantage are certainly a factor in the formation of ascriptive identities. Particularly for group dominance theorists, "the sharing of a common economic position in society is the very basis of group consciousness."[97] Of course, sociological studies in Brazil do, indeed, document significant outcome disparities along color lines. However, several studies have documented that those disparities increase with class position, and, at least in the lower stratum of Brazilian society, Telles claims, "race loses salience to class."[98]

The results lend some credence, then, to an interpretation of the possible relative importance of class over racial identification in Brazil as concerns attitudinal stances. Although these findings do not dismiss the effect of racial identification on the cognitive organization of ideological stances, they indicate that overlapping identities must be taken into account, thereby complicating frameworks that are mono-group based.

Explaining Support

These results reveal significant majority support among Brazilians of all color categories for race-targeted initiatives as measured through the 2000 CEAP/DataUff survey. How might we explain this support?

One possible explanation for the support of race-targeted initiatives may be found in a concept put forth by Schuman and Harding labeled "sympathetic identification."[99] These researchers sought to understand the variable ways in which individuals identify with the social underdog and specifically with an ethnic minority facing discrimination. They found that majority members who were sympathetic to cases of discrimination against minorities had "the capacity to identify at least as strongly with the minority member . . . as with fellow majority members."[100]

Two factors in Brazil may work to stimulate "sympathetic identification" across color lines: racial ambiguity and class-based identification. Regarding the former, ambiguous racial identification is correlated with relatively high rates of intercategory marriage in Brazil and only moderate spatial segregation.[101] That is, just as strong lines of demarcation are significant for the production of robust particularist identification, their absence may lessen "we/they" mentalities. Furthermore, class-based identification appears to cut across racial category lines in Brazil, at least as pertains to the lower class, which is the majority segment of the country.

However, there are alternative explanations possible for the apparent greater support for affirmative action initiatives by individuals of the white category in Brazil as compared to the United States. As I discussed, there is little history of race-targeted initiatives in Brazil. Sympathetic identification may be easier to express when the question has been hypothetical. That is, where there is no real perceived threat for those who would not be beneficiaries of these policies, a principled agreement is less problematic. This dynamic is born out in the comparison of support for quotas in commercials to those in employment. White opinions on the commercial quota issue are much closer to those of nonwhites (65 percent of both whites and nonwhites support these initiatives) in comparison to employment quotas (48 percent of whites versus 66 percent of nonwhites support them), perhaps due to the fact that very few whites (or nonwhites, for that matter) would ever be directly affected by such a policy on commercials. Now that race-targeted policies are being widely adopted in Brazil, perceived threat may indeed grow and result in white opposition.

Tempering this outcome to some extent, however, is the fact that the central realm in which quotas are being most widely adopted, higher education, is still a sphere of privilege and does not directly affect the lives of the great masses of Brazilians. The ability of those masses to successfully complete basic education or compete for university admittance through rigorous entrance exams is severely limited. Nonetheless, the symbolic repercussion of the negative effect of racial quotas on just a few could reverberate widely, influencing public opinion.

The central explanation that I wish to offer here for this outcome, however, is a derivative of what has been called in the literature "a matter of principle approach."[102] Kinder and Sanders argue, with some noted skepticism, that opinions about issues of race are based in part on abstract principles. Addressing the American context, they claim, following Myrdal, for example, that Americans are unified by a commitment to a "'creed'—a set of governing principles that guides their views on politics and society."[103] These principles stem in large part from the "American creed." Kinder and Sanders identify those principles as ideas of equality, economic individualism, and limited government in the American context, and after an exhaustive examination of American public opinion, they claim that these principles "do matter" (that is, that they significantly influence public opinion about race).[104] This formulation is consistent too with Zaller's predispositions or values framing for understanding influences on the formation of public opinion.[105]

Perhaps Myrdal is the researcher who most clearly posited the effect of abstract principles or values on matters of race in the United States. In his study of American race relations, which, of course, he found to be incredibly cruel and backward, he was optimistic about Americans being able to confront racial inequality. Key to that challenge was the set of principles espoused in the American creed. He wrote: "Americans of all national origins, classes, regions, creeds, and colors, have something in common: a social ethos, a political creed. It is hard to avoid the judgement that this 'American Creed' is the cement in the structure of this great and disparate nation."[106] This formulation is strikingly close to a view of the myth of racial democracy as an ethos shared by all strata of Brazilian society that may act as a yardstick with which to measure its unequal structure. That is, recall that a number of scholars believe that the myth of racial democracy may have a positive side, acting as a utopian dream that envisions Brazilian society as one based on a "myth of an interrelating people."[107] Although skin-color inequality exists in Brazil, the racial democracy orientation may constitute a moral high ground common to all Brazilians that both recognizes and repudiates discrimination, as discussed extensively in Chapter 5.

Therefore, beyond an ideology leading Brazilians of varying degrees of African descent to believe that they live in a "racial paradise,"[108] rather than some type of "Brazilian ignorance" stance, or instead of an ideology that legitimizes white privilege, racial democracy may reflect a deep-seated desire for a society that is not segmented along racial lines and that is essentially equal for all peoples. As such, this antiracialism imagery may provide Brazilians a yardstick with which to measure their unequal status, thereby enabling them or leading them to desire to confront that inequality. Hence, far from precluding antiracism, the myth may act as a valued and accepted principle, a "matter of principle,"[109] a legitimate utopian ideal that can lead to support for reverting the reality that so strongly contradicts the creed: racialized inequality.

Conclusion

In sum, group dominance perspectives, in general, and SDT, in particular, do not adequately capture the influence of the ideology of racial democracy in the state of Rio de Janeiro, Brazil, or in much of the nation, as represented in the 1995 DataFolha data set. The findings show this myth to be a nearly consensual construct that recognizes a discriminatory basis in the production of *negro* disadvantage. In addition, they also show that, as a stratification belief, the myth generates hypothetical support for confronting the causes of that reality, leading a majority of Brazilians in that state to express favor toward several possible race-targeted policy initiatives in 2000.[110]

An important caveat is in order, however. At the time this survey was conducted, the affirmative action boom had not yet begun at Brazilian universities, although there had been national media discussions of that approach as well as limited experiments in some state agencies and in the private business realm. Hence, we should again keep in mind Bobo's focus on "perceived threat" as determinant of attitudes toward antiracism.[111] If the actual threat is low, white racial attitudes may be less reactionary. Widespread and well-publicized implementation of racial quotas, then, could certainly shift the dynamics that I have captured in this early survey, leading to the development of more polarized, group-based "conflict attitudes."

Beyond this hypothetical support for race-targeted strategies in Brazil that my findings in this chapter suggest, sorting public resources along the lines of race in a society that has traditionally embraced racial ambiguity is sure to raise other issues for students of public opinion and racialized dynamics. I look at two of these in the final two empirical chapters of this book. The first explores the practical problem of racial sorting for beneficiary identification in the implementation of race-targeted policies, and the second confronts the race-making dynamics that these policies may stimulate. Both are sure to significantly affect race-targeted measures and racialized dynamics in a myriad of ways in the coming years.

8 Racial Sorting

ALONG WITH THE QUESTION POSED just a few years back as to whether affirmative action would ever be a reality in Brazil, a practical question has always accompanied that doubt. Namely, would the ambiguous nature of racial identification in Brazil be an obstacle to the adoption and/or successful implementation of race-targeted policy? Regarding the former, racial ambiguity certainly has proved not to be an obstacle to the policy's adoption. Brazilian universities have moved forward with surprising efficiency since the State University of Rio de Janeiro's initial foray into racial quotas in 2001. As to actually identifying beneficiaries for the policy's implementation being an obstacle, there are two schools of thought on this issue. On the one hand, a group of Brazilianist scholars has viewed the question of diffuse identification as a possible daunting obstacle, including Andrews, Reis, Sansone, Da Matta, and Fry.[1] Representative of this perspective, Skidmore writes:

> In practical terms, how will [Brazil] establish eligibility for the beneficiaries of [affirmative action]? For a long time now Brazilians have affirmed the fluidity of racial distinctions that characterize its society. It is at times said that Brazil doesn't have clearly-defined racial categories ... To establish racial categories would be undoubtedly one of the greatest practical difficulties for implementing affirmative action in Brazil.[2]

Other scholars find such a question regarding beneficiary identification in Brazil less problematic and possibly even absurd.[3] Bertulio writes, "Throughout Brazilian history and even including the present, I know of no difficulty that the white community has had in identifying a black individual in order to deprive him of his basic rights . . . I believe that the most sensible answer to this worry . . . is that *negros* are *negro* individuals."[4] Bertulio goes on to argue that the state ought to eliminate color distinctions other than *negro* and white. In fact, that is exactly what state actors are doing in terms of the administration of affirmative action strategies, as noted earlier. Hence, unlike the changes being proposed for the national census discussed in Chapter 4, the de jure adoption of dichotomous classification in *negro* and white by state actors is a reality in present-day Brazil for the administration of racial quotas. The move, then, toward "monoracial" categorization, that is, classification reflecting only one racial heritage,[5] hopes to remove racial ambiguity in a multiracial context.

The problematic nature of mixed-race or ambiguous identification for the administration of race-targeted policies came to the forefront of discussions in the United States when the 2000 Census allowed respondents to "mark one or more" races for the first time.[6] The difficulty is, as laid out by Goldstein and Morning, that race-targeted legislation in general relies on "single-race categories that unequivocally distinguish between those who are members of minority groups and those who are not."[7] Hence, scholars in the United States warn of the dangers of mixed-race categories for the enactment of policies built on the assumption of single-race classification.[8] In fact, Skerry claims that "multiracialism may well be the silver bullet that finishes off the affirmative action regime."[9]

The Brazilian move toward dichotomous categorization in *negro* and white for the administration of race-targeted policy could be considered an instance of administrative pragmatism, of bureaucracies grappling with "ambiguously raced bodies," as framed by Golub in his discussion of the historic Plessy court decision in the United States. In that instance, he reveals "the Court's deep anxiety regarding mixed-race individuals," and the "social and legal processes of racial sorting . . . of purportedly natural and discrete racial groups."[10] As in the Plessy case, falling on one side or the other of the sometimes ambiguous racial divide had serious consequences. In Brazil, what might be the consequences of adopting monoracialism in a society that has traditionally viewed itself as embracing mixed racial origins? In the short term, will the institutionalization of dichotomous classification help realize the legislative intent of identifying the diverse Brazilian population of varying degrees of African ancestry for targeted intervention? For example, if faced with a choice between white and *negro* in a bureaucratic context, into which category will multi-racial browns classify or be classified by a third party?

These questions are of utmost importance in Brazil for the success of affirmative action policies, as well as potentially for other regions in Latin America with histories of mestizo identification. In addition, they provide an important comparative case to the United States that may find itself more deeply embroiled in the same problem for the administration of civil rights legislation and affirmative action as mixed-race identification, newly institutionalized in the 2000 Census, increases in saliency. The comparative stance takes on even more importance if, as some researchers claim, U.S. classification trajectories are moving toward a Latin American model.[11]

To address these issues I draw on data from the 2002 PESB national survey that included items on affirmative action and, importantly, captured self- and other-classification dynamics in various formats: open-ended, census, monoracial (or dichotomous), and by comparison to photographs.

Background

Recall that in October of 2001, officials at the two state universities in Rio de Janeiro initiated racial quotas with the following legislation: "It is hereby established a minimum quota of up to 40 percent for brown and *negro* populations in the filling of openings at the university level at the State University of Rio de Janeiro (UERJ) and the State University of Norte Fluminense."[12] However, soon the problem of mixed-race categorization became more evident, and the groundbreaking legislation was changed from "brown and *negro*" in 2001 to only "*negro*" in 2003.[13] This switch to dichotomous classification was in part a response to apparent racial fraud, or white individuals self-classifying as browns for quota inclusion.[14] The expressed logic in that regard was that although a white individual might try to pass for brown, it is unlikely that he or she would go so far as to claim to be *negro*, the *negro* movement's proposed umbrella term for browns and *pretos*.[15] The term *negro* may carry more negative connotations or may be associated with darker skin tones in popular parlance than the mixed-race term and hence appear a less attractive option for whites.[16] In addition, César claims that opting for *negro* was a way "to incorporate a political connotation that implies a race conscience and not one based only on phenotype."[17] Finally, Peria reports that the decision to drop the brown term was based on argumentation offered by *negro* movement actors who cited the custom of sectors of academia and the *negro* movement to

join together browns and *pretos* based on their similar positions of socioeconomic disadvantage.[18]

In contrast, then, to the previous color classification scheme,[19] joining
together as *negros* those individuals with some "discernible" degree of African ancestry in a dichotomous white versus nonwhite classification may be
viewed as approximating the U.S. understanding of racial group membership.[20] Nobles, for example, writes that using the *negro* term for browns and
pretos in Brazil "would virtually duplicate U.S. census schedules insofar as
the categories 'white' and 'black' are concerned."[21] Although the use of the
term *negro* has a long history in Brazilian *negro* movements, a first step in its
adoption by state actors was taken in the 1980s. I quote Brazilianist historian
Andrews on this issue:

> [The Department of Social Studies and Indicators within the IBGE] decided
> in 1980 to begin analyzing and publishing racial data in dichotomous form,
> dividing the population into whites (*brancos*) and blacks (*negros*). This quiet,
> seemingly routine decision by a group of government researchers and tech-
> nocrats was actually rather far-reaching in its implications. While not aban-
> doning the traditional three-category concept of race, . . . IBGE had moved
> toward an alternative conceptualization of Brazilian race relations, in which
> people of both pure and mixed African ancestry are seen as a single racial
> group—in short, a North American vision of race.[22]

That is, similar to the United States, where mixed-race mulattoes were eventually merged into a solo black category,[23] in Brazil mixed-race browns are
joined with *pretos* as *negros* for race-targeted policy administration. This, in
my estimation, in effect represents a move toward "unmixing" the population
of mixed racial heritage employing a similar logic to the U.S. rule of hypodescent, as preeminent Brazilianist historian Thomas Skidmore wrote: "Several universities, such as the University of the State of Rio de Janeiro, have
also set quotas from minority admissions. In looking for some mechanism
to decide which candidates are eligible for a system like Affirmative Actions,
they have actually adopted the one-drop rule!"[24] As laid out by Zack, the logic
of that rule can be explained as follows: "A person, P, is black if P has one black
ancestor, any number of generations back. And a person, Q, is white if Q has
no black ancestors, any number of generations back, and no other nonwhite
ancestors of other races."[25] In general practice, however, the rule is based on
"discernible" African admixture, or "traces" of African heritage readable in

the faces of the raced individuals.[26] That is, one-drop of black blood, as traditionally stated, generally matters because it has colored or "stained" the phenotype of its possessor. Racial passing for those whose skin color was not "obviously" colored despite African admixture, for example, has a long history in the United States.[27]

A central goal of the historic rule of hypodescent in the United States was to ensure white purity through which the exploitation of nonwhites was furthered.[28] In Brazil, whiteness is clearly not marked by a similar level of "purity" or exclusivity.[29] For example, many whites, when given the chance in an open-format survey context, actually prefer to self-classify as *moreno*, that ambiguous "nonwhite" identification that I addressed in Chapter 3.[30]

Nonetheless, as Sheriff reports, even though many Brazilians prefer not to self-classify or even other-classify according to a dichotomous racial scheme, they may be cognizant of the discourse on racism that employs that scheme.[31] Hanchard, as I mentioned earlier, writes that color is not "a free-floating signifier for Brazilians, but [operates] within long-standing parameters of white and *negro*."[32] Other scholars agree that underlying what is traditionally viewed as racial ambiguity may be a bipolar scheme that structures social interaction.[33] Hence, affirmative action administrators appear to be counting on Brazilians to indeed call on that posited underlying bipolarity and to distinguish race in *negro* and white.

However, even though "nonwhiteness" is correlated with disadvantage in Brazil and scholars perceive underlying bipolar dynamics, there do seem to be some issues with sorting the population into discrete dichotomous racial categories. Consider the following 2004 quota legislation at the federal university in Brazil's capital city, Brasília. It reads: "To compete for the openings reserved through the quota system for *negros*, a candidate should: be of brown or *preto* color, declare one's self *negro*, and specifically opt for the quota system for *negros*."[34] The candidate is then photographed. Subsequently, that photograph goes before a specially constituted committee made up of an anthropologist, a sociologist, a student representative, and three *negro* movement actors whose identities are kept *sub secreto*.[35] In reviewing the photographs, if the committee does not consider a candidate a *negro/a*, then he or she is disqualified. The applicant can, however, appeal the decision and appear in person before the committee to argue his or her racial classification.[36] Similarly, the State University of Mato Grosso do Sul has also adopted the use of photographs and a verification committee for a quota system.[37] At that institution, the committee is made up of two university representatives and three *negro* movement ac-tors.[38] At least two other universities (Federal University of São Paulo and of Paraná) mandate personal interviews with a special committee to verify an applicant's racial classification.

These unusual modi operandi surely stem from the racial ambiguity born of a context that for approximately 140 years has officially embraced multi-racial categorization. At present, about 40 percent of the national population self-classifies in an intermediate category in the national census, and outside the constraints of the survey contexts, Brazilians prefer a multitude of color labels, as shown in Chapter 3. In an apparent effort to reduce that ambiguity in Brazil, affirmative action policies are centrally adopting, then, monoracialism. The generally stated intention of the policies is to include browns and *pretos*.[39]

The use of photographs and a verification committee are controversial measures due in part to parallels in de jure discrimination of past racist so-cieties.[40] Of course, the central and dramatic difference is that in Brazil the policies address the *inclusion* of a subordinate population, not its *exclusion*.[41] Nonetheless, they have stirred great debate in Brazil.[42] Moreover, even these boards of "race experts" appear to have problems sorting into *negro* and white. Consider the following two cases.

Testifying to the tenuous character of the verification process, the national media in Brazil reported in 2007 that two *identical* twin brothers declared themselves *negros* for quotas at the University of Brasília, and only one had that race status certified. They were part of a group of 3,791 students that de-clared themselves *negros* and requested quota inclusion. Of that group, 1,551 were rejected, and sixty-nine of those rejected individuals appealed to the photograph-examination board to argue their racial classification. On further deliberation, the committee certified the formerly excluded twin as a *negro*, as it also did for twenty-two other students whom the board had previously clas-sified as non-*negros*, that is, by default, whites.[43]

Similarly, in another case, two siblings (not twins) also applied for *negro* quotas at the University of Brasília, and again one was rejected.[44] The rejected sibling went so far as to sue the university, and a federal judge heard her case. Because it reached beyond the anonymous and confidential race board at the University of Brasília, there is a record of testimony of the applicant as well as from a participant from the race examination board. The university com-mission's rejection, according to that race board member called to testify, was based on the fact that although the rejected sibling may be of brown color, in her interview before the commission she contradicted her previous signed declaration of being a *negra*.[45] Her brother, of the same color *parda*, did claim to be a *negro*. In his ruling, according to the judge, it would be absurd to consider two siblings of identical color, born of the same family, to be of two different "races." In addition, the judge wrote that "the criteria for defining a person as a member of the *negro* race are still not sufficiently defined." The formerly rejected sibling, then, won her case.

Hence, racial sorting, even when carried out by official race boards of "experts" in racial classification, does appear problematic and to be an issue meriting empirical exploration. As the two above-mentioned cases bear out, there may be material consequences to the introduction of de jure white versus *negro* racial classification for race-targeted policies in Brazil, namely, the exclusion of those not deemed *negro* enough by third parties or those who prefer not to discretely racialize their ambiguously raced bodies. Racial sorting, then, may not be a straightforward or unambiguous bureaucratic process. Before turning to the data, I briefly review literature addressing the sources of possible sorting errors when targeting specific populations for public policy intervention.

Sorting Error

Problems concerning dichotomous categorization for targeted intervention in Brazil may centrally stem from a phenomenon noted in the literature: a slippery mapping of beneficiary categories onto those disadvantaged populations that policies attempt to address.[46] I want to suggest here that this possible incongruity between the official map and the reality of disadvantage can result from both the application of "hard" concepts onto "soft" phenomena[47] and from a disconnect between policy and popular classification schemes.[48]

Regarding the former, Ford argues that group-keyed preferences must make "hard" the boundaries of "soft" or "muddy variables" for determining the exact dimensions of the targeted population.[49] When the population's targeted characteristic is its race, as opposed to sex for example, it may be especially difficult to delimit. He claims that sex-based differentiation permits a fairly consistent and empirically manageable classification. There is a clear biological grounding for unambiguous sexual differentiation in almost every case. (Questions of gender identification are a muddier area, but sex differentiation is of a different kind.) Removing the biology from race, as indeed we must, for there is no biology to support racial differentiation as a valid scientific endeavor, we are left with a socially constructed classification whose boundaries suffer from high levels of ambiguity, contingency, and subjectivity that fluctuate over time.[50]

A dramatic example of the problem of the combination of "hard" legal categories of race and "soft" racial identification dynamics is found in an exploration of the landmark *Plessy v. Ferguson* Supreme Court case of 1892. Obliviously, in this case, the state was sorting by race for exclusionary purposes as opposed to inclusionary ones, but the difficulty of discerning the race of "ambiguously raced bodies" or in "convert[ing] racial ambiguity into orderly legal categories" is similar to some of the dynamics Brazil is facing in its administration of de jure monoracial classification for race-targeted policy.[51] Golub points out that the context of this legal dispute was the city of New Orleans, whose population diversity and racial common sense were uniquely shaped by French and Spanish colonial histories. Present there were high rates of interracial sexual contact and a "racial hierarchy that followed the three-tiered pattern of the Spanish and French empires rather than the American two-tiered model."[52] It was in that context that Jim Crow laws of segregation resulted in the legal requirement for clear rules for defining racial classification in black and white. Golub writes, "The existence of growing interracial populations in the nineteenth century created difficulties for legislation designed to enforce the separation of the races";[53] thus the challenge posed by Plessy, whom the law considered one-eighth Negro. American race-thinking presupposed discrete or pure racial kinds. This thinking required, then, the hardening of racial boundaries through the denial of mixed-race heritages, thereby clearly delimiting ambiguously raced bodies. As a result, the imposition of Jim Crow witnessed a dynamic in which softer racial boundaries located on a color continuum were hardened into stark black versus white categories delimited by the rule of hypodescent.

Regarding the repercussion of a possible disconnect between policy and popular classification schemes for administering targeted public policy, de Zwart addresses this dynamic in the case of affirmative action in India.[54] That country's policies institutionalized a simple dichotomy in 1951 between "the backward" and "the forward" classes in a society with a multiplicity of highly salient caste distinctions. De Zwart comments that affirmative action strategies generally employ salient social categories that are used outside of the policy context to avoid some classification problems. Government officials did not do this in the Indian example on which he reports; rather, they instituted a "backward classes" category in an attempt to locate the central cleavage in that society as class based instead of caste based. Since then, according to de Zwart, officially appointed "Backward Classes Commissions" have continuously struggled to identify who actually deserves beneficiary status.[55]

Perhaps most pertinently, however, debates in the United States leading up to the 2000 Census also addressed the possible disjuncture between the rigid language of antiracism legislation and the slippery, subjective, and overlapping nature of racial classification, in part born of increasing rates of racial intermarriage and the increasing popularity of multiracialism. Reflecting on this phenomenon, Perlmann and Waters write:

> [T]he government, while relying on a subjective definition of race, also placed an unrealistic restriction on that subjectivity—only one race could be chosen (even as it routinely accepted multiple parental birthplaces and ethnic ancestries). In order to have clear-cut racial categories for legal purposes we have created a system of counting that ignores an increasingly widespread reality. Denying that members of different races marry is like treating them as members of different biological species . . . Yet we also have an interest in ensuring that civil rights legislation, which rests on clear counts of racial membership, is not hobbled by ambiguities.[56]

As a reflection of this tension, the stage was set for a struggle between multiracial social movements in the United States, which argued the right to self-identify as of mixed-racial heritage and sought to alter the official single-race classification scheme in the 2000 Census, and black movement actors who were strongly opposed to institutionalizing multiracialism. (Other civil rights organizations and representatives of Hispanics, Native Americans, and Asians and Pacific Islanders joined the black movement in their opposition to the adoption of multiracialism in the U.S. Census).[57]

These organizations and representatives argued, for example, that if multiracial categorization was institutionalized in the U.S. Census, the resulting disconnect between official classification and existing civil rights and other race-targeted legislation could leave vulnerable a population who may have previously been identified as black.[58] Perlmann and Waters write that "If, for example, a person who is black can be counted in various ways, it will be much harder to enforce laws promoting racial equality—antidiscrimination efforts, affirmative actions, and voting rights could all be affected."[59]

Due in large part to black movement opposition, the multiracial category option was defeated. Instead, a compromise was reached allowing citizens to

"mark one or more" races in the 2000 Census. This format was judged preferable for protecting race-targeted legislation as it could be partnered with a
system of "aggregation and allocation" to revert the effects of the new format.[60] Under that system, anyone self-classifying in more than one race in
the U.S. Census can be bureaucratically reclassified back into single-race categories, thereby overcoming the gap between official and popular classification schemes. The process laid out by the Office of Management and Budget's
guidelines for aggregation and allocation reads, "Federal agencies will use
the following rules to allocate multiple race responses for use in civil rights
monitoring and enforcement . . . Responses that combine one minority race
and white are allocated to the minority race."[61] In a sense, this method of
reallocation essentially can be viewed as constituting a bureaucratic post hoc
reinstatement of the rule of hypodescent in the national census to establish
the legal racial status of ambiguously raced bodies.

Indeed, then, there appear to be serious issues to confront regarding sorting targeted racialized populations. In the specific case of Brazil, due to the
historic lack of race-targeted public policy and traditional racial ambiguity,
these issues are sure to surface, as indeed they have. In the following section,
then, I explore what may be consequences of deciding to sort into "black and
white" in a context where the vast majority of the population of some degree
of African ancestry self-classifies as "neither black nor white."[62]

Findings

This analysis focuses on attitudes toward differing formats of color or race
classification, race-targeted policy, and, importantly, the relationship between
these two, to detect the possible consequences of obligatory dichotomous racial sorting for the identification of affirmative action beneficiaries. Employing the 2002 PESB data set, six survey items refer to color or race in open-
ended, official census, and dichotomous formats, the latter two according to
both self- and other-classification. The open-ended and census formats were
reported in Chapter 3, along with other-classification in the census format according to photographs. I will briefly recall those results here for comparison
to the novel dichotomous format questions. Question wording for all survey
items is listed in Table 8.1 (in their order of appearance in the survey).

Table 8.1 Survey items on racial classification and race-targeted policy

Survey item	Format
1. What is your color or race?	Open
2. Which of these terms best describes your color or race?	Census
3. What is your color according to *preto* or white? (Restricted to census browns.)	Dichotomous
4. What is the color or race of each one of the photographed individuals?	Census
5. What is the color of each individual using only *preto* and white?	Dichotomous
6. Which person (or persons) deserves to get a good public sector job through quotas?	Eight photos

SOURCE: PESB 2002.

Classification Schemes

Self-Classification. Official classification in the census format (item 2, Table 8.1) offers a baseline measurement for comparison. It is very important, for, as put forth by the head of the Ministry of Racial Inequality, the state views *negros*, the proposed beneficiaries of race-targeted policies, as those who self-classify as brown or *preto* in the census format.[63] In Table 3.2, we saw that when presented with the ternary census choices, the sample self-classified in the following way: 49 percent white, 39 percent brown, and 12 percent *preto*. Hence, in the state's formulation, *negros* would total 51 percent of the sample. However, when given an open-ended choice, Table 3.2 revealed a dynamic that is well documented in Brazil: a preference for noncensus terms in the general population. In that format, the *moreno* category stands out at 24 percent of the overall sample population. Of note, the noncensus *negro* term draws a significant percentage of the sample at 8 percent. Category switching and a demonstrated preference for noncensus terms in the open format also means, of course, that the census terms lose membership: The white category loses 6 percentage points (from 49 to 43); the brown, 23 (from 39 to 15); and finally the *preto* category shrinks to only 3 percent of the sample population, down from 12 in the official format.

We can draw at least two important conclusions from these first two classification schemes. First, they attest to the "problematic" inconsistency of racial categorization in Brazil that race-policy administrators face.[64] Most importantly, though, they reveal that in a population in which 57 percent prefer nonwhite categories in an open format, or in which 51 percent would theoretically be deemed *negros* by the state using the census format, only 8 percent show preference for the *negro* category when given a chance to choose freely. These results hint at the possible disconnect between official policy and popular classification schemes.

Sorting Photographs.   As noted earlier, a few universities have resorted to race classification committees or in-person interviews to establish race status for quota inclusion. Hence, other-classification dynamics in Brazil become very important to understand. The color sorting of photographs of individuals spanning the color continuum (see Figure 3.1) mimics some of the dynamics that may be involved, especially in those contexts that employ the use of photographs, as mentioned above. Results presented in Table 3.5 reveal how respondents classified the photographs according to the census format (Table 8.1, item 4). It reveals generally high levels of agreement among respondents (close to 90 percent) as to who should be classified as white, brown, and *preto* as regards seven out of eight photos. Photograph 4 was the only one that divided opinions more significantly: Twenty-five percent said he was white, 73 percent said he was brown. According to these results, and considering that the intent of racial quotas to include the population of varying degrees of African ancestry, that is, browns and *pretos*, the individuals in photographs 5, 6, 7, and 8 undoubtedly meet the color criterion. In addition, three-fourths of the sample claimed that even the individual of photograph 4 was brown and hence theoretically deserving of quota inclusion.

Quota administrators, however, are called on to sort according to a binary vision and division of the population. Census whites should theoretically fall on one side of that divide, and census browns and *pretos* should move to the other side. Mimicking the other-classification dynamics of the race classification boards, the survey asked respondents to divide the sample along a binary cleavage (Table 8.1, item 5).

The survey's question format for this experiment used the terms white versus *preto* rather than white versus *negro* found in some race-targeted legislation. The use of the white versus *negro* format would have been preferable. Nonetheless, studies reveal that, although the two terms may be differentiated by affirmative action administrators, who suggest that *negro* subsumes both the brown and *preto* census terms, this distinction may be somewhat context specific. Júnior, for example, claims that "*negro* and *preto* are synonymous" in everyday language.[65] Moreover, Telles writes, as reported earlier: "*Negro* in the popular system, like *preto*, refers only to those at the darkest end of the color continuum."[66]

Moreover, I present a cross-tabulation of those who self-classified as *negro* and those who self-classified as *preto* in the open-ended question by a skin-tone measure that I detail below. The results will confirm the lack of differentiation between these two categories in terms of location along the color continuum in the 2002 survey context.[67] Finally, I present results below from a localized 2003 survey in Brazil involving a group of affirmative action candidates that reveal that when brown candidates were asked to self-classify as *negro* for beneficiary inclusion, they reacted very similarly to the way browns did toward the *preto* term in the PESB survey.[68] Hence, I believe that available evidence suggests that the use of the *preto* term in a *constrained* white versus *preto* survey format in 2002 should have invoked fundamentally similar racial understandings as would have a white versus *negro* format, although the popular connotations of these terms may be currently shifting.

Interestingly and as noted, administrators in Rio de Janeiro chose the combination "brown and *negro*" as beneficiary categories in 2001. *Negro* was clearly a substitute for the *preto* term in that formulation. The actual quota categories vary throughout the new legislation and discourse about affirmative action, from *afro-descendente* (Afro-descendant) or *afro-brasileiro* (Afro-Brazilian), which César defines as "*negros, pretos* and browns," to browns and *negros*, to just *negros*, and, finally, to browns and *pretos*.[69] The assumed legislative intent in each case is to include as beneficiaries those defined by the census as browns or *pretos*.[70]

The results presented in Table 8.2 present some problems for sorting Brazilians into a dichotomous format for affirmative action. Overwhelmingly, photographs 1, 2, and 3 (column 1) were judged as whites, and photographs 7 and 8 as *pretos* (column 2). However, photographs 4, 5, and 6 present some problems. Well over one-third of the respondents now define the individuals in photographs 5 and 6 as white, and about three-fourths of the respondents claim that the individual in photograph 4 is white. Three-fourths had considered the individual in photograph 4 to be brown in the census format question.

These disagreements highlight a substantial potential problem: Significant swaths of the population who should be eligible for race-targeted benefits when judged according to the color yardstick of being either brown or *preto* might easily be denied assistance under a system imposing dichotomous racial

Table 8.2 Percent distribution of other-classification of photographs in dichotomous format: Adult population in Brazil, 2002 (row-percentaged)

Photograph	White	Preto
1	99.3%	0.7%
2	98.0	2.0
3	96.8	3.2
4	73.5	26.5
5	37.5	62.5
6	37.4	62.7
7	1.2	98.8
8	1.0	99.0

SOURCE: PESB 2002, data adapted from Bailey 2008.

divisions. In other words, in this other-classification experiment, browns and *pretos* do not straightforwardly collapse into one side of the dichotomous scheme. Brazilians clearly disagree with one another about where to draw the line between whiteness and blackness.

Self-Classification into a Binary Divide.   Other-classification is not the most frequently used format for establishing racial classification status in Brazil for the administration of race-targeted quotas. Self-classification is definitely the preferred mode. Self-classification is also, of course, the long-accepted procedure in the United States. Hence, I return to that more accepted format and explore whether *self*-classification into a constrained white versus *preto* scheme facilitates the inclusion of browns for race-targeted quotas.

Respondents who self-classified in the mixed-race brown category in the census format (item 2, Table 8.1) were asked to reclassify as either white or *preto* (item 3, Table 8.1). In that very novel experiment, fully 44 percent of respondents who formerly said that they were brown now opt for the white category, while 56 percent reclassified in the nonwhite category *preto*.

This is an intriguing result. It forces a binary vision onto the population's general custom of ternary categorization, potentially leading some legitimate quota beneficiaries to lose that possibility due to a preference for the wrong side of that divide. However, does this survey experiment really capture *self*-exclusionary dynamics on the part of browns? That is, would these mixed-race individuals act in that same way even when faced with real loss in a real-world situation? Or does the use of *preto* as opposed to *negro* in the 2002 survey item somehow vitiate the experiment?

Table 8.3 Percent distribution of self-classified whites, browns, and *pretos* of the census format choosing to self-identify as *negro* for affirmative action inclusion, 2003

Self-Classification in Census Format	N	Identify as Negro for Beneficiary Inclusion
White	304	3%
Brown	296	46
Preto	289	97

SOURCE: Adapted from Rosemberg 2004, International Program of Graduate Scholarships of the Ford Foundation (*Programa Internacional de Bolsas de Pós-Graduação da Fundação Ford*).

I present results from that localized survey in 2003 of a students applying for affirmative action scholarships mentioned earlier that suggest the validity of the 2002 PESB format and the self-exclusionary dynamic that it may capture on the part of browns, as reported by Rosemberg.[71] On being asked to self-classify as *negro* (as opposed to *preto*) to gain beneficiary status, approximately half of 296 self-classified browns did so (at 46 percent) while the other half (51 percent) excluded themselves from *negro* benefit status, as shown in Table 8.3. In addition, and tellingly in terms of the similar connotations of *negro* and *preto*, of the 289 self-classified *preto* candidates, 97 percent chose to reclassify as *negros* for inclusion. The percentage of browns that opted to reclassify as *negro* in the 2003 survey, then, is very similar to the percentage of browns in the PESB sample who opted for the *preto* term, that is, roughly half. Hence, the two surveys appear to capture almost identical self-exclusionary dynamics on the part of browns asked to reclassify as either *pretos* or *negros*.

However, are the browns who opt for whiteness so different in terms of skin tone from those who opt for the *preto* category that the general population might likely not consider them eligible candidates for racial quotas structured by dichotomous categorization anyway? I can address this question by cross-tabulating brown respondents, divided into their chosen white and *preto* categories, by the skin tone variable (Table 8.4). To operationalize skin tone I use two survey items. First, I employ item 4 (Table 8.1), which asked respondents to classify the photographs according to the white, brown, and *preto*. Using respondents' *combined* opinions, I positioned the photographs along a continuum lightest to darkest.[72] Because some of the photographs occupied almost identical positions along the continuum, I collapsed categories to form a five-point spectrum. The skin tone categories are as follows: "very light" (photograph 1), "light" (photographs 2 and 3), "light medium" (photograph 4), "medium" (photographs 5 and 6), and "dark" (photographs 7 and 8).

Table 8.4 Percent distribution of self-classification in white and preto by skin tone for self-classified browns: Adult population in Brazil, 2002

Skin tone	White	Preto
Very light	3.2%	1.0%
Light	20.7	5.7
Light medium	41.9	30.3
Medium	31.6	51.2
Dark	2.7	11.8
TOTAL	100.0	100.0
N	361	456

SOURCES: Bailey 2008, PESB 2002.

The results in Table 8.4 show that the brown-to-white individuals have lighter skin tones on average than the brown-to-*preto* individuals. For example, whereas 21 percent of browns who reclassified as white have a "light" skin tone, only 6 percent of browns who reclassified as *preto* share that color. However, fully one-third of the former claim to look like the individuals in photographs 5, 6, 7, or 8, who all have medium or dark skin tones. These individuals challenge any notion of white category exclusivity. Another 42 percent of the brown-to-white population self-classify as having a "light medium" skin tone, like the individual in photograph 4, which appears particularly ambiguous. However, that same "light medium" skin tone also characterizes 30 percent of the brown-to-*preto* population. Hence, neither the exclusivity of the white category nor the clearly "darker" tone of the *preto* category has been maintained.

Who Deserves Quotas?

The PESB survey also contained a very unique question regarding the public's opinion on what type of person would be deserving of inclusion in a racial quota system. Respondents were asked to look at each photographed individual and opine as to just that (Table 8.1, item 6). I present the percent distribution of "yes" opinions on each photograph. This item allows an exploration of the direct effect of a potential recipient's skin color on those opinions. That is, what color of person actually deserves to be a beneficiary in the minds of the survey respondents?

Table 8.5 shows the percentages of the sample who support the inclusion as a quota beneficiary of the individual in each photo.[73] Results show that, according to the PESB sample, not all nonwhite individuals deserve *negro* quo-

Table 8.5 Percent distribution of opinions on which photographed individuals deserve a public sector job through a quota system by skin tone: Adult population in Brazil, 2002

Photo	Skin tone	Deserves Quota
1	Very light	26.6%
8	Light	24.6
7	Light	26.8
4	Light medium	26.7
5	Medium	34.2
2	Medium	30.1
3	Dark	61.1
6	Dark	64.9

SOURCES: Bailey 2008, PESB 2002.

tas. Only about a third of respondents believe that the two medium skin-toned individuals of photographs 5 and 6 deserve inclusion. Recall that overwhelming majorities of the sample earlier had categorized these two individuals as browns. The only two individuals whom a significant majority of the sample (over 60 percent in each case) say deserve quotas are those in photographs 7 and 8, the two with the darkest skin tones. These results clearly suggest the possibility that many browns might be excluded from beneficiary status due to third-party judgments.

In some sense, however, these results are not surprising, for state actors have chosen to institutionalize the less salient term *negro* to designate beneficiaries in much of the affirmative action policies. But, as I suggested earlier, that term may refer more to the darker end of the color continuum in the population's mind-set rather than to the entire nonwhite population, as the state stipulates. To illustrate this disconnect between bureaucratic and popular classification schemes, I turn to results presented in Table 8.6. It is a cross-tabulation of individuals who self-classify as *negro* and those as *preto* in the open-ended question by the skin-tone variable (columns 1 and 2). The table reveals that, in terms of skin tone, 51 percent of *negros* and 52 percent of *pretos* say that they possess the same skin colors as the dark skin-toned individuals of photographs 7 and 8. In contrast, only about 6 percent of browns (column 3) claim to look like the individuals in those two photos. Brown, then, appear to be located differently along the dark to light color continuum than *negros* and *pretos*.[74] Hence, it is almost obvious that, when asked who deserves

Table 8.6 Percent distribution of select categories of color-race from the open format by skin tone: Adult population in Brazil, 2002

Skin Tone	Negro	Preto	Brown	White
Very light	1.0%	1.0%	0.8%	40.2%
Light	2.8	0.0	11.6	42.1
Light medium	11.6	10.2	43.8	14.7
Medium	33.7	36.9	38.1	2.9
Dark	50.9	51.9	5.7	0.3
TOTAL	100.0	100.0	100.0	100.0
N	160	67	351	969

SOURCES: Bailey 2008, PESB 2002.

quotas, in most affirmative action legislation that targets *negros*, only those of the darkest skin tone receive significant support. This finding suggests a real disconnect between official state race categories and the categories embedded in the general population's racial common sense. Because Brazilian society may be keyed more toward *negro* as a dark color as opposed to a collective nonwhite racial group, the very language of the quota legislation may prejudice the possible inclusion of browns.[75] The state's map and the population's racial landscape diverge.

Discussion

What, then, are the possible consequences of institutionalizing binary racial categorization for the administration of race-targeted policy in a traditionally mixed-race society? Will the adoption of the dichotomous format achieve the legislative intent of identifying the nonwhite population for targeted intervention, thereby resulting in a match between the state's official map (racial categories in *negro* and white) and the real distribution of racial disadvantage?

State and movement actors clearly posit a binary vision of "races" in Brazil. For example, the Secretary of Racial Inequality Matilde Ribeiro writes, "the *negra* population is made up of those who self-classify as *pretos* and browns."[76] My results indicate, however, that the general public may experience that binary racial divide quite differently, possibly making beneficiary identification problematic. I found that in an open format question, 57 percent of the sample self-classified in nonwhite categories, but only 7 percent did so in the *negro* category. When those who self-classified as browns were forced into opting for one side or another of that racial divide, fully 44 percent preferred the white category. Moreover, a very significant portion of these newly self-declared whites (one-third) claimed to have the medium and dark skin tones that Ribeiro, Nascimiento, and others claim are marks of *negro* race membership; in addition, a third of the browns who chose to move to the *preto* side of the racial divide were of medium light skin tones. Finally, mixed-race individuals did not fare well when it came to the respondents' opinions on who deserves *negro* quotas—a majority of the sample would exclude them from such benefits.

These results suggest a real disconnect between the state's attempt to map racial disadvantage and its actual distribution in Brazilian society. That is, a significant portion of the brown or mixed-race population could suffer exclusion from racial quotas in Brazil either through self- or other-elimination due to the problematic nature of the *negro* category. Self-elimination would be the case when a brown individual does not view him- or herself as a *negro or negra* and hence not a member of the beneficiary population. Burdick has examined this dynamic closely, which he conceptualizes as "color-identity alienation" or, in the view of *negro* movements actors, "the refusal of the majority of Afro-Brazilians to acknowledge their blackness."[77] According to Burdick, as reported earlier, the *negro* movement's insistence that all nonwhites call themselves *negros* hampers the antiracism agenda. As one of his subjects reported, "I could call myself *negra*, . . . but I just don't feel it." Would a brown individual continue to view him- or herself as a non-*negro* or non-*negra* when material benefits are at stake? The data cited from Rosemberg's study revealed that only 50 percent of students who had previously self-classified as brown using the census format later opted to self-classify as *negro* in the dichotomous format to qualify for benefits.[78] It appears, then, that self-elimination of potential beneficiaries is a significant possibility.

As regards other-elimination, well over a third of sample respondents viewed the individuals in photographs 5 and 6 as white. In addition, two-thirds said that people with a similar skin color to those two photographs do not deserve quotas, including 60 percent of those who claimed to be that color. The actual criteria used to evaluate *negro* status by the verification commissions at the Universities of Brasília and Mato Grosso do Sul are not totally known.[79] In a 2007 interview, the rector of the University of Brasília stated, "The [racial classification] board is going to interview and opine if the candidates meet the requisites for *negros* and *pardos*. The selection is based on appearance, on the phenotype of the student."[80] According to a *negro* movement member of the Mato Grosso do Sul commission, a *negro* or *negra* was judged to be a person with a "flat nose, large lips, and coarse hair."[81] My data suggest, however, that the rejection of some browns may be a real possibility, as the experience of the identical twins and the two siblings with the race board at the University of Brasília I mentioned earlier suggests.

I argue, then, that these self- and other-elimination dynamics in part result from a slippery mapping of policy categories that speak of *negros* in a dichotomous scheme onto the racially continuous and ambiguous common sense of the majority of Brazilians.[82] State and *negro* movement actors have opted for targeting the population as a collection of races. From that racialist perspective, that option conceives of distant, diffuse, and multiple ancestries as singular and enduring, as African or European. It then equates those distilled ancestries with races in *negro* and white. Finally, that race option verifies race membership through a color scheme using a white/less-than-white palette. However, ordinary Brazilians, who continually invoke multiple color differences, neither equate these differences with singular ancestral divides, as I laid out in Table 4.3, nor with dichotomous understandings of race or color.

The possible exclusion from racial quotas of a significant portion of the brown population in Brazil either through self-elimination or third-party decisions may seem unproblematic for those who might argue that it is the darker population (represented by photographs 7 and 8) who are really disadvantaged and hence deserving of racial quotas. However, as mentioned earlier, some studies dispute the existence of a "mulatto escape hatch," that browns in Brazil are significantly better off in terms of many socioeconomic indicators than census *pretos*.[83] Moreover, the stated intention of the policies is to include self-declared browns and *pretos*.[84] Hence, browns' exclusion is clearly problematic if the logic of quotas is to target the underprivileged population of varying degrees of African ancestry.[85]

Why does it appear that Brazilians distinguish blackness from whiteness so differently in this constrained-choice survey context when compared to the way that is generally observed in the United States? I believe that historian Barbara Fields provides a key insight that may help explain this difference. She recounts the following anecdote from the United States of a young white boy's exchange with his mother regarding his description of an African American playmate to illustrate race socialization:

> The creators and re-creators of race include as well a young woman who chuckled appreciatively when her four-year-old boy, upon being asked whether a young [African American] friend whose exploits he was recounting was black,

answered: "No, he's brown." The young woman's benevolent laughter was for the innocence of youth. . . . It taught the little boy that his empirical description was cute but inappropriate.[86]

Fields recounts this anecdote to place in evidence the fact that "physical description follows race, not the other way around."[87] That is, as Washington claims, "Only she who is *disposed* to divine a 'difference' . . . divines it" [emphasis in original].[88] There is no obvious, natural dichotomous division between whites and blacks as structured by hypodescent, as we have so stridently developed in the United States.[89] That line is clarified only after the historic imposition of a race ideology that embeds its racial categories and rules of division in the population's racial worldview. The "black" or "African American" category is indeed generally efficient in the United States to identify black beneficiaries of race-targeted policy and to exclude whites. However, as Morning and Sabbagh remark, the United States is unique in that "the official use of racial categories preceded antidiscrimination legislation by three hundred years."[90] U.S. society had thoroughly internalized the rule of hypodescent via extreme and overlapping contexts of racial categorization over centuries before using that same rule for antidiscrimination purposes.

If dichotomous understandings of race do become the dominant racial ideology in Brazil, then the line between white and *negro* racial groups may eventually become as obvious for everyday Brazilians as it is for everyday Americans. Will that racial division, which Andrews calls a "North American vision of race" come to dominate?[91] In the next chapter I address just that question: the race-making effect of state policies of inclusion.

9   Race Making in Black and White

IN THE PREVIOUS CHAPTER, I examined the material consequences of adopting racial dualism for the administration of race-targeted policies, that is, the possible exclusion from benefits "qualifying" nonwhite individuals. I now turn to another type of consequence that could result from adopting de jure classification in white versus *negro*/nonwhite for these policies, but this time a symbolic effect as opposed to a material one. I frame as a symbolic effect the possibility that these policies will have repercussions for racial identification trajectories in Brazil. The importance of this issue cannot be overplayed. This is a time of racial category instability in Brazil born in large part of the political struggle of the *negro* movement to have its voice heard on issues of socioeconomic disadvantage but also in terms of its vision of the proper label for its proposed constituency. The passage of affirmative action legislation at dozens of universities throughout the country was and is an important *political stake* in the struggle against racialized disadvantage, as discussed in Chapter 7. However, I argue that, in addition, the legislation, which uses the idiom of the *negro* movement's vision of Brazilian racial dynamics in *negro* and white,[1] also constitutes a "*weapon*" in an ongoing "classificatory battle" to have that dichotomous worldview become central to the national racial common sense.[2]

That might seem a tall order for a society in which almost 40 percent of the population self-classifies as "neither black nor white" but somewhere in between. Through the adoption of de jure racial dualism for affirmative action policies, however, the *negro* movement has joined with an ally of considerable weight in the classification struggle—the Brazilian state. According to Bourdieu, states wield considerable "symbolic power" that can change the way individuals view their social world. The state's power is a force that can at times be employed "to impose the legitimate definition of the divisions of the social world and, thereby, to *make and unmake groups*" through institutionalizing social cleavages.[3] A state's decision to target specific social categories in public policy may be a good example.[4] As discussed in previous chapters, the *negro* movement in Brazil has historically struggled to build a *negro* constituency, a failure attributed in part to a low salience of "racial consciousness."[5] The new racial quota laws in Brazil could now help broaden that racial consciousness and solidify the *negro* movement's constituency.[6]

This chapter analyzes, then, the possible symbolic consequences of the introduction of race-targeted policies in Brazil through the lens of social scientific theories of "race making." By symbolic consequences, I mean specifically the institutionalization of a conceptual distinction that may "generate feelings of similarity and group membership."[7] According to Lamont and Molnár, symbolic resources, such as conceptual distinctions, interpretive strategies, and cultural traditions, can be harnessed for "creating, maintaining, contesting, or even dissolving institutionalized social differences."[8] To address possible symbolic consequences, I draw again on the 2002 national probability survey, which includes items on affirmative action and importantly captures possible classification repercussions from the introduction of those policies. This final empirical chapter, then, seeks centrally to understand the role of the state as a "group-maker" and specifically its role in "race making" through inclusive state policies.

Background

As discussed previously, there appears to be an historic lack of robust *negro* subjectivity in Brazil, typified in part by the embrace of the racially ambiguous, intermediate brown category in the national census. Many *negro* movement actors view this dynamic as problematic. Some research suggests that, regardless of the distinction between brown and *preto* within the color continuum, members of these two categories may be treated similarly by Brazil's informal systems of social stratification.[9] Findings regarding the similar structural position of browns and *pretos* go against the traditional belief in a "mulatto escape hatch" as theorized by Degler, that is, that an intermediate category provides an escape from the stigma of blackness.[10] Hence, movement actors note a common status of relative deprivation on the parts of browns and *pretos* (in relation to whites) in which they partly base their vision of racial divisions in that context.[11]

To challenge situations of collective disadvantage, researchers posit that strong collective identification is generally necessary.[12] This perspective is supported by Anthony Marx in his comparative examination of racial dynamics in Brazil, the United States, and South Africa. Marx writes, for example, "only when identity is consolidated does the logic of response to structural conditions apply."[13] In other words, only when Brazilians of varying degrees of African ancestry embrace race as a common social identity will they be likely to mobilize against racism.

This view of the need to embrace race as an identity to confront race-based discrimination is surely based in large part on the history of the struggle of the descendents of slaves to confront centuries of exclusion in North America. In that context, the eventual embrace of race for mulattos and Negroes, in the language of that period, as a counter-dominance identity and strategy can be clearly seen in events such as the Harlem renaissance of the 1920s and 1930s and reinforced by black pride movements of the civil rights era. Regarding the former, Davis writes, "The development of a new American black culture was both symbolized and led by the 'Black Renaissance' of the 1920s."[14] He claims that renaissance "was led by mulatto poets, novelists, musicians, dancers, and other artists who, in expressing black ideas and feelings, had implicitly adopted the one-drop rule."[15] This vision of a unified blackness had been rejected by Marcus Garvey, for example, who contended that "mulattoes were not really blacks," influenced by Jamaican dynamics where socially dominant mulattoes discriminated against "unmixed" blacks.[16]

The end result, then, according to Davis, was that African Americans implicitly embraced the one-drop rule (or were forced to do so) for discerning racial group memberships in black and white, a fact that continues today largely untouched. For example, when given the chance to recognize multiple racial heritages in the 2000 census, only about 1.6 percent of Americans did so, excluding Hispanics.[17] White and black Americans both were the least likely to avail themselves of this new format that many thought might actually challenge the one-drop tradition.[18] It has not seriously done so up to this point.

Why is "black" or *negro* racial group consciousness weaker in Brazil than in the United States and South Africa? Hanchard and Marx contend that, unlike in the other two cases, *negro* movement actors in Brazil did not have an explicit target against which to stimulate the construction of an oppositional *negro* identity, as I mentioned in Chapter 6 on the *negro* movement's struggle to build a constituency. The cases of the United States and South Africa were characterized by extreme de jure discrimination in the form of Jim Crow and apartheid. Scholars posit that those forms of blatant race-based exclusion ironically provided the conditions for their confrontation by the excluded through the embrace of race. In contrast, Marx writes of the Brazilian context:

> With no formal rules of racial domination, Brazil's social order has been maintained without presenting an explicit target for identity formation that might otherwise have provided an external basis for mobilization and redress. This presented activists with the difficult task of seeking to consolidate an identity unilaterally, which in the US and South Africa had been enforced by state policy and could be exploited by [minority] population leaders.[19]

How, then, could *negro* movement actors consolidate a *negro* race identity in Brazil that has lacked an explicit race-based approach by the state? Some, as explored earlier, have turned to the demonization of the myth of racial democracy to constitute a target. In addition, according to Marx, "to meet this challenge, activists turned to essentialist claims of African origins, trying to counter long-entrenched images of a physical continuum diluting racial identity."[20] One example of this turn is the project of reethnization of blackness that I described in Chapter 4. In the United States, due to centuries of exclusion and segregation, Americans of varying degrees of African ancestry constructed a common "community of culture" and of institutions, in Cornell's idiom discussed in that previous chapter. Recall that according to Hanchard, race-specific, self-sufficient institutions, such as black churches in the United States, are "the perverse silver-lining of racial segregation," supporting contrastive identity construction.[21] Due to this construction, Davis, for example, writes that African Americans are a "self-conscious social group with an ethnic identity."[22] In contrast, in Brazil, Sansone documents in his extensive ethnographic research that, in his words, Brazil is a case of "blackness without ethnicity."[23] *Negro* movement actors fight, then, to establish a unified *negro* identity through recuperating cultural symbols that had over the years been identified more with Brazilian national identity than exclusively an Afro-Brazilian community.

Before turning to the data to gauge the consequences of the new de jure classification in Brazil on identity formation, and beyond the *negro* movement's own efforts at identity construction, it is instructive to explore more systematically why Brazil's classifications have *not* been structured dichotomously, that is, why Brazilians have long embraced intermediacy. To do so, I briefly touch on two issues: the power of external categorization in the development of racial identification and how categorization has historically helped in the production of dichotomous racial classification in the United States, the illustrative case.[24]

Contexts of Categorization

To understand how social boundaries of division between populations are accomplished, I focus on the processes, principles, or mechanisms promoting boundary construction, as opposed to taking the existence of "races" for granted.[25] Viewing social identities as the result of internal and external dynamics that produce, maintain, or weaken boundaries,[26] several researchers who focus more intently on external definition examine those contexts where more powerful "others" exercise their power through labeling. In certain contexts, under certain conditions, these agents can promote social identification through naming, in effect a dynamic that can lead to the production of social groups *out of* social categories.[27]

To explore some of these processes, Jenkins examines "contexts of categorization," similar to Cornell and Hartmann's "construction sites," Tilly's "social sites" of boundary change, and to Bourdieu's sites of "objectification."[28] These are social spaces or practices that structure interaction along categorical lines. Jenkins proposes a typology of these contexts organized on a continuum from most informal (routine public interaction) to the most formal (official classification, for example, in national censuses).[29] Bourdieu frames the contexts slightly differently, as on the continuum between two extremes—the insult and official naming—in a process of "objectification."[30] Through structuring interaction along categorical lines, these contexts provide fertile ground for group formation.

Of course, the internalization of categorization is always contingent; we cannot clearly predict when a category of individuals may assimilate, in whole or part, the terms by which it is defined by an "other." Several scenarios are possible, based on factors such as the authority of the categorizer and whether force is used.[31] Regarding the former, the ultimate authority in any territory is the state; and, as I will argue below, its symbolic power is key for turning categories into groups. However, also important for that process can be the "mutual reinforcement of categorization in overlapping social contexts."[32] That is, in some instances, the conversion of a category into a group may be "over-determined" by the fact that the categorized are confronted with a definition of themselves in several important realms of interaction at the same time.[33]

In fact, in the following section I posit that "overdetermination" born of overlapping contexts of categorization may help explain in part the conversion of a category into a group in the United States in the exemplary case of the construction of the boundaries of the social identity embraced by African Americans. As I lay out those overlapping contexts of categorization, I show at the same time how those contexts differed in Brazil, leading to a different outcome.

Marking Boundaries through Hypodescent

The United States constitutes an illustrative case of creating a *category* of persons, African slaves and their descendents, into a robust *group,* African Americans. It did so through employing the rule of hypodescent, defined by the U.S. Census Bureau for the 1860 Census, for example, as moving into a nonwhite category "all persons having any perceptible trace of African blood."[34] Some researchers argue that "the rule [of hypodescent] is unique in that it is found *only* [emphasis added] in the United States and not in any other nation in the world."[35] In this section, I lay out the historical "contexts of categorization" that may have significantly contributed to the development of the boundaries of race in the United States and see how those contexts were either absent or differed significantly in Brazil.[36] I posit that an exceptional combination in the United States of the racial defense of slavery, race science, census race categorization, and race legislation over a period of some 300 years came together to help most rigorously produce racial group subjectivity in black and white. Although none of these contextual factors in and of itself was a sufficient cause for its development, and although these are intimately interconnected phenomena, I briefly lay out each separately.

Racial Defense of Slavery.   One difference that may help account in part for the unique understanding of race in the United States compared to Brazil was the fact that the United States combined slavery with *radical* republicanism.[37] Wacquant writes that a way had to be found for "reconciling the 'self-evident truth' that 'all men are created equal' and endowed 'with certain unalienable rights' with the arrant violation of these very same truths by the bondage of millions of blacks."[38] A radical disqualification was needed to exempt African Americans as candidates for equality, and race became the system on which this disqualification was based. Thus, Americans took part in an elaborate racial defense of slavery. It had to be stipulated that blacks were "racially inferior to whites and therefore natural slaves."[39] According to Degler, "many hours of mental labor and many pages of print were consumed in developing and propagating a racial defense of slavery in the US."[40] The resultant radical "other" ontology of slaves as race not only justified their enslavement, but it followed that racial mixing was an unnatural act and its product also unfit for equality with whites. Conveniently, this disqualification also meant the extension of property rights over mixed progeny.

In Brazil, slavery coexisted with monarchism rather than republicanism. There was only a philosophy of hierarchy, and, therefore, no need to rigorously defend differing levels of social status.[41] Nobles comments, "Abolitionist rhetoric [in Brazil] focused little on race as such, mostly because the supporters of slavery did not defend it in terms of the racial inferiority of non-whites or their suitability as slaves. They argued, when required to argue at all, that slave labor was the basis of the country's economy."[42] A republican form of government was not installed in Brazil until 1889, a year after the official abolition of slavery. In the United States, there was almost a full century of radical republicanism and slavery (1776 through 1865).

Race Science.   At the time of the dawn of the U.S. nation, the racial divide posited by advocates of slavery was still a folk perspective. Importantly, in the mid-nineteenth century, race science began to make its way onto the scene, coinciding with a growing antiabolitionist movement.[43] This new influence of science "substantiated and strengthened the ideology of race, reifying it as part of a natural ordering system."[44]

Helping to effectuate this reification was the American School of Ethnology. It brought polygenism, or the belief in the existence of a number of different human species of separate origins, to the forefront in the early-nineteenth-century United States.[45] Polygenists were particularly interested in the result of black and white racial species intermixing—mulattos. These scientists were obsessed with mulatto degeneracy and purported to demonstrate, for example, higher rates of madness and shorter life spans of mulattos due to their biologically degenerate nature. Even with the arrival of Darwinism, "American scientists remained deeply committed to the distinctness of races."[46] For example, even if all humans had common ancestors, this did not mean that each race had evolved with the same capacities. In this way, Darwinism did not replace polygenist thought about race and racial mixture but joined it. For

American polygenists, mulatto frailty was paramount: The mixed type was bound to either die off or revert back to the "dominant type," the black race.[47]

Some Brazilian race scientists in the late nineteenth and early twentieth centuries stipulated the opposite. Instead of positing the absolute degeneracy produced by racial mixing, they argued that better living conditions and the power of "white blood" would lead to a gradual absorption of mixed-race individuals into whiteness.[48] In this way, miscegenation, unthinkable and prohibited in much of the United States, accomplished two positive outcomes in Brazil. It would strengthen the white stock for life in the tropics and also reduce the presence of the *negro* race, a combination leading to a whiter future for Brazil. This notion of biological whitening gradually subsided in the first half of twentieth-century Brazil. During those years, prominent social scientist Gilberto Freyre, for example, focused on the hybrid strength resulting from miscegenation. He believed that racial mixing was slowly creating a Brazilian "metarace," a *moreno* (brownish) people, not a white one. In this way he posited a bright future for Brazil, a future denied it by mulatto degeneracy theories popular in the United States.[49]

Meanwhile, in continuing to focus on mulatto degeneracy, U.S. race scientists furthered the nation's obsession with white purity, aided in a racial defense of slavery, and assured the mulatto's fate of relegation to the inferior black race. Interestingly, much of the evidence that U.S. race scientists brought to bear in their degeneracy investigations came from their use of the national census.

Census Categorization.   In response to the legislative need of representational apportionment in a nascent U.S. democracy, the first national census in 1790—almost a century before Brazil's first census in 1872—began sorting its population into citizenship-status categories of free white males, free white females, all other free persons, and slaves. However, it was in 1850 that the national census joined forces with race science to move decisively from considerations of citizenship status to the biology of race. The 1850 census introduced a separate slave schedule and added the mulatto category. Its introduction came at the bequest of race scientists who felt the need to muster evidence of mulatto degeneracy.[50] However, the influence of science on census category choice reached a high point in 1890, when race scientists convinced legislators to measure the exact degree of distance from pure whiteness of all individuals of mixed race, leading the census to reflect a "growing concern among southern politicians over racial purity."[51] Hence, the quadroon and octoroon categories were added.

In 1900, the census jettisoned those two categories due to their unwieldy na-ture.[52] In the 1930 U.S. census, the mulatto and black categories were collapsed into the single race category "Negro," and that definition of black racial group membership based in the rule of hypodescent would define U.S. understand-ings of race for the rest of the twentieth century.

According to Nobles, Brazilian census officials "emphasized racial 'mix-ture' with the same vigilance that their U.S. counterparts have emphasized racial 'purity.'"[53] Even though this emphasis on mixture was used by Brazil-ian elites to promote the idea of whitening, the Brazilian census never ad-opted the rule of hypodescent. There was simply less pressure to define the exact nature and boundaries of those social divisions in Brazil.

Race Legislation.   Following the brief and anomalous Reconstruction era in the United States, state and local legislatures responded to the new sta-tus of blacks with segregation laws and statutes that aimed to isolate them from access to white institutions. This radical exclusion was later enshrined by the 1896 *Plessy* precedent decision marking the ultimate support for de jure discrimination structured by hypodescent. The Supreme Court ruled against Homer Plessy, who presumed to ride in a coach reserved for whites. In that ruling, the Court took "judicial notice" of what was common knowl-edge: A Negro, or black, is any person with any black ancestry (even if only one-eighth, as was Mr. Plessy).[54] This landmark decision dovetailed well with budding Jim Crow legislation (enforced into the 1960s). Segregation laws were less concerned with distinguishing between blacks and mulattoes than with rigidly separating their social interactions from whites.

According to Degler, "The systematic separation of the races, whether le-gally or customarily, is a North American phenomenon. It has no analog in Brazil."[55] Racial discrimination, though, did continue in Brazil after slavery's abolition through informal mechanisms. In fact, as mentioned earlier, some point to a lack of a clear target, such as Jim Crow legislation, as one factor that hampered antiracism mobilization in Brazil.[56] In the Jim Crow United Staes, the civil rights movement finally brought an end to de jure discrimination and led to the enactment of legislation like the Voting Rights Act and race-based policy to counter centuries of exclusion. However, enforcement of that legislation would appear to require continuing to sort the nation's population by the very categories invented to protect white purity: race as defined by the perversity of the rule of hypodescent.[57]

In sum, in the United States, aided by a combination of the racial defense of slavery, race science, census race categorization, and race-based de jure discrimination, racialism defined by hypodescent has become an enduring feature of American thought and organization. Each of these factors constituted individually a formal context of racial categorization.[58] Overlapping one another, reinforcing and legitimizing the goals of each other, they helped to overdetermine the unique embrace of hypodescent in the United States.

Brazil's Adoption of Race-Based Policy

As we have seen, Brazil's history does not include those overlapping contexts of dichotomous classification structured by hypodescent. However, race-targeted policy based in dichotomous racial understandings is now ascendant. Most notably, no fewer than thirty state and federal universities are adopting a racial quota system to counteract the dramatic underrepresentation of nonwhites in higher education.[59] Quota systems are also being adopted in other realms, such as employment, and for actors in state-sponsored commercials.[60] These strategies are controversial[61] but appear to mark a growing trend. Moreover, in classifying in a single nonwhite or *negro* race category all mixed-race individuals with discernible African ancestry, administrators appear clearly to be moving toward the logic of the rule of hypodescent, as claimed by Skidmore: "they [Brazilian universities] have actually adopted the one-drop rule!"[62] Faced with this legislation, what might be the consequences of categorizing in a *negro* versus white format individuals who have long embraced racially ambiguous categorization?

Findings

This final empirical chapter looks at the possible consequences of the institutionalization of hypodescent on future classification tendencies. I approach this issue in two central ways. First, I compare how adopting a dichotomous format would alter the distributions of whites and nonwhites, as judged through the survey context. To do so, I compare distributions of folk, official, and dichotomous classification schemes from the 2002 PESB survey. That is, I compare the percentages of the sample who self-classified as white according to the open-ended format (folk scheme), the census format (official scheme), and the dichotomous format (structured by the logic of hypodescent).

Results, presented in Table 9.1, reveal that 43 percent of the sample chose to self-classify as white when given a chance in an open-ended question. That percentage rose to 49 percent in the official ternary format of the national census. However, in the dichotomous format, the proportion of whites rose to 67 percent of the sample population. What occurred in that binary experiment was that the white category became swollen with the 44 percent of self-classified browns who were made to choose between white and *preto* categories and chose the former, as reported in the previous chapter. The nonwhite population (census browns and *pretos*) were actually a slight majority, then, in the official format; according to the dichotomous format, they became a real minority population.[63] In a sense, then, forced classification in a dichotomous racial format appears to do more to whiten the Brazilian population overnight than all the years of the reign of the "whitening ideology."[64] Hence, the results suggest that a possible unintended consequence of forced dichotomous classification, as viewed from the *negro* movement perspective, could be a dramatic move toward whiteness in terms of an official accounting of the color composition of Brazilian society.

Second, I gauge the specific effect of the introduction of race-targeted policy on classification tendencies through an experimental survey method incorporated into the 2002 PESB questionnaire. This method consists of what is known as a split-ballot experiment. Instead of all respondents being subjected to the same questionnaire, two versions are employed, splitting the sample down the middle. In this way, when a variation, generally such as in word use or question format, is introduced in one and not the other, then the effect of that difference can be clearly discerned through comparing responses from the two versions.

In the PESB survey, only one version of the questionnaire (version 2) began the race relations module of that survey with a special text on the implementation of racial quotas for *negros*. That text read:

> The subject of color or race is very important in Brazil. The government is now creating quotas for public-sector employment for *negros* because they have had fewer opportunities than whites to obtain good public-sector jobs. Before this change, to get those public-sector jobs individuals took the same qualifying exams, and those scoring best got the job. Now *negros* are guaranteed some good public-sector jobs even though their exam scores may not be the best.

The interviewer read the text; and, immediately after having heard this text read aloud, respondents in that half of the sample began the race module of the survey with the same initial question with which the other half of the

Table 9.1 Percent distributions of whites, browns, and *pretos* by self-classification in open-ended, census, and dichotomous formats: Adult population in Brazil, 2002

	Open-Ended	Census	Dichotomous
White	42.7%	49.1%	66.7%
Brown	15.4	38.6	—
Preto	2.9	12.4	33.3
TOTAL	—	100.0	100.0
N	1,330	2,082	2,203

SOURCE: PESB 2002.

sample began (but without hearing the text): self-classification in the open format. Hence, we can detect whether the mention of the quota legislation in that text actually affected racial self-classification through comparing the answers of those who heard the text with those who did not hear it.

Table 9.2 presents frequency distributions of the open-ended format self-classification question by the two versions to isolate any difference in modes of self-classification that may have arisen as a result of the introduction of that text. To examine this question, we focus in on the pertinent *negro* term. The table shows that whereas in version one, the questionnaire given to those not hearing the text about affirmative action, 4.8 percent self-classified as *negro*, in version two that percentage rose to 8.8 percent of the split sample. Hence, in this survey context, it appears that the mere mention of racial quotas for *negros* nearly doubled the *negro* population.

This finding suggests, then, that singling out *negros* for race-targeted policies may result in significant growth regarding the percentage of those choosing to self-classify as such. Importantly, though, this possible trend growing the *negro* population needs to be considered in conjunction with the previous mentioned result showing that 44 percent of browns opt for whiteness when forced into the dichotomous format. That is, both findings together suggest that a *negro* classification may be consolidated and grow due to the necessity of self-classifying as *negro* to receive state-controlled resources, but its percentage of the overall population appears significantly limited by an opposing trend toward consolidating whiteness. The latter may constitute, then, an unexpected symbolic consequence of institutionalizing a dichotomous classification scheme in Brazil. That whiteness, though, would appear not to mirror whiteness in the United States, which is premised on white racial purity. In

Table 9.2 Percent distribution of self-classification in open-ended format and by questionnaire version: Adult population in Brazil, 2002

Color/Race	Version 1	Version 2
White	44.3%	41.1%
Moreno	24.9	23.1
Brown	14.8	16.1
Negro	4.8	8.8
Preto	3.4	2.4
Moreno claro	2.5	3.1
Amarelo	2.0	1.4
Mixed	0.7	1.0
Claro	0.8	0.8
Mulatto	0.5	0.8
Indian	0.2	0.6
Mestiço	0.4	0.1
Others	0.7	0.9
TOTAL	100.0	100.0
N	1,200	1,106

SOURCE: PESB 2002.

contrast, in Brazil the data suggest that the expansion of whiteness may be one characterized by the inclusion of many individuals of varying degree of African ancestry who previously self-classified as nonwhites.

Discussion

Boundary Effects

I began this chapter with one central question: What are the symbolic consequences of obligatory dichotomous classification for the administration of race-targeted policy in a society that has traditionally viewed itself as multiracial? Specifically, how might the institutionalization of that conceptual distinction affect social boundary change?[65]

Two results of my analysis are particularly relevant to this question. First, the distribution of color classification using the ternary census format places the white portion of the sample at 49 percent; however, when browns are forced into a binary racial scheme, the proportion of white increases to two-thirds (or 67 percent). In addition, using the split ballot experiment, the percentage of individuals choosing to declare themselves *negros* nearly doubled in that version of the questionnaire that planted the question of racial quotas for *negros* compared to the versions that did not mention quotas.

Regarding the effect of the racial quota question, are these fluctuations merely a result of a survey experiment, or will the distribution of resources along monoracial categorical lines truly affect classification dynamics in Brazil? Of course, estimating future trajectories is by definition speculative. Jenkins's and Tilly's framings on the power of categorization for the internalization of racial group subjectivity are instructive to further explore this issue.[66] In his typology of the contexts of categorization, Jenkins includes "administrative allocation," where rewards and penalties are distributed within and from public and private-sector formal organizations along categorical lines. Tilly addresses this same dynamic conceptualized as "incentive shift," or the distribution of "rewards or penalties that affect their pursuit of within-boundary relations, cross-boundary relations, and representations of the boundary zone."[67] Viewing race-targeted policy in Brazil as a formal "context of categorization" (or an instance of an "incentive shift" mechanism), there are at least three possible scenarios that deserve mention here in terms of how the institutionalization of dichotomous racial group categories may affect future classification trajectories: nonboundary effect, a reactive boundary effect, and a race-making effect.

Nonboundary Effect.   It may be the case that the institutionalization of racial group distinctions in *negro* and white fails to produce a "significant activation of social boundaries," what Tilly calls a "non-boundary effect."[68] That is, state-mandated categorization may not generate feelings of similarity and group membership. One way this nonboundary effect could play out would be if individuals choose to self-classify as *negros* only in the bureaucratic context where material benefits come into play but choose not to do so outside that context, that is, they do not internalize *negro* identification.

As a possible illustration of this scenario, recall the case presented in the previous chapter of the two siblings applying to the University of Brasília. Of the two, one was rejected while her brother was admitted. In appearing before the race-verification board, the rejected sibling, who had apparently claimed in her quota application to be of *parda* color and of the *negra* race, contradicted herself and this time claimed to be *parda* but not a *negra*. That is, even though her color and her brother's color were similar, the brother apparently accepted membership in the *negra* race (or at least was not pushed on this issue), but the sister did not do so consistently. The judge ruled in this case that it is the color criterion that should be decisive and not whether individuals state or "feel" *negra* race membership.[69] Others, too, without an emotional or philosophic attachment to a *negro* racial group, may simply claim a *negro* status for beneficiary inclusion.

One could frame such a dynamic as illustrating the operation of "simple self-interest" or attitudes that reflect the perception of possible "tangible losses or gains to an individual or his or her immediate family," as opposed to reflecting group-based sentiments.[70] In essence, it could be the case that self-interests trump group-based interests.

In addition, Jenkins claims that "categorization may be less likely to 'stick' where it is markedly at odds with existing boundaries."[71] That is, "de facto and de jure meanings . . . do not always match up," thereby at times thwarting official classification projects.[72] The category *negro* is not embraced by the vast majority of nonwhites in Brazil, as suggested by the data I present in previous chapters, because they do not see themselves as located easily within that category. Finally, as I argued in Chapter 4, racial categories and racialized culture are not strongly associated in that context. That is, I did not find evidence of a robust *negro* "community of culture" that might sustain collective *negro* identification; or, as framed by Sansone, blackness in Brazil is not robustly ethnicized.[73] Hence, these factors may negatively condition the internalization of the *negro* category.

Reactive Boundary Effect.   It could also be the case that the boundaries that are activated by affirmative action strategies in Brazil are not the ones that are institutionalized by the state, that is, named in the state's targeted policies. Instead, the official naming and targeting for state benefits of one population may stimulate the appearance of unnamed and even heretofore nonexistent "groups." Such a dynamic may be framed as an unintended consequence. Nagel writes regarding this type of reactive boundary effect:

> The political recognition of a particular ethnic group can not only reshape the designated group's self-awareness and organization, but can also increase identification and mobilization among ethnic groups not officially recognized, and thus promote new ethnic group formation. This is especially likely when official designations are thought to advantage or disadvantage a group in some way.[74]

Nagel frames this process of one of "resource competition"[75] and offers several examples, including the heightened ethnic self-awareness of whites in the United States in reaction to affirmative action policies for disadvantaged ethnic and racial minorities in that context.

De Zwart also illustrates a similar scenario in his study of the effects of affirmative action policies on identity formation in India and Nigeria.[76] He demonstrates how the state's naming and institutionalization of a certain category may produce no boundary effect in terms of the named category (that is, a nonboundary effect), but, yes, stimulate the unintended appearance of competing categories. In explaining how this could come to pass, he begins by claiming that affirmative action policies generally employ social categories that are commonly used outside the policy context. To the contrary, however, as noted in the previous chapter, India institutionalized a simple dichotomy in 1951 between "the backward" and "the forward" classes in a society with a multiplicity of highly salient caste distinctions. The idea was to get beyond caste and move toward categorization based on social class. The result, however, was the increased salience of caste identification as differing caste-based populations struggled for inclusion. He argues, then, that when state actors choose unpopular or nonsalient official umbrella categories to incorporate into public policy, contrary to unifying a population, the result can be to stimulate the appearance of competing splinter groups in the distribution fray. Hence, instead of simplifying classification schemes, forced classification in unpopular categories can have the opposite effect. De Zwart ironically finds that in the Indian case, "the collectivities that emerged are precisely those that replacement was meant to supersede."[77]

The example offered by de Zwart may be especially useful for understanding possible outcomes in Brazil due to the apparent lack of saliency for self-classification of the state's chosen *negro* term. The overwhelming majority of nonwhites who do not prefer this term, including those who outright reject it, may attempt to mobilize under a different banner, perhaps as mixed-race *mestiços* or *morenos*. There is, in fact, an organization that has formed under the name "*Movimento Pardo-Mestiço Brasileiro—Nação Mestiça*" (Brazilian Brown-Mestizo Movement—Mestizo Nation) that claims to fight for the rights of mestizos in Brazil and rejects the *negro* label.[78] According to their home page, they are:

> . . . a NGO dedicated, among other things, to the valorization of the process
> of miscegenation among the diverse ethnic groups from which Brazilian

nationality was born, to the promotion and defense of the brown-mestizo identity, and to the recognition of browns-mestizos as the cultural and territorial heirs of the peoples from whom they descended.

The seriousness or reach of this organization is hard to gauge at present, but, as I laid out in Chapter 3, the popularity of the *moreno* term is certainly undeniable. It consistently ranks as the second most popular category for self-classification in Brazil behind white without ever having been adopted by the state as an official census term.

While at this juncture a significant multiracial movement influencing a reactive boundary effect in Brazil is hard to imagine, the example of the United States is instructive. In that context, a very small multiracial movement waged an intense classificatory struggle and influenced a very significant change in the 2000 Census: the addition of the "mark one or more" races format to the racial composition question.[79] Seemingly insignificant movements can take flight, especially when backed by certain powerful political interests, as happened in the United States. In Brazil, the construction or strengthening of a mixed-race identity due to a nascent mixed-race movement reacting to the institutionalization of the *negro* term for affirmative action could permanently establish intermediate identification as wholly separate from *negro*. From a *negro* movement perspective, such a development would constitute a serious negative unintended consequence of the state's institutionalization of the *negro* identification.[80]

Race-Making Boundary Effect. The final possible scenario would be that of a direct boundary effect, in this case, a race-making effect in terms of those categorized as *negros*. According to Jenkins, the "targeting of resources and interventions at a section of the population which is perceived to have particularly urgent or specialized 'needs', may call into existence a new social categorization, or strengthen existing categorization."[81] Jenkins argues that this type of "administrative allocation" is particularly powerful for the internalization of externally defined categories because it makes categories really count in the lives of the categorized.[82] Simply structuring rewards (and penalties), then, along categorical lines can stimulate group boundary formation along the lines of *negro* subjectivity.

In addition, in the case of quotas in Brazil, these policies structure a zero-sum competition between groupings of individuals, and research, including that of Nagel mentioned above, shows that resource competition is a strong incentive for group making. As Banton remarks, "when people compete as individuals, this tends to dissolve the boundaries that may define groups; when they compete as groups, this reinforces group boundaries."[83]

The group-making effect resulting from race-targeted policy is indeed recognized in Brazil. For example, prominent University of São Paulo sociologist Antonio Sérgio Guimarães names identity construction as "one of the goals of affirmative action policies."[84] He writes that as Brazil establishes race-targeted policies, "the legislator will be helping to create, through legislation, the community [of *negros*] over which it seeks to legislate."[85] Moreover, as opposed to an act of inventing something new, many activists and researchers view strategies for strengthening *negro* racial subjectivity structured by a similar logic to that of the rule of hypodescent as "nothing more than a re-working of the substance of a group whose boundaries and identity have already been delimited by the system of racial domination."[86]

It is certainly unclear at this point, however, whether or not racial identification in *negro* and white will be widely internalized by Brazilians. Racial worldviews are bound by history and context.[87] The processes that led to the naturalization of white and black races as defined by hypodescent in the United States played out over centuries of overlapping contexts of categorization that generally have no clear parallels in Brazil. There was no strident racial defense of slavery, race science did not generally vilify race mixing, the national census did not employ monoracial categories, and de jure discrimination was never a part of Brazilian history in postabolition years. Without these processes, the internalization of hypodescent in Brazil is far from assured.

The Symbolic Power of the State

Nonetheless, even absent those historic processes, because the Brazilian state has now entered the arena of the officialization of race categories in *negro* and white, the probability of race making may be greater due to the legitimizing role a state plays. Scholars have long pointed to the role of states as "worldmakers."[88] As mentioned earlier, Bourdieu, for example, argues that states wield "symbolic power," constituted through social capital acquired in previous struggles, to make their visions and divisions of the social world "stick."[89]

Historically, state naming along racial lines has been most notably carried out for purposes of exclusion. Along those lines, Anthony Marx examines the state's power for race making in his influential book *Making Race and Nation: A Comparison of South Africa, the United States, and Brazil*. He writes:

> States then play a central role in imposing the terms of official domination, with unintended consequences. Official exclusion, as by race, legitimates these categories as a form of social identity . . . In the short run, such exclusion benefits those included and hurts others. But in the longer run, institutional exclusion may further reconsolidate subordinate identity and encourages self-interested mobilization and protest.[90]

From a very different optic but similar logic, I posit that in addition to creating identities by legislating *exclusion,* states also have the power to impose the terms of official *inclusion* that may have "world-making" capacity.[91] That is, official inclusion through institutionalizing race in social policy may legitimatize race as form of social identity; hence, the key role of the state in race making. This race-making argument resulting from state official categorization has also been made by Ford, for example, who points out its irony:

> But this attention [on the part of the state] may solidify the very social divisions beyond which preferential programs were ostensibly designed to move us. Many will thus doubtless suggest that there is something profoundly wrong with an "anti-discrimination" ethic which calls for such jurisprudential segregation and brands badges of racial identity onto the face of public life, insisting that the real problem lies deeper in the group-essentialist paradigm rather than merely at the level of procedural propriety.[92]

The efficacy of a state's symbolic power to "make groups" is not absolute, nor is the state alone in its effort to reorder racial categorization dynamics and effectuate boundary change in Brazil. Regarding the first issue, the efficacy of symbolic power depends in part on what Bourdieu calls the "theory effect."[93] This effect refers to the degree to which a proposed category resonates among the named due to its basis in "objective affinities" that characterizes them. That is, if there is some internal homogeneity and agreement of conditions that buttress an external ascription, the likelihood of group formation increases.[94]

An example of a "theory effect" can be found in Fields, who argues, for example, that in early colonial times the descendents of Africans were not enslaved because of race; rather, their enslavement under subhuman conditions later provided the "evidence" on which to name them as a race apart. She reasons that it was much more convincing to conceive a population as an inferior race when they were already oppressed, that is, the theory effect of labeling black slaves as a race was based "in [the] reality" of their common degradation.[95] Studies continually demonstrating the common relative disadvantage of browns and *pretos* in Brazil, then, may also provide a strong basis for a "theory effect" and hence increase the chance that the *negro* label will stick in Brazil.[96]

Moreover, as I commented earlier and also explored in Chapter 7, the state is joining with other actors to clarify racial boundaries in Brazil. It has "partnered" with both *negro* movements in this endeavor as well as with science, that is, with a significant sector of social scientists who have adopted the race concept in *negro* and white for social analysis—those ascribing to the racialist paradigm of scientific analysis. Each of those two actors, academia and social movements, also possesses levels of symbolic power and hence the ability to challenge the way the social world is conceptualized. Regarding movement actors, Brubaker points to categorizing actions of "ethnopolitical entrepreneurs":

> By *invoking* groups, they seek to *evoke* them, summon them, call them into being. Their categories are for doing—designed to stir, summon, justify, mobilize, kindle, and energize. By reifying groups, by treating them as substantial things-in-the-world, ethnopolitical entrepreneurs may, as Bourdieu notes "contribute to producing what they apparently describe or designate."[97]

Similarly, Petersen writes: "A transition from category to group is usually pioneered by a small band of intellectuals, who may propagandize for decades or perhaps generations before their arguments are accepted, if ever, by the sector of the population of which they have appointed themselves representatives."[98]

Regarding the participation of science in boundary-clarification dynamics, the early works of social demographers Hasenbalg and Silva in the late 1970s and 1980s clearly illustrate that process.[99] Hasenbalg and Silva began analyzing quantitative data on racialized discrimination and found that the utility of the ternary color division captured in the national census (white, brown and *preto*) was not supported by their analyses. Instead, they began to collapse brown and *preto* into a category "nonwhite" in juxtaposition to white. Silva wrote, "to consider blacks [*pretos*] and mulattoes [browns] as composing a homogeneous 'nonwhite' racial group does no violence to reality. Rather than being a mere simplification, the joint analysis of Blacks and mulattoes constitutes a sensible approach to the analysis of racial discrimination in Brazil."[100]

Silva and Hasenbalg, then, modified the boundary debate by providing a strong basis for a binary vision of discrimination dynamics in Brazil. Subsequent social researchers of the racialism stage that I laid out in Chapter 2 carry the work of Silva and Hasenbalg into another dimension, however, when they label "nonwhites" as members of a *negro* racial group.[101] The move is from color to race, from an attempt to capture skin-color variation to the adoption of something very similar to the rule of hypodescent for dichotomous racial identification in Brazil. Interestingly, Hasenbalg states (in a published interview with Guimarães), "It should be added that when we [Hasenbalg and Silva] study [racial] inequalities juxtaposing whites and nonwhites (pretos and browns), we are referring strictly to processes of socioeconomic stratification. When we examine other dimensions of social life involving the sociability of individuals (for example, in marriage and friendship), that [binary] juxtaposition is not adequate, [due to] browns distinguishing themselves from pretos and moving closer to whites."[102] Hence, it would appear, for example, that proposals to change the terms of the national census from capturing a ternary color continuum to a binary racial group divide, as discussed in Chapter 4, as well as racialist researchers' adoption of the conceptualization of race in *negro* and white for their social analyses, might have the effect of hiding significant differences within the population of nonwhites in certain social spheres.[103] Nonetheless, the use of *negro* in juxtaposition to white is now dominant in the growing field of Brazilian race relations studies, and hence the symbolic power of academia in the clarification of boundaries in Brazil falls on the side of a binary racial vision.[104]

In many cases political struggle pits symbolic powers against one another, each trying to define the legitimate vision of the social world. These contests, as claimed by Bourdieu, may be conceptualized as "classificatory struggles" or struggles "for the monopoly over legitimate naming."[105] In the case of Brazil, however, there appears at this historic moment to be a confluence of important symbolic powers behind furthering a dichotomous racial vision in Brazil—the state, social movements, and the dominant social science perspective; the opposing side in the "struggle" seems only to be the stubborn and ambiguous classificatory tendencies of ordinary citizens and a less dominant group of "antiracialist" social scientists.[106]

This confluence of these actors sets up a scenario mimicking the overlapping contexts of categorization, systematically reviewed above in the case of the United States, that are key to making categories stick. That is, there is no doubt that this is a period in Brazilian history during which racial dualism is beginning to restructure formal and possibly informal contexts of categorization. As I laid out in Chapter 2, the dominant racialist perspective among race relations researchers who study the Brazilian case has wholly embraced the logic and correctness of dichotomous categorization.[107] Hence, it can be said that the existence of white and *negro* races in Brazil is now clearly buttressed and legitimized by science. As I discussed in Chapters 3 and 4, there are those who propose census adoption of the *negro* category defined by hypodescent.[108] Diverse media outlets write and report in *negro* and white, and the culture industry invests heavily in that vision.[109] Brazil's small (but growing) *negro* movement has opted for the *negro* term defined by a rhetoric of racial descent delimited through a rule similar to that of hypodescent,[110] as have some government agencies.[111] Finally, as I discussed in this Chapter 7, race-based legislation in higher education structured by racial dualism is now ascendant. Will these contexts of categorization reach into the lives of everyday Brazilians in such consequential ways as to modify their racial worldviews? Only time will tell. However, what is clear from this discussion is that although the rule of racial dualism is understood by bureaucrats, scholars, and activists, everyday Brazilians continue to self-classify and other-classify in ways that defy its logic. White purity is "sullied" in Brazil, and the all-encompassing integrity of the one-drop rule fails to enclose all traceable evidence of African ancestry in a *negro* race category.

Lastly, the de jure adoption of dichotomous racial classification may have serious unintended consequences. First, as analyzed in the preceding chapter, that scheme appears to prejudice the inclusion of many brown individuals of mixed racial heritage as quota beneficiaries either through self-classificatory dynamics or through third parties, such as the University of Brasília's race board. Second, results presented in this chapter also suggest another possible unintended consequence: a significant move toward whiteness in terms of the country's overall color composition.[112] That is, the policies may actually expand the boundaries of whiteness, which means the boundaries of the *negro* identity would be constricted. That appears to be the case even though the dichotomous classification scheme may actually aid in increasing the salience of *negro* identification for those who do not see themselves as fitting into the expanded white category or that are rejected by others as candidates for whiteness. The actual size, then, of the newly formed *negro* racial group may be much less than the one that the *negro* movement now claims to be its putative constituency—all browns and *pretos*, or about half of the national population.[113]

Conclusion

From a comparative perspective with the United States, a very interesting irony is beginning to play itself out: "It may be the case that racial identity in the United States is becoming more Brazilian in character [i.e., multiracial] while Brazil appears to be more like North America [i.e., monoracial]."[114] The 2000 U.S. Census for the first time institutionalized multiracialism, and a couple of years later some Brazilian institutions have been adopting racial dualism or monoracialism. According to Hochschild, "It may be a deep irony that the Census Bureau is introducing the United States to a whole new way of thinking about race in the twenty-first century. But so it is; there is no point in resisting Americans' desire to check more than one box."[115] Lee and Bean report on studies that show that one in forty Americans claimed to be multiracial in the 2000 census, and as many as one in five may do so by the year 2050.[116] As Hochschild metaphorically puts it referring to the institutionalization of multiracialism in the United States, "it is not possible to put the genie back in the bottle."[117] Hence, policies based on monoracial identification in the United States may be in jeopardy[118] at the same time that Brazil is betting on that very formulation.

Hence, although the "one-drop rule ... is in retreat in the US," as noted by Cornell and Hartmann,[119] something approaching the rule of hypodescent is ascendant in Brazil.[120] In effect, in Brazil, the "unmixing" has begun. Cornell and Hartmann further comment on this type of process:

> The task for those who promote this "unmixing of peoples" (Brubaker 1995) is to root out ambiguity and multiplicity and to preserve and protect above all else the integrity, rights, and independence of the group. Their rhetoric is the essentialist rhetoric of primordialism, finding ultimate links among persons if not in blood then in a cultural endowment too deep and fundamental to be ignored or in a historical experience too indelible to ever disappear. The unmixing of peoples involves perpetuating or establishing those links—real or imagined—as the bases of human organization, identity, and action.[121]

There is no doubt that those supporting the institutionalization of the rule of hypodescent in Brazil are doing so in the interest of antiracism. Brazilian society is stratified in part according to racialized characteristics. The systems producing or maintaining that disadvantage evident in the lives of census browns and *pretos* must be ended and their effects reverted. Morning and

Sabbagh comment that "the adoption of anti-discriminatory policy leads to some mechanism for categorizing disadvantaged groups. If ethnic discrimination is the target, a means of classifying the population by ethnicity normally follows."[122] In Brazil, if race-based discrimination is the target, then classifying by race would seem to follow.

Supporting that logic, Guimarães claims that "if blacks [in Brazil] do not believe in the existence of races, they would also have to believe that they themselves do not fully exist as people, given that they are partially perceived and classified as race by others."[123] He adds, "It would be very difficult to imagine a way of fighting against an imputation or discrimination without granting it a social reality."[124] From this perspective, robust racial identification becomes the sine qua non of antiracism. However, there may be a deeply flawed logic at work here. Returning once more to Barbara Fields's insights, a perspective that necessitates the embrace of race because of the existence of racism "transforms the act of a subject [the discriminator] into an attribute of the object [the discriminated]."[125] In effect, obligatory classification according to the one-drop rule, so that Brazilians will learn to believe in the existence of races because of racist treatment, makes those discriminating racists the true architects of population diversity in Brazil in *negro* and white.

Is "unmixing" for race making the only viable strategy for combating racial inequality? If so, in Brazil, along with obligatory file photos for university entrance and anonymous race boards, racial identity cards and official race registries may also be forthcoming.[126] Putting "the genie back in the bottle" may require these measures and more.[127]

10   Conclusion

THIS SURVEY OF RACIAL ATTITUDES IN BRAZIL has produced many counterintuitive results, a few of which I will briefly summarize in view of offering a framing capable of explaining the contours of public opinion in that context. My findings are "unexpected" against the backboard of dominant theories of racial attitudes that, I submit, are based largely on the experience of "race relations" in the United States. Various scholars characterize that particular experience as "racialist," that is, reflecting the generalized belief that "there are heritable characteristics possessed by members of our species that allow us to divide them into a small set of races."[1] Although most of the hard biological racist racialism of the past, with its attendant racial hierarchies, is no longer embraced by the scientific community nor by the lion's share of everyday Americans, the belief in biological races still predominates among the generalized population and, according to one study, among many in the American scientific community.[2]

According to the field's leading scholars on racial attitudes, dynamics in the racialist context lead to three specific assumptions that are core to framings explaining attitudinal stances: (1) individuals identify with their own racial groups; (2) interests are perceived as racial group specific; and (3) ideologies are embraced along group lines.[3] It is not my contention that societal interaction in the Brazilian context does not involve racialized understandings and identification dynamics. Rather, it is the intensity, clarity, and primary nature of those understandings in the racialist context that differentiates it, as argued by Waters in her comparative examination of the divergent racial worldviews experienced inside and outside the United States.[4] I characterized in this book the divergent racial common sense in Brazil as antiracialist, following in large part Antonio Sérgio Guimarães.[5] The use of the concept antiracialism in Brazil describes a common sense that embraces racial ambiguity and "mixing" as the very essence of "Brazilianness" and as expressed in that nation's founding "myth of the three races."[6] As a result, the racial common sense in Brazil historically rejected the notion of particularist racial group memberships as legitimate building blocks of the national community.

The most rigorous scientific theories are generally predictive in nature. What happens when theories based, then, in the historical experience of racialism are employed to frame skin color dynamics in Brazil? That is, what happens when the three core assumptions of U.S. racialism are treated as hypotheses and empirically tested in Brazil? Under those conditions, my results reveal them as less than rigorous in the case of racial attitudes.

For example, I found that far from the assumption that individuals identify with "their own racial group," Brazilians continue to embrace racial ambiguity in the three surveys spanning the years 1995 through 2002.[7] The great majority of nonwhite Brazilians prefer the intermediate or mixed-race term of the national census, claiming to be neither "black nor white." When forced into a white and nonwhite dichotomous scheme, the newly formed race-based division is very unlike the one that academics, activists, and state bureaucrats posit—that is, census whites on one side, browns and *pretos* on the other. Instead, under such conditions, the white side of the equation becomes swollen with over 40 percent of census browns. Outside the bounds of the census, Brazilians prefer a multitude of racial and color labels that are context specific. A corollary of this lack of clear racial group subjectivity is my finding that race does not clearly delineate cultural communities in Brazil, as it is perceived to in contexts characterized by racialism.[8] In the racialist United States, for example, the racial and cultural ambiguity that is so strongly embraced in Brazil was rejected historically through the institutionalization of hypodescent and racial segregation. Americans of African and European ancestries now embrace classification in black and white, even when given the chance to recognize historic category intermixing through the new "mark one or more" races format in the 2000 census.[9]

Second, my data suggest that interests are not primarily interpreted along racial boundaries in Brazil. I laid out significant hypothetical support from individuals who self-classify as white for antiracism strategies of every sort, from participation in antiracism protest events to supporting affirmative action policies. Whites' stated support of these strategies was oftentimes almost equal to that of nonwhites in Brazil. Clearly, then, a majority of whites expressed interests that went against their own apparent "racial interests." This finding strongly contradicts the U.S. context, where whites have been shown to over-whelmingly reject affirmative action strategies and black movement politics,[10] described by leading scholars as contributing to veritable "culture wars" in the United States.[11]

Finally, as to ideologies being group specific, I show that ideological stances that make up the core of the myth of racial democracy are not embraced along group lines. In fact, the population's interpretation of the myth is not what the literature would have it to be at all during the 1995 through 2002 period, that is, a hierarchy-enhancing legitimizing ideology. Framing the myth in large part as a stratification belief, my data reveal that color or race is not a signifi-cant predictor of beliefs about Brazilian racial disadvantage. Again, this find-ing strongly contradicts the dramatic racial divide in the United States, where blacks and whites appear many times to see the world from entirely differing perspectives, and where whites blame blacks for their own disadvantage while blacks blame discrimination.[12]

None of these results is easily explained by dominant theories: Individu-als embrace racial ambiguity; interests cut across racial lines; racial category does not predict core ideological stances. Group conflict, sociocultural, and social identity theories stipulating robust in-group subjectivity whether due to group-based interests, out-group prejudice, or in-group favoritism, respec-tively, fail to offer explanations for these dynamics, as detailed in each chap-ter. The exercise becomes one of trying to fit round pegs into square holes, that is, the reality of racial dynamics in Brazil into inadequate theoretical fram-ings. These "general" theories need revision to take into account contexts that differ significantly from the particular U.S. experience.

In that pursuit, I argue that a critique of those theories should begin by fo-cusing on their central common analytic concept: the "racial *group*." Address-ing dynamics born of group-based interests, out-group hostility, or in-group favoritism, these are all "group qua group" framings.[13] However, adopting a "racial group" conceptualization is, in its very name, suggestive of scenarios that should be empirical questions, as opposed to embedded assumptions: namely that the boundary of a population thus named is robust enough to merit the analytic status of a sociological group.

Social boundaries come in varying intensities. Some are blurred or bright, hard or soft, strong or weak, symbolic or otherwise.[14] Social boundaries, then, run along a "groupness" continuum. Those that are sufficiently strong and bright, that are embraced by the so-labeled populations and by those with whom they relate, may be conceptualized as social groups. In contrast, boundaries that are dim or weak should be conceptualized differently. Some boundaries are best framed as categories that may not be embraced by the categorized at all. Others may enclose mere aggregate populations. The point I make here, which may seem a question of semantics but that has important consequences when ignored, is that the scientific study of racial attitudes recorded in the literature may be overly "groupist" in orientation. In beginning with the epistemological assumption that racialized boundaries merit group status, assumptions of group-based identities, interests, and ideologies follow, assumptions that unravel in the Brazilian context. Hence, it is not a question of semantics, as my counterintuitive results suggest.

I argue, then, that to reconcile these theories to the Brazilian context requires the explicit recognition of variable boundary salience, or varied levels of groupness, in the idiom of Loveman, Brubaker, and their colleagues Cooper and Stamatov.[15] Once this recognition is called forth, the intensity of boundaries becomes an empirical issue on which the nature of the attitudes under study rests. Where individuals do not clearly and subjectively embrace discrete categories of race, where interests may be organized or perceived differently, for example, according to class understandings as opposed to primarily racial ones, and where ideologies do not fall along the lines of color, a scholar is sure to find racial boundary salience to be less than robust. To assume robust boundaries weakens the explanatory and hence predictive rigor of theory.[16]

A second major point I would like to emphasize in regards to revising existing framings has to do with the specific nature and effect of the so-labeled myth of racial democracy. Abundant evidence from the survey data from 1995 through 2002 reveals its nature and those effects to be quite different than portrayed by the dominant Brazilianist perspective put forth by scholars such as Hanchard, Winant, Twine, and Guimarães,[17] nor as would be expected according to general theories addressing racial attitudes, as those posited by Sears, Bobo, and Sidanius.[18] Several scholars have raised this question regarding the framing of this myth as an important point of debate in Brazil, as to whether this myth represents an insidious lie or a legitimate utopia.[19] In the social science jargon of general theories, it is either a hierarchy-enhancing legitimizing myth or one of counterdominance or delegitimization of the status quo.[20] As the former, it would constitute a belief or ideology that leads to opposition to challenges to the racial status quo; as the latter, it could lead to support for those challenges.[21] The opposition or support that the Brazilian racial common sense may engender toward challenges to the racial status quo can be measured by attitudes toward antiracism strategies, as I explored explicitly in Chapters 6 and 7.

I found strong evidence suggesting that an insidious lie framing the myth of racial democracy does not fit the data. First, the majority stratification belief in Brazil, believed by scholars and activists to constitute the ideological core of the myth of racial democracy, is not a denial of racial discrimination but its recognition. Secondly, I found that this recognition is associated with support for antiracism strategies from affirmative action to antiracist mobilization, and not the opposite, that is, necessarily hierarchy enhancing, as predicted in the literature. Hence, I argue that the nature of the myth of racial democracy captured in my data, far from a cruel hoax responsible for perpetuating nonwhite disadvantage, is more consistent with the view of it as a legitimate utopian stance. Most Brazilians do not want to live in a society where skin color disadvantages the chances of some and privileges those of others. Racism is repugnant to the average Brazilian. As such, the myth of racial democracy constitutes a type of egalitarian predisposition or creed, or a "dream of equality" in Sheriff's phrasing. That creed appears to serve as a yardstick with which to measure the real conditions and hence influence attitudinal stances toward many racialized issues in Brazil.[22]

As I detailed earlier, sectors of Brazilian *negro* movements did once embrace the myth of racial democracy as an egalitarian creed and yardstick device with which to speak to issues of existing inequality.[23] Recall Guimarães' conclusion from his study of that earlier rhetorical use: "It has to be recognized that in ideological terms, the belief in a racial democracy and a mixed origin of the Brazilian people served to solidify the formal position of equality of black and mulattos in Brazilian society."[24] Hence, Guimarães concludes: "The ideas and the name racial democracy, far from constituting an achievement created by the white dominant classes, as some activists and sociologists want to make it today, was for many years a way of integration forged by black militancy."[25]

Used in that way, as a commonly held values orientation that finds racism repugnant, it parallels to some degree the American creed and its use at certain pivotal times to call that nation to be responsible to the values that it holds as most dear. As a centerpiece of the American political common sense, the American creed wields significant sway over public opinion on many issues. As Gunnar Myrdal wrote, "Americans of all national origins, classes, regions, creeds, and colors, having something in common: a social ethos, a political creed . . . the 'American Creed.' "[26]

And it was that common ethos that Martin Luther King Jr., for example, called on in his famous speech at the Washington mall in 1963:

> Now, I say to you today my friends, even though we face the difficulties of today and tomorrow, I still have a dream. It is a dream *deeply rooted in the American dream.* I have a dream that one day this nation will rise up and live out the true meaning of its *creed:* we hold these truths to be self-evident. That all men are created equal.

Insistence on the basic values of American idealism, then, formed the basis of the struggle to overcome the structures and relationships that were born of American racist racialism. The American creed was a platform from which the voices of an oppressed racialized population could argue its equal creation and hence equal rights. In essence, these basic rights, which include equality, justice, liberty, and the pursuit of happiness, became the "master ideas" that were forgotten by some, ignored by others, excised from the public realm, and then recalled by prophetic voices of change to hearken their implementation.

As opposed to group-based interests, out-group bias, or in-group favoritism, Kinder and Sanders posit that the driving force behind public opinion on many racial issues can be these "master ideas," "matters of principle," or "values predisposition," like the American creed, that speak to a common set of values embraced by a population.[27] This "principles" framing of determinants of American public opinion on racial issues, although finding empirical support in the work of Kinder and Sanders, as well as in that of Sniderman and his colleagues, has been significantly criticized by other prominent scholars in the field, such as Bobo, Sears, and Sidanius.[28] In this debate among American scholars on the U.S. context, the "principled stance" framing is centrally considered a race-neutral set of values, such as political equality and individualism. At the core of the critiques, then, is the perspective that to pretend race-neutral principles influence attitudes toward racial issues is to feign ignorance of the underlying racial interests and prejudice that are central.

Although I do not necessarily disagree with some of the criticisms of the "matters of principle" stance as applied to the U.S. context, I would point out that, different from the core values of the American creed, the racial democracy creed is far from race neutral. It is, instead, centrally about racialized dynamics. Hence, the master ideas of the racial democracy creed do not pretend color blindness; rather they situate color within the ideas of antiracialism, including a repugnance of color discrimination. Unfortunately, the only reigning creed about race in the United States for centuries was one of white racial supremacy.

Hence, I wish to propose that a "matters of principle" or a "values predisposition" framing of the myth of racial democracy is consistent with my findings, as opposed to group conflict, sociocultural, and social identity theories. Understanding the myth of racial democracy as a set of master ideas regarding the equality of all individuals, regardless of skin color, the value of racial mixing and ambiguous identification dynamics, the rejection of rigid racial group memberships as the building blocks of a national community, and the repugnant nature of skin-color discrimination, provides an efficient explanation of the attitudes of Brazilians that I have presented throughout this book.

Importantly, a set of commonly held master ideas do not ensure that these will be fully realized; gaps and gulfs between real culture and ideal culture are commonplace. Racial stereotypes, prejudice, and discrimination are a part of Brazilian societal dynamics, and these must be constantly confronted in pursuit of a just society for all. However, history shows that matters of principle can form the basis from which to call a nation to task, to challenge it or shame it into action.[29] Deeply seated and commonly held egalitarian creeds can be viewed, then, as essential tools when wielded in the fight against racialized discrimination, as they were indeed in the United States.

Today, however, strategies in Brazil put forth by many movement, state, and academic actors appear not to agree with this characterization of the myth of racial democracy as a type of egalitarian creed. In contrast, as discussed, it has been framed as a racist ideology propagated by whites and embraced by "anesthetized" nonwhites, historically leading Brazilians to believe they live in a racial paradise and hampering antiracism in general.[30] Why adopt a strategy of the "demonization" of this myth, using Fry's phrasing?[31] I want to suggest two possible answers.

A first answer is suggested by the perspective that has historically viewed the absence of significant antiracist mobilization in Brazil as stemming from the lack of a clear target against which to mobilize.[32] In postabolition years in much of the United States, individuals of African ancestry lived in a virtual police state ruled formally by Jim Crow segregation.[33] Raw racial hate and violence were commonplace, expressed through lynching, castelike aversions, and beliefs in white supremacy. The starkness of these concrete and de jure abominations against the American creed made the call to mobilization reverberate strongly among African Americans and even among many European Americans who joined their struggle.

In contrast, Brazilian society was not ruled by de jure race-targeted exclusionary measures in postabolition years,[34] and lynching, caste dynamics, and white supremacy groups were notably absent. Nonetheless, Brazilians of varying degrees of African ancestry suffered disproportionately disadvantaged life chances and continue to do so. That is, the absence of formalized discrimination was not enough to ensure a context in which the formerly excluded could thrive among equals.

To reverse that situation in the absence of the affront of de jure discrimination, movement actors may have felt compelled to decide on a different target to rally the disadvantaged population. The strategy became not to call a nation to live up to its antiracialist ideas but to renounce those ideas as a type of "false consciousness." The racial democracy *creed* became, in effect, the *myth* of racial democracy, the target against which *negro* movement actors sought to mobilize against the status quo.[35] Evidencing this dramatic shift, the fight against and an eventual demise of the myth of racial democracy in Brazil is viewed by some scholars as parallel to the struggle and eventual demise of Jim Crow segregation in the United States.[36] Hence, one reason for the myth's demonization was utilitarian—the need to find a target.

A second element prompting the strategy of the demonization of the racial democracy creed, rather than utilitarian, may be framed as philosophical because the myth is thoroughly antiracialist in character: It celebrates racial mixture and color ambiguity.[37] In contrast, examples of antiracist struggle to which the Brazilian *negro* movement historically looked for inspiration used strategic essentialism, which required an investment in racialism. The civil rights movement in the United States, for example, employed the language of race and discrete groups in conflict to identify and mobilize its constituency. In doing so, the movement successfully challenged de jure exclusion and many aspects of structural inequality. That is, antiracist racialism can indeed be a transformative weapon against racialized oppression.

The logic of this embrace of racialism is echoed in academic literature, perhaps most illustratively in a comparative formulation by Talcott Parsons, who wrote, "I take the position that the race relations problem has a better prospect of resolution in the United States than Brazil, partly *because* the line between white and [black] has been so rigidly drawn in the United States because the system has been sharply polarized."[38]

More recently, Winant echoes the "advance" that could be gained through racialist development in Brazil:

The public articulation and exploration of racial dualism would itself be a major advance [in Brazil]. Many black people undoubtedly still succeed in denying the significance of their racial identity. They are "avoiders," as Twine (199[8]) documents at length. Their ability not only to deny, but to *avoid* their own racial identity is aided by the tremendous depth of the ideology of racial democracy. What good is an ideology, after all, if it cannot effectively identify its adherent's identity . . . ?[39]

Lastly, Guimarães similarly endorses strategic racialism in Brazil. In his extensive and important work on Brazilian racial dynamics and antiracism, he writes: "If blacks do not believe in the existence of races, they would also have to believe that they themselves do not fully exist as people."[40] Hence, the embrace of race in *negro* and white, for Guimarães and other scholars, becomes an absolute necessity for antiracism.

Scholars, activists, bureaucrats, and various types of organizational actors both in and outside of Brazil, then, attempt to overcome a history of ambiguous racial boundaries through *negro* identity mobilization and the unification of all Brazilians with some degree of African ancestry as a step toward struggling against racism. Simply put, antiracialism is not straightforwardly compatible with such a vision. Hence, on philosophical grounds, the antiracialist myth of racial democracy became a target.

Would an embrace of anitracialism necessarily preclude antiexclusionary strategies? My findings are not consistent with that line of reasoning. Instead, they support a revisionist examination of the myth as by Alejandro de la Fuente, for example, who argues that the myth can be and has been harnessed in ways that protect and promote subordinate populations.[41] For example, he argues that the myth of racial democracy, which is found in various countries of Latin America, is inclusionary in principle and has thereby historically restricted the political options of white elites and provided grounds on which the excluded can demand full participation: "[The myth of racial democracy] embodies a set of socially acceptable ideals that can be turned into opportunities for participation and advancement by those at the bottom of the socioracial hierarchy."[42] That view is indeed consistent with my findings.[43]

Furthermore, non–race-specific coalitions, such as women's groups,[44] labor unions and urban social movements,[45] that mobilize around issues perhaps disproportionately important to Brazilians of varying degrees of African descent may find fertile ground in a context oriented by the racial democ-racy perspective. One especially notable example is the Movement of Landless Workers. Segato cautions regarding that movement that "introducing seg-mentation by race into those popular fronts would not only be spurious but would also have disastrous consequences."[46]

Directly opposing the racialist stances of Parsons and Winant concern-ing antiracism strategies, Marvin Harris and his colleagues wrote, "We fail to see why Brazil cannot destroy racism without destroying its unique system of ambiguous and flexible race-color boundaries."[47] That is, according to these scholars, antiracialism does not necessarily negate antiracism. How to mus-ter antiracialism as a movement strategy, however, is not specified by those scholars. Indeed, that would be a daunting task, just as has been employing strategic essentialism as a strategy in a population in which 40 percent self-classify in an intermediate category. Placing both stances in perspective, Se-gato concludes:

> If we decide that the founding myth of Latin American nations is mere decep-tion, then we have to endorse the notion that only after establishing segregation as the point zero of racial truth can we initiate a truly antiracist politics ... Con-versely, if we see, from a Latin American perspective, segregation ... as a dysto-pia of conviviality, we are compelled to envisage alternative political roads.[48]

As I detailed in the previous chapter, however, the political road that has been chosen by many *negro* movement, academic, and state actors in Bra-zil is one that, as Ford describes it, rests on "jurisprudential segregation ... [that] brands badges of racial identity onto the face of public life."[49] The re-cent adoption of race-targeted policies in *negro* and white may indeed be the mechanism that produces a significant shift in racial classification dynamics from antiracialism toward racialism.

Importantly, Bourdieu claims that "to change the world, one has to change the ways of world-making, that is ... the practical operations by which groups are produced and reproduced."[50] The contemporary story in Brazil appears to be the adoption of one such "practical operation" capable of overcoming ra-cial ambiguity and in sociological terms producing a group *out of* a statistical category, that is, a *negro* racial group out of the category "nonwhites" (browns and *pretos*).[51] Inspired in Marxist theoretical language, the effect could be framed as a push to move a "race-in-itself" to becoming a "race-for-itself." It may, however, be well to keep in mind Bourdieu's criticism of this Marx-ian conceptualization. He writes that the move from a category to a group is "always celebrated as a real ontological advance . . . it is presented as the effect of an 'awakening of consciousness'" under "enlightened leadership."[52] When that move by movement actors to constitute the group is joined by the state, as in this case through de jure inclusionary policies, and even by science, the created group, in Boltanski's words, may become "as if it had been there for all eternity."[53] Hence, it is undeniably crucial to analyze the mechanisms of its construction.

I would like to end my discussion, however, with a last thought on the implications of those race-making policies for the social scientific theorizing of racial attitudes in Brazil. I have stipulated that during the period of 1995 through 2002, the contours of racial attitudes in Brazil confound those predicted by group conflict, sociocultural, and social identity theories. Bobo, in a seminal piece published in 1988 entitled "Group Conflict, Prejudice, and the Paradox of Contemporary Racial Attitudes," concluded, "To recapitulate, conditions of inequality and ethnocentrism establish conflicting group interests, which, in turn, translate into interpretive tendencies on the part of dominant and subordinate group members."[54]

Conditions of inequality surely exist in Brazil, as social science has documented and has proposed as falling along a white versus nonwhite cleavage. However, scholars have long held that nonwhites deny racial discrimination and buy into hegemonic, white ruling ideas that, in effect, are based in white racial interests.[55] According to Bobo's framing, what can dramatically change the contours of Brazilians' interpretive tendencies, that is, their racial common sense, is ethnocentrism (the corollary of which is racial subjectivity), exactly that which scholars view as traditionally weak in Brazil. Inasmuch as the state's legitimization of race in *negro* and white through official de jure classification and distribution of resources along those lines leads to the strengthening of binary racial subjectivity, then attitudinal stances, that is, "interpretive tendencies," should indeed become more polarized, expressed through increasingly group-based identities, interests, and supporting ideologies. Hence, I posit that I have captured a period in the history of Brazilian racial attitudes that is, indeed, in transition. With state, social movement, and science race making in *negro* and white, the framings that I have found inefficient for the Brazilian context using 1995 through 2002 survey data may slowly begin to fit. That is, the round pegs of Brazilian racial dynamics will be whittled and planed in such a way that the square holes of existing U.S.–based theories of racial attitudes may eventually seem a "natural" fit.

Reference Matter

Notes

Chapter 1

1. Henceforward I use the term *race* without quotation marks.

2. Gilberto Freyre 1946, 1959, 1974. The actual phrase *racial democracy* may have first been used by Freyre in the early 1960s. See Guimarães 2002.

3. According to Guimarães 2002, p. 309, Freyre's writings "broke decisively with the Brazilian ideological establishment of the Old Republic (1889–1930) which was strongly characterized by racism . . . and the idea of biological and cultural whitening."

4. Freyre, 1959, pp. 7–8.

5. Freyre 1959, p. 4, cited in Silva 1998, p. 219.

6. Nobles 2000.

7. Telles 2004, p. 4.

8. Freyre 1946, 1974.

9. The term *pardo* is an official census term in Brazil often translated into English as brown or mulatto. It should be considered an intermediate term between two other official census categories, *branco* or white on one end of a color continuum and *preto* or black on the other.

10. Silva 1996, p. 120.

11. Munanga 1996, pp. 186, 190.

12. Guimarães 1999. Guimarães's statement that the racial democracy myth implies a racial paradise scenario surely refers to Freyre's 1959, pp. 8–9, statement in which, in comparison to the ills of Jim Crow de jure discrimination of African Americans in the United States, he claimed, "There is in all likelihood no earthly paradise,

but in respect of race relations the Brazilian situation is probably the nearest approach to a paradise to be found anywhere in the world" (cited in Motta 2000, p. 669).

13. Maio 2001.

14. Wagley 1952a, p. 7.

15. The meaning of the *negro* term varies historically from encompassing all individuals of varying degree of African ancestry to only those at the darkest end of the white-to-black color continuum. In contemporary Brazil, it is conceptualized by *negro* movement actors as a term of racial affirmation embedded in a dichotomous racial scheme juxtaposed to white.

16. Wagley 1952b, p. 152.

17. Wagley 1952b, p. 153.

18. Wagley 1952b, p. 151.

19. Wagley 1952b, p. 154.

20. Marx 1998.

21. Guimarães 2002.

22. Guimarães 2001a; Nascimento and Nascimento 2001.

23. Hasenbalg 1985; Silva 1985.

24. Lovell 1999; Telles 1992, 1993, 1994, 2004.

25. See, for example, Guimarães 2001a.

26. Agier 1993; Andrews 1991; Nascimento and Nascimento 2001; Santos 1999.

27. Hanchard 1999; Winant 2001.

28. Skidmore 1974.

29. In the general literature on public opinion, Zaller 1992 posits a decisive elite effect on the formation of the opinions of the masses. Zaller's framing, then, may support in theory the commonly hypothesized association between elite and nonelite attitudes toward racial issues in Brazil. My data will show, however, that such an assumption in Brazil may not be warranted.

30. Hasenbalg 1998, p. 237; Sidanius et al. 2001; Winant 2001.

31. For example, Da Matta 1997; Fry 2000; Reis 1997; Sheriff 2001; Silva 1998.

32. Sheriff 2001, p. 221.

33. See Fry 2000; Sheriff 2001.

34. See Hochschild 1995; Kinder and Sanders 1996; Myrdal 1944.

35. Bobo 1988a, p. 94; Myrdal 1944; Sidanius and Pratto 1999.

36. This lacuna is noted by Hanchard 1994, p. 63; Hasenbalg and Silva 1999, pp. 165–166; and Winant 1994, p. 149. There have been sporadic earlier works, but much of it used nonrandom samples. See, for example, Bicudo 1946; Degler 1971; and Willems 1949.

37. Sheriff 2001; Twine 1998.

38. Hasenbalg and Silva 1999, p. 165–166. Winant 1994, p. 149, notes: "Brazilian racial attitudes have not been studied in depth since the late 1950s and early 1960s. . . .

As far as I know there has never been a comprehensive, methodologically sophisticated survey of racial attitudes, something on the order of Schuman, Steeh, and Bobo's *Racial Attitudes in America*."

39. I provide details on these data sets in the following chapter.

40. Bonilla-Silva 2004; Skidmore 2003.

41. Daniel 2006.

42. Appiah 1990; Waters 1999.

43. Guimarães 1999, 2001a. See also Waters 1999 on "nonracialism," a proximate construct.

44. Brubaker 2002; Brubaker and Cooper 2000; Brubaker, Loveman, and Stamatov 2004; Loveman 1999a.

45. Powell 1997.

46. The 1986 data on Brazilians' stratification beliefs come from Hasenbalg and Silva 1999, which I will discuss more fully below.

47. Burdick 1998a; Telles 1999.

Chapter 2

1. Schuman et al. 1997, p. 2.

2. Schuman et al. 1997, p. 2.

3. Krysan 2000; Schuman et al. 1997.

4. Krysan 2000, p. 5.

5. Burstein 1985.

6. Bobo 1997, p. 10.

7. Krysan 2000. Other points of criticism of public opinion research address "social desirability bias" and "race-of-interviewer" bias. See Bickart and Flecher 1996. I will return to both issues in subsequent chapters.

8. Sears et al. 2000c.

9. Krysan 2000.

10. See, for example, Bobo and Tuan 2006 and Hunt 2007.

11. Kinder and Sanders 1996; Pettigrew and Meertens 1995; Sears 1988.

12. Bobo 1988a; Jackman 1994; Sidanius and Pratto 1999.

13. Tajfel and Turner 1986.

14. Other theoretical models utilized in the study of racial attitudes do exist. See Sears et al. 2000b and Sidanius and Pratto 1999 for more complete reviews of theoretical stances.

15. Allport 1954; Meertens and Pettigrew 1997.

16. Kinder and Sears 1981; Sears 1988; Sears et al. 2000a. Although Symbolic Racism is essentially a confrontation of the U.S. context, other sociocultural approaches are employed outside the United States. For example, Meertens and Pettigrew 1997 employ a similar approach to explain prejudice in France, Germany, Great Britain, and the Netherlands.

17. Allport 1954.

18. Kinder and Sears 1981, p. 416.

19. Kinder and Sears 1981, p. 416.

20. Kinder and Mendelberg 2000, p. 77.

21. See also Meertens and Pettigrew 1997 on subtle versus overt racism.

22. Kinder and Sanders 1996.

23. Bobo 1988a,b; Campbell 1965; Jackman 1994; Sidanius and Pratto 1999. I call this collection of theoretical perspectives "group conflict theories" following Krysan 2000. Sears and his colleagues (Sears et al. 2000b) label them "social structural theories."

24. Bobo 1988a, 2000; Blumer 1958.

25. Bobo 2000, p. 142.

26. Blumer 1958.

27. Bobo 2000, p. 142.

28. See and Wilson 1989, p. 379.

29. Bobo 2000, p. 160.

30. Sidanius, Peña, and Sawyer 2001; Sidanius and Pratto 1999.

31. Sidanius et al. 2000, p. 230–31. See also Jackman 1994.

32. Sidanius et al. 2000.

33. Sidanius et al. 2000, p. 196.

34. Sidanius et al. 2000, p. 197.

35. Sidanius et al. 2000, p. 228.

36. Sears et al. 2000b, p. 22.

37. Tajfel and Turner 1986.

38. Tajfel and Turner 1986, p. 9.

39. Tajfel and Turner 1986, p. 16.

40. Tajfel and Turner 1986, p. 14.

41. Sears et al. 2000b, p. 22.

42. Dawson 2000, p. 350.

43. Jenkins 1994.

44. Brubaker 2002; Brubaker and Cooper 2001; Brubaker, Loveman, and Stamatov 2004; Loveman 1999a.

45. Appiah 1990, p. 5, italics added.

46. Zack 1999, p. 307.

47. Nonphysical or unobvious criteria may also be possible, as in the instance of Irish immigrants to the United States who were once categorized as nonwhites.

48. Appiah 1990, p. 5. See also Goldberg 1993, p. 51.

49. Sears et al. 2000b, p. 9.

50. Waters 1999.

51. Waters 1999, p. 76.

52. Waters 1999, p. 81.

53. Waters 1999, pp. 28–29.

54. Guimarães 1999, 2001a.

55. Johnson 2000; Silva 1998; Skidmore 1992, 1997; Wade 1997.

56. Guimarães 2001a, pp. 157–158.

57. Guimarães 2001a, p. 158.

58. Guimarães 2001a, p. 158.

59. Silva 1998, p. 218.

60. Silva 1998, p. 203.

61. Wade 1997, pp. 25–26.

62. Munanga 1996.

63. Wade 1993.

64. Wright 1990.

65. Whitten 1981.

66. Purcell and Sawyers 1993.

67. Torres-Saillant 1998.

68. Lancaster 1992.

69. Freyre 1974.

70. Freyre 1974.

71. Wade 1993, p. 11.

72. Fry et al. 2007; Guimarães 2001a.

73. Freyre 1946.

74. Degler 1986 [1971]; Harris 1952, 1964, 1970; Hutchinson 1952; Pierson 1967; Wagley 1952c; Willems 1949. I do not include, for example, Sérgio Buarque de Holanda nor Caio Prado Jr., whose central work I view as part of the Freyrean period for these purposes.

75. Wagley 1952a, p. 9. At the time of the UNESCO studies, Wagley, p. 9, comments, "Since Brazil is predominantly a nation of rural dwellers, these communities are representative of an important segment of the whole country. Over 70 percent of the total of more than 52 million Brazilians live in small towns of less than 5,000 people." He bases these figures on the 1950 census.

76. Harris 1970.

77. Harris 1964, pp. 60–61.

78. Hutchinson 1952; Pierson 1967.

79. Harris 1964, p. 57.

80. Harris 1964, p. 59.

81. Harris 1964, p. 56.

82. Nogueira 1985.

83. Wagley 1952b, p. 154.

84. Willems 1949, pp. 407, 408. See also Bicudo 1947 and Nogueira 1985.

85. Harris 1952.

86. Degler 1971; Harris 1970.

87. Harris 1970, pp. 1–2.

88. Hutchinson 1952, p. 38.

89. Wagley 1965, p. 543.

90. Degler 1971; Wagley 1952a, p. 14.

91. Harris 1952, p. 64.

92. Guirmarães 1999.

93. Skidmore 1992.

94. Fernandes 1969.

95. Gonzalez 1985.

96. Hasenbalg 1985; Silva 1985.

97. Guimarães 1999.

98. Skidmore 1992.

99. Bastide and Fernandes 1955.

100. Fernandes 1969. See Silva 1998, p. 206, for a statement on that blame.

101. Fernandes 1969.

102. Guimarães 1999, p. 83.

103. Guimarães 1999.

104. Guimarães 1999.

105. Guimarães 1999, p. 63.

106. Guimarães 1999, p.63.

107. Fontaine 1985.

108. Nascimento 1978.

109. Skidmore 1992.

110. Hasenbalg 1985; Silva 1985.

111. Guimarães 1999, p. 65. This "hard" evidence was so important due in part to the fact that, as Skidmore 1992 claims, the so-called São Paulo school pointed to these same dynamics but never produced rigorous data to support their analysis: In Skidmore's words, "Yet neither he [Fernandes] nor any of the São Paulo school conducted empirical research to document the message for which they became famous" (1992, p. 10).

112. Guimarães 1999, p. 66; Hasenbalg 1985; Silva 1985.

113. Dzidzienyo 1971; Fontaine 1985; Nascimento 1978.

114. Hanchard 1999, p. 13.

115. Camara 1998; Segato 1998.

116. Gilliam 1992; Hanchard 1994; Winant 1994.

117. Guimarães 1999, p. 39.

118. Guimarães 1999, p. 25.

119. Guimarães 1999, p. 68.

120. Guimarães 1999, p. 13.

121. Hanchard 1999, p. 19.

122. Winant 1999, p. 112.

123. Winant 1994, p. 169.

124. Twine 1998.

125. Guimarães 1999; Hanchard 1994; Marx 1998; Nobles 2000; Winant 1999.

126. Twine 1998.

127. Manifesto 2006. Available online at: http://alex.nasc.sites.uol.com.br/manifestopelascotas.htm.

128. Bourdieu and Wacquant 1999. See Telles's 2003 response.

129. Bairros 1996; Camara 1998; Fry 1996; Harris et al. 1993; Reis 1997; Segato 1998; Silva 1998; Sansone 2003.

130. Fry et al. 2007; Maio and Santos 2005.

131. Hanchard 1994; Winant 1994.

132. See Goldberg 1992 on the conceptualization of "ethnorace." See Sansone 2003 for a detailed discussion of conceptualizations of race and ethnicity in the social sciences and specifically on how the case of the United States unduly influences the study of racial dynamics in Brazil.

133. Segato 1998.

134. Silva 1998.

135. Hanchard 1994.

136. Segato 1998.

137. Silva 1998, pp. 223, 207.

138. Silva 1998., pp. 207, 212.

139. Silva 1998, p. 212.

140. Silva 1998, p. 212.

141. Silva 1998.

142. Fry 1996, p. 132.

143. Silva 1998, p. 228.

144. Segato 1998, p. 137.

145. Fry 1996, p. 134. See also de la Fuente 1999; Fry 1996; Reis 1997; Sansone 1998; Sheriff 1997; and Souza 1997.

146. Nobles 1995, p. 9.

147. Nobles 1995, p. 212. For more on how national identity conditions ethnic and racial particularism, see Hanchard 1999, p. 4; Segato 1998, p. 137; and Skidmore 1985, p. 16.

148. Maggie 2005; Sansone 1998; Santos and Maio 2005.

149. Fry et al. 2007.

150. Fry et al. 2007, p. 345.

151. See Simon Schwartzman's (2008) reflection on the lack of transformational potential of recent racial quota policies in higher education. Available online at: www .schwartzman.org.br/simon/cotas2008.pdf.

152. Edward E. Telles, program officer of the Ford Foundation in Rio de Janeiro at the time, was instrumental in funding the CEAP survey (as well as the PESB survey discussed below). Telles was also on the faculty of the Department of Sociology at the University of California, Los Angeles, where he served as cochair of my dissertation committee and facilitated my participation in the survey project. He is presently professor of sociology at Princeton University.

153. The DataUff research team for the CEAP survey was headed by Carlos Alberto Almeida and Zairo Cheibub.

154. Telles and Lim 1998.

155. Turra and Venturi 1995.

156. Telles and Lim 1998.

157. PESB 2002.

Chapter 3

1. Dawson 2000, p. 350. Dawson also recognizes within-group variation but claims it as a lesser phenomenon to between-group variation.

2. Kinder and Sanders 1996, pp. 287–88.

3. Kinder and Sanders 1996; Schuman et al. 1997; Sears et al. 2000c; Tuch and Martin 1997.

4. Brubaker 2002.

5. Alba 2005.

6. Banton 1983.

7. Cornell and Hartman 1998.

8. Hirschman, Alba, and Farley 2000, p. 390.

9. Brubaker et al. 2004.

10. Loveman 1999b, p. 916.

11. Cited in Fry 2000, p. 100.

12. Exceptionally, national censuses in some countries of Latin American countries do not, however, include racial composition questions, perhaps due to national ideologies of *mestizaje*.

13. Anderson 1990; Lee 1993; Nobles 2000.

14. Nobles 2000.

15. The decision to exclude the color question in 1970 was made during the years of military dictatorship. Racial or color composition questions were not included in the censuses of 1900 and 1920. No censuses were conducted at all in 1910 and 1930. See Nobles 2000.

16. Nobles 2000.

17. Davis 1991.

18. Guimarães 2001a.

19. In my use of quotations of texts in English, I maintain the authors' usages of color and race terms. The reader will note, however, that most Brazilianist scholars writing in English generally use the term *black* when referring to nonwhites in Brazil, paralleling the use of *black* or *African American* in the United States.

20. Araujo 1987, p. 15; Bailey and Telles 2006; Nobles 2000, p. 5.

21. Leslie 1999, p. 365.

22. Andrews 1991, p. 254, italics added.

23. Da Matta 1997, p. 71.

24. Brubaker 2002.

25. Byrne et al. 1995; Harris et al. 1993, 1995. However, they also write that "other salient identities should [also] be explored," although they do not specify which would be the other terms in a format that would include *moreno*.

26. According to Harris et al. 1993, p. 459, an emic classification system is based on the principle of self-identification, where "individuals [are] permitted to categorize themselves . . . according to their own sense of identity." Its opposite is an etic system, where it is the outsider or community of scientists who classifies.

27. Harris et al. 1993, p. 454. See also Sansone 1996, pp. 180–81.

28. Harris et al. 1993, p. 459.

29. See Oliveira 1999, p. 172.

30. Bertulio 1997, p. 204; Oliveira e Oliveira 1974.

31. Sansone 1993, 1995, 2003.

32. Sansone 1995, p. 72. See also Butler 1998, pp. 7, 57.

33. Maggie 1991.

34. Barcelos 1999, p. 163.

35. Bailey and Telles 2006.

36. Cunha 1998, p. 224.

37. Hanchard 1994.

38. Ribeiro 2007; Wood 1991, p. 94.

39. Hanchard 1999.

40. Nascimento and Nascimento 2001, p. 108.

41. Andrews 1991, p. 250; Guimarães 2001a, p. 172; Hanchard 1994, pp. 24–25; Nobles 2000, p. 171; Reichmann 1999, p. 2; Skidmore 2003.

42. Silva 1996, p. 93. See also Piza and Rosemberg 1999, p. 47.

43. Nobles 2000.

44. Noguiera 1985.

45. Olivera et al. 1985, p. 12.

46. Butler 1998, p. 52.

47. Sansone 1995, p. 72.

48. Piza and Rosemberg 1999, p. 47.

49. Barth 1969. Nagel 1994 highlights this distinction in the language of structure versus agency in ethnic boundary formation.

50. Longman 2001; Omi and Winant 1994.

51. Jenkins 1994, pp. 198–99.

52. Nagel 1994.

53. Barth 1969, p. 10.

54. Barth 1969, p. 11.

55. Omi and Winant 1994.

56. Jenkins 1994; Tilly 2004; Washington 2004.

57. Handelman 1977; Loveman 1999a; Petersen 1987.

58. Jenkins 1994.

59. This latter stage may be viewed as a coming together of external and internal definition, where historic racist ascription was countered by adopting and infusing the racial label with positive characteristics. See Appiah 2000; Davis 1991; Omi and Winant 1994; and Segato 1998.

60. Jenkins 1994.

61. Brubaker and Cooper 2001, p. 14.

62. Brubaker and Cooper 2001, p. 20; Brubaker et al. 2004.

63. Brubaker and Cooper 2000, p. 19.

64. Brubaker and Cooper 2000, p. 10.

65. Petersen 1987.

66. Yancey et al. 1976, p. 360.

67. Yancey et al. 1976, p. 400. Both Yancey et al. and Cohen subsume race under ethnicity. The former make reference to Cohen 1974, p. xv.

68. Jenkins 1994, p. 21.

69. Brubaker and Cooper 2000, p. 14.

70. Jenkins 1994; Brubaker and Cooper 2000.

71. Harris and Sim 2002.

72. Davis 1991; Hirschman, Alba, and Farley 2000; and Rodriguez 2000 all corroborate the embedded consistency between interview and self-classification in the U.S. censuses. Regarding blacks (Davis 1991, p. 12) and black Hispanics (Rodriguez 2000, p. 135), these researchers compared the percentages of these populations recorded when interviewer classification was used with subsequent measures when self-classification was employed. They report the percentages were the same. As a result, Davis 1991, p. 12, states that black Americans "generally apply the one-drop-rule to themselves." Commenting on this switch to self-classification, Hirschman, Alba, and Farley 2000, p. 381, also comment that "The overall patterns of racial composition . . . suggest that most Americans identified themselves by race largely as census enumerators had classified them."

73. Bailey and Telles 2006; Hasenbalg and Silva 1991; Silva 1996; Telles 2002, 2004; Telles and Lim 1998; Turra and Venturi 1995.

74. Telles and Lim 1998.

75. As I will address below, I do not mean to imply that opting for equivalent terms, such as black as opposed to African American in the United States, for example, is associated with low levels of groupness.

76. Brubaker 2002; Brubaker and Cooper 2000; Goldberg 1992; Jenkins 1994; Schwartzman 1999, p. 86.

77. Tajfel and Turner 1986.

78. Hirschman et al. 2000, p. 383.

79. Hirschman et al. 2000, p. 383.

80. Hirschman et al. 2000, p. 385.

81. Hirschman 2004, p. 405.

82. Telles 2002; Twine 1998.

83. Brazilian Institute of Geography and Statistics (IBGE) 1999; Silva 1996.

84. Hirschman et al. 2000.

85. Brubaker 2002; Jenkins 1994.

86. Alba 2005, p. 23.

87. Bailey and Telles 2006; Telles 2004.

88. Byrne et al. 1995; Harris et al. 1995.

89. Freyre 1974; Guimarães 1999.

90. Sansone 1995.

91. Nascimento and Nascimento 2001.

92. Nobles 2000, p. 126.

93. Nobles 2000, p. 127.

94. Telles 2004, pp. 86–87.

95. Burdick 1998a.

96. Guirmarães 2001a.

97. Schuman and Converse 1971.

98. I have changed the numbering of the photographs to facilitate subsequent data presentation. To view the original numbering and also the original color photographs, see https://webfiles.uci.edu/xythoswfs/webui/_xy-5837890_1 (or request directly from the author).

99. Nogueira 1985, p. 89. See also Piza and Rosemberg 1999 and Silva 1996.

100. For example, Leslie 1999.

101. Harris and Sim 2002.

102. Hirschman et al. 2000.

103. In addition, individuals who switched to other categories do not simply congregate in similar categories but form entirely new ones, like the *moreno* term, as I analyze below.

104. Miles and Torres 1996; Silva 1998.

105. Sears et al. 2000b, p. 22.

106. Alba 2005.

107. Alba 2005, p. 41.

108. Alba 2005, p. 43.

109. Barth 1969, p. 17.

110. Segato 1998, p. 148.

111. Brubaker and Cooper 2000, p. 37.

112. Guimarães 1999, 2001a.

Chapter 4

1. On the conceptualization of "monoracial," see Harris and Sim 2002. See Nobles 2000 for a comparative study of census classification debates in the United States and Brazil.

2. Perlmann and Waters 2002.

3. Perlmann and Waters 2002.

4. Bertulio 1997; Brasil 1996; and Santos 1999.

5. Lovell 1999, p. 413; see also Daniel 2006; Nobles 2000; Skidmore 1993.

6. Lee and Bean 2004; Perlmann and Waters 2002.

7. Telles 1992, 2004.

8. More limited discussions of the adoption of a monoracial classification scheme actually have a long history in Brazil (see Pinto 1990). According to Oliveira e Oliveira 1974, p. 73, the term *negro* was adopted formally by *negro* activists in 1929 as a substitute for the then commonly used designation "man of color" (*homen de cor*).

9. Guimarães 2001a.

10. For example, see Pizzorno 1978, a key piece in the social movement literature on the mobilization of collective identities.

11. Bertulio 1997; Santos 1999; Turner 2002; Winant 2001.

12. Cornell 1996, p. 279. On the conceptualization of "levels of racial groupness," see Loveman 1999a and Brubaker and Cooper 2000.

13. Santos 1999; Turner 2002.

14. Cornell and Hartmann 1998.

15. Barth 1969; Cornell and Hartmann 1998; Jenkins 1994; Nagel 1994.

16. Cornell 1996, p. 266.

17. Cornell 1996, p. 278.

18. Silva 1996.

19. Carvalho, Wood, and Andrade 2004; Telles 2004. Both these studies also report a less frequent shift from the white to the brown category framed as a type of "darkening" as opposed to "whitening" dynamic.

20. See Skidmore 1974 on "whitening" and Degler 1971 on "mulatto escape hatch."

21. Nogueira 1985; Walker 2002.

22. Snipp 2003.

23. Degler 1971; Guimarães 2001a. There are, however, exceptions, such as individuals from Northern Brazil who may self-classify as brown without any clear tie to African ancestry.

24. Hasenbalg 1985; Lovell 1999; Silva 1985. See Telles 2004 and Telles and Lim 1999 for a more critical stance—their research does document significant difference between browns and *pretos* in terms of some socioeconomic indicators.

25. Wood and Lovell 1992. Findings regarding the similar treatment of browns and *pretos* go against the traditional belief in a "mulatto escape hatch" as theorized by Degler 1971, that is, that an intermediate category provides some escape from nonwhite disadvantage.

26. Schwartzman 1999.

27. Winant 2001, p. 26 (emphasis in original).

28. Hanchard 1994, p. 22.

29. Andrews 2004. There have been, however, limited mobilizations in the past, such as insurrections and the formation of *quilombos* ("runaway" slave communities) in preabolition years and other forms of cultural and political movements throughout the twentieth century (Oliveira e Oliveira 1974 and Pinto 1990). Hanchard 1994, p. 139, comments, however, that there was no significant (in terms of number and effects) *negro* mobilization in the 1970s and 80s: "There were no Afro-Brazilian versions of boycotting, sit-ins, civil disobedience." Recently, however, as I will discuss, the *negro* movement has taken on greater significance in the public sphere, and mobilizing events have become more common.

30. Gonzalez 1985; Hanchard 1994; Twine 1998; Winant 2001.

31. Burdick 1998a, p. 150.

32. Turner 2002; Winant 2001.

33. Santos 1999, p. 29. In that same vein, Silva 1999b, p. 18, noted that "the use of these identifiers [various nonwhite terms] causes a serious loss of [black] identity."

34. Bertulio 1997; Brasil 1996. Importantly, and as I will address in Chapter 8, this institutionalization is now being enacted in affirmative action legislation all over the country.

35. Nobles 2000, p. 172, writes, for example, that the result of unifying browns and *pretos* as *negros* "would be that the Brazilian census schedule would virtually duplicate U.S. census schedules insofar as the categories 'white' and 'black' are concerned." See also Guimarães 2001a, p. 172; Nascimento and Nascimento 2001, p. 108; and Reichmann 1999, p. 2 .

36. Gonzalez 1985.

37. Costa 2001, p. 150; Cunha 1998.

38. Guimarães 2001a.

39. Agier 1993, p. 104.

40. Burdick 1998b.

41. Brubaker and Cooper 2000.

42. This assumption rests in part on the folk equation of ethnicity and culture, although, as Lopez and Espiritu 1990, p. 201, remark, this assumption is also prevalent in much social scientific literature. As I will discuss, both are dynamic concepts, but very strong ethnic group boundaries can exist even in the absence of shared culture of the traditional sort, as Barth 1969 argues.

43. Sansone 2003; Segato 1998.

44. Brown 1999; Prandi 2000; and Walker 2002.

45. This difference between the United States and Brazil does not reflect a "kinder" nature of Brazilian slavery. Prandi 2000 claims that the survival of African religions in Brazil is due to the conditions born of the concentration in cities of African peoples brought to Brazil during the final period of slavery.

46. Prandi 2000; Walker 2002.

47. Fry 1982; Sansone 1998; Sheriff 1999.

48. Agier 1993; Riserio 1999.

49. Brown 1999, p. 213.

50. According to Gonzalez 1985, p. 131, "with the Estado Novo, a long period of co-optation and manipulation of the Black masses by Brazilian populism was inaugurated." See also Costa 2001.

51. Andrews 2004, p. 165.

52. This did not just happen on the level of state actors, however, but also coincided with existing and growing intellectual debates about the nature of the Brazilian nation and its people. See Bacelar 1999; Costa 2001; Guimarães 1999.

53. Andrews 2004, p. 165.

54. Andrews 2004, p. 171. As Brown 1999 writes of this process: "This occurred during the process of state building and represents effort to integrate Afro-Brazilians and their culture into the modern state both through the creation of political alliances and through the dissemination and promotion of national political [and racial] ideologies" (p. 216).

55. Andrews 2004; Fry 1982; Riserio 1999; Sheriff 1999.

56. Sheriff 1999.

57. Sheriff 1999, p. 14.

58. Sheriff 1999, p. 14.

59. Bacelar 1999.

60. Prandi 2000.

61. Brown 1999.

62. Brown 1999; Prandi 2000.

63. Prandi 2000, p. 642.

64. Brown 1999, p. 221.

65. Andrews 2004, p. 169.

66. Gonzalez 1985, p. 127; Hanchard 1994. Brown 1999, for example, writes that "Syncretism is the fruit . . . of an act of cultural violence" (p. 255).

67. Brown 1999, p. 213.

68. Andrews 2004, p. 171.

69. Gonzalez 1985; Hanchard 1994.

70. Gonzalez 1985, p. 123.

71. Riserio 1999, p. 255; Agier 1993; Gonzalez 1985; Hanchard 1994.

72. Cunha 1998, p. 220.

73. Agier 1993, 106.

74. Brown 1999. Riserio 1999 comments, however, that "this anti-syncretism stance is, in Brazil and other places, more an intellectual attitude than a popular one" (p. 256).

75. Agier 1993, p. 110.

76. Brown 1999; Cunha 1998.

77. Agier 1993.

78. Hanchard 1994, p. 138.

79. Cunha 1998.

80. Riserio 1999, p. 257.

81. Riserio 1999, p. 255; Agier 1993; Sansone 2003.

82. Brown 1999, p. 225.

83. Brown 1999, p. 226.

84. Brown 1999.

85. Nobles 2000, p. 130.

86. Cornell 1996, p. 269.

87. Cornell 1996, p. 269; Yancey et al. 1976.

88. Cornell and Hartmann 1998, pp. 274–75. See Coser 1956 on the generally strong relationship between structural disadvantage and social group formation.

89. Yancey et al. 1976.

90. Hanchard 1994; Twine 1998; Winant 2001.

91. Sansone 2003.

92. Cornell 1996, pp. 265, 283.

93. Cornell and Hartmann 1998; Nagel 1994.

94. Barth 1969, p. 15.

95. Nagel 1994, p. 162.

96. Cornell 1996.

97. Cornell 1996 comments, "what they share can be tremendously diverse, from physiological features to behavioral practices to cognitive schemas" (p. 268).

98. Cornell 1996, p. 270; Yancey et al. 1976.

99. Cornell 1996, p. 275.

100. Barth 1969, p. 16; Cornell 1996.

101. Cornell and Hartmann 1998.

102. Cornell 1996, p. 268.

103. Cornell 1996, pp. 272, 271. Cornell draws on Alba 1985, Gans 1979, and Waters 1990 for this conceptualization.

104. Nagel 1994, p. 162.

105. Sheriff 1999.

106. According to Pitanga 1999, p. 39, "Axé music, as samba-reggae has become known, is today the most important movement of the cultural affirmation of Brazilian Blacks."

107. Sansone 2003, p. 18.

108. Walker 2002, p. 17.

109. Walker 2002, p. 17.

110. Guimarães 2001a.

111. That nonwhites claim cultural ownership of "whiter" sports is important because it speaks to a two-direction flow of appropriation. See Segato 1998.

112. Sansone 2003, p. 192.

113. Walker 2002, p. 20.

114. Nagel 1994; Cornell and Hartmann 1998.

115. We chose to ask whites and browns about *negro* ancestors as opposed to African ancestors believing that these two terms carry the same connotation but that *negro* was more familiar to ordinary Brazilians. The PESB data that I present below proves that assumption to be weak, at best.

116. Cornell 1996; Fry and Maggie 2004; and Sansone 1998, 2003.

117. Segato 1998, p. 131.

118. Brown 1999; Hanchard 1994.

119. Segato 1998, pp. 148–49.

120. Segato 1998, p 131. Alternatively, on p. 147, she also writes that "whiteness in Brazil is impregnated by blackness."

121. Sansone 2003, p. 165. Davis 1991, p. 18, also recognized this dynamic when he wrote, "A group that is racially distinctive in a society may be an ethnic group as well, but not necessarily."

122. A popular Brazilian food originating among slaves. See Fry 1982. See also Silva's 1998 discussion of *feijoada* as an element of Brazilian national culture.

123. Fry and Maggie 2004, p. 157.

124. Costa 2001; Reis 1997; Segato 1998; Silva 1998.

125. Cornell 1996.

126. Nobles 2000.

127. Sansone 2003, p. 12.

128. Barth 1969, p. 35. See also Brubaker and Cooper 2001 and Cornell and Hartmann 1998.

129. Barth 1969, p. 35.

130. Hanchard 1994, p. 83.

131. Hanchard 1994.

132. Cornell 1996, p. 270.

133. On denial of discrimination, see Guimarães 2001a; Hanchard 1994; Twine 1998; and Winant 2001.

134. Mitchell 1977; Hasenbalg and Silva 1999.

135. Hanchard 1994. See also Brown 1999; Cunha 1998; Gonzalez 1985; and Segato 1998.

136. Hanchard 1994, p. 138, refers to "the fetishization of cultural artifacts and expressions."

137. Hanchard 1994, p. 141.

138. Cunha 1998.

139. Fry et al. 2007; Maggie and Fry 2004.

140. Daniel 2006.

141. Santos 1999; Silva 1999a,b.

142. Guimarães 2001a; Hanchard 1994; Parsons 1968; Twine 1998; Winant 2001.

143. Fry and Maggie 2004; Fry et al. 2007; Harris et al. 1993; Reis 1997; Sansone 1998, 2003; Segato 1998.

144. Munanga 1996, p. 186.

Chapter 5

1. Guimarães 2002; Hanchard 1994, p. 74.

2. Hasenbalg 1998; Hasenbalg and Silva 1999.

3. Guimarães 1999, 2001a; Telles 2004.

4. Degler's 1986[1971] seminal book is titled *Netither Black nor White*. Similarly, Skidmore 1974 uses the phrase "black into white" to describe Brazil. See Freyre 1979 on metarace.

5. Segato 1998; Silva 1998.

6. Nobles 2000.

7. Da Matta 1981.

8. Guimarães 2001a; Winant 1999.

9. Hanchard 1994; Santos 1999.

10. Cunha 1998; Hasenbalg 1998; Twine 1998.

11. Apostle et al. 1983.

12. Bairros 1989, p. 23.

13. Guimarães 2002, p. 330, for example, uses the phrase "With the death of racial democracy . . ."

14. Hunt 2007; Schuman and Krysan 1999; Schuman et al. 1997; Sears, Sidanius, and Bobo 2000c; Sidanius and Pratto 1999; Tuch and Martin 1997.

15. Apostle et al. 1983; Kluegel 1990.

16. Bobo and Kluegel 1993; Kluegel 1990.

17. For example, Krysan 2000.

18. Kinder and Sanders 1996; Sears, Henry, and Kosterman 2000a.

19. Bobo 1988b; Sidanius and Pratto 1999.

20. Dawson 2000; Kinder and Sanders 1996.

21. Sidanius and Pratto 1999, p. 123.

22. Hasenbalg and Huntington 1982, p. 245.

23. Pierson 1967; Wagley 1952c.

24. Degler 1986[1971], p. xv.

25. Fernandes 1969; Hasenbalg and Huntington 1982.

26. Hasenbalg and Huntington 1982, p. 256.

27. Fernandes 1969, pp. 138–39.

28. Bastide and Fernandes 1955; Fernandes 1969.

29. Dzidzienyo 1971.

30. Fernandes 1969, p. 138; Hasenbalg and Huntington 1982, p. 82.

31. See, for example, Hasenbalg 1985, 1999; Lovell 1999; Silva 1985; and Telles 2004.

32. Sidanius and Pratto 1999.

33. Guimarães 1999, p. 62.

34. Bairros 1989; Guimarães 1999, 2001a; Hasenbalg 1998; Marx 1998; Nascimento and Nascimento 2001; Santos 1999; Winant 1999, 2001.

35. Hanchard 1994, p. 56.

36. Winant 1999, p. 110.

37. Twine 1998, p. 8.

38. Twine 1998, p. 8.

39. Guimarães 2001b, p. 137.

40. Hasenbalg 1998, p. 237.

41. Sidanius, Peña, and Sawyer 2001; Sidanius and Pratto 1999.

42. Lovell 1999.

43. Segato 1998, p. 137. See also de la Fuente 1999; Fry 1996; Nogueira 1985; Reis 1997; Sansone 1998, 2003; and Souza 1997. In setting up these opposing two views of the myth of racial democracy, I follow the lead of Segato 1998 and Sheriff 2001. Sheriff 2001, p. 130, asks, for example, whether the racial democracy orientation in Latin America is a "misleading myth or a legitimate utopia." It should be noted that Sheriff appears to conclude that the myth is both of those things; that is, she opposes the reduction of racial democracy to a misleading myth that most of the dominant literature emphasizes (for example, Hanchard 1994 and Twine 1998) without the recognition of its utopian side.

44. Guimarães 2001b, p. 137. He refers to Fry 1995.

45. Sheriff 2001.

46. Nobles 1995, p. 9.

47. For more on how Brazilian national identity conditions positive racial identification, see Hanchard 1999, p. 4; Segato 1998, p. 137; and Skidmore 1985, p. 16.

48. Sheriff 2001, p. 221.

49. Nogueira 1985, p. 26

50. Guimarães 2002, p. 308.

51. Allport 1954; Kinder and Sanders 1996; Meertens and Pettigrew 1997.

52. Sears et al. 2000a, p. 77.

53. Bobo 1988a; Jackman 1994; Sidanius and Pratto 1999.

54. Sidanius and Pratto 1999.

55. Sidanius and Pratto p. 123.

56. Fernandes 1965; Guimarães 1999; Hasenbalg 1998; Turra and Venturi 1995.

57. Guimarães 2001b.

58. Guimarães 2002; Hanchard 1994.

59. Hasenbalg and Huntington 1982; Twine 1998.

60. Sears et al. 2000a.

61. Sidanius and Pratto 1999.

62. Hasenbalg and Huntington 1982.

63. Because prejudice does not necessary stem from power relationships (Tajfel and Turner 1986), this question was included in the survey. However, a similar question about whether *negros* discriminate against whites was not asked. The literature generally identifies discrimination as the purview of superordinate groups that are in a position to impose their specific racial interests.

64. In addition to the options that point to discrimination or lack of capitalizing on existing opportunities, participants in the DataFolha survey were also given the choices of "both" and "don't know." I classify the "both" response as a structuralist explanation (see Schuman et al. 1997 and Krysan 2000), and I treat the "don't know" responses (5 percent) as missing data. Interviewees offered other responses freely which I collapse into one of the two central categories that I evaluate as most appropriate. "Other" responses collapsed into the structuralist stance are: a. "the government," b. "lack of opportunities," c. "the society/the system." "Other" responses collapsed into the individualist stance are: a. "the prejudice of *negros*," b. "there is no difference/ *negros* and whites have the same opportunities." Importantly, fully 84 percent of responses fell into one of the two structuralist ("1") or individualist ("2") responses before any collapsing of categories.

65. Twine 1998.

66. Andrews 1991, p. 8.

67. Mitchell and Wood 1998.

68. See, for example, Degler 1986 [1971] and Hasenbalg and Huntington 1982.

69. See, for example, Schwartzman 1999; and Telles 2004.

70. Degler 1986 [1971]; Twine 1998; Winant 2001.

71. Dzidzienyo 1971.

72. Degler 1986 [1971], p. 272.

73. Lovell 1999; Schwartzman 1998; Silva 1985, 2000.

74. Telles 2004, p. 172.

75. See Guimarães 2006, p. 266, an interview of Carlos Hasenbalg.

76. Telles 2004, p. 150.

77. Sidanius and Pratto 1999.

78. Sidanius and Pratto 1999, p. 106. Hasenbalg 1998, p. 237, also uses the concept of "false consciousness" to frame the myth of racial democracy in Brazil.

79. Dawson 2000; Kinder and Sanders 1996; Sears et al. 2000b.

80. Banton 1983, pp. 125–26.

81. Alba 2005.

82. Kluegel and Smith 1986.

83. Kluegel and Smith, p. 241. See also Gurin, Miller, and Gurin 1980; Smith and Kluegel 1984; and Waters 1990. Regarding the effect of boundary salience, Waters 1990, p. 160, explains that white ethnic identification in the United States leads to a "lack of understanding of the ethnic or racial experience of others," especially regarding obstacles to social mobility. Stated alternatively, she finds that ethnic boundary salience among U.S. whites influences an individualist account of racial and/or ethnic inequality.

84. For a discussion of the Brazilian context as characterized by both a relative lack of segregation or separation and by "interracial intimacy," see Segato 1998 and Silva 1998.

85. See, for example, Harris 1970.

86. Silva 1998, p. 213.

87. Harris 1970, p. 2.

88. Kluegel and Smith 1986; Silva 1998. Kluegel and Smith 1986 use racial group membership in the United States in their comparison as exemplifying a high degree of group membership salience. This chapter makes use of that same comparison.

89. Kluegel and Smith 1986; Smith and Kluegel 1984; Waters 1990. However, other-classification, color categories, or discrimination based on imputed characteristics can exist beyond particularist group subjectivity. Racial discrimination and prejudice are about how others categorize an individual and not primarily about how an individual chooses to self-identify. See Telles and Lim 1998 and Wade 1997, p. 72.

90. See Segato 1998, p. 148. The lack of significance of the color construct for predicting attitudinal stances, or the cognitive domain, does not negate its significance for structuring socioeconomic outcomes.

91. de la Fuente 1999; Fry 1995; Nogueira 1985, p. 26; Reis 1997; Segato 1998.

92. Guimarães 1999.

93. Guimarães 1999, p. 62.

94. Hasenbalg and Silva 1999, pp. 170–71.

95. Mitchell 1977.

96. Telles 2004, p. 10. He adds, p. 46, "It was only in the mid-1990s that the Brazilian state began to recognize racism."

97. Guimarães 2002; Santos 1999; Silva 1999a; Daniel 2006.

98. Andrews 1996, pp. 496–97.

99. Winant 1999, p. 110. See also Guimarães 2001a, Lovell 1999, and Daniel 2006.

100. Lee 2002; Zaller 1992.

101. Zaller 1992, p. 6.

102. Zaller 1992, p. 8.

103. Andrews 1991; Guimarães 1999; Nobles 2000.

104. Lee 2002, p. 19.

105. Zaller 1992, p. 22.

106. Hasenbalg 1998, p. 237.

107. Hasenbalg and Silva 1999, pp. 165–66. Interestingly, although Hasenbalg generally embraces the dominant interpretation in his work, he does admit that the results from that 1986 election survey that he reports in 1998, p. 244, and with Silva in 1999 indicate that everyday Brazilians are not ignorant or clouded by deception about racism: "They know that prejudice and racism exists." However, at the same time Hasenbalg 1998, p. 244, affirms this, he also claims that this recognition is vacuous, for it nevertheless "is continuously hampering the realization of the dream [i.e., the legitimate utopia or a true racial democracy]."

108. Guimarães 2002, p. 306.

109. Cited in Guimarães 2002, p. 306.

110. Guimarães, p. 312.

111. Guimarães, p. 313.

112. Guimarães, p. 313.

113. Guimarães, p. 324.

114. Guimarães, p. 313.

115. Guimarães, p. 329.

116. Guimarães, p. 329.

117. Silva 1998, p. 329.

118. Bacelar 1999, p. 96.

119. Guimarães 2001a, p. 161.

120. Kluegel 1990.

121. Schuman et al. 1997, p. 171.

122. Schuman and Krysan 1999.

123. See also Kinder and Sanders 1996, pp. 98–106.

124. See also Bailey 2002.

Chapter 6

1. For examples, Andrews 2000; Burdick 1998a; Hanchard 1994; Hasenbalg 1998. Although throughout I refer to "the Brazilian *negro* movement," I am actually using this label as an umbrella term representing a large array of sometimes disconnected organizations that "place an explicit emphasis on struggling against racism and building a positive black identity" (Burdick 1998, p. 137), recognizing too that "a movement is a field of actors, not a unified entity" (Gamson and Meyer 1996, p. 283).

2. According to bipolar schemes of white versus *negro* racial classification generally employed by *negro* movements in Brazil, the "*negro* constituency" would refer to all nonwhite Brazilians, excluding those self-classifying as either Indian or of Asian descent (Nascimento and Nascimento 2001).

3. Cunha 1998.

4. Twine 1998, p. 8.

5. Winant 1994, 2001.

6. Andrews 1991, 2000; Bacelar 1999.

7. Bertulio 1997; Santos 1999.

8. Hasenbalg 1998; Silva 1998.

9. See, for example, Bobo 1988b; Kinder and Sanders 1996; and Schuman et al. 1997.

10. Hanchard 1994, p. 63.

11. Twine 1998.

12. Hanchard 1994.

13. Benedita 1999b; Nascimento and Nascimento 2001; Santos 1999.

14. Hanchard 1994; Winant 1994.

15. Alexander 1987, p. 25.

16. Bobo 1988b, p. 287.

17. It is certainly possible to go even further back in Brazilian history to find numerous instances of *negro* struggle for rights and survival. One clear example is the history of *quilombos*, or runaway slave communities. See Mitchell 1977 for a history of racialized mobilization and conflict in Brazil.

18. Guimarães 2001b, p. 130.

19. See Andrews 1991; Fiola 1980.

20. Guimarães 2001b; Soares and Silva 1985.

21. Andrews 1991, p. 193.

22. Guimarães 2001b, p. 132.

23. Guimaraes 2001b, p. 132.

24. Andrews 1991, p. 194.

25. Andrews 1991, p. 194.

26. Johnson 2001; Reichmann 1999.

27. Andrews 1991. Evidence is lacking, however, that this concession of including antiracism in those political platforms was widely translated into public discourse at the time.

28. Telles 2004.

29. Peria 2004.

30. Guimarães 2001a, p. 183.

31. Nascimento and Nascimento 2001.

32. Sansone 1996.

33. See, for example, Hanchard 1999.

34. Burdick 1998a,b; Hanchard 1994.

35. Hanchard 1994, p. 139.

36. Burdick 1998a.

37. Andrews 2000, p. 100.

38. Andrews 1991; Telles 2004; Winant 2001.

39. See, for example, Twine 1998.

40. Burdick 1998a, p. 139.

41. Winant 1999, p. 103.

42. Guimarães 2001b, p. 128. See also Marx 1998.

43. Guimarães 1999.

44. Twine 1998.

45. Fiola 1990.

46. Burdick 1992, p. 25.

47. Bacelar 1999, p. 97.

48. Andrews 1991, p. 198.

49. Andrews 2000, p. 100.

50. See, for example, Bertulio 1997 and Guimarães 2001a.

51. Santos 1999.

52. Santos-Stubbe 1998.

53. Santos-Stubbe, 1998, p. 55.

54. Fiola 1990, p. 41.

55. Nobles 2000, p. 147.

56. Burdick 1992, p. 24.

57. Bertulio 1997; Guimarães 2001a; Santos 1999.

58. Twine 1998; Winant 2001.

59. Bobo 1988a,b; Schuman et al. 1997.

60. Bobo 1988b, p. 289.

61. Bobo 1988b, p. 287.

62. According to that perspective, "whites' negative attitudes toward the black political movement reflect the learning of negative feelings and beliefs towards blacks

in general" (Bobo 1988b, p. 287). Importantly, as concerns sociocultural framings, Bobo remarks, "Prejudice theories do not provide clear guidance for developing expectations regarding the attitudes of blacks towards the black political movement" (1988b, p. 290),

63. Bobo 1988b, p. 287.

64. Bobo 1988b.

65. Bobo 1988b, p. 290.

66. Bobo 1988b, p. 290.

67. Those sociodemographic variables are age, a continuous variable; sex, a dummy variable denoted by male; education level, treated as a continuous variable with 5 values: (1) illiterate/primary incomplete, (2) primary complete/junior incomplete, (3) junior complete/secondary incomplete, (4) secondary complete/superior incomplete, and (5) superior complete; and color according to various formats.

68. Andrews 2000; Bacelar 1999.

69. For example, as commented previously, some *negro* movement actors refer to the difference between *pretos* and *negros* as between the "common black" and the "Africanized black" (Barcelos 1999, p. 163), respectively, intimating that *negros* are more racially conscious than *pretos*.

70. See, e.g., Hanchard 1994; Twine 1998; Burdick 1998; Hasenbalg 1998; and Andrews 2000.

71. Sears et al. 2000c.

72. Bonilla-Silva 1999, p. 903. See also Bonilla-Silva 1996.

73. Bonilla-Silva 1996, p. 473.

74. Hanchard 1994; Sidanius and Pratto 1999.

75. Bobo 1988a, 1988b.

76. Sidanius and Pratto 1999.

77. Bobo 1988b.

78. Bobo 1988a, p. 97.

79. Bobo 1988a, 1988b; Bonilla-Silva 1996, 1999; Sidanius and Pratto 1999.

80. Bobo 1988b, p. 290.

81. Twine 1998; Winant 2001.

82. Nascimento 2001.

83. Guimarães 2001a; Twine 1998.

84. Fry 1996; Hasenbalg 1998; Silva 1998. Burdick 1998a, 1998b; Sansone 1998, 2003.

85. Silva 1998, p. 224.

86. Appiah 1990, p. 5.

87. Appiah 1990, p. 5.

88. Bourdieu 1989, cited in Wacquant 1997, p. 127.

89. Nascimento and Nascimento 2001, p. 108.

90. Guimarães 2001a, p. 172.

91. Guimarães 2001a, p. 177.

92. Nonphysical or unobvious criteria may also be possible, as in the instance of Irish immigrants in the United States, who were once categorized as nonwhites.

93. Nascimento and Nascimento 2001.

94. Nascimento and Nascimento 2001, p. 125.

95. Racialism as a social movement strategy is rarely contemporarily criticized. It is an accepted notion not only among black social movements but also in academic, government, and nongovernmental organization circles. Some movement activists would disagree strenuously with this conceptualization of their discourse as tied to biological lineage or inheritable traits. They claim, for example, that the collective black category is a construct that unites individuals sharing perceived common shades of color associated with experiences of discrimination and culture. Again, what makes this discourse racialist in my view is that those perceived common shades of color are treated as a mark of origin, despite mixture, and are equaled to race. See Nascimento and Nascimento 2001; and Nascimento 2001.

96. Guimarães 1999, 2001a.

97. Whether or not, in the historic Brazilian worldview, ancestry equals race as it does in social movement mind-set is a question I cannot address here.

98. Cunha 1998, p. 226.

99. Silva 1998.

100. Fry 1996, p. 132.

101. Burdick 1998a, p. 151.

102. Burdick 1998a, p. 150.

103. Burdick 1998a, p. 151.

104. Fry 1996; Hasenbalg 1998; Silva 1998. See also Nobles 2000.

105. Guimarães 2001a, p. 166.

106. Sheriff 1999.

107. Hasenbalg 1998.

108. Hasenbalg 1998, p. 245.

109. Hasenbalg 1998, p. 246.

110. Andrews 2000; Bacelar 1999.

111. Lovell 1994.

112. Telles 1994, p. 59.

113. Telles 1994, p. 59.

114. Telles 1994, p. 46.

115. Bailey and Telles 2006.

116. Sansone 1996.

117. See also Bailey 2004.

Chapter 7

1. Andrews 1997; Fry 2000; Hanchard 1994.
2. Andrews 1997, p. 142.
3. Hanchard 1994, p. 21.
4. Marx 1998.
5. Instituto de Política Econômica Aplicada 2003.
6. Marx 1998.
7. Apostle et al. 1983; Kluegel and Smith 1986; Sidanius and Pratto 1999.
8. Andrews 1997; Reskin 1998.
9. Hochschild 1999. See also Andrews 1997.
10. Guimarães 1999.
11. Araujo 2001; Fry and Maggie 2004; Fry et al. 2007; Reichmann 1999; Maio and Santos 2005.
12. Oppenheimer 1996.
13. Weisskopf 2008, p. 669.
14. Weisskopf 2008, p. 669.
15. Oppenheimer 1996, p. 926.
16. Guimarães 2001a, p. 173.
17. Guimarães 2001a, p. 173.
18. Stubrin 2005.
19. Weisskopf 2008.
20. Asembléia Legislativa 2001. The categories defining beneficiaries were subsequently changed in Rio de Janeiro's state universities, dropping the intermediate brown term, as I discuss in subsequent chapters.
21. Jeter 2003; Resende 2007; Weber 2007.
22. Ribeiro 2007.
23. Paim 2005.
24. Marx 1998.
25. Marx 1998. See also Hanchard 1994.
26. See Bailey 2008 for a "political opportunity" (McAdam 1982) framing explaining this development. Several researchers have explored the importance of one or both of these variables, including Htun 2004; Instituto de Política Econômica Aplicada 2003; Peria 2004; Reichmann 1999; and Telles 2004. Htun 2004 also mentions a political opportunity framing.
27. Htun 2004; Reichmann 1999.
28. Marx 1998.
29. See Cardoso and Ianni 1962.
30. Pinheiro and Neto 1997.
31. Brasil 1996.

32. Instituto de Política Econômica Aplicada 2003.

33. Htun 2004; Reichman 1999; Telles 2004.

34. Cited in Htun 2004, p. 80.

35. Instituto de Política Econômica Aplicada 2003; Telles 2004.

36. Instituto de Política Econômica Aplicada 2003; Telles 2004.

37. Asembléia Legislativa 2001.

38. Universidade do Estado da Bahia 2002.

39. Guimarães 2001a; Hanchard 1994.

40. Andrews 1997, 2000; Bertulio 1997; Hanchard 1994; Martins 1996.

41. Nobles 2000, p. 19.

42. Apostle et al 1983; Kluegel and Smith 1986; Sears et al. 2000b.

43. Hughes and Tuch 2000, p. 170.

44. On group conflict theory, see Bobo 1988a and Jackman 1994; on group position theory, see Blumer 1958; on social dominance theory, see Sidanius and Pratto 1999; and on neoclassical hegemony models, see Gramsci 1971.

45. Sidanius, Pratto, and Bobo 1996.

46. Federico and Sidanius 2002; Sidanius et al. 2001; Sidanius and Pratto 1999.

47. For example, Sears et al. 2000c.

48. Sidanius et al. 2001.

49. See Krysan 2000.

50. For example, Sidanius and Pratto 1999, p. 48.

51. Sidanius and Pratto 1999, p. 48.

52. Sidanius and Pratto 1999, p. 49.

53. The relative levels of this orientation, according to Sidanius and Pratto (1999, p. 49), also depend on other socialization factors such as religious practices, biologically based "temperamental predispositions" and personalities, and gender.

54. Sidanius and Pratto 1999, pp. 43–44.

55. On "false consciousness," see Marx and Engels 1846/1970, and on "ideological hegemony," see Gramsci 1971.

56. Sidanius and Pratto 1999, pp. 22–23.

57. Sidanius and Pratto 1999, p. 45.

58. Sidanius et al. 2001.

59. Hanchard's 1994 theoretical framework can be most clearly categorized as a neoclassical hegemony model (Gramsci 1971). As such, it falls under the category of "general group dominance perspective" (Sidanius et al. 1996).

60. Sidanius and Pratto 1999.

61. I created this variable using scale construction techniques, centrally principal factor analysis. Two of the questions had only two response categories representing support or a lack thereof for said policies. The other two had four response categories measuring levels of agreement and disagreement using the "strongly or in part"

format. I collapsed the levels of agreement to a single agree response and did likewise for the disagreement measures. Therefore, all variables have two possible responses, support or lack of support for specific race-targeted initiatives, to be used in variable construction. Employing the four items, the first goal was to ensure that they all appear to be measuring a common underlying dimension. Principal factor analysis technique showed a very significant eigenvalue on a primary factor at 2.7, and the eigenvectors, or factor loadings, were all highly significant at >0.5. Scores on the four items were subsequently standardized. I then created a new variable combining and averaging the four standardized items. Lastly, I converted the scale to a range from 0 to 1. Thirty-four unique values were recorded through the averages of the standardized values, and hence I treat this dependent variable as continuous.

62. Education is a continuous variable with five values: (1) illiterate/primary incomplete, (2) primary complete/junior incomplete, (3) junior complete/secondary incomplete, (4) secondary complete/superior incomplete, and (5) superior complete.

63. The color measure has three categories in a first model—white, brown, and *preto*—and two categories in a second as a dummy variable (1 = white, 0 = nonwhite).

64. Sidanius et al. 2001.

65. Kinder and Sanders 1996, p. 17.

66. Kinder and Sanders 1996, p. 17.

67. Bobo and Kluegel 1993; Kinder and Sanders 1996.

68. Kinder and Sanders 1996, p. 262.

69. Bobo and Kluegel 1993, p. 453.

70. Sidanius and Pratto 1999.

71. Warren 2002, pp. 234–35.

72. Hanchard 1994.

73. On "façade," see Jackman 1994, and on "neat trick," see Sidanius et al. 2001, p. 847.

74. Sidanius and Pratto 1999, p. 39.

75. Sidanius et al. 2001, p. 846.

76. Sidanius et al. 2001, p. 848.

77. Brubaker 2002.

78. Handelman 1977, p. 187.

79. For more on this point, see Loveman 1999a.

80. Jenkins 1994.

81. Goldberg 1997, p. 191.

82. Brubaker 2002, p. 164.

83. Brubaker 2002, p. 164.

84. Reskin 2003.

85. Reskin 2003, p. 5.

86. Sidanius and Pratto 1999, p. 48.

87. Reskin 2003, p. 6.

88. Sears et al. 2000b.

89. Hasenbalg and Silva 1999.

90. Hanchard 1994; Nobles 2000.

91. Brubaker 2002, pp. 2, 3.

92. Reskin 2003.

93. Reskin 2003, p. 5.

94. Hwang, Fitzpatrick, and Helms 1998, p. 377.

95. Kinder and Sanders 1996.

96. Harris 1964, pp. 60–61.

97. Hwang et al. 1998, p. 369.

98. Telles 1994, p. 46.

99. Schuman and Harding 1963. See also Krysan 2000.

100. Schuman and Harding 1963, p. 238. See also Hasenbalg 1998, p. 245, where he writes of white empathy as a factor influencing attitudes in Brazil.

101. On intermarriage, see Telles 1993; and on spatial segregation, see Telles 1992.

102. Kinder and Sanders 1996.

103. Kinder and Sanders 1996, p. 128; Myrdal 1944.

104. Kinder and Sanders 1996, p. 158.

105. Zaller 1992.

106. Myrdal 1944, cited in Kinder and Sanders 1996, p. 129.

107. de la Fuente 1999; Fry 1996; Nogueira 1985; Reis 1997; Sansone 1998; Segato 1998, p. 137; Sheriff 2001; Souza 1997.

108. Guimarães 2002, p. 308, referring to a use of that phrase by Freyre.

109. Kinder and Sanders 1996.

110. See also Bailey 2004.

111. Bobo 1988a,b.

Chapter 8

1. Andrews 1997; Da Matta 1997; Fry et al. 2007; Reis 1997; Sansone 1998; Skidmore 1997.

2. Skidmore 1997, p. 134.

3. Bertulio 1997; Guimarães 1997, 1999.

4. Bertulio 1997, p. 204.

5. Morning and Sabbagh 2005.

6. Hochschild 2002; Prewitt 2002.

7. Goldstein and Morning 2002, p. 119.

8. Harrison 2002; Prewitt 2002.

9. Skerry 2002, p. 338.

10. Golub 2005, p. 564.

11. Bonilla-Silva 2004; Skidmore 2003.

12. Asembléia Legislativa 2001.

13. Asembléia Legislativa 2003.

14. César 2005; Merola 2003.

15. Merola 2003.

16. Guimarães 1997; Júnior 2004.

17. César 2005, p. 60.

18. Peria 2004, p. 100.

19. Nogueira 1985.

20. Guimarães 2001a, p. 172; Hanchard 1994, pp. 24–25.

21. Nobles 2000, p. 171.

22. Andrews 1991, p. 250.

23. Davis 1991; Golub 2005; Petersen 1987.

24. Skidmore 2003.

25. Zack 1999, p. 304.

26. Golub 2005; U.S. Census Bureau 1979.

27. Davis 1991; Golub 2005.

28. Davis 1991.

29. Sansone 2003.

30. Bailey and Telles 2006.

31. Sheriff 2001.

32. Hanchard 1999, p. 19.

33. Twine 1998; Winant 2001.

34. Universidade de Brasília 2004.

35. Maio and Santos 2005; Weber 2007.

36. Universidade de Brasília 2004. The official procedure for the designation of racial quotas beneficiaries was modified at the University of Brasília in 2008 to exclude mandatory photographing of *negro* applicants (Universidade de Brasília 2008). However, these individuals still must appear before an "interviewing committee" to have their *negro* racial status officially verified.

37. Universidade Estadual de Mato Grosso do Sul 2004.

38. Corrêa 2003.

39. Ribeiro 2007.

40. Golub 2005.

41. A special edition of the Brazilian academic journal *Perspectivas Antropológicas* (issue no. 23, 2005) addresses this debate.

42. Fry et al. 2007; Maio and Santos 2005.

43. Weber 2007.

44. Resende 2007.

45. See the judicial decision online at http://conjur.estadao.com.br/static/text/56134,1.

46. Ford 1994; Harrison 2002; Skerry 2002.

47. Ford 1994.

48. Golub 2005.

49. Ford 1994, p. 1241.

50. See Perlmann and Waters 2002 and Zack 1995.

51. Golub 2005, p. 565. See also de Zwart 2005, p. 155, for the distinction between the effects of categorization for exclusion versus inclusion.

52. Golub 2005, p. 569.

53. Golub 2005, p. 563.

54. de Zwart 2005.

55. See de Zwart 2005, p. 159, on cognitive resonance.

56. Perlmann and Waters 2002, p. 11.

57. Perlmann and Waters 2002.

58. Harrison 2002; Prewitt 2002.

59. Perlmann and Waters 2002, p. 13.

60. Perlmann and Waters 2002.

61. Office of Management and Budget 2000, Section II (cited in Perlmann and Waters 2002, p. 15).

62. Degler 1971.

63. Ribeiro 2007.

64. Bailey and Telles 2006; Sansone 2003.

65. Júnior 2004, p. 304.

66. Telles 2004, pp. 86–87.

67. Using a probability sample, Bailey and Telles 2006 also document that the skin colors of the individuals who prefer the *preto* and *negro* categories appear very similar.

68. Rosemberg 2004.

69. César 2005, p. 65.

70. Paim 2005; Ribeiro 2007.

71. Rosemberg 2004.

72. Almeida, Young, and Pinto 2002.

73. Five percent of the sample consistently said that they could not answer the question solely by viewing a photo.

74. Bailey and Telles 2006.

75. Telles 2004, pp. 86–87.

76. Ribeiro 2007.

77. Burdick 1998a, p. 149.

78. Rosemberg 2004.

79. Côrrea 2003; Resende 2007; Weber 2007.

80. Russo 2007. Notice how even the rector of the University of Brasília uses the *negro* term on this occasion as equal to the census *preto* term in his formulation, distinguishing both from those who self-classify as browns.

81. Côrrea 2003.

82. Bailey 2008; Harrison 2002; Skerry 2002.

83. Hasenbalg 1985; Lovell 1999; Silva 1985. Nonetheless, Telles and Lim (1998, p. 473; see also Telles 2004, p. 146) document "some support for Degler's [1971] mulatto escape hatch theory, thus refuting Silva's (1985) well-known challenge."

84. Ribeiro 2007.

85. César 2005; Paim 2005, Ribeiro 2007; Skidmore 2003.

86. Fields 1990, p. 118.

87. Fields 1990, p. 118.

88. Washington 2004, p. 8.

89. Davis 1991; Snipp 2003.

90. Morning and Sabbagh 2005, p. 58.

91. Andrews 1991, p. 250.

Chapter 9

1. Telles 2004.

2. Bourdieu 1991; Goldberg 2003. See also Bourdieu 1989, p. 21, on "strategies that aim at imposing a new construction of social reality by jettisoning the old political vocabulary."

3. Bourdieu 1991, p. 221, italics in original. See also Boltanski 1984; Bourdieu 1989; Goldberg 2003; Haney López 1996; Petersen 1987.

4. Cornell and Hartmann 1998; Tilly 2004.

5. Hanchard 1994; Nobles 2000; Twine 1998.

6. Ford 1994; Golub 2005; Haney López 1996.

7. Lamont and Molnár 2002, p. 168.

8. Lamont and Molnár 2002, p. 168.

9. Hasenbalg 1985; Lovell 1999; Silva 1985. See Telles 2004 and Telles and Lim 1998 for a more critical view.

10. Degler 1971.

11. Telles 2004.

12. Hanchard 1994; Pizzorno 1978; Winant 2001.

13. Marx 1998, p. 266.

14. Davis 1991, p. 58.

15. Davis 1991, p. 59.

16. Davis 1991, p. 59.

17. Farley 2002.

18. Hochschild 2002; Perlmann and Waters 2002.

19. Marx 1998, p. 262.

20. Marx 1998, p. 260.

21. Hanchard 1994, p. 83.

22. Davis 1991, p. 15.

23. Sansone 2003. The title of his 2003 book is, in fact, *Blackness without Ethnicity*.

24. Davis 1991.

25. Brubaker 2002; Tilly 2004; Washington 2004.

26. Barth 1969; Nagel 1994.

27. Jenkins 1994.

28. See Cornell and Hartmann's 1998 "construction sites," Tilly's 2004 "social sites," and Bourdieu's 1991 sites of "objectification."

29. Jenkins 1994.

30. Bourdieu 1991, p. 239. On objectification see p. 243.

31. Jenkins 1994; Tilly 2004; Washington 2004.

32. Jenkins 1994, p. 216.

33. Tilly 2004, p. 216; Washington 2004.

34. U.S. Bureau of the Census 1979, p. 18.

35. Davis 1991, p. 13; Smedley 1993, p. 9. Washington 2004 holds that the United States is not totally unique in this respect. He points to examples such as modern China, Nazi Germany, and Rwanda as adopting very similar rules at certain moments in their histories regarding specific populations.

36. I do not pretend here a complete accounting of why hypodescent developed in the United States; rather, I point out some of the more significant differences with the Brazilian case addressed in the literature.

37. Degler 1971; Fields 1990; Wacquant 2005.

38. Wacquant 2005, p. 127; see also Fields 1990.

39. Degler 1971, p. 85.

40. Degler 1971, p. 86.

41. Degler 1971.

42. Nobles 2000, p. 88; Degler 1971, p. 86.

43. Smedley 1993.

44. Smedley 1993, p. 323; Snipp 2003.

45. Nobles 2000.

46. Nobles 2000, p. 53

47. Nobles 2000, p. 54.

48. Nobles 2000; Skidmore 1974.

49. Nevertheless, whitening continues to affect popular racial understandings to some extent in Brazil, where white skin color is ideal and, for example, may be sought after through the desirability of marriage to a whiter partner.

50. Nobles 2000.

51. Snipp 2003, p. 566.

52. The mulatto category was also excluded that year, but it was added again to the 1910 and 1920 censuses.

53. Nobles 2000, p. 87.

54. Degler 1971.

55. Degler 1971, p. 5.

56. Hanchard 1994; Marx 1998.

57. Morning and Sabbagh 2005.

58. Jenkins 1994.

59. César 2005; Ribeiro 2007.

60. Araujo 2001.

61. Fry and Maggie 2004 and Maio and Santos 2005.

62. Skidmore 2003.

63. Guimarães 2001a.

64. Nobles 2000; Skidmore 1974.

65. Lamont and Molnár 2002; Tilly 2004.

66. Jenkins 1994; Tilly 2004.

67. Tilly 2004, p. 220.

68. Tilly 2004, p. 222.

69. Resende 2007. See the judicial decision online at http://conjur.estadao.com.br/static/text/56134,1.

70. Bobo and Kluegel 1993.

71. Jenkins 1994, p. 216.

72. Washington 2004, p. 15.

73. Sansone 2003.

74. Nagel 1994, p. 157.

75. Banton 1983.

76. de Zwart 2005.

77. de Zwart 2005, p. 155.

78. See their website at www.nacaomestica.org/.

79. Daniel 2006.

80. Although I focus here on the effects of these policies on the strengthening of brown or mixed-race identification, a parallel reactive effect surely could be an increase of racial groupness among white Brazilians.

81. Jenkins 1994.

82. Jenkins 1994, p. 214.

83. Banton 1995, p. 486.

84. Guimarães 1999, p. 192.

85. Guimarães 1999, p. 191.

86. Agier 1993, p. 104.

87. de la Fuente 2002; Loveman 1999a.

88. Goldberg 2003; Goodman 1978.

89. Bourdieu 1989.

90. Marx 1998, p. 6.

91. Bailey 2008; de Zwart 2005; Ford 1994; Petersen 1987.

92. Ford 1994, p. 1285. See also de Zwart 2005 and Petersen 1987.

93. On "theory effect," see Bourdieu 1987, p. 17. See de Zwart 2005 on "cognitive consonance."

94. Bourdieu 1991.

95. Fields 1990.

96. Recall, however, that not all research agrees on the common disadvantaged position of browns and *pretos* in Brazil. See, for example, Telles 2004 and Telles and Lim 1998.

97. Brubaker 2002, p. 166, italics in original. Brubaker cites Bourdieu 1991, p. 220. See also Bourdieu on the genesis and functioning of group spokespeople, which he calls the mystery of ministry: "The spokesperson is the person who, speaking about a group, speaking on behalf of a group, surreptitiously posits the existence of the group in question, institutes the group, through that magical operation which is inherent in any act of naming" (p. 250).

98. Petersen 1987, p. 207.

99. Hasenbalg 1985; Silva 1985.

100. Silva 1985, p. 43.

101. See Andrews 1991, p. 250, who documents this dynamic on the part of IBGE researchers. See also Telles: "Silva's conclusion became widely accepted and for many researchers it served to legitimize the collapsing of browns and blacks into a single *negro* or nonwhite category. Moreover, black-movement leaders used it as 'proof' that browns and blacks received similar levels of discrimination and therefore should unite as *negros*." (2004, p. 146).

102. Guimarães 2006, p. 263.

103. Brubaker and Cooper 2000, p. 9, offer a framing of this type of "groupist" dynamic adopted by some social scientists as the "flattening rubric of identity."

104. Guimarães 2001a; Hanchard 1994; Twine 1998; Winant 1999, 2001. See Bourdieu on "science proposing a truth" (1991, pp. 222–23). On the role of science in creating "race" in the first place, see Gould 1993. On the interaction of race scientists and the state in creating "race" along the lines demarcated by rule of hypodescent in the United States, see Nobles 2000.

105. On "classificatory struggles," see Bourdieu 1991, p. 241, and Goldberg 2003. See Bourdieu 1989, p. 21, on struggles "for the monopoly over legitimate naming."

106. Fry et al. 2007.

107. Hanchard 1994; Twine 1998; Winant 2001; Guimarães 1002a.

108. Bertulio 1997. See discussion in Bailey and Telles 2006.

109. Bacelar 1999; Sansone 2003.

110. Santos 1999; Guimarães 2001a.

111. IPEA 2003; Ribeiro 2007.

112. Bailey 2008.

113. Guimarães 2001a; Ribeiro 2007.

114. Lovell 1999, p. 413; see also Daniel 2006; Nobles 2000; Skidmore 2003.

115. Hochschild 2002, pp. 350–51.

116. Lee and Bean 2004.

117. Hochschild 2002, p. 251.

118. Harrison 2002; Prewitt 2002; Skerry 2002.

119. Cornell and Hartmann 1998, p. 224.

120. Skidmore 2003.

121. Cornell and Hartmann 1998, p. 248, and Brubaker 1995.

122. Morning and Sabbagh 2005, p. 58.

123. Guimarães 2001a, p. 162.

124. Guimarães 1999, p. 25. Brazilians, however, may not actually deny the existence of races. The founding myth of the Brazilian nation envisions its people as a mixture of Europeans, Africans, and Indians. Moreover, the very notion of multiracialism rests on a belief in racial origins. See Nobles 2000 and Zack 1999. What they do not evidently embrace is a conception of racial group membership defined by hypodescent.

125. Fields 2001, p. 40.

126. Guimarães 1997.

127. Hochschild 2002, p. 350.

Chapter 10

1. Appiah 1990, p. 5; Guimarães 1999, 2001a; Waters 1999.

2. Morning 2004.

3. Dawson 2000; Kinder and Sanders 1996; Sears et al. 2000b.

4. Waters 1999.

5. Guimarães, 1999, 2001a.

6. Da Matta 1981.

7. Of course, there is no biological racial group to which anyone actually belongs, as the science of human biology shows. Many theorists, however, treat race as a substratum reality structured in black and white. See Silva 1998.

8. See Sansone's 2003 extensive ethnographic research on this question of the lack of association between blackness and culture or ethnicity in Brazil.

9. Perlmann and Waters 2002.

10. Bobo 1988b; Kinder and Sanders 1996.

11. See, for example, Hochschild 1999.

12. Dawson 2000; Kinder and Sanders 1996.

13. Sidanius and Pratto 1999.

14. Dim or bright (Alba 2005); hard or soft (Banton 1983); strong or weak (Cornell 1996); symbolic or otherwise (Gans 1979); symbolic or social (Lamont and Molnár 2002).

15. Brubaker 2002; Brubaker and Cooper 2000; Brubaker, Loveman, and Stamatov 2004. See also Alba 2005, who makes a similar argument in terms of comparative studies of immigrant population dynamics.

16. In addition, to treat less than robust social boundaries as enclosing sociological groups also reifies those populations. As Brubaker 2002, p. 166, points out, citing Gil-White 1999, p. 803, "as 'analysts of naturaliziers,' we need not be 'analytic naturalizers.'" Brubaker 2002 also notes that some of the groupist language may merely be an "intellectual bad habit."

17. Guimarães 2001a; Hanchard 1994; Twine 1998; Winant 1999.

18. Sidanius et al. 2001 and Sidanius and Pratto 1999.

19. Guimarães 2002; Hasenbalg 1998; Segato 1998; Sheriff 2001; Sansone 2003; Silva 1998. Suggestive of this very debate, Sheriff's 2001 influential ethnography is titled *Dreaming Equality*. Sheriff's research, however, draws attention to the prescriptive essence of the myth of racial democracy at the same time that she argues that it also contains a descriptive, obscurantist element.

20. Sidanius and Pratto 1999. Specifically on "counterdominance" ideologies, see p. 39.

21. Sidanius and Pratto 1999.

22. Sheriff 2001. The egalitarian nature of this creed should be understood as couched in a society that is drastically unequal on many levels but most especially in terms of the distribution of wealth and the enormous gulfs between the rich and the poor. Certainly, notions of equality in such a setting may have much more to do with perceived opportunities than real outcomes. As I mentioned in Chapter 6, the *negro* movement in Brazil did once dream of a more egalitarian socialist society in which to forge a racial democracy.

23. Nobles 2000, p. 19—"The racial democracy ideal, in other words, did not require racially segregatory public policies and, indeed, found them repellent."

24. Guimarães 2002, p. 329.

25. Guimarães 2002, 329.

26. Myrdal 1944, p. 3, cited in Kinder and Sanders 1996, p. 129.

27. See Hochschild 1995; Kinder and Sanders 1996, p. 129; Myrdal 1944; Zaller 1992.

28. Sniderman and Carmines 1997; Sniderman, Crosby, and Howell 2000. See Bobo 2000; Bobo and Tuan 2006; and Sears et al. 2000c for criticisms of the "principled stance" framing.

29. For example, de la Fuente 2001.

30. Guimarães 2001a; Hanchard 1994; Twine 1998; Winant 1999.

31. Fry 2000.

32. Guimarães 2001a; Hanchard 1994; Marx 1998; Winant 1999.

33. Wacquant 2002.

34. Immigration policies may be the exception.

35. Guimarães 2001a; Hanchard 1994.

36. Daniel 2006, p. 1.

37. Silva 1998.

38. Parsons 1968, pp. 352–53; italics in original.

39. Winant 2001, p. 256; italics in original.

40. Guimarães 2001a, p. 162.

41. de la Fuente 1999, 2001; Segato 1998.

42. de la Fuente 1999, p. 68.

43. It should be noted that antiracialism as a movement *strategy*, as opposed to a *description* of the reigning racial common sense in Brazil, has not really been pursued in contemporary Brazil. The current movement strategy of strategic essentialism comes, then, not as an alternative to the previously employed strategy of strategic antiracialism in contemporary Brazil. Since the democratic opening of the 1980s, black movements have generally adopted a "radical racialism," as Guimarães 2001a claims, against the backdrop of the racial status quo.

44. Lovell 2000.

45. Bacelar 1999; Maggie 2001.

46. Segato 1998, p. 136.

47. Harris et al. 1995, p. 1614.

48. Segato 1998, pp. 130–31.

49. Ford 1994, p. 1285.

50. Bourdieu 1989, p. 23.

51. On creating a group out of a category, see Petersen 1987, pp. 206–07; and Jenkins 1994.

52. Bourdieu 1991, p. 233.

53. Boltanski 1984, p. 488.

54. Bobo 1988a, p. 100.

55. Hanchard 1994; Twine 1998; Winant 2001.

References

Agier, Michel. 1993. "Ethnopolítica: A Dinâmica do Espaço Afro-Baiano." *Estudos Afro Asiáticos,* 22: 99–115.

Alba, Richard. 1985. Italian Americans: Into the Twilight of Ethnicity. Englewood Cliffs, NJ: Prentice-Hall.

Alba, Richard. 2005. "Bright vs. Blurred Boundaries: Second-Generation Assimilation and Exclusion in France, Germany, and the United States." *Ethnic and Racial Studies,* 28(1): 20–49.

Alexander, Jeffrey C. 1987. "The Centrality of the Classics." In *Social Theory Today,* ed. Anthony Giddens and Jonathan H. Turner. Stanford, CA: Stanford University Press.

Allport, Gordon H. 1954. *The Nature of Prejudice.* Reading, MA: Addison-Wesley.

Almeida, Alberto Carlos, Clifford Young, and Andréia Soares Pinto. 2002, April–June. "Qual é a Cor do Brasileiro? *Insight Inteligéncia,* 30–39.

Anderson, Margo. 1990. *The American Census: A Social History.* New Haven, CT: Yale University Press.

Andrews, George R. 1991. *Blacks and Whites in São Paulo, Brazil, 1888–1988.* Madison: University of Wisconsin Press.

———. 1996. "Brazilian Racial Democracy, 1900–90: An American Counterpoint." *Journal of Contemporary History,* 31(3): 483–507.

————. 1997. "Ação Afirmativa: Um Modelo para o Brasil?" In *Multiculturalismo e Racismo: uma comparação Brasil–Estados Unidos,* ed. J. Souza. Brasilia: Paralelo 15.

————. 2000. "Forms of Black Political Response in Brazil." In *Beyond Racism: Embracing an Independent Future,* vol. 4. Comparative Human Relations Initiative, Atlanta, GA: The Southern Education Foundation.

————. 2004. *Afro-Latin America.* Oxford, U.K.: Oxford University Press.

Appiah, Kwame Anthony. 1990. "Racisms." In *Anatomy of Racism,* ed. David Theo Goldberg. Minneapolis: University of Minnesota Press.

————. 2000. "Racial Identity and Racial Identification." In *Theories of Race and Racism,* ed. Les Black and John Solomon. London: Routledge.

Apostle, Richard A., Charles Y. Glock, Thomas Piazza, and Marijean Suelzle. 1983. *The Anatomy of Racial Attitudes.* Los Angeles: University of California Press.

Araujo, Clara. 2001. "Potencialidades e Limites da Politica de Cotas no Brasil." *Estudos Feministas,* 9: 231–52.

Araujo, Tereza Cristina N. 1987. "A Classificação de 'Cor' nas Pesquisas do IBGE: Notas para uma Discussão." *Cadernos de Pesquisa,* 63: 14–16.

Asembléia Legislativa do Estado do Rio de Janeiro. 2001. "Lei Estadual 3708/2001." Retrieved December, 2007, from www.alerj.rj.gov.br/.

————. 2003. "Lei Estadual 4151/2003." Retrieved December, 2007, from www.alerj .rj.gov.br/.

Bacelar, Jeferson. 1999. "Blacks in Salvador: Racial Paths." In *Black Brazil: Culture, Identity, and Social Mobilization,* ed. Larry Crook and Randal Johnson. Los Angeles: UCLA Latin American Center Publications.

Bailey, Stanley R. 2002. "The Race Construct and Public Opinion: Understanding Brazilian Beliefs about Racial Inequality and Their Determinants." *American Journal of Sociology,* 108(2): 406–39.

————. 2004. "Group Dominance and the Myth of Racial Democracy: Antiracism Attitudes in Brazil." *American Sociological Review,* 69: 728–47.

————. 2008. "Unmixing for Race-Making in Brazil." *American Journal of Sociology,* 118(3): 577–614.

Bailey, Stanley R., and Edward E. Telles. 2006. "Multiracialism vs. a Collective Black: Census Debates in Brazil." *Ethnicities,* 6(1): 74–101.

Bairros Luíza. 1989. "Brazil: Birthplace of Racial Democracy?" In *Introspectives: Contemporary Art by Americans and Brazilians of African Descent,* ed. J. J. Drewal and D. C. Driskell. Los Angeles: The California Afro-American Museum.

———. 1996. "Orfeu and Poder: Uma Perspectiva Afro-Americana sobre a Política Racial no Brasil." *Afro-Ásia,* 17: 173–186.

Banton, Michael. 1983. *Racial and Ethnic Competition.* Cambridge, U.K.: Cambridge University Press.

———. 1995. "Rational Choice Theories." *American Behavioral Scientist,* 38(3): 478–97.

Barcelos, Luiz C. 1999. "Struggling in Paradise: Racial Mobilization and the Contemporary Black Movement in Brazil." In *From Indifference to Inequality: Race in Contemporary Brazil,* ed. Rebecca Reichmann. University Park: Pennsylvania State University Press.

Barth, Fredrik. 1969. *Ethnic Groups and Boundaries.* Boston: Little, Brown and Company.

Bastide, Roger, and Florestan Fernandes. 1955. *Relaçoes raciais entre negros e branco em São Paulo.* São Paulo: Editora Anhembi.

Bertulio, Dora De Lima. 1997. "Enfrentamento do Racismo em um Projeto Democrático." In *Multiculturalismo e Racismo: Uma Comparação Brasil--Estados Unidos,* ed. Jesse Souza. Brasilia: Paralelo 15.

Bickart, Barbara, and E. Marla Felcher. 1996. "Expanding and Enhancing the Use of Verbal Protocols in Survey Research." In *Answering Questions: Methodology for Determining Cognitive and Communicative Processes in Survey Research,* ed. N. Schwarz and S. Sudman. San Francisco, CA: Jossey-Bass Publishers.

Bicudo, Virgínia Leone. 1947. "Atitudes Raciais de Pretos e Mulatos em São Paulo." *Sociologia* 9(3): 195–219.

Blumer, Herbert. 1958. "Race Prejudice as a Sense of Group Position." *The Pacific Sociological Review,* 1: 3–7.

Bobo, Lawrence. 1988a. "Group Conflict, Prejudice, and the Paradox of Contemporary Racial Attitudes." In *Eliminating Racism: Profiles in Controversy,* ed. P. A. Katz and D. A. Taylor. New York: Plenum Press.

———. 1988b. "Attitudes toward the Black Political Movement: Trends, Meaning, and Effects on Racial Policy Preferences." *Social Psychology Quarterly,* 51(4): 287–302.

———. 1997. "Race, Public Opinion, and the Social Sphere." *Public Opinion Quarterly,* 61: 1–15.

———. 2000. "Race and Beliefs about Affirmative Action." In *Racialized Politics: The Debate about Racism in America,* ed. David. O. Sears, Jim Sidanius, and Lawrence Bobo. Chicago: University of Chicago Press.

Bobo, Lawrence, and James R. Kluegel. 1993. "Opposition to Race-Targeting: Self Interest, Stratification Ideology, or Racial Attitudes?" *American Sociological Review,*
58: 443–64.

Bobo, Lawrence D., and Mia Tuan. 2006. *Prejudice in Politics: Group Position, Public
Opinion, and the Wisconsin Treaty Rights Dispute.* Cambridge, MA: Harvard University Press.

Bonilla-Silva, Eduardo. 1996. "Rethinking Racism: Toward a Structural Interpretation." *American Sociological Review,* 62: 465–80.

———. 1999. "The Essential Social Fact of Race." *American Sociological Review,* 64:
899–906.

———. 2004. "From Bi-Racial to Tri-Racial: Towards a New System of Racial Stratification in the US." *Ethnic and Racial Studies,* 27(6): 931–50.

Boltanski, Luc. 1984. "How a Social Group Objectified Itself: 'Cadres' in France, 1936–
45." *Social Science Information,* 23(3): 469–91.

Bourdieu, Pierre. 1989. "Social Space and Symbolic Power." *Sociological Theory,* 7(1):
14–25.

———. 1991. *Language and Symbolic Power.* Cambridge, MA: Harvard University
Press.

Bourdieu, Pierre, and Wacquant, Loic. 1999. "On the Cunning of Imperialist Reason."
Theory, Culture & Society, 16: 41–58.

Brasil, Ministério da Justiça, Secretaria Nacional de Direitos Humanos. 1996. *Programa Nacional de Direitos Humanos.* Brasilia: Imprensa Nacional.

Brazilian Institute of Geography and Statistics (IBGE). 1999. "What Color Are You?"
In *The Brazil Reader: History, Culture, Politics,* ed. Robert Levine and John Crocitti. Durham, NC: Duke University Press.

Brown, Diane. 1999. "Power, Invention, and the Politics of Race: Umbanda Past and
Future." In *Black Brazil: Culture, Identity, and Social Mobilization,* ed. Larry Crook
and Randal Johnson. Los Angeles: UCLA Latin American Center Publications.

Brubaker, Rogers. 1995. "Aftermaths of Empire and the Unmixing of Peoples: Historical and Comparative Perspectives." *Ethnic and Racial Studies,* 18(2): 189–218.

———. 2002. "Ethnicity without Groups." *Archives Européènes de Sociologie,* XLIII(2):
163–89.

Brubaker, Rogers, and Frederick Cooper. 2000. "Beyond 'Identity.' " *Theory and Society,* 29: 1–47.

Brubaker, Rogers, Mara Loveman, and Peter Stamatov. 2004. "Ethnicity as Cogni-
tion." *Theory and Society,* 33: 31–64.

Burdick, John. 1992. "Brazil's Black Consciousness Movement." *NCCA Report on the Americas, 25:* 23–46.

———. 1998a. "The Lost Constituency of Brazil's Black Movements." *Latin American Perspectives,* 25: 136–55.

———. 1998b. *Blessed Anastácia: Women, Race, and Popular Christianity in Brazil.* New York: Routledge.

Burstein, Paul. 1985. *Discrimination, Jobs, and Politics: The Struggle for Equal Employment Opportunity in the United States since the New Deal.* Chicago: University Chicago Press.

Butler, Kim D. 1998. *Freedoms Given, Freedoms Won: Afro-Brazilians in Post-Abolition São Paulo and Salvador.* New Brunswick, NJ: Rutgers University Press.

Byrne, Bryan, Marvin Harris, Josildeth Gomes Consorte, and Joseph Lang. 1995. "What's in a Name? The Consequences of Violating Brazilian Emic Color-Race Categories in Estimates of Social Well-Being." *Journal of Anthropological Research,* 51: 389–97.

Camara, Evandro. 1998. Review of Francis Winddance Twine, *Racism in a Racial Democracy: The Maintenance of White Supremacy.* New Brunswick, NJ: Rutgers University Press, 1998. *American Journal of Sociology,* 104 (3): 911–13.

Campbell, Donald T. 1965. "Ethnocentric and Other Altruistic Motives." In *Nebraska Symposium on Motivations,* ed. Robert Levine. Lincoln: University of Nebraska Press.

Cardoso, Fernando Henrique, and Octávio Ianni. 1962. *Côr e Mobilidade Social em Florianópolis: Aspectos das Relações entre Negros e Brancos numa Comunidade do Brasil Meridional.* São Paulo: Companhia Editora Nacional.

Carvalho, José Alverto Magno De, Charles H. Wood, and Flávia Cristina Drumond Andrade. 2004. "Estimating the Stability of Census Based Racial/Ethnic Classifications: The Case of Brazil," *Population Studies,* 58(3): 331–43.

César, Raquel Coelho Lenz. 2005. "Políticas de Inclusão no Ensino Superior Brasileiro: Um Acerto de Contas e de Legitimidade." *Revista ADVIR,* 19: 55–64.

Cohen, Abner. 1974. "Introduction." In *Urban Ethnicity,* ed. Abner Cohen. London: Tavistock.

Cornell, Stephen. 1996. "The Variable Ties That Bind: Content and Circumstance in Ethnic Processes." *Ethnic and Racial Studies,* 19: 265–89.

Cornell, Stephen, and Douglas Hartmann. 1998. *Ethnicity and Race: Making Identities in a Changing World.* Thousand Oaks, CA: Pine Forge Press.

Corrêa, Hudson. 2003, December 15. "Em MS, Foto diz quem entra or cotas para ne-gros." *A Folha de São Paulo.*

Coser, Lewis A. 1956. *The Functions of Social Conflict.* London: Routledge & K. Paul.

Costa, Sérgio. 2001. "A Mestiçagem e Seus Contrários: Ethnicidade e Nacionalidade no Brasil Contemporâneo." *Tempo Social,* 13(1): 143–58.

Da Cunha, Olivia Maria Gomes. 1998. "Black Movements and the 'Politics of Identity' in Brazil." In *Cultures of Politics. Politics of Cultures: Re-Visioning Latin American Social Movements,* ed. Sonia E. Alvarez et al. Boulder, CO: Westview Press.

Da Matta, Roberto. 1981. *Relativizando: Uma Introdução à la Antropologia Social.* Petrópolis: Editora Vozes.

———. 1997. "Notas Sobre o Racismo Á Brasileira." In *Multiculturalismo e Racismo: uma comparacão Brasil–Estados Unidos,* ed. J. Souza. Brasilia: Paralelo 15.

Daniel, G. Reginald. 2006. *Race and Multiraciality in Brazil and the United States: Converging Paths?* University Park: Pennsylvania State University Press.

Davis, F. James. 1991. *Who Is Black.* University Park: Pennsylvania State University Press.

Dawson, Michael C. 2000. "Slowly Coming to Grips with the Effects of the American Racial Order on American Policy Preferences." In *Racialized Politics: The Debate about Racism in America,* ed. David O. Sears, Jim Sidanius, and Lawrence Bobo. Chicago: University of Chicago Press.

Degler, Carl N. 1971. *Neither Black nor White: Slavery and Race Relations in Brazil and the United States.* Madison: University of Wisconsin Press.

de la Fuente, Alejandro. 1999. "Myths of Racial Democracy: Cuba, 1900–1912." *Latin American Research Review,* 34: 39–73.

———. 2001. *A Nation for All: Race, Inequality, and Politics in Twentieth Century Cuba.* Chapel Hill: University of North Carolina Press.

de Zwart, Frank. 2005. "The Dilemma of Recognition: Administrative Categories and Cultural Diversity." *Theory and Society,* 34: 137–69.

Dzidzienyo, Anani. 1971. *The Position of Blacks in Brazilian Society.* London: Minority Rights Group.

Farley, Reynolds. 2002. "Racial Identities in 2000: The Response to the Multiple-Race Response Option." In *The New Race Question: How the Census Counts Multiracial Individuals,* ed. J. Perlmann and M. Waters. New York: Russell Sage Foundation.

Federico, Christopher M., and Jim Sidanius. 2002. "Sophistication and the Anteced-ents of Whites' Racial Policy Attitudes." *Public Opinion Quarterly,* 66: 145–76.

Fernandes, Florestan. 1965. *A Integração do Negro na Sociedade de Classes.* São Paulo: Dominus Editora.

———. 1969. *The Negro in Brazilian Society.* New York: Columbia University Press.

Fields, Barbara. 1990. "Slavery, Race and Ideology in the United States of America." *New Left Review,* 181: 95–118.

———. 2001. "Whiteness, Racism, and Identity." *International Labor and Working-Class History,* 60: 48–56.

Fiola, Jan. 1990. "Race Relations in Brazil: A Reassessment of the 'Racial Democracy' Thesis." *Occasional Papers Series, No. 24.* Latin American Studies Program: University of Massachusetts at Amherst.

Fontaine, Pierre-Michel. 1985. "Introduction." In *Race, Class, and Power in Brazil,* ed. P. Fontaine. Los Angeles: UCLA Center for Afro-American Studies.

Ford, Christopher A. 1994. "Administering Identity: The Determination of 'Race' in Race Conscious Law." *California Law Review,* 82: 1231–85.

Freyre, Gilberto. 1946. *The Masters and the Slaves.* New York: Alfred A. Knopf.

———. 1959. *New World in the Tropics: The Culture of Modern Brazil.* New York: Knopf.

———. 1974. *The Gilberto Freyre Reader.* New York: Alfred A. Knopf.

Fry, Peter. 1982. *Para Inglês Ver.* Rio de Janeiro: Zahar Editores S.A.

———. 1995. "O Que a Cinderela Negra Tem a Dizer Sobre a 'Politica Racial' no Brasil." *Revista USP,* 28: 122–35.

———. 2000. "Politics, Nationality, and the Meanings of 'Race' in Brazil." *Daedalus* 129: 83–118.

Fry, Peter, and Yvonne Maggie. 2004. "Cotas Raciais: Construindo un País Divido?" *Econômica,* 6(1): 153–61.

Fry, Peter, Yvonne Maggie, Marcos Chor Maio, Simone Monteiro, and Ricardo Ventura Santos, eds. 2007. *Divisões Perigosas: Política Raciais no Brasil Contemporâneo.* Rio de Janeiro: Civilização Brasileira.

Gamson, William A., and David S. Meyer. 1996. "Framing Political Opportunity." In *Comparative Perspectives on Social Movements,* ed. Doug McAdam, John D. McCarthy, and Mayer N. Zald, pp. 275–90. Cambridge, U.K.: Cambridge University Press.

Gans, Herbert J. 1979. "Symbolic Ethnicity: The Future of Ethnic Groups and Culture in the Future of America." *Ethnic and Racial Studies,* 2: 1–20.

Gilliam, Angela. 1992. "From Roxbury to Rio—And Back in a Hurry." In *African-American Reflections on Brazil's Racial Paradise,* ed. David J. Hellwig, pp. 173–81. Philadelphia: Temple University Press.

Gil-White, Francisco. 1999. "How Thick Is Blood? The Plot Thickens . . . : If Ethnic Actors Are Primordialists, What Remains of the Circumstantialist/Primordialist Controversy?" *Ethnic and Racial Studies,* 22(5): 789–820.

Goldberg, Chad Alan. 2003. "Haunted by the Specter of Communism: Collective Identity and Resource Mobilization in the Demise of the Workers Alliance of America." *Theory and Society,* 32: 725–73.

Goldberg, David Theo. 1992. "The Semantics of Race." *Ethnic and Racial Studies,* 15: 543–69.

———. 1993. *Racist Culture: Philosophy and the Politics of Meaning.* Oxford, U.K.: Blackwell.

———. 1997. *Racial Subjects: Writing on Race in America.* New York: Routledge.

Goldstein, Joshua R., and Ann J. Morning. 2002. "Back in the Box: The Dilemma of Using Multiple-Race Data for Single-Race Laws." In *The New Race Question,* ed. Joel Perlmann and Mary M. Waters, pp. 119–36. New York: Russell Sage Foundation.

Golub, Mark. 2005. "Plessy as 'Passing': Judicial Responses to Ambiguously Raced Bodies in *Plessy v. Ferguson.*" *Law and Society Review,* 39(3): 563–600.

Gonzalez, Lélia. 1985. "The Unified Black Movement: A New Stage in Black Political Mobilization." In *Race, Class, and Power in Brazil,* ed. Pierre-Michel Fontaine. Los Angeles: UCLA Center for Afro-American Studies.

Goodman, Nelson. 1978. *The Ways of Worldmaking.* Indianapolis, IN: Hackett Publishing.

Gould, Stephen Jay. "American Polygeny and Craniometry before Darwin: Blacks and Indians as Separate, Inferior Species." In *The "Racial" Economy of Science: Toward a Democratic Future,* ed. S. Harding, pp. 84–115. Indianapolis: Indiana University Press.

Gramsci, Antonio. 1971. *Selections from the Prison Notebooks of Antonio Gramiaci,* trans. and ed. Q. Hoare and G. Smith. New York: International Publishers.

Guimarães, Antonio S. 1997. "A Desigualdade que Anula a Desigualdade: Notas sobre a ação afirmativa no Brasil." In *Multiculturalismo e Racismo: uma comparacão Brasil—Estados Unidos,* ed. J. Souza. Brasilia: Paralelo 15.

———. 1999. *Racismo e Anti-Racismo no Brasil.* Sao Paulo: Editora 34.

———. 2001a. "The Misadventures of Nonracialism in Brazil." In *Beyond Racism: Race and Inequality in Brazil, South Africa, and the United States,* ed. Charles Hamilton et al. Boulder, CO: Lynne Rienner Publishers.

———. 2001b. "A questão racial na política brasileira." *Tempo Social,* 13(2): 143–67.

————. 2002. "Democracia racial: el ideal, el pacto y el mito." *Estudios Sociológicos,* 20: 59: 305–33.

————. 2006. "Entrevista com Carlos Hasenbalg." *Tempo Social,* 18(2): 259–68.

Gurin, Patricia, Arthur H. Miller, and Gerald Gurin. 1980. "Stratum Identification and Consciousness." *Social Psychology Quarterly,* 43: 30–47.

Hanchard, Michael. 1994. *Orpheus and Power: The Movimento Negro of Rio de Janeiro and São Paulo, Brazil, 1945–1988.* Princeton, NJ: Princeton University Press.

————. 1999. "Introduction." In *Racial Politics in Contemporary Brazil,* ed. Michael Hanchard. Durham, NC: Duke University Press.

Handelman, Don. 1977. "The Organization of Ethnicity." *Ethnic Groups,* 1: 187–200.

Haney López, Ian. 1996. *White by Law: The Legal Construction of Race.* New York: New York University Press.

Harris, David R., and Jeremiah Joseph Sim. 2002. "Who Is Multiracial? Assessing the Complexity of Lived Race." *American Sociological Review,* 67: 4614–27.

Harris, Marvin. 1952. "Race Relations in Mina Velhas, a Community in the Mountain Region of Central Brazil." In *Race and Class in Rural Brazil,* ed. Charles Wagley. Paris: UNESCO.

————. 1964. *Patterns of Race in the Americas.* New York: Walker and Company.

————. 1970. "Referential Ambiguity in the Calculus of Brazilian Racial Identity." *Southwestern Journal of Anthropology,* 26:1–12.

Harris, Marvin, Josildeth Gomes Consorte, Joseph Lang, and Bryan Byrne. 1993. "Who are the Whites? Imposed Census Categories and the Racial Demography of Brazil." *Social Forces,* 72: 451–62.

————. 1995. "A Reply to Telles." *Social Forces,* 73: 1613–14.

Harrison, Roderick J. 2002. "Inadequacies of Multiple-Response Race Data in the Federal Statistical System." In *The New Race Question,* ed. Joel Perlmann and Mary M. Waters, pp. 137–60. New York: Russell Sage Foundation.

Hasenbalg, Carlos. 1985. "Race and Socioeconomic Inequalities in Brazil." In *Race, Class, and Power in Brazil,* ed. Pierre-Michel Fontaine. Los Angeles: UCLA Center for Afro-American Studies.

————. 1998. "Entre o Mito e os Fatos: Racismo e Relações Raciais no Brasil." In *Raça, Ciência e Sociedade,* ed. M. Maio and R. Santos. Rio de Janiero: Editora Fiocruz.

————. 1999. "Perspectives on Race and Class in Brazil." In *Black Brazil,* ed. L. Crook and R. Johnson, pp. 61–84. Los Angeles: UCLA Latin American Center Publications.

Hasenbalg, Carlos, and Suellen Huntington. 1982. "Brazilian Racial Democracy: Reality or Myth?" *Humboldt Journal of Social Relations,* 10: 245–58.

Hasenbalg, Carlos, and Nelson do Valle Silva. 1991. "Raça e Oportunidades Educacionais no Brasil." In *Desigualdade Racial no Brasil Contemporâneo,* ed. Peggy Lovell. Belo Horizonte, MG: MGSP Editores Ltda.

———. 1999. "Notes on Racial and Political Inequality in Brazil." In *Racial Politics in Contemporary Brazil,* ed. Michael Hanchard. Durham, NC, and London: Duke University Press.

Hirschman, Charles. 2004. "The Origins and Demise of the Concept of Race." *Population and Development Review,* 30(3): 385–415.

Hirschman, Charles, Richard Alba, and Reynolds Farley. 2000. "The Meaning and Measurement of Race in the U.S. Census: Glimpses in the Future." *Demography,* 37: 381–93.

Hochschild, Jennifer L. 1995. *Facing up to the American Dream: Race, Class, and the Soul of the Nation.* Princeton, NJ: Princeton University Press.

———. 1999. "Affirmative Action as Culture War." In *The Cultural Territories of Race: Black and White Boundaries,* ed. Michell Lamont. Chicago: University of Chicago Press.

———. 2002. "Multiple Racial Identifiers in the 2000 Census, and Then What?" In *The New Race Question,* ed. Joel Perlmann and Mary M. Waters. New York: Russell Sage Foundation.

Hughes, Michael, and Steven A. Tuch. 2000. "How Beliefs about Poverty Influence Racial Policy Attitudes." In *Racialized Politics: The Debate about Racism in America,* ed. David O. Sears, Jim Sidanius, and Lawrence Bobo. Chicago: University of Chicago Press.

Hunt, Matthew O. 2007. "African-American, Hispanic, and White beliefs about Black/White Inequality, 1977–2004." *American Sociological Review,* 72: 390–415.

Hutchinson, Harry. 1952. "Race Relations in a Rural Community of the Bahian Recôncavo." In *Race and Class in Rural Brazil,* ed. Charles Wagley. Paris: UNESCO.

Htun, Mala. 2004. "From 'Racial Democracy' to Affirmative Action: Changing State Policy on Race in Brazil." *Latin American Research Review,* 39(1): 60–89.

Hwang, Sean-Shong, Kevin M. Fitzpatrick, and David Helms. 1998. "Class Differences in Racial Attitudes: A Divided Black America?" *Sociological Perspectives,* 41: 367–80.

Instituto Brasileiro de Geografia e Estadística [IBGE]. 1999. "What Color Are You?" In *The Brazil Reader: History, Culture, Politics,* ed. Robert Levine and John Crocitti. Durham, NC: Duke University Press.

Instituto de Política Econômica Aplicada [IPEA]. 2003. "Igualdade Racial." *Boletim de Políticas Sociais,* 7: 74–79.

Jackman, Mary. 1994. *The Velvet Glove: Paternalism and Conflict in Gender, Class, and Race Relations.* Los Angeles: University of California Press.

Jenkins, Richard. 1994. "Rethinking Ethnicity: Identity, Categorization and Power." *Ethnic and Racial Studies,* 17: 197–223.

Jeter, Jon. 2003, June 16. "Affirmative Action Debate Forces Brazil to Take Look in the Mirror." *The Washington Post,* A01.

Johnson, Ollie A. 2001. "Racial Representation and Brazilian Politics: Black Members of the National Congress, 1983–1999." *Journal of Interamerican Studies and World Affairs,* 40(4): 97–118.

Júnior, João Feres. 2004. "Ação Afirmativa no Brasil: Fundamentos e Críticas." *Econômica,* 6(2): 291–312.

Kinder, Donald R., and Tali Mendelberg. 2000. "Individualism Reconsidered: Principles and Prejudice in Contemporary American Opinion." In *Racialized Politics: The Debate about Racism in America,* ed. D. O. Sears, J. Sidanius, and L. Bobo. Chicago: University of Chicago Press.

Kinder, Donald R. and Lynn M. Sanders. 1996. *Divided by Color: Racial Politics and Democratic Ideas.* Chicago: University of Chicago Press.

Kinder, Donald R. and David O. Sears. 1981. "Prejudice and Politics: Symbolic Racism versus Racial Threats to the Good Life." *Journal of Personality and Social Psychology,* 40: 414–31.

Kluegel, James R. 1990. "Trends in Whites' explanations of the Black–White Gap in Socioeconomic Status, 1977–1989." *American Sociological Review,* 55: 512–25.

Kluegel, James R., and Eliot R. Smith. 1986. *Beliefs about Inequality: Americans' Views of What Is and What Ought to Be.* New York: Aldine de Gruyter.

Krysan, Maria. 2000. "Prejudice, Politics, and Public Opinion: Understanding the Sources of Racial Policy Attitudes." *Annual Review of Sociology,* 26: 135–168.

Lamont, Michéle, and Virág Molnár. 2002. "The Study of Boundaries in the Social Sciences." *Annual Review of Sociology,* 28: 167–95.

Lancaster, Roger. 1992. *Life Is Hard: Machismo, Danger, and the Intimacy of Power in Nicaragua.* Berkeley: University of California Press.

Lee, Jennifer, and Frank Bean. 2004. "America's Changing Color Lines: Immigration, Race/Ethnicity, and Multiracial Identification." *Annual Review of Sociology,* 30: 221–42.

Lee, Sharon. 1993. "Racial Classification in the U.S. Census: 1890–1990." *Ethnic and Racial Studies,* 16: 75–94.

Lee, Taeku. 2002. *Mobilizing Public Opinion: Black Insurgency and Racial Attitudes in the Civil Rights Era.* Chicago: University of Chicago Press.

Leslie, Michael. 1999. "The Representation of Blacks on Commercial Television in Brazil: Some Cultivation Effects." In *Black Brazil,* ed. L. Crook and R. Johnson. Los Angeles: UCLA Latin American Center.

Longman, Timothy. 2001. "Identity Cards, Ethnic Self-Perception, and Genocide in Rwanda." In *Documenting Individual Identity: The Development of State Practices in the Modern World,* ed. Jane Caplan and John Torpey. Princeton, NJ: Princeton University Press.

Lopez, David, and Yen Espiritu. 1990. "Panethnicity in the United States: A Theoretical Framework." *Ethnic and Racial Studies,* 13(2): 198–224.

Lovell, Peggy A. 1994. "Race, Gender, and Development in Brazil." *Journal of Latin American Studies,* 26: 7–35.

———. 1999. "Development and the Persistence of Racial Inequality in Brazil: 1950–1991." *Journal of Developing Areas,* 33: 395–418.

———. 2000. "Gender, Race, and the Struggle for Social Justice in Brazil." *Latin American Perspectives,* 27: 85–103.

Loveman, Mara. 1999a. "Is 'Race' Essential? A Comment on Bonilla-Silva." *American Sociological Review,* 64: 891–98.

———. 1999b. "Making 'Race' and Nation in the United States, South Africa, and Brazil: Taking 'Making' Seriously." *Theory and Society,* 28: 903–27.

Maggie, Ivonne. 1991. "A Ilusão do Concreto." Concurso de Professor Titular Thesis, Ciência Sociais, UFRJ, Rio de Janeiro.

———. 2001. "Os Novos Bacharéis: A Experiência do Pré-Vestibular para Negros e Carentes." *Novos Estudos: CEBRAP,* 59: 193–202.

———. 2005. "Políticas de Cotas e o Vestibular da UnB ou a Marca que Cria Sociedades Divididas." *Horizontes Antropológicos,* 11(23): 289–91.

Maggie, Yvonne, and Peter Fry. 2004. "A Reserva de Vagas para Negros nas Universidades Brasileiras." *Estudos Avançados,* 18(50): 67–80.

Maio, Marcos Chor. 2001. "UNESCO and the Study of Race Relations in Brazil: Regional or National Issue?" *Latin American Research Review,* 36: 118–36.

Maio, Marcos Chor, and Ricardo Ventura Santos. 2005. "Política de Cotas Raciais, Os 'Olhos da Sociedade' e os Usos da Antropologia: O Caso de Vestibular da Universidade de Brasília (UNB)." *Horizontes Antropológicos*, 11(23): 181–214.

Manifesto. 2006. Available online at: http://alex.nasc.sites.uol.com.br/manifestopelas cotas.htm.

Martins, Sergio da Silva. 1996. "Ação Afirmativa e Desigualdade Racial no Brasil." *Estudos Feministas*, 4: 203–08.

Marx, Anthony W. 1998. *Making Race and Nation: A Comparison of the United States, South Africa, and Brazil*. Cambridge, U.K.: Cambridge University Press.

Marx, Karl, and Friedrich Engels. 1846/1970. *The German Ideology*. New York: International Publishers.

McAdam, Doug. 1982. *Political Process and the Development of Black Insurgency*. Chicago: University of Chicago Press.

Meertens, Roel W., and Thomas F. Pettigrew. 1997. "Is Subtle Prejudice Really Prejudice?" *Public Opinion Quarterly*, 61: 54–71.

Merola, Ediane. 2003, September 9. "Não Haverá Distorções." *O Globo*, 3.

Miles, Robert, and Rudy Torres. 1996. "Does 'Race' Matter? Transatlantic Perspectives on Racism after 'Race Relations.'" In *Re-Situating Identities: The Politics of Race, Ethnicity, Culture*, ed. Vered Amit-talai and Caroline Knowles. Orchard Park, NY: Broadview Press.

Ministerio da Justicia. 1998. *Programa Nacional de Direitos Humanos*. Brasilia: Secretaria Nacional dos Direitos Humanos.

Mitchell, Michael. 1977. "Racial Consciousness and the Political Attitudes and Behavior of Blacks in São Paulo, Brazil." Ph.D. diss., Indiana University.

Mitchell, Michael, and Charles Wood. 1998. "Ironies of Citizenship: Skin Color, Police Brutality and the Challenge to Democracy in Brazil." *Social Forces*, 77(3): 1001–20.

Morning, Ann. 2004. "The Nature of Race: Teaching and Learning about Human Difference." Dissertation, Princeton University.

Morning, Ann, and Daniel Sabbagh. 2005. "From Sword to Plowshare: Using Race for Discrimination and Antidiscrimination in the United States." *International Journal of Social Science*, 57(183): 57–73.

Motta, Roberto. 2000. "Paradigms in the Study of Race Relations in Brazil." *International Sociology*, 15(4): 665–682.

Munanga, Kabengele. 1996. "As facetas de um racismo silenciado," In *Raca e Diversidade*, org. L. M. Schwarcz and R. S. Queiroz, pp. 213–229. São Paulo: Edusp.

Myrdal, Gunnar. 1944. *An American Dilemma*. New York: McGraw-Hill.

Nagel, Joanne. 1994. "Constructing Ethnicity: Creating and Recreating Ethnic Identity and Culture." *Social Problems,* 41(1): 152–76.

Nascimento, Abdias do. 1978. *O Genocidio do Negro Brasileiro: Processo de um Racismo Mascarado.* Rio de Janeiro: Paz e Terra.

Nascimento, Abdias do, and Elisa Larkin Nascimento. 2001. "Dance of Deception: A Reading of Race Relations in Brazil." In *Beyond Racism: Race and Inequality in Brazil, South Africa, and the United States,* ed. Charles Hamilton et al. Boulder, CO: Lynne Rienner Publishers.

Nascimento, Elisa Larkin. 2001. "It's in the Blood: Notes on Race Attitudes in Brazil from a Different Perspective." In *Beyond Racism: Race and Inequality in Brazil, South Africa, and the United States,* ed. Charles Hamilton et al. Boulder, CO: Lynne Rienner Publishers.

Nobles, Melissa. 1995. "'Responding with Good Sense': The Politics of Race and Censuses in Contemporary Brazil." Ph.D. dissertation, Department of Political Science, Yale University.

———. 2000. *Shades of Citizenship: Race and the Census in Modern Politics.* Stanford, CA: Stanford University Press.

Nogueira, Oracy. 1985. *Tanto preto, Quanto Branco: Estudo de Relações Raciais.* São Paulo: EDUSP.

Office of Management and Budget [OMB]. 2000, March 9. *Guidance on Aggregation and Allocation of Data on Race for Use in Civil Rights Monitoring and Enforcement.* Bulletin 00-02. Washington, DC: U.S. Government Printing Office.

Oliveira, Cloves Luiz Pereira. 1999. "Struggling for a Place: Race, Gender, and Class in Political Elections in Brazil." In *From Indifference to Inequality: Race in Contemporary Brazil,* ed. Rebecca Reichmann. University Park: Pennsylvania State University Press.

Oliveira, Lucia Elena, Rosa Maria Porcaro, and Tereza Cristina Araújo Costa. 1985. *O Lugar do Negro na Força de Trabalho.* Rio de Janeiro: IBGE.

Oliveira e Oliveira, Eduardo De. 1974. "Mulato, um Obstáculo Epistemológico." *Argumento,* 1: 65–73.

Omi, Michael, and Winant, Howard. 1994. *Racial Formation in the United States: From the 1960s to the 1980s.* New York: Routledge.

Oppenheimer, David Benjamin. 1996. "Understanding Affirmative Action." *Hastings Constitutional Law Quarterly,* 23(4): 921–97.

Paim, Paulo. 2005. "Projeto de Lei do Senado no. 6264/2005 [PLS 213/2003]— Estatuto da Igualdade Racial." Available online at www.camara.gov.br/sileg/integras/359794.pdf.

Parsons, Talcott. 1968. "The Problem of Polarization on the Axis of Color." In *Color and Race*, ed. J. H. Franklin. Boston: Houghton Mifflin.

Peria, Michelle. 2004. "Ação Afirmativea: Um Estudo Sobre a Reserva de Vagas para Negros nas Universidades Públicas Brasileiras. O Caso do Estado do Rio de Janeiro." Universidade Federal do Rio de Janeiro, Museu Nacional. Programa de Pós-Graduação em Antropologia Social.

Perlmann, Joel, and Mary C. Waters. 2002. "Introduction." In *The New Race Question: How the Census Counts Multiracial Individuals*, ed. J. Perlmann and M. Waters. New York: Russell Sage Foundation.

Petersen, William. 1987. "Politics and the Measurement of Ethnicity." In *The Politics of Numbers*, ed. William Alonso and Paul Starr, pp. 187–233. New York: Russell Sage Foundation.

Pettigrew, Thomas, and Roel W. Meertens. 1995. "Subtle and Blatant Prejudice in Western Europe." *European Journal of Social Psychology*, 25 (1): 57–75.

Pierson, Donald. 1967. *Negroes in Brazil: A Study of Race Conflict in Bahia*. Carbondale: Southern Illinois University Press.

Pinheiro, Paulo Sérgio, and Paulo de Mesquita Neto. 1997. "Programa Nacional de Direitos Humanos: Avaliação do Primeiro Ano e Perspectivas." *Estudos Avançados*, 11(30): 117–134.

Pinto, Regina Pahim. 1990. "Movimento Negro e Ethnicidade." *Estudo Afro Asiáticos*, 19: 109–23.

Pitanga, Antônio. 1999. "Where Are the Blacks?" In *Black Brazil: Culture, Identity, and Social Mobilization*, ed. Larry Crook and Randal Johnson. Los Angeles: UCLA Latin American Center Publications.

Piza, Edith, and Fulvia Rosemberg. 1999. "Color in the Brazilian Census." In *From Indifference to Inequality: Race in Contemporary Brazil*, ed. Rebecca Reichmann. University Park: Pennsylvania State University Press.

Pizzorno, Alessandro. 1978. "Political Exchange and Collective Identity in Industrial Conflict." In *The Resurgence of Class Conflict in Western Europe since 1968*, ed. Colin Crouch and Alessandro Pizzorno. New York: Holmes & Meier.

PESB. 2002. *Pesquisa Social Brasileira*. Federal Fluminense University, directed by Alberto Carlos Almeida and Zairo Cheibub. Funding: Ford Foundation.

Powell, John A. 1997. "The 'Racing' of American Society: Race Functioning as a Verb Before Signifying as a Noun." *Law And Inequality*, 15: 99–125.

Prandi, Reginaldo. 2000. "African Gods in Contemporary Brazil: A Sociological Introduction to Candomblé Today." *International Sociology*, 15(4): 641–63.

Prewitt, Kenneth. 2002. "Race in the 2000 Census: A Turning Point." In *The New Race Question*, ed. Joel Perlmann and Mary M. Waters, pp. 354–61. New York: Russell Sage Foundation.

Purcell, Trevor W., and Kathleen Sawyers. 1993. "Democracy and Ethnic Conflict: Blacks in Costa Rica." *Ethnic and Racial Studies* 16(2): 298–322.

Reichmann, Rebecca. 1999. "Introduction." In *From Indifference to Inequality: Race in Contemporary Brazil*, ed. Rebecca Reichmann. University Park: Pennsylvania State University Press.

Reis, Fabio Wanderley. 1997. "Mito e Valor da Democracia Racial." In *Multiculturalismo e Racismo: uma Comparacão Brasil–Estados Unidos*, ed. J. Souza. Brasilia: Paralelo 15.

Resende, Elaine. 2007, May 31. "Cor da Família: Irmãos Têm o Mesmo Direito de Concorrer por Cota de Negros." *Revista Consultor Jurídico*. See the judicial decision at: http://conjur.estadao.com.br/static/text/56134,1.

Reskin, Barbara. 1998. *The Realities of Affirmative Action in Employment*. Washington, DC: American Sociological Association.

———. 2003. "Including Mechanisms in Our Models of Ascriptive Inequality." *American Sociological Review*, 68: 1–21.

Ribeiro, Matilde. 2007. "Inclusão Social." *O Globo*, June 11: 6.

Riserio, Antônio. 1999. "Carnival: The Colors of Change." In *Black Brazil: Culture, Identity, and Social Mobilization*, ed. Larry Crook and Randal Johnson. Los Angeles: UCLA Latin American Center Publications.

Rodriguez, Clara. 2000. *Changing Race: Latinos, the Census, and the History of Ethnicity in the United States*. New York: New York University Press.

Rosemberg, Flúvia. 2004. "O Branco no IBGE Continua Branco na Ação Afirmativa?" *Estudos Avançados*, 18(50): 61–66.

Russo, Iris. 2007, January 10. "UnB muda sistema de cotas para negros." *G1: O Portal de Notícias da Globo*.

Sansone, Livio. 1993. "Pai Preto, Filho Negro: Trabalho, Cor e Diferenças de Geração." *Estudos Afro-Asiáticos*, 25: 73–98.

———. 1995. "O Local e o Global na Afro-Bahia Contemporânea." *Revista Brasileira de Ciencias Sociais*, 29: 65–84.

———. 1996. "Nem Somente Preto ou Negro: O Sistema de Classificacão Racial no Brasil que Muda." *Afro-Asia,* 18: 165–87.

———. 1998. "As Relações Raciais em Casa-Grande & Senzala Revisitadas à Luz do Processo de Internacionalização e Globalização." In *Raça, Ciência e Sociedade,* ed. M. Maio and R. Santos, pp. 207–17. Rio de Janiero: Editora Fiocruz.

———. 2003. *Blackness without Ethnicity: Constructing Race in Brazil.* New York: Palgrave Macmillan.

Santos, Thereza. 1999. "The Black Movement: Without Identity There Is No Consciousness or Struggle." In *Black Brazil: Culture, Identity, and Social Mobilization,* ed. Larry Crook and Randal Johnson. Los Angeles: UCLA Latin American Center Publications.

Santos-Stubbe, Chirly Dos. 1998. "Cultura, Cor e Sociedade: A Questão da Etnicidade entre as Empregadas Domésticas." *Estudos Afro-Asiáticos,* 33: 51–70.

Schuman, Howard, Charlotte Steeh, Lawrence Bobo, and Maria Krysan. *Racial Attitudes in America.* Cambridge, MA: Harvard University Press.

Schuman, Howard, and Jean Converse. 1971. "The Effects of Black and White Interviewers on Black Responses in 1968." *Public Opinion Quarterly,* 35(1): 44–68.

Schuman, Howard, and J. Harding. 1963. "Sympathetic Identification with the Underdog." *Public Opinion Quarterly,* 27: 230–41.

Schuman, Howard, and Maria Krysan. 1999. "A Historical Note on Whites' Beliefs about Racial Inequality." *American Sociological Review,* 64: 847–55.

Schuman, Howard, Charlotte Steeh, Lawrence Bobo, and Maria Krysan. 1997. *Racial Attitudes in America: Trends and Interpretations.* Cambridge, MA: Harvard University Press.

Schwartzman, Simon. 1999. "Fora de Foco: Diversidade e Identidades Étnicas no Brasil." *Novos Estudos CEBRAP,* 55: 83–96.

———. 2008. "A medida da lei de cotas para o ensino superior." Available online at: www.schwartzman.org.br/simon/cotas2008.pdf.

Sears, David O. 1988. "Symbolic versus Realistic Group Conflict." In *Eliminating Racism: Profiles in Controversy,* ed. P. A. Katz and D. A. Taylor. New York: Plenum Press.

Sears, David O., P. J. Henry, and Rick Kosterman. 2000a. "Egalitarian Values and Contemporary Racial Politics." In *Racialized Politics: The Debate about Racism in America,* ed. D. O. Sears, J. Sidanius, and L. Bobo. Chicago: University of Chicago Press.

Sears, David O., John J. Hetts, Jim Sidanius, and Lawrence Bobo. 2000b. "Race in American Politics: Framing the Debates." In *Racialized Politics: The Debate about Racism in America*, ed. D. Sears, J. Sidanius, and L. Bobo. Chicago: University of Chicago Press.

Sears, David O., Jim Sidanius, and Lawrence Bobo, eds. 2000c. *Racialized Politics: The Debate about Racism in America*. Chicago: University of Chicago Press.

See, Kathleen O'Sullivan, and William Julius Wilson. 1989. "Race and Ethnicity." In *Handbook of Sociology*, ed. N. J. Smelser. Beverly Hills, CA: Sage.

Segato, Renata L. 1998. "The Color-Blind Subject of Myth; Or, Where to Find Africa in the Nation." *Annual Review of Anthropology*, 27: 129–51.

Sheriff, Robin. 1997. "'Negro Is a Nickname That the Whites Gave to the Blacks': Discourses on Color, Race and Racism in Rio de Janeiro." Ph.D. dissertation, Department of Anthropology, City University of New York.

———. 1999. "The Theft of *Carnaval*: National Spectacle and Racial Politics in Rio de Janeiro." *Cultural Anthropology*, 14(1): 3–28.

———. 2001. *Dreaming Equality: Color, Race, and Racism in Urban Brazil*. New Brunswick, NJ: Rutgers University Press.

Sidanius, Jim, Yesilernis Peña, and Mark Sawyer. 2001. "Inclusionary Discrimination: Pigmentocracy and Patriotism in the Dominican Republic." *Political Psychology*, 22(4): 827–51.

Sidanius, Jim, and Felicia Pratto. 1999. *Social Dominance*. Cambridge, U.K.: Cambridge University Press.

Sidanius, Jim, Felicia Pratto, and Lawrence Bobo. 1996. "Racism, Conservatism, Affirmative Action, and Intellectual Sophistication: A Matter of Principled Conservatism or Group Dominance." *Journal of Personality and Social Psychology*, 70: 467–90.

Sidanius, Jim, Pam Singh, John Hetts, and Chris Federico. 2000. "It's Not Affirmative Action, It's the Blacks: Continuing Relevance of Race in American Politics." In *Racialized Politics: The Debate about Racism in America*, ed. D. Sears, J. Sidanius, and L. Bobo. Chicago: University of Chicago Press.

Silva, Benedita da. 1999a. "The Black Movement and Political Parties: A Challenging Alliance." In *Racial Politics in Contemporary Brazil*, ed. Michael Hanchard. Durham, NC: Duke University Press.

Silva, Benedita da. 1999b. "Race and Politics in Brazil." In *Black Brazil: Culture, Identity, and Social Mobilization*, ed. Larry Crook and Randal Johnson. Los Angeles: UCLA Latin American Center Publications.

Silva, Denise Ferreira da. 1998. "Facts of Blackness: Brazil Is Not (Quite) the United States . . . and Racial Politics in Brazil?" *Social Identities*, 2: 201–34.

Silva, Nelson do Valle. 1985. "Updating the Cost of Not Being White in Brazil." In *Race, Class, and Power in Brazil*, ed. Pierre-Michel Fontaine. Los Angeles: Center for Afro-American Studies.

———. 1996. "Morenidade: Modo de Usar." *Estudos Afro-Asiaticos*, 30: 79–98.

———. 2000. "Extent and Nature of Racial Inequalities in Brazil." In *Beyond Racism: Embracing an Independent Future*, vol. 4. Comparative Human Relations Initiative. Atlanta, GA: The Southern Education Foundation.

Skerry, Peter. 2002. "Multiracialism and the Administrative State." In *The New Race Question*, ed. Joel Perlmann and Mary M. Waters, pp. 327–39. New York: Russell Sage Foundation.

Skidmore, Thomas E. 1974. *Black into White: Race and Nationality in Brazilian Thought*. New York: Oxford University Press.

———. 1985. "Race and Class in Brazil: Historical Perspectives." In *Race, Class and Power in Brazil*, ed. P. Fontaine. Los Angeles: UCLA Center for Afro-American Studies.

———. 1992. "Fact and Myth: Discovering a Racial Problem in Brazil." Working Paper #173. Notre Dame, IN: Kellogue Institute, University of Notre Dame.

———. 1993. "Bi-racial U.S.A. vs. Multi-Racial Brazil: Is the Contrast Still Valid?" *Journal of Latin American Studies*, 25: 373–86.

———. 1997. "Ação Afirmativa no Brasil? Reflexões de um Brasilianista." In *Multiculturalismo e Racismo: Uma Comparacão Brasil—Estados Unidos*, ed. J. Souza. Brasilia: Paralelo 15.

———. 2003. "Racial Mixture and Affirmative Action: The Cases of Brazil and the United States." *The American Historical Review*, 108(5): 1391–96.

Smedley, Audrey. 1993. *Race in North America: Origin and Evolution of a Worldview*. Boulder, CO: Westview Press.

Smith, Eliot R., and James R. Kluegel. 1984. "Beliefs and Attitudes about Women's Opportunity: Comparisons with Beliefs about Blacks and a General Perspective." *Social Psychology Quarterly*, 47: 81–95.

Sniderman, Paul M., and Edward G. Carmines. 1997. *Reaching Beyond Race*. Cambridge, MA: Harvard University Press.

Sniderman, Paul M., Gretchen C. Crosby, and William G. Howell. 2000. "The Politics of Race." In *Racialized Politics: The Debate about Racism in America*, ed. David. O. Sears, Jim Sidanius, and Lawrence Bobo. Chicago: University of Chicago Press.

Snipp, C. Matthew. 2003. "Racial Measurement in the American Census: Past Practices and Implications for the Future." *Annual Review of Sociology*, 29: 563–88.

Souza, Jesse. 1997. "Multiculturalismo, Racismo e Democracia: Por Que Comparar Brasil e Estados Unidos?" In *Multiculturalismo e Racismo: Uma Comparacão Brasil-Estados Unidos*, ed. J. Souza. Brasilia: Paralelo 15.

Stubrin, Florencia. 2005. "Um Retrato das Desigualdades no Ensino Superior: Alguns Dados." *Revista ADVIR*, 19: 72–74.

Tajfel, Henri and John C. Turner. 1986. "The Social Identity Theory of Intergroup Behavior." In *Psychology of Intergroup Relations*, ed. S. Worchel and W. Austin. Chicago: Nelson Hall.

Telles, Edward E. 1992. "Residential Segregation by Skin Color in Brazil." *American Sociological Review*, 57: 186–97.

———. 1993. "Racial Distance and Region in Brazil: The Case of Marriage among Color Groups." *Latin American Research Review*, 28: 141–162.

———. 1994. "Industrialization and Racial Inequality in Employment: The Brazilian Example." *American Sociological Review*, 59: 46–63.

———. 1999. "Ethnic Boundaries and Political Mobilization among African Brazilians: Comparisons with the U.S. Case." In *Racial Politics in Contemporary Brazil*, ed. Michael Hanchard. Durham, NC: Duke University Press.

———. 2002. "Racial Ambiguity among the Brazilian Population." *Ethnic and Racial Studies*, 25(3): 415–41.

———. 2003. "U.S. Foundations and Racial Reasoning in Brazil." *Theory, Culture & Society*, 20(4): 31–47.

———. 2004. *Race in Another America*. Princeton, NJ: Princeton University Press.

Telles, Edward, and Lim, Nelson. 1998. "Does It Matter Who Answers the Race Question? Racial Classification and Income Inequality in Brazil." *Demography*, 35: 465–74.

Tilly, Charles. 2004. "Social Boundary Mechanisms." *Philosophy of the Social Sciences*, 34(2): 211–36.

Torres-Saillant, Silvio. 1998. "The Tribulations of Blackness: Stages in Dominican Racial Identity." *Latin American Perspectives*, 25(3): 126–46.

Tuch, Steven A., and Jack K. Martin, eds. 1997. *Racial Attitudes in the 1990s: Continuity and Change*. Westport, CT: Praeger.

Turner, J. Michael. 2002. "The Road to Durban—and Back." *NACLA Report on the Americas*, 35(6): 31–35.

Turra, Cleusa, and Gustavo Venturi. 1995. *Racismo Cordial*. São Paulo: Editora Ática.

Twine, Francis Winddance. 1998. *Racism in a Racial Democracy: The Maintenance of White Supremacy*. New Brunswick, NJ: Rutgers University Press.

U.S. Bureau of the Census. 1979. *Twenty Censuses: Population and Housing Questions 1790–1980*. Washington, DC: U.S. Government Printing Office.

Universidade de Brasília. 2004. *Edital de Abertura*. Available online at: www.cespe .unb.br/vestibular/ arquivos/2004-2/ED_2004_2_VEST_2004_3_ABT_I.PDF.

———. 2008. *Edital de Abertura*. Available online at: www.cespe.unb.br/vestibular/ 1VEST2008/arquivos/ED_4_2008_1_VEST_2008_ABT.PDF

Universidade do Estado da Bahia. 2002. *Resolução No. 196/2002*. Available online at www.uneb.br/atos/atos_consu_196_25-07-02.pdf.

Universidade Estadual de Mato Grosso do Sul (UEMG). 2004. *Edital PROE/UEMS no 003/2004*. Available online at: www.ifcs.ufrj.br/~observa/universidades/uems _edital_2005.pdf.

Wacquant, Loic. 1997. "Towards an Analytic of Social Domination." *Political Power and Social Theory,* 11: 221–34.

Wacquant, Loic. 2002. "From Slavery to Mass Incarceration." *New Left Review,* 13: 41–60.

———. 2005. "Race as Civic Felony." *International Social Science Journal,* 183: 127–41.

Wade, Peter. 1993. *Blackness and Race Mixture: The Dynamics of Racial Identity in Colombia*. Baltimore: Johns Hopkins University Press.

———. 1997. *Race and Ethnicity in Latin America*. London: Pluto Press.

Wagley, Charles. 1952a. "Introduction." In *Race and Class in Rural Brazil,* ed. Charles Wagley. Paris: UNESCO.

———. 1952b. "From Caste to Class in North Brazil." In *Race and Class in Rural Brazil,* ed. Charles Wagley. Paris: UNESCO.

———. ed. 1952c. *Race and Class in Rural Brazil*. Paris: UNESCO.

———. 1965. "On the Concept of Social Races in the Americas." In *Contemporary Cultures and Societies in Latin America,* ed. D. B. Heath and R. N. Adams. New York: Random House.

Walker, Sheila S. 2002. "Africanity vs. Blackness: Race, Class and Culture in Brazil." *NACLA Report on the Americas,* 35(6): 16–20.

Warren, Jonathan. 2002. *Racial Revolutions: Antiracism & Indian Resurgence in Brazil*. Durham, NC: Duke University Press.

Washington, Scott. 2004. "Principles of Racial Taxonomy." Available at: www.iserp
.columbia.edu/news/conferences/categories/downloads/washington.pdf .

Waters, Mary C. 1990. *Ethnic Options: Choosing Identities in America*. Berkeley: University of California Press.

———. 1999. *Black Identities: West Indian Immigrant Dreams and American Realities*.
Cambridge, MA: Harvard University Press.

Weber, Demétrio. 2007, June 7. "UNB Agora Aceita Inscrição do 'Gêmeo Branco.'"
O Globo.

Weisskopf, Thomas E. 2008. "Quota Systems" In *International Encyclopedia of the Social Sciences, 2nd edition,* ed. William A. Darity, pp. 668–70. Farmington Hill, MI:
Macmillan Reference USA.

Whitten, Norman. 1981. "Introduction." In *Cultural Transformations and Ethnicity in
Modern Ecuador,* ed. N. Whitten. Urbana: University of Illinois Press.

Willems, Emilio. 1949. "Racial Attitudes in Brazil." *The American Journal of Sociology,* 54(5): 402–08.

Winant, Howard. 1994. *Racial Conditions: Politics, Theory, Comparisons*. Minneapolis: University of Minnesota Press.

———. 1999. "Racial Democracy and Racial Identity: Comparing the United States
and Brazil." In *Racial Politics in Contemporary Brazil,* ed. Michael Hanchard.
Durham, NC: Duke University Press.

———. 2001. *The World Is a Ghetto*. New York: Basic Books.

Wood, Charles. 1991. "Categorias Censitarias e Classificações Subjetivas de Raça no
Brasil." In *Desigualdade Racial no Brasil Contemporâneo,* ed. Peggy Lovell. Belo
Horizonte, MG: MGSP Editores Ltda.

Wood, Charles, and Lovell, Peggy. 1992. "Racial Inequality and Child Mortality in
Brazil." *Social Forces,* 70: 703–24.

Wright, Winthrop. 1990. *Cafe con Leche: Race, Class and National Image in Venezuela*. Austin: University of Texas Press.

Yancey, William L., Eugene P. Ericksen, and Richard N. Juliani. 1976. "Emergent
Ethnicity: A Review and Reformulation." *American Sociological Review,* 41(3):
391–403.

Zack, Naomi. 1995. "Life after Race." In *American Mixed Race: Constructing Micro-
diversity,* ed. N. Zack. Lanham, MD: Rowman & Littlefield.

———. 1997. "Philosophy and Racial Paradigms." *Journal of Value Inquiry,* 33: 299-317.

Zaller, John. 1992. *The Nature and Origins of Mass Opinion*. Cambridge, U.K.: Cambridge University Press.

Index

Note: Tables and figures are indicated by *t* or *f,* respectively, following the page number.

Abertura democrática, 29–30, 119

Affirmative action, 8, 11. *See* Race-targeted public policy

African ancestry, 45, 81–82, 81*t,* 172–73

African-derived culture, 70–74; nationalization of, 71–72, 83; re-Africanization of, 72–74

Age, and attitudes toward *negro* movement, 129, 143–44, 144*t*

Agier, Michel, 73

Alba, Richard, 40, 51–52, 55, 64, 107

Alexander, Jeffrey, 118

Alger, Horatio, 6

Almeida, Carlos Alberto, 234*n*153

Amarelo, 41

American Creed, 6, 167, 218–20

American School of Ethnology, 196

Andrews, George Reid, 43, 71, 72, 100, 109–10, 119, 121, 122, 145, 169, 172, 189

Antiblack affect, 16–18, 96, 105

Antiracialism, 9; in Brazil, 22–30, 215; challenges to, 28–30, 111; defined, 22–23, 35; and *negro* movement, 139; proponents of, 34; racial democracy myth and, 108–13, 222; as strategy, 264*n*43. *See also* Racial democracy myth; Racialism

Antiracism: participation in, 127–32, 128*t,* 215–16; racial identification as prerequisite for, 212–13, 221–22. *See also* Race-targeted public policy

Apartheid, 193

Appiah, Kwame Anthony, 20–21, 137–38

Attitudes, behavior in relation to, 14–15

Attitudinal complex, 13–14

Axé music, 77, 78*t,* 242*n*106

Bacelar, Jeferson, 115, 122

Bailey, Stanley R., 143

Bairros, Luíza, 32, 89

Banton, Michael, 107, 207

Barth, Fredrik, 47, 64–65, 75, 85

Bastide, Roger, 29

Bean, Frank, 212

Behavior, attitudes in relation to, 14–15

Beneficiaries, of race-targeted policies, 169, 178–87

Bertulio, Dora de Lima, 169–70

Binary classification. *See* Dichotomous classification

Black, as racial category, 235*n*19. See also terms beginning with *Negro*

Black Renaissance, 192

Blocos, 73
Blumer, Herbert, 17
Bobo, Lawrence, 14, 15, 17–18, 21, 63, 118,
    124, 135–36, 160, 168, 217, 219, 224,
    250n62
Boltanski, Luc, 224
Bonilla-Silva, Eduardo, 134–35
Bossa nova, 77, 78t
Bourdieu, Pierre, 32, 191, 194, 207–10,
    223–24, 261n97
Branca aristocratic class, 3
Branco: as census category, 41, 227n9;
    defined, 42
Brazil: ancestry in, 68, 80–83, 81t, 139;
    founding myth of, 93, 215, 262n124;
    inequalities in, 263n22; monoracialism
    in, 8, 66–67, 69, 87; racial attitudes in,
    3–5, 7, 26–27; racial boundaries in,
    49–65; racial composition of, 41–48; as
    racial democracy, 1–8, 29–30, 34; U.S. vs.,
    24, 65, 171–72, 211, 214–16, 224
Brazilian ignorance stance, 5, 92, 104, 116
Brazilian Institute of Geography and
    Statistics (IBGE), 41, 46, 172
Brazilian metarace, 1–2, 24, 34, 56, 82, 88,
    115, 139, 197, 262n124
Brazilian *Negro* Front. *See Frente Negra
    Brasileira*
British Social Attitudes (BSA), 37
Brown, Diane, 72, 73
Brown. *See* Miscegenation; *Morenos*
Brubaker, Rogers, 20, 44, 48, 49, 65, 70, 162,
    164, 209, 217
Buarque de Holanda, Sérgio, 23
Burdick, John, 58, 69, 121, 122, 140, 187
Burstein, Paul, 14
Butler, Kim D., 46

Camara, Evandro, 32
Candomblé, 70, 72, 73, 78
Capitalism, 119
Capoeira, 71, 78–79, 78t
Cardoso, Fernando Henrique, 41, 111,
    148–49
Carnaval, 71, 73, 78t, 79
Categories, sociological definition of, 47–48,
    161–62
Catholicism, 70, 73
CEAP. *See Centro de Articulação de
    Populações Marginalizadas*
CEAP/DataUff survey, 7, 35–37, 234n152,
    234n153

Census categorization of race: binary vs., 84,
    120, 180–83, 187, 191, 261n101; in Brazil,
    41–46, 58–60, 68, 120, 198; color and,
    46, 58–60, 68; *negro* movement and, 84,
    120, 123, 138, 172; other-categorization
    according to, 180; proposed alterations of,
    44–45; race making and, 67, 74; ternary,
    43–44, 66, 179; in U.S., 66, 170–72,
    177–78, 192, 195, 197–98, 206, 211–12. *See
    also* State, racial classification role of
*Centro de Articulação de Populações
    Marginalizadas* (CEAP), 35
César, Raquel Coelho Lenz, 171, 181
Cheibub, Zairo, 234n153
China, 259n35
Circumstantialism, 74
Civil Rights Act (1964), 14
Class: antiracialism and, 23, 26; discrimina-
    tion based on, 27, 102–5, 103t; identities
    based on, 165, 166; *negro* movement and,
    122, 142–43; racism and, 142–43
Colombia, 8, 24
Color, vs. race, 46, 58–60, 61t, 68
Common sense. *See* Public opinion
Community of culture, 75, 83, 85
Community of interests, 75, 86–87
Conflict attitudes. *See* Group conflict
    attitudes
Cooper, Frederick, 48, 49, 70, 217
Cornell, Stephen, 67–68, 74–76, 83–85, 193,
    194, 212
Costa, Sérgio, 84
Cuba, 8, 24, 71
Cultivation effect, 43
Culture: African-derived, 70–74, 78t, 83;
    communities of, 75, 83, 85; race and,
    66–87. See also *Negro* culture
Cunha, Olivia Maria Gomes da. *See* Gomes
    da Cunha, Olivia Maria

Da Matta, Roberto, 43, 169
Daniel, G. Reginald, 8, 87
Darwinism, 196
DataFolha Instituto de Pesquisas, 37
DataFolha survey, 7, 37
DataUff, 36
Davis, F. James, 192, 193
Dawson, Michael C., 20
Degler, Carl N., 26, 91, 104, 108, 191, 196, 198
de la Fuente, Alejandro, 108, 222
Democratic Social Party, 120
De Zwart, Frank, 176–77, 205

Dichotomous classification, 11–12; boundary effects of, 202–7; direct boundary effect of, 206–7; *negro* movement and, 120, 191; nonboundary effect of, 203–4; race making and, 199–213; race-targeted policies and, 170–73, 180–89; reactive boundary effect of, 204–6; unintended consequences of, 182–83, 185, 187, 200, 204–6, 211; whitening effect of, 84, 200–201, 211
Discrimination. *See* Racial discrimination
Dominican Republic, 24, 152, 161

Ecuador, 8, 24
Education: attitudes on race-targeted policies influenced by, 156*t*, 159; and attitudes toward *negro* movement, 129, 131; non-white disadvantage influenced by, 104–5. *See also* University entrance policies
Elites: public opinion influenced by, 110, 112–13, 228*n*29; and racial democracy myth, 4–5, 110, 115
Emic classification system, 235*n*26
Ericksen, Eugene P., 74
Etic classification system, 235*n*26

False consciousness, 106, 151–52, 160, 221, 246*n*78, 253*n*55
Farley, Reynolds, 40, 52
Favoritism, in-group, 19, 51
Federal Fluminense University, Rio de Janeiro, 36
Federal University of Paraná, 174
Federal University of São Paulo, 174
Fernandes, Florestan, 28–29, 108, 119, 232*n*111
Ferreira da Silva, Denise, 137
Fields, Barbara, 188–89, 208–9, 213
Fiola, Jan, 123
Folha de São Paulo (newspaper), 37
Ford, Christopher A., 175, 208, 223
Frente Negra Brasileira (Brazilian *Negro* Front), 69, 114, 118–19
Freyre, Gilberto, 1, 5, 23, 24, 90, 197
Fry, Peter, 32, 33, 84, 108, 140, 169, 220
Funk music, 77

Garvey, Marcus, 192
General Social Survey (GSS), 37
Germany, 259*n*35
Goldberg, David Theo, 161–62
Goldstein, Joshua R., 170

Golub, Mark, 170, 176
Gomes da Cunha, Olivia Maria, 72, 139–40
Gonzalez, Léila, 69
Group-based interests, 134–36
Group conflict attitudes, 124, 134–35, 168
Group conflict theories, 17–19, 94–95, 106, 124, 151, 216, 230*n*23
Groupism, 161–65, 217
Groupness, 20, 48, 216–17
Group position model, 17, 151
Groups, sociological definition of, 47–48, 161–62
Guimarães, Antonio S., 22–23, 29–31, 42, 65, 92, 93, 108, 113–15, 119, 120, 122, 138, 141, 147, 207, 212, 215, 217, 218, 222

Hanchard, Michael, 30–31, 33, 69, 73, 85, 86, 92, 117, 120–21, 145, 153, 160, 173, 192, 193, 217
Harding, J., 165
Harlem renaissance, 192
Harris, David R., 50
Harris, Marvin, 26–28, 32, 44, 56, 107, 165, 223, 235*n*26
Hartmann, Douglas, 67–68, 75, 194, 212
Hasenbalg, Carlos, 4, 7, 30, 88, 91, 92, 105, 108, 113, 141–42, 163, 209–10, 247*n*107
Hirschman, Charles, 40, 51–52
Hochschild, Jennifer L., 146, 212
Horatio Alger myth, 6
Hughes, Michael, 150
Huntington, Suellen, 91
Hutchinson, Harry, 26–27
Hwang, Sean-Shong, 164
Hypodescent, 42, 68, 172–73, 176, 178, 189, 195–99. *See also* One-drop rule

IBGE. *See* Brazilian Institute of Geography and Statistics
Identities. *See* Racial groups
Ideology, social dominance theory and, 151–52
Immigrants, assimilation and exclusion of, 64
India, 176, 205
Indígena, 41
In-group favoritism, 19, 51
Institutional community, 75
Instituto Brasileiro de Geografía e Estadísticas (IBGE), 36
Intermarriage, 67, 166
International Conference on Racism (Durban, South Africa, 2001). *See*

International Conference on Racism
(continued)
World Conference against Racism,
Racial Discrimination, Xenophobia,
and Related Intolerance (Durban, South
Africa, 2001)
International Monetary Fund, 41

Jenkins, Richard, 47, 49, 161, 194, 203,
204, 206
Jim Crow laws, 1–3, 17, 105, 115, 176, 193,
198, 220
Juliani, Richard N., 74
Júnior, João Feres, 180

Kinder, Donald R., 39, 159, 165, 167, 219
King, Martin Luther, Jr., 219
Kluegel, James R., 107, 160
Krysan, Maria, 14–16, 116

Lamont, Michéle, 191
Latin America: census categories in, 234n12;
emigration from, 8; *mestizaje* ideology
of, 24
Lee, Jennifer, 211–12
Lee, Taeku, 110, 112–13
Legislation, race, 198
Legitimizing myths, 152
Leslie, Michael, 43
Lim, Nelson, 50
Lovell, Peggy A., 66
Loveman, Mara, 20, 217
Lula da Silva, Luiz Inácio, 149

Maggie, Yvonne, 84
Marx, Anthony, 192–93, 207–8
Marx, Karl, 152
Marxism, 29, 151, 223
Matters of principle, 166–67, 219–20
Media, public opinion influenced by, 110–11
Mestizaje, 24. *See also* Miscegenation
Metarace. *See* Brazilian metarace
Ministry of Racial Inequality, 179
Miscegenation: and Brazilian metarace, 1, 56,
82, 115, 139, 197, 262n123; bureaucratic
difficulties concerning, 170–71, 173–79,
185–87; negative view of, 29, 196–97; and
perceptions of ethnic ancestries, 80–81;
positive view of, 197; race science and,
196–97; racial democracy myth and, 1–2,
34, 88, 90, 114–15, 139. *See also Morenos*
Mitchell, Michael, 109

MNU. See *Movimento Negro Unificado*
Molnár, Virág, 191
Monoracialism, 8, 66–67, 69, 87, 170
Morenos: as Brazilian metarace, 1, 56; and
negro movement, 131–32, 141; self-
classification of, 53–56; as social group,
44, 54–56, 206
Morning, Ann J., 170, 189, 212
Motive-based theories, 162–63
Movement of Landless Workers, 223
Movimento Negro Unificado (MNU), 69, 114,
119–20
*Movimento Pardo-Mestiço Brasileiro–Nação
Mestiça*, 205–6
Mulatto escape hatch, 68, 188, 191
Mulattos. *See* Miscegenation
Multiracialism, 8, 66–67, 170, 177–78, 192,
206, 211–12
Munanga, Kabengele, 2, 24, 87
Music, 77, 78t
Myrdal, Gunnar, 167, 218–19
Myth of racial democracy: antiracialism
and, 108–13, 222; as attitudinal complex,
88; criticisms of, 3–5, 29–30, 32, 89, 92,
217–18, 220–22; as an ideal, 6, 34, 93, 108,
113–15, 167–68, 217–20, 263n19, 263n22;
meanings of, 88–89; miscegenation and,
1–2, 34, 88, 90, 114–15, 139; proponents
of, 1–3, 6, 34, 93; race-targeted policies
and, 150, 160–61, 167–68; racial attitudes
and, 90–93; Vargas and, 71. *See also*
Antiracialism

Nagel, Joanne, 75, 204–6
Nascimento, Abdias do, 45, 114, 138–39, 187
Nascimento, Elisa Larkin, 45, 138–39
National Human Rights Program, 149
Negro culture, 10, 76–87; African derivation
of, 72–74; community of interests
and, 86–87; and perceptions of ethnic
ancestries, 80–83, 81t; and perceptions
of ethnic distinctiveness, 79–80; public
policy and, 86–87; repertoires of, 77–79,
78t, 80t
Negro Experimental Theater. See *Teatro
Experimental do Negro*
Negro movement, 117–44; age and, 129,
143–44, 144t; antiracialism and, 139;
antiracism participation and, 127–32,
128t, 130t, 131t; background on, 118–20;
Brazilian attitudes toward, 125–44; class
and, 122, 142–43; and collective black

category, 45, 57–58, 120, 138, 171–72, 248*n*2; defined, 248*n*1; discrimination as target of, 4, 119–22; education as influence on attitudes toward, 129, 131; group-based interests and, 134–36; group conflict theories, 124; mobilization of, 11, 117–18, 120–23, 127–28, 143–44, 192–93, 220–21, 239*n*29; need for participation in, 126–27, 127*t*; and race-targeted policies, 149; and racial democracy myth, 4, 113–15, 220–21; and racial subjectivity, 67, 69–70, 120, 123, 137–42, 191, 193, 222; sociocultural approaches to, 124, 251*n*62; transparency of, 132–33, 133*t*; visibility of, 132, 133*t*, 143

Negros: and African ancestry, 45; as census category, 67, 69, 74, 76, 82, 84; defined, 44–45, 228*n*15; discrimination against, 97–102; as distinct category, 66; identity of, 29–30; prejudice against, 3, 96–97; *pretos* vs., 42, 44–45, 120, 180–81, 250*n*69; self-classification of, 56–58, 76, 121, 123, 140–41, 179–80, 183; as social group, 54–58, 67–70. See also *Negro* culture; *Negro* movement

Neoclassical hegemony models, 151

Nicaragua, 24

Nigeria, 205

Nobles, Melissa, 34, 41, 57, 74, 123, 150, 172, 196, 198

Nogueira, Oracy, 27, 46, 60, 93

Nonwhite disadvantage: explanations of, 91, 97–99, 98*t;* police discrimination, 100; in university admissions, 147; in U.S., 94, 104, 116

Nonwhites, 43, 45, 68–69

One-drop rule, 22, 172–73, 192, 199, 211–13. *See also* Hypodescent

Oppenheimer, David Benjamin, 147

Orixás, 72, 78, 78*t*

Other-categorization, racial, 49–51, 60*t*, 194–95

Pagode, 77, 78*t*

Pardo: as census category, 41, 227*n*9; defined, 42, 68; as distinct category, 43–44

Parsons, Talcott, 221

Paternalistic racism, 18

Perceived threat, 124, 136, 166, 168

Peria, Michelle, 171

Perlmann, Joel, 177

PESB survey, 7, 37–38

Pesquisa Nacional Brasiliera (PESB), 37

Petersen, William, 209

Phenotypes, 55, 58–60

Pierson, Donald, 26

Piza, Edith, 46

Plessy, Homer, 198

Plessy v. Ferguson (1892), 176, 198

Police, discrimination by, 100, 102

Policy. *See* Race-targeted public policy

Polygenism, 196–97

Prado, Caio, Jr., 23

Pratto, Felicia, 94–95, 106, 134–35

Preferences systems, 147

Prejudice. *See* Racial prejudice

Preto: as census category, 41, 227*n*9; defined, 42; *negro* vs., 42, 44–45, 120, 180–81, 250*n*69

Preto velho, 72

Public opinion: bottom-up approach to, 112; criticisms of surveys of, 14–15; formation of, 110–13; predispositions and, 113–15; on race-targeted policies, 154–68, 155–57*t;* on racial discrimination, 110–13, 247*n*107; top-down approach to, 110

Quilombos, 239*n*29, 248*n*17

Quota systems: defined, 147; deserving beneficiaries of, 184–86, 185*t;* exclusion of beneficiaries from, 182–83, 185, 187; in university admissions, 147–48. *See also* Racial sorting

Race legislation, 198

Race making, 190–213; background on, 191–94; boundary effects and, 202–7; dichotomous classification and, 199–213; other-categorization and, 194–95; race science and, 196–97; race-targeted policies and, 199–213; state role in, 207–11; in United States, 195–99. *See also* Racial groups: formation of

Race science, 196–97

Race-targeted public policy, 11, 12, 145–68; adoption of, 148–50, 199–213; education as influence on attitudes toward, 159; *negro* culture and, 87; public opinion on, 154–68, 155–57*t;* race as influence on attitudes toward, 158–59, 159*t;* racial democracy myth and, 150, 160–61, 167–68; racial identification influenced by, 199–213; support for, 165–68;

Race-targeted public policy *(continued)*
theoretical perspectives on, 150–52; types
of, 146; in U.S., 146, 158, 164–65. *See also*
Racial sorting
Racial attitudes: in Brazil, 3–5, 7, 26–27;
group conflict theories, 17–19; and racial
democracy myth, 90–93; research on,
15–19, 35–38; social identity theory and,
19; sociocultural approaches to, 16–17; in
U.S., 7–8, 39, 104, 116, 214; white, 16–17
Racial boundaries: in Brazil, 49–65; category
loyalty and, 51–54, 53*t*, 54*t*, 56*t;* census
categories and, 41–46, 58–60; cognitive
effects of, 107; dichotomous classification
and, 202–7; direct effect, 206–7; external
vs. internal definition of, 47, 49–51, 51*t*,
60*t;* immigrants and, 64; nonboundary
effect, 203–4; phenotype distinctions
and, 55, 58–60; reactive boundary
effect, 204–6; stratification beliefs and,
107–8, 246*n*83; variability of, 39–40, 64,
107–8, 166, 169–70, 215–17. *See also* Race
making; Racial groups; Racial sorting
Racial democracy myth. *See* Myth of racial
democracy
Racial discrimination: in Brazil, 97–102, 98*t*,
101*t*, 108–16, 153–54, 218; class-based vs.,
27, 102–5; decline in, 101–2; existence of,
3–4, 27–28; individualist vs. structuralist
accounts of, 89–90, 94–96, 98–99, 104–7,
245*n*64; *negro* movements and, 4, 119–22;
prejudice vs., 95; racial democracy myth
and denial of, 4–5, 10, 28, 32, 89, 91–92,
103–4, 121–22
Racial groups, 9–10; alternative category
preferences as, 54–58; continuum of,
20–22, 216–17; formation of, 47–49, 67,
74–76, 223–24 (*see also* Race making);
membership in, 40; monochrome
identification of, 164–65; social dominance theory and, 161–65; spokespeople
for, 261*n*97; theoretical perspectives on,
74–76; as units of analysis, 39; within-
category ideological homogeneity of,
162–64. *See also* Racial boundaries
Racial identities. *See* Racial groups
Racialism, 9; assumptions of, 21, 138, 251*n*95;
in Brazil, 22–25, 30–32; challenges to,
32–34; defined, 20, 32, 35, 137–38; lack
of, 21–22; *negro* movement and, 137–42;
proponents of, 31–32, 221–22; in U.S.,
20–22. *See also* Antiracialism

Racial prejudice: in Brazil, 96–97, 97*t*, 109;
discrimination vs., 95
Racial sorting, 169–89; background on,
171–75; in Brazil, 178–89; bureaucratic
difficulties concerning, 170–71, 173–79,
185–87; dichotomous classification and,
170–73, 180–89, 182*t*, 199; errors in,
175–78; photographs and, 59*f*, 180–82,
182*t*, 184–86, 185*t;* self-classification
and, 179–80, 182–84, 183*t*, 184*t;* in
U.S., 176–78, 188–89. *See also* Other-
categorization, racial; Racial boundaries;
Self-classification, racial
Racism: class and, 142–43; cultural emphasis
as obstacle to combating, 86. *See also*
Antiracism
Reis, Fabio Wanderley, 32, 84, 108, 169
Religious expression: African-derived, 70–72,
240*n*45; *negro* culture and, 77–78
Reskin, Barbara, 162–64, 163*f*
Ribeiro, Matilde, 186, 187
Rio de Janeiro, 148, 149, 171
Riserio, Antônio, 73
Rosemberg, Fulvia, 46, 183, 187
Rwanda, 259*n*35

Sabbagh, Daniel, 189, 212
Samba, 71, 77
Sanders, Lynn M., 39, 159, 165, 167, 219
Sansone, Livio, 32, 44–45, 77, 80, 82–85, 169,
193, 204
Santos, Ivair dos, 149
Santos, Thereza, 69
Santos-Stubbe, Chirly Dos, 123
São Paulo school, 28–29, 232*n*111
Schuman, Howard, 13, 116, 165
Schwartzman, Simon, 234*n*151
SDT. *See* Social dominance theory
Sears, David, 15, 20, 21, 63, 217, 219
Second Conference of the Tradition of the
Orixás, 73
See, Kathleen O'Sullivan, 18
Segato, Renata L., 30–32, 65, 83, 84, 108, 223
Self-classification, racial, 49–51, 53–58, 53*t*,
54*t*, 56*t*, 61*t*, 76, 121, 123, 140–41, 179–80,
182–84, 183*t*, 184*t*, 201*t*, 202*t*
Self-interest, 158–59, 204
Sheriff, Robin, 6, 71, 93, 173, 218, 244*n*43, 263*n*19
Sidanius, Jim, 15, 18, 21, 63, 94–95, 106,
134–35, 217, 219
Silva, Nelson do Valle, 4, 7, 24, 30, 32, 33, 46,
84, 88, 108, 113, 115, 163, 209–10, 261*n*101

Sim, Jeremiah Joseph, 50
Skerry, Peter, 170
Skidmore, Thomas E., 28, 169, 172, 199, 232n111
Slavery: African-derived religious expression and, 70, 72, 74; race making and, 208–9; racial defense of, 195–96; in U.S. vs. Brazil, 196
Smith, Eliot R., 107
Sniderman, Paul M., 219
Social constructivism, 74–75
Social dominance theory (SDT): and negro movement, 134–35; and race-targeted policies, 151–52, 161–65; racial attitudes and, 18; and stratification beliefs, 106
Social identity theory, 19, 51, 216
Sociocultural theories, 16–17, 94, 105, 216
South Africa, 193
Split-ballot experiment, 200
Spokespeople, group, 261n97
Sports, 78–79
Stamatov, Peter, 217
State, racial classification role of, 149, 170, 172, 179–80, 185–88, 190–91, 207–11. See also Census categorization of race
State University of Bahia, 149
State University of Mato Grosso do Sul, 173–74, 187
State University of Norte Fluminense, 148, 171
State University of Rio de Janeiro (UERJ), 148, 169, 171, 172
Stratification beliefs: Brazilian, 105–8; group conflict theories, 94–95, 106; individualist vs. structuralist bases of, 89–90, 105–7; race-targeted policies and, 154–55; racial boundaries and, 107–8, 246n83; racial democracy myth and, 89; sociocultural approaches to, 94, 105
Stubrin, Florencia, 147
Symbolic communities, 76
Symbolic racism, 16–17
Sympathetic identification, 165–66

Tajfel, Henri, 19–20
Teatro Experimental do Negro (Negro Experimental Theater) (TEN), 69, 114, 119
Telles, Edward, 50, 58, 104–5, 109, 142–43, 165, 181, 234n152
TEN. See Teatro Experimental do Negro
Theory effect, 208–9

Tilly, Charles, 194, 203, 206
Tuch, Steven A., 150
Turner, John C., 19–20
Twine, Francis Winddance, 7, 92, 117, 217, 222

Umbanda, 72, 73
Unified Negro Movement to Combat Racial Discrimination. See Movimento Negro Unificado
United Nations, 3, 120, 149
United Nations Educational, Scientific and Cultural Organization (UNESCO), 3
United States: Brazil vs., 24, 65, 171–72, 212, 214–16, 224; census categorization in, 66, 68, 172, 177–78, 195, 197–98; ideals of, 6, 167, 218–19; Jim Crow laws in, 1–3, 17, 105, 115, 176, 193, 198, 220; Latin American immigration to, 8; monoracialism in, 66; multiracialism in, 8, 66–67, 170, 177–78, 192, 206, 212; nonwhite disadvantage in, 94, 104, 116; race legislation in, 198; race making in, 195–99; race relations in, 1–3, 32–33, 90, 167; race-targeted policies in, 146–47, 158, 164–65; racial attitudes in, 7–8, 39, 104, 116, 214; racial attitudes research in, 15–16; racial defense of slavery in, 195–96; racial identification in, 49–52, 63–64, 68, 236n72; racialism in, 20–22; racial mobilization in, 192; racial sorting in, 176–78, 188–89
University entrance policies, 147–49, 169, 171–74, 187–88, 199, 203–4
University of Brasília, 174, 187–88, 203–4, 256n36

Vargas, Gertulio, 71, 118
Venezuela, 8, 24
Vestibular, 147

Wacquant, Loïc, 32, 195
Wade, Peter, 24
Wagley, Charles, 26–28
Walker, Sheila S., 80
Warren, Jonathan, 160
Washington, Scott, 189, 259n35
Waters, Mary, 21–22, 177, 214, 246n83
West Indies, 21–22
Whitening: biological, 197; class and, 26; dichotomous classification and, 84, 200–201, 211; of negro culture, 71; in popular imagination, 259n49; racial

Whitening *(continued)*
   identification and, 68, 123; of religion, 72;
   in São Paulo, 29
Willems, Emilio, 26–27
Wilson, William Julius, 18
Winant, Howard, 31–33, 69, 92, 110, 121–22,
   217, 222
World Conference against Racism, Racial
   Discrimination, Xenophobia, and
Related Intolerance (Durban, South
   Africa, 2001), 120, 132, 149

Yancey, William L., 48, 74

Zack, Naomi, 20, 172
Zaller, John, 110, 112–13, 167, 228*n*29